THE ETRUSCANS
IN THE MODERN IMAGINATION

McGILL-QUEEN'S STUDIES IN THE HISTORY OF IDEAS
Series Editor: Philip J. Cercone

The Etruscans
in the Modern Imagination

Sam Solecki

McGill-Queen's University Press
Montreal & Kingston • London • Chicago

ISBN 978-0-2280-1463-8 (cloth)
ISBN 978-0-2280-1576-5 (ePDF)
ISBN 978-0-2280-1577-2 (ePUB)

Legal deposit fourth quarter 2022
Bibliothèque nationale du Québec

Printed in Canada on acid-free paper that is 100% ancient forest free
(100% post-consumer recycled), processed chlorine free

This book has been published with the help of a grant from the Canadian
Federation for the Humanities and Social Sciences, through the Awards
to Scholarly Publications Program, using funds provided by the Social Sciences
and Humanities Research Council of Canada.

Funded by the   Financé par le
Government   gouvernement
of Canada   du Canada

Canada Council   Conseil des arts
for the Arts   du Canada

We acknowledge the support of the Canada Council for the Arts.

Nous remercions le Conseil des arts du Canada de son soutien.

Library and Archives Canada Cataloguing in Publication

Title: The Etruscans in the modern imagination / Sam Solecki.

Names: Solecki, Sam, author.

Series: McGill-Queen's studies in the history of ideas; 85.

Description: Series statement: McGill-Queen's studies in the history
of ideas; 85 | Includes bibliographical references and index.

Identifiers: Canadiana (print) 20220254591 | Canadiana (ebook)
20220254796 | ISBN 9780228014638 (cloth) | ISBN 9780228015765
(ePDF) | ISBN 9780228015772 (ePUB)

Subjects: LCSH: Europe—Civilization—Etruscan influences. |
LCSH: Etruscans.

Classification: LCC CB203 .E87 2022 | DDC 940.2/8—dc23

This book was typeset by Marquis Interscript in 10.5/13 New Baskerville.

For my son André, with whom I explored the Acqua Alta Valley at Norchia and followed D.H. Lawrence's footsteps from Tarquinia's Tombs of the Rasenna to his grave at Kiowa Ranch, New Mexico.

A: Why were you always so interested in the Etruscans?
S: Because they almost weren't there.

Like the corpses of the Etruscan kings ready to sink into ashes
at the first unbarring of the door of the sepulchre.

John Ruskin

I can imagine myself as a Greek or Roman, perhaps even as an Egyptian,
but the imagination stops short at the Etruscans. They don't quite
come into focus.

Al Purdy

I admire the Etruscans: they built wooden houses to live in and cities
of rock for the dead.

François Truffaut

And in the wars of the gods, I now take the side of the defeated gods.

Heinrich Heine

We can have no idea what sort of things are going to become history one day.
Perhaps the past is still largely undiscovered: it still needs so many
retroactive forces for its discovery.

Friedrich Nietzsche

Nous autres, civilisations, nous savons maintenant que nous sommes
mortelles.

Paul Valéry

Contents

Illustrations

Preface:
The Return of the Repressed

The Etruscans are an archaeological culture wrecked several times over.

Nigel Spivey

All art is a dialogue. So is all interest in the past. And one of the parties lives and comprehends in a contemporary way. In the end, it can be only a dialogue in the present, about the present.

M.I. Finley[1]

The Etruscans in the Modern Imagination tells the story of a people who, after being gradually conquered and assimilated by the Romans between the fourth and first centuries BCE, disappeared for nearly two millennia from the historical record before being resurrected during the past three centuries by antiquarians, historians, archaeologists, and artists to take their place beside the Phoenicians, Greeks, and Romans in the history of the Mediterranean world. Until recently they were invariably described as "mysterious," an epithet that owed less to any specific aura than to the fact that they had been forgotten, had a contested origin, left few ruins and no literary remains, were widely considered as deeply superstitious, and spoke a unique language that long resisted translation. Put simply, they were little known and remained in the long shadows cast by Egypt, Greece, and Rome, the A-list of ancient history. For two millennia the Etruscans belonged to what Czesław Miłosz describes as the "mythologies of the unlucky conquered nations,"[2] most of which have been overlooked, repressed, or forgotten.

My argument follows the chronological arc implicit in the next section's title: Etruscan history from empire to defeat, assimilation, a

---

1 Spivey, *Etruscan Art*, 194; Finley, "Introduction: Desperately Foreign," in *Aspects of Antiquity*, 14.

2 Miłosz, "World and Justice," in *Unattainable Earth*, 69.

lengthy disappearance, and finally, beginning in the eighteenth century, the return into the cultural imagination of the West. But I want to be clear that this book is not a history of the Etruscans, though that history is briefly and with inevitable loss of nuance sketched in the opening section as a backstory to their surprising return from oblivion. That return is my focus, and the classical background provides the historical context. If the book has a tutelary spirit, it is Janus: even as the story moves forward in time in its discussion of the Etruscan presence in art and thought, from Johann Joachim Winckelmann in the eighteenth century to Anne Carson in the twenty-first, it inevitably looks back repeatedly to the civilization whose extinction is the point of departure for the argument. As my title suggests, this book's overall approach falls within the genre of studies of cultural transmission, dissemination, and influence between ancient and modern civilizations. Each chapter deals with the nature, quality, and extent of that influence in a particular figure and work. Even a glance at the table of contents reveals a hybrid genre as well as the kinds of readers it anticipates: classical scholars interested in the Etruscans and similar "vanished kingdoms," to use Norman Davies's evocative phrase; literary scholars attentive to modes of cross-cultural influence; humanists and others with a general interest in the classical world, like readers of *Minerva* and *Archaeology Today*; and readers nurtured on the popular books of Leonard Cottrell, C.W. Ceram, James Wellard, Mary Renault, and Michael Wood – even these occasionally venture into scholarly books with endnotes.

I begin with Winckelmann's classic *History of the Art of Antiquity* (1764) because it shows cultural dissemination and influence at play across the civilizations of Egypt, Greece, Etruria, and Rome without forgetting the lesson he wants his contemporaries to learn: in art, *return to the Greeks*. The leading creative figures of his age, like Christoph Willibald von Gluck, Antonio Canova, and Jacques-Louis David, would have nodded in agreement. Instead of the Greeks, I focus on the Etruscans and their unexpected return, which begins with Renaissance scholars, antiquarians, and amateur archaeologists before the Etruscans are repurposed for the arts in the late eighteenth century. Each of the twenty-four chapters is an episode in that homecoming; taken together, they are its history. Though the story of Etruscan scholarship, or Etruscology, is inseparable from my narrative, I deal with its major figures only in passing. Their story has been well told by members of the field, beginning with Massimo Pallottino's thorough account in *The Etruscans* and essays in Nancy Thomson de Grummond's indispensable *Encyclopedia of the History of Classical Archaeology*. At one point I considered devoting a chapter to Pallottino, but I quickly realized that it would require a degree of fluency in Italian I don't possess. He remains, nevertheless, one of the book's tutelary spirits, the necessary counterpoint to D.H. Lawrence who flirts with counterfactual history to argue for an imagined past that is simultaneously possibility and prophecy. A general point worth making at the outset is that the further we move forward in time from Winckelmann, the more Etruscan material artists have to work with. Another way of putting this is that the "horizon of expectation" – the general state of knowledge – with respect to the Etruscans is much greater for Raymond Queneau, Margaret Drabble, and Anne Carson than it was for Winckelmann, Stendhal, and Nathaniel Hawthorne. By the later decades of the twentieth century, the breadth of knowledge about the Etruscans – what is available for study and for art – reaches what might be called, borrowing from the physicists, a critical mass. We know more about the Etruscans than anyone has since the Roman Republic. Even since the mid-eighteenth century that knowledge has grown exponentially and has gradually altered the cumulative historical construct that is our image of the Etruscans.

I visualize that growth as a series of four maps of Europe – one each for the seventeenth, eighteenth, nineteenth, and twentieth centuries – all with red dots indicating some event associated with the Etruscans: sales and shipments of artifacts, discoveries, publications, conferences, forgeries, etc. The increase in the number of dots between the first and fourth maps is astonishing. The first two maps would record a great deal of antiquarian and archaeological research, early books on the Etruscans, and the mania for Etruscan gems, vases, and artistic values; the one for the nineteenth century would add to these the Etruscan presence in literature and travel writing, and an increasing volume of studies by first-class archaeologists as well as cranks convinced they had cracked the mystery of the Etruscan origin and deciphered their language; the twentieth century would show an unprecedented growth in all these areas but especially in the professionalization of Etruscology and the frequency of casual references to the Etruscans in various discourses.

My more specifically literary critical approach in the chapters devoted to fiction and poetry owes much to the tradition of biographical and historical criticism, as well as to what I call a soft version of

reader-reception theory. The latter I extend beyond its usual focus
on the reader's subjective engagement with the text. Instead, I begin
by examining the relationship between my authors and their Etruscan
material – *their primary text,* so to speak – before they turn that material into art, the text that we read. I need to know what William Blake
knew about the Etruscans before writing "An Island in the Moon" in
1784. Blake's use of Etruscan material in a minor satire tells us something about the general state of knowledge of the Etruscans in
England at that time. Other questions include: What liberties does
the author take with the historicity of the Etruscan sources? What
does the text tell us about what the authors think their readers know
about the Etruscans, what Hans Robert Jauss calls "the structure of
expectations the reader brings to his reading"?[3] What is the text's
vision – whether a dream of Sigmund Freud's or a poem of Zbigniew
Herbert's or Anne Carson's – of the Etruscans? I'm also interested
in how the creative interaction between the artist and the often fragmented or isolated Etruscan materials recreates the past as something
contemporary. The artist is inevitably dominant in the dialectical
encounter since so much about the Etruscans demands completion,
translation, and interpretation. As we know from our reading of
Sappho, the mind is impatient of gaps, and for later poets her "work
and the lacunae in it doubled for the pool of Narcissus."[4] The artist
fills them with his or her own self just as the historian produces
imaginative interpolations to fill the gaps in the historical record.
Both our art and our history are permeated by our present. Another
way of putting this is that every use of the Etruscans in the present
makes their past a presence in our history.

Each of my authors turns an aspect of the past into a modern work
of art or discourse; its modernity is confirmed and reinforced with each
contemporary reading. My critical interpretations begin with Anne
Carson's comment that "A scholar is someone who takes a position.
From which position certain lines become visible"[5] and Kenneth Burke's
suggestion that "The main ideal of criticism ... is to use all that there is
to use."[6] In other words, I use whatever approach seems appropriate to

3 Holub, "Constance School of Reception Aesthetics [Reception Theory]," 15.
4 Raphael, *Antiquity Matters,* 306.
5 Carson, *Plainwater,* 93.
6 Kenneth Burke, *The Philosophy of Literary Form,* 23.

the individual and work at hand. If not quite a theory, it's more than just a bricolage. As mentioned, most of my readings are grounded in history and biography; at least two draw on psychoanalysis; six rely on art history; myth history, film theory, and music history appear in one chapter each. Considering that there are twenty-four chapters and a lengthy appendix it is not surprising that there are inevitable centrifugal tendencies, with some chapters seeming to ride off in different directions. I have tried to maintain a sense of unity with a network of repetitions, prolepses, and analepses among the chapters, and with Winckelmann and Lawrence making periodic appearances as tutelary spirits throughout. In my more reflective moments, I also think of the book's unity in terms of the hermeneutic circle: in other words, the reader's understanding of the book as a whole is established by reference to the individual chapters, while the understanding of each of the chapters is, in turn, established by reference to the whole. Like a jigsaw puzzle, the whole is established gradually and incrementally until the last piece falls in place in the summative afterword.

Another unifying aspect is the underlying narrative *topos*: the story on which my argument hangs is one of disappearance and return, an archetype that has taken forms as different as the story of the Jews in the Old Testament and history, *The Odyssey*, the sixteenth-century story of *The Return of Martin Guerre*, Shakespeare's romances, Balzac's *Colonel Chabert*, Dumas's *The Count of Monte Cristo*, Hawthorne's "Wakefield," and Alejandro G. Iñárritu's *The Revenant*. To extend the metaphor of Etruscan history as a fragmented narrative, it has provided us with a mystery story with nearly countless revelations over the centuries. Even today, when we know more about the Etruscans than anyone has since the Romans, their story remains a puzzle with many important pieces missing and continuing disagreements about some of the key evidence. In the language, for instance, Tim Cornell points out that the meanings of only two hundred words have been established, and he adds in a footnote that "understandable irritation at popular misconceptions has caused some experts to exaggerate the level of scholarly knowledge of Etruscan."[7] We are the heirs of the Renaissance humanist interest in the remote, once seemingly lost past, from ancient manuscripts to the histories of Italian city states whose Etruscan past played an important

7 Cornell, *The Beginnings of Rome*, 46.

part in nascent Italian nationalism. The archaeology of the past three centuries – since the eighteenth-century rediscovery of the cities destroyed by Vesuvius – has been predicated on some such assumption: there is something of interest and value to be brought back into the light of history. Freud's favourite metaphor of the mind as a multi-layered Rome is inseparable from the two centuries of widely reported archaeological excavations that preceded it. The Etruscan excavations in the eighteenth and nineteenth centuries were a sideshow to the main events, so to speak, at Pompeii, Egypt, and Babylon and to the general interest in the ancient Mediterranean world. Those last three provided much more spectacular finds. The Etruscans, however, had the advantage of being a comparative novelty that even as it became more widely known remained a "mystery" because of controversy over origins, the lack of large ruins, the absence of a literature, and, most famously, a language that teasingly used a version of the Greek alphabet but resisted translation. Over the centuries, this last attracted cranks and scholars who proposed over fifty languages including Ancient Egyptian, Hebrew, Armenian, Ibero-Celtic, Albanian, Urnordic, and Finnish as keys. The great Michael Ventris, who deciphered Linear B in 1952, was long convinced of a relationship between it and Etruscan.[8] The 13,000 short surviving inscriptions, mostly epitaphs and dedications full of lexical curiosities, provide a small sample for scholarship. Further frustration comes with the fact that Etruscan is not part of the Indo-European family of languages.

Gaps in the historical record allowed and continue to allow room for imaginative reconstructions – from the writings of German historian Barthold Niebuhr to New Age novels and Etruscan zombie films – but the evidential paucity also poses difficulties. Nothing indicates the precarity of the small nation more clearly than the poverty of its remains, which often leave us addressing the unknowability of the past not simply with questions but with guesses. The study of the Etruscans simply does not offer the scholar or the artist sufficiently rich and varied cultural material to work on. They didn't even leave a post-conquest chronicle on the model of the Mayan Books of Chilám Balám written in Mayan using the Latin alphabet. The current record of

8 Chadwick, *The Decipherment of Linear B*, 34.

reception in the arts reflects this in the reappearance of the same small body of Etruscan objects in modern works: vases, jewellery, certain sarcophagi, tomb paintings, and a handful of pieces of sculpture. Even the magnificent Sarcophagus of the Married Couple at Rome's Museo di Villa Giulia,[9] the most famous image they left, had to be reassembled from hundreds of fragments. I can imagine someone speculating about the cultural unconscious of the Greeks but not of the Etruscans. The same situation faces students of the Cycladic islands, another culture lacking a written record and known mainly from tombs and a partly understood art. Tombs can tell us much, but we should never forget that, like history itself, they are graveyards of aristocracy (the phrase is Vilfredo Pareto's).[10]

My objective is to show the growing diffusion of Etruscan awareness after the mid-eighteenth century, primarily but not exclusively in the arts. The individual chapters discuss representative sightings and encounters in chronological order, with the length depending on the extent, intensity, and significance of the engagement. These can be roughly divided into three groups. In the first, there is often a casual reference to things Etruscan in a text or work of art that provides local colour, a touch of mystery/exoticism, semantic texture, or an image with suggestive figurative potential (Blake, Prosper Mérimée, Gustave Flaubert, Don Siegel). In the second, the Etruscan material is more prominent, though it plays a supporting role to other concerns and themes as in Nathaniel Hawthorne's *The Marble Faun*, Anatole France's *The Red Lily*, Raymond Queneau's *The Bark Tree*, and Anne Carson's poems. In the final group are works whose focus is entirely Etruscan: Winckelmann's Etruscan chapter, George Dennis's *The Cities and Cemeteries of Etruria*, Mika Waltari's novels, D.H. Lawrence's *Etruscan Places*, and Rika Lesser's *Etruscan Things*. In this group, the chapters on Waltari, Aldous Huxley, and Lawrence stand apart in their sympathetic and eudemonic argument that the mysterious Etruscans offer a life-affirming vision of individual and social being lacking in modernity and preferable to anything on offer from the Greeks and Romans. The various perspectives are inflected by the individual's place, time, and approach – Niebuhr's scientific

9 Henceforth simply Villa Giulia.
10 Quoted in Spivey, *Etruscan Art*, 160.

history, Johann Jakob Bachofen's myth criticism, Ralph Waldo Emerson's Transcendentalism, Lawrence's vitalism, and Anne Carson's post-modernism. A title for this sort of cultural appropriation might be "The Uses of the Etruscans."

The individuals and examples discussed are intended as representative types and classes; other examples can be found in the footnotes and in the appendix, "Etruscan Sightings." The result is a totality that is a mosaic predicated on the interplay between chapter and whole and I think more comprehensive and truer to the complexity of its subject matter than any single approach could be. By the end, the reader will have a clear sense of how the Etruscans were rediscovered and how they have been understood in the different phases since the Enlightenment. The approach is chronological to allow readers to follow the expansion of interest and to trace lines of affinity and influence among the individuals and works involved. In rare cases I deviate from chronology to show several responses from different times to the same Etruscan work. If I sometimes offer more description and quotation than analysis, it is because many of the works are unfamiliar and need to be introduced and contextualized. Though it was never my intention to write another introduction to the Etruscans in an already crowded field, I think readers will find enough information in the brief introduction to have a sense of the ancient history that is the matrix for the narrative of their rise, decline, disappearance, and rebirth. Since that ancient history is of necessity in the form of a survey, it goes without saying that richness of detail, variety, and nuance are sometimes sacrificed – for example, not all the versions of different Etruscan myths and gods are mentioned, the controversies surrounding the parentage of Servius Tullius are ignored, and the Etruscan decline omits some positive aspects of Romanization. Summaries and surveys inevitably simplify, if only by omitting facts irrelevant to the argument, but they don't necessarily distort.

A different sort of epistemological problem arises when I think of the book's perspective on the Etruscans. I interpret Claude Lévi-Strauss's suggestion that anthropology is the product of Europe's "strong feelings of remorse" as also applicable to history. I think of his "redemptive quest" to save from vanishing the customs and languages of the Caduveo, Bororo, and Nambikwara, at least in print, as nearly identical to the work of Etruscologists, historians, and artists who have engaged with the Etruscans.[11] Such an engagement inevitably involves binaries with moral implications – Bororo/Brazil, Etruscan/Roman, destroyed/destroyer, victim/conqueror – and secular reflections on eschatology and history. The Etruscans, like the Amazonian peoples, have benefited from the fact that modern writers almost always take the side of history's losers in an unequal contest, especially if they are opposed to their own society's values. Lévi-Strauss's praise of the Amazonian way of being in the world and his criticism of Western civilization are almost identical with Lawrence's views of the Etruscans and of the West. In this argument, Europe lacks a true sense of community and the sacred and offers instead a calcified monotheism, its secular replacement progress, industrialism, and overpopulation. In the Etruscans/Romans binary, Rome is the harbinger of European instrumental reason and imperialism and Etruria is the exemplary victim whose remains offer us the aesthetics of the dispossessed and the melancholy always inherent in ruins. That we can never know them – the perennially elusive Etruscans – as well as we know the Egyptians, Greeks, and Romans doesn't hurt their cause either. A civilization that leaves behind mostly ruins, fragments, and no significant literary remains ensures that it will continue to remain unknowable to some degree and therefore continue to pique the interest of posterity. What has been erased by time constitutes the site and symbol of mystery, an emptiness impossible to overcome. It becomes a world of abandoned meanings. We can never feel as close to anything Etruscan as we do to Greek lyrics or Roman busts and temples, but that doesn't prevent spiritual affinities of the sort felt by George Dennis, Lawrence, and Huxley. We may be moral relativists reluctant to blame those in the past on the basis that "they should have known better," but I suspect that our sympathies will inevitably lie with history's victims, a people subjugated, absorbed, and almost erased from history. Martha Nussbaum addresses the issue of seemingly anachronistic judgments in *The Cosmopolitan Tradition*: "The ancient Greeks and Romans did not have our data, and very likely their world contained fewer inequalities between nations, perhaps even smaller internal inequalities, than does our world. Still the differences were large enough, and philosophers such as Cicero, Seneca and Marcus [Aurelius], well-traveled and

11 Lévi-Strauss, *Tristes Tropiques*, 388.

busily engaged in projects of imperial expansion, *should not have neglected them*" (my italics).[12] Inevitably anyone writing about the Etruscans is involved in a long-deferred act of historical redemption and a bias may occasionally show, though it need not always be an instance of retrospective disapproval. Admirers of Rome, like Hegel, Niebuhr, and Bachofen, will shake their heads in disagreement. They console themselves that history dealt Rome a better hand. Like Polybius they celebrate the triumph of a world historical power that changes the course of civilization.

By the book's end, however, I think readers will agree that the Etruscans have a definite place today not just among Etruscologists but in the long cultural afterlife of antiquity in the Western imagination, or what cultural studies calls our "imaginary." They are an exception to Eugenio Montale's comment that "Disappearing is the destiny of destinies" / ("Svanire / è dunque la ventura delle venture").[13] Their fate might not be quite what Hegel meant by the "cunning of history," but it does raise doubts concerning teleological historiographies.

12 Nussbaum, *The Cosmopolitan Tradition*, 6.
13 Montale, "Portami il girasole ch'io lo trapianti," in *Collected Poems 1920–1954*, 46–7.

Acknowledgments

I first became interested in the Etruscans in the autumn of 1965, while taking a course on Livy at the University of Toronto with the great Livy scholar the late Robert Maxwell Ogilvie, the author of *A Commentary on Livy: Books I–V*. A passing reference in one of his lectures directed me to Massimo Pallottino's classic *The Etruscans*. In graduate school the interest was rekindled during research for a PhD thesis on D.H. Lawrence, whose imaginative *Etruscan Places* was the perfect complement to Pallottino's academic study. Over the next several decades, the Etruscans remained a non-professional interest. I continued to read some of the scholarship in English and French and kept an Etruscan notebook recording random Etruscan references. Looking back, I see that the Etruscans were part of a more comprehensive interest in the ancient history of the Mediterranean that, like a magnet, organized much of my reading outside my research and writing before retirement. In the 1990s the two came together when I spent a decade writing a book on Al Purdy and helping edit several of his books of poetry and prose. He was as fascinated by the Etruscans as he was by Lawrence, who was a lifelong touchstone for his poetry. When Purdy visited the Etruscan sites in 1998, two years before his death, his guidebook was *Etruscan Places*.

Because I travelled often to Italy and lived in Siena in the mid-1990s I had the opportunity to visit most of the Etruscan sites and museums several times. The notebooks began to pile up, though I had no intention of writing anything. The idea of a book would not have occurred to me if I hadn't reread Pallottino's classic work – especially the section "A Short History of Etruscan Studies" – and then James Wellard's popular *The Search for the Etruscans* (1973), and several scholarly articles about their survival and return after what might be called a post-colonial assimilation into the Roman Empire. Three articles were seminal, and their influence is evident in my study. Roger T. Macfarlane's essay on the Etruscans in the Latin poets directed me to their presence in Roman writing in general, just as Ogilvie's lectures and books had shown me their place in Roman history. Nancy Thomson de Grummond's essay "Rediscovery" established a trail from Latin literature to George Dennis's classic travel book of 1848, with many informative stops in between. And Martin Korenjak's recent "The Etruscans in Ancient Literature" provided an exhaustive survey of the ancient literary sources.

It was while reading de Grummond's magisterial and beautifully designed *Etruscan Myth, Sacred History, and Legend* (2006) a decade ago that I began to wonder whether anyone had studied the Etruscan presence and influence in nineteenth- and twentieth-century literature, art, and thought. When it became evident that the answer was no, a second question arose: was there enough material for a monograph focusing on the past two or three centuries? *The Etruscans in the Modern Imagination* is the answer. My notebooks provided me with a long preliminary list of historians, poets, travel writers, artists, novelists, and thinkers who had noticed the Etruscans, shown an interest in Etruscan matters, or mentioned them in passing. Further reading and hours on the web provided me with enough new material for a study of the Etruscan presence since the eighteenth century, or from Johann Joachim Winckelmann's *History of the Art of Antiquity* (1764) to recent poems by Anne Carson. Among other Etruscan scholars whose work I found indispensable were Jacques Heurgon, Emeline Richardson, Larissa Bonfante, Nigel Spivey, Stephan Steingräber, and Sybille Haynes. More generally I have drawn on the work of Fernand Braudel, M.I. Finley, Walter Burkert, Arnaldo Momigliano, Norman Davies, Ralph W. Mathisen, Greg Woolf, David Abulafia, and Richard Jenkyns.

And I'd like to offer my particular thanks to the two anonymous readers for the press. Their very close reading of the manuscript and their many suggestions, small and large – especially in the historical section – saved me from stumbling through Etruscan and Roman places and helped make this a much stronger book. At McGill-Queen's University Press, Jonathan Crago and Kathleen Fraser guided the manuscript through the press. Catherine Marjoribanks, my meticulous copy editor, did the rest.

In Toronto, I found patient listeners in seminars at University College and in the English department, and in W.J. Keith, Lynd Forguson, J.M. Cameron, Josef Škvorecký, D.F.S. Thomson, Michael Ondaatje, Henry and Jane Auster, T.H. Adamowski, Karen Mulhallen and Guy and Alberta Nokes, Krystyna Sieciechowicz, Walter Buczynski, Emmett Robbins, Desmond Conacher, Dr M.L. Smith, Neal Dolan, Richard Greene, and Paul Meyer. In Italy, Alfredo Rizzardi of the University of Bologna enlightened me about Etruscan Bologna and Marzabotto; Dr Sandro Forconi and Laura Ferri of Siena patiently showed me sites in the area and in the Maremma; Elias Polizoes took me to Murlo; and Caterina Ricciardi helped with information about Etruscan sites near Rome. Thanks also to my father, Tadeusz Solecki, who had a long interest in the ancient Mediterranean world, its ships in particular.

Sam Solecki
Professor Emeritus
Department of English
University of Toronto

PART ONE

Antique Matters

Introduction:
The Etruscans from Empire to Defeat ...
Assimilation ... Return

I

From Empire to Defeat

The Etruscans were [Rome's] hereditary foes.

George Dennis[1]

Whether the Etruscans came across the Mediterranean from Lydia (Herodotus) or were an indigenous people (Dionysius of Halicarnassus) or are a combination of the two is tangential to this book's focus, though the question continues to provoke discussion and even DNA testing.[2] There is a growing consensus around the third option. I begin, however, with the generally accepted view of them as appearing sometime around 1000 BCE as an Early Iron Age civilization called Villanovan – after the site near Bologna where it was identified in 1853 – and evolving in an unbroken sequence from it. In David Ridgway's carefully precise definition, "the peninsular Iron Age culture conventionally termed 'Villanovan' represents the outward and visible sign

---

1 Dennis, *Westminster Review*, 173.

2 For a realistic assessment of the evidence see Ulf: "The ancient written sources hold contradictory views as to who the Etruscans were and from where they originated. Modern scholarship has been content to pick out one of the ancient concepts and to support it with historical, archaeological or linguistic arguments." "An Ancient Question: The Origin of the Etruscans," in *Etruscology*, 11–34. For the use of DNA, see Perkins, "DNA and Etruscan Identity," 109–20.

of the Etruscans in their Iron Age stage."³ The civilization becomes "Etruscan" over the next three centuries as it moves south and establishes itself in cities in central and southern Italy as far as Capua and other sites in Campania. In the seventh and sixth centuries we can speak of an Etruscan empire. We often forget that the beginnings of Etruscan civilization are roughly contemporaneous with those of Greece and Rome, whose traditional foundational dates are 776 and 753 BCE. At their empire's greatest extension between the seventh and fifth centuries there were Etruscan cities in most parts of the peninsula, and Rome was ruled by Etruscan kings approximately from 616 to 509 BCE.⁴ Their steady decline began in the fourth century and ended in the third after a series of defeats in conflicts with Rome that led to complete assimilation by the Augustan era. Like many other ancient and modern peoples, they and their almost empire gradually vanished from the historical record and were forgotten almost as completely as countless species killed by earth's various cataclysms. The people merged over time with Latins (and others); the language and customs left their mark on Latin and Roman life and religion; and the accidentally surviving durable remnants of material culture began the long wait for rediscovery.

The rise of the Roman empire couldn't have been accomplished without the conquest and assimilation of the many historically inconsequential peoples of the Italian peninsula who, when they lost their independence, assumed gradually what today we would call a post-colonial status. The following partial list is long and to most ears filled with

3 Quoted in Cornell, *The Beginnings of Rome*, 46.

4 For a discussion of the suggested dates of the fall of the Tarquin monarchy, see Ogilvie, below. Cornell has equally strong doubts about the dates: "One can argue about details, and speculate endlessly about what might really have happened during these years; but the important question is whether the broad outline of events is correct. Is it true to say that at the end of the sixth century BC Rome ceased to be ruled by a monarch, and became a republic governed by annual consuls? The historicity of Lucretia, Brutus, Horatius and the rest is a secondary issue in comparison with this basic question. Equally it is of little consequence whether the change took place in a matter of days, as tradition maintains, or over a period of a few years, during which the city may have been occupied by the forces of Lars Porsena. The same point can be made about the chronology. Whether the Roman Republic began in 509 BC, or 507 or 504 or 502, is not of great importance at this distance. What matters is that an approximate date should be established; and tradition clearly points to a date shortly before 500 BC." Cornell, *The Beginnings of Rome*, 218.

unfamiliar names: Ligurians, Samnites, Umbrians, Faliscans, Capenates, Volsci, Oscans, Campanians, Iapygians, Messapians, Lucanians, Oenotrians, Bruttians, Sicanians, Elymians, Sabines, and the people at the heart of this book, the Etruscans. The chances of vanishing are greater if, like the Etruscan, a civilization leaves behind no substantial stone or marble ruins and no extensive written record of its language, religion, society, and history. As a result, we know almost nothing about most of the peoples on the list, and much of what we know directly about the Etruscan world comes from ruins, tombs, and grave goods. Writing about the Ligurians in his *Origines*, Cato the Elder (234–149 BCE) suggests that the "Ligurians have no memory of where they came from," a suggestion that Cornell extends to most of the pre-Roman peoples: "It is most improbable that the Italian peoples had any historical literature of their own," though he adds that "the Etruscans are a possible exception."[5] Without a written record, without what George Steiner calls the "instruments of remembrance and quotation,"[6] we can't imagine a culture's mindscape and its way of being in the world. The less we know about them, the more mysterious they remain. The obvious contrast here is with the Jews. Titus destroyed Jerusalem and the Temple in 70 CE, but the Jewish language and the Jewish people – whose book Heinrich Heine described as "ein portatives Vaterland," a portable Fatherland – survived and eventually regained the status of a nation-state that could write its own ancient and modern histories.[7] Unlike the Etruscans, their return is real, not a figure of speech. By contrast, we read about Etruscan history in texts written by Greek and Latin authors which refer to them as Tyrrheni (Greek) or Tusci/Etrusci (Roman), not Rasna or Rasenna, their proper name. In other words, we communicate with them through interpreters and the subjects, events, and individuals they chose as significant. The situation is further complicated because the Romans wrote about the Etruscans only after conquering and then assimilating them as citizens. For the Roman writers they are the "other," a people who had to be overcome if Rome was to become the city we remember as an empire. They represent values and a way of life antithetical to that of the Romans and, from their viewpoint, inferior. The same can be said

---

5 Cornell, *The Beginnings of Rome*, 37.
6 Steiner, "Zion," in *My Unwritten Books*, 127.
7 Quoted in Hofmann, "Heine's Heartmobile," 42.

of the Roman attitude to the Phoenicians. Martin Korenjak summarizes this situation as follows:

The quantity of evidence provided by ancient authors about the Etruscans stands in inverse proportion to the political and cultural vitality of the latter. Close to nothing is transmitted from the heyday of Etruscan power and prosperity in the Archaic period. Most relevant texts come from Hellenism, during which the Etruscans were already losing their political identity, and above all from the Roman Empire, by which time Etruscan culture had disappeared as a whole. This, too, in a number of ways conditions the kind and quality of information we get and the resulting image of the people. To begin with, the belatedness of the sources means that most of our information is second-hand at best, which multiplies the possibilities for misunderstandings and distortions.[8]

The absence of an Etruscan literature gives them the posthumous status of an almost prehistoric people, their history and fate similar in some ways to those of North American Indigenous Peoples whose languages vanished with them. A current website lists over a hundred names just under the letter *A* (Atenas, Attakapas, Attikamigues, Abitibi), most with a date indicating a last sighting or recorded use of the language. Linguists remind us that languages vanish almost monthly, and that of the seven thousand or so currently spoken, half will probably be gone by the end of the century because of the economically driven hegemony of English.[9] Some linguists describe this as linguicide. A recent example is the death, on 7 October 1992, of Tevfik Esenç, the last speaker of Ubykh, a language of the western Caucasus which a century ago was spoken by approximately 50,000 people. As I wrote earlier, Etruscan survives in roughly 13,000 inscriptions on sarcophagi, urns, statues, vases, and on a remarkable corpus of bronze mirrors.[10] The Phoenicians have left a similarly meagre written record. We have a small collection

---

8 Korenjak, "The Etruscans in Ancient Literature," 46.

9 In Europe, the Czechs (in the 1620s) and the Poles (in 1790s) were conquered and forbidden to teach their own languages and histories and disappeared as nations from the European map until the Treaty of Versailles.

10 There is a similarity here with the Phoenicians, who also have no literary remains. There are, as with the Etruscans, over ten thousand inscriptions, almost all votive or funerary. And, again like the Etruscans, they have traditionally been "underappreciated

of Etruscan words and a rudimentary grammar, but there is nothing to read that would provide the sort of insights we get about the daily and inner lives of Romans from Cicero and Pliny's letters, the Augustan poets, or Tacitus. The last Etruscan in the historical record is a diviner summoned to help the Roman army trying to stop King Alaric and his Visigoths in 408 CE by calling down thunderbolts. After him the Etruscans fell off history's radar screen and thus never became part of the historico-cultural furniture of our minds.

I want to emphasize the difference between their fate and the sort of "end of the world" scenario the poet Adam Zagajewski describes when dealing with the decline and fall of Rome.

A historian will say our epoch has been preceded by countless ends of the world. Mighty Babylon fell. The Romans looked with horror at the barbarians and at the Christians. Byzantium fell. For the people living in those civilizations like bees in a hive these were terrifying catastrophes, real ends of the world (Carthage fell). After all, they could not have known that in one hundred, two hundred, or five hundred years the scar would heal and something of ancient Rome would be preserved in Christian Europe.[11]

With his eye on Rome, Zagajewski, following Hegel, overlooks the crucial fact that the Babylonians and Carthaginians, like the Etruscans, were not "preserved in Christian Europe." They fell out of historical memory while Rome and Byzantium lived on. Pagan Rome slowly evolved into Christian Rome. Latin remained alive as it mutated into the Romance languages. Poland, Zagajewski's real subject when he reflects on vanished kingdoms, was erased from Europe's map in the 1790s and was ruled by Prussia, the Hapsburg Empire, and Russia until the Treaty of Versailles restored it to history. The Etruscans, by contrast, belong to the category of nations that disappeared through a gradual cultural genocide. I can

by classical historians and archaeologists, who are more interested in the glory that was Greece and the grandeur that was Rome." See Quinn, *In Search of the Phoenicians*, xxii, xv. Quinn doesn't mention the Etruscans.

11 Zagajewski, *Solidarity, Solitude*, 112. Worth noting is Gibbon's description of "the ruin of Paganism, in the age of Theodosius" as "perhaps the only example of the total extirpation of any ancient and popular superstition [which] may therefore deserve to be considered, as a singular event in the history of the human mind." Gibbon, *The History of the Decline and Fall of the Roman Empire*, 3:334.

indicate more precisely what I mean by referring to a narrowly averted cultural genocide of the twentieth century, Stalin's attempt in the 1940s to eliminate ethnic groups like the Kalmyks, Karachai, Chechens, Ingush, and Crimean Tartars by deporting them from their homelands and then wiping "their homelands off the map, eliminating the names of the deported from official documents, abolishing their republics, destroying cemeteries, renaming villages and towns, and removing all references to them from history books." Stalin failed only because he ran out of time.[12] Russian was to have replaced the native languages, which within a generation or two would no longer be spoken. A Kalmyk was to be as deracinated and assimilated as the Etruscans under Augustus.

Though they may not have realized it, at that point the historical file on them began to close because old Etruria and the Etruscans no longer existed: there were no state archives or chronicles, no literature, the religion was gradually forgotten (or assimilated), and the language was spoken less often. They ceased to be referred to by Roman and pre-modern historians and were neglected by their successors. Their few material remains existed as insignificant ruins, grave goods, sarcophagi, terracotta and bronze sculpture, vases, jewellery, and the chromatically audacious paintings in underground tombs. If they were to survive, they would have to be rediscovered to become a Lazarus nation. What differentiates the Etruscans from the other Italian nations that disappeared after conquest by Rome – and this is my argument – is that after nearly two millennia their cold case was reopened in the eighteenth century by antiquarians, archaeologists, forgers, scholars, intellectuals, and artists. The main part of this book tells the story of the last two and a half centuries of that gradual but persistent rediscovery, the gradually increasing diffusion and reception of Etruscan culture, and their return to their proper place in the history of the Mediterranean. This is a rare example of culture correcting and redeeming history.

Between the ninth and seventh centuries they established cities in Etruria (modern Tuscany, Umbria, and Lazio) and were trading in the Mediterranean. Over time their influence spread through the Italian peninsula and their cities loosely organized in three confederations of twelve. Like the Greek city states, they had a common language, religion, and customs but that did not prevent occasional hostilities among them,

12 Applebaum, *Gulag*, 428–9.

though these were never as fratricidal as those in Greece. Sybille Haynes describes the federation as follows: "The principal Etruscan cities were autonomous and only loosely linked in a (religious) association. Separately they had developed their cultural identity and their political and economic institutions and spheres ... [T]his diversity is reflected in the artistic individuality and varying funerary customs of the different cities."[13] Haynes's emphasis on a "religious" association – centred on the recently rediscovered Fanum Voltumnae near Orvieto – is substantiated by the absence in the ancient sources of any reference to a military action involving a united Etruscan army. It is possible that the federation that met here never came together for military reasons. In other words, the Etruscan people may have been a nation, but they were never a homogeneous nation-state or a nation in the modern senses of the word. This is one of the reasons I refer to them more often as a people than a nation, though perhaps the last might have quotation marks around it in the phrase Etruscan "nation." One other possibility would be to invoke Jacques Derrida's *sous rature* and present the word with an "X" through it to indicate that it doesn't carry its usual weight and meaning. Despite the long-term success of their disharmonic confederation, they never completely overcame their "city-state particularism."[14]

We can gather how difficult it is to group them within a single unitary concept from Otto-Wilhelm von Vacano's definition by negatives: "The Etruscans were not in any way a homogeneous race, nor were they a people united by common ties of ancestry and language, or a nation, and they were not even primarily an economic union or defensive alliance, but a religious confederation, whose members were city-states of the western part of Central Italy, in many cases extremely diverse in origin and composition, each capable of creating its own history and working out its own development."[15] For von Vacano they were "an archaic creation" of the sort that had flourished in the eight and seventh

---

13 Haynes, *Etruscan Civilization*, 135. On the question of the nature of the Etruscan confederation, see also Cornell: "In fact it is highly questionable whether the assembly that met at the shrine of Voltumna ever functioned as a political or military league. There is no historically verified instance in the sources of an action involving an Etruscan federal army, and many scholars have supposed that the league of Voltumna was a purely religious association. On the other hand, there is abundant evidence of antagonism and warfare between the Etruscan cities." *The Beginnings of Rome*, 312.

14 Finley, *The Use and Abuse of History*, 129.

15 von Vacano, *The Etruscans in the Ancient World*, 48.

centuries throughout the ancient world – a loosely defined coalition of city states most closely bound by their religion and with fluid boundaries. Oswald Spengler argues that "*an Etruscan nation never existed. In Tuscany, as in the Peloponnese, there were only city-states, national points which in the period of colonization could only multiply, never expand.*"[16] He might have added that they failed to federate. Perhaps they were too tribal, schismatic, or disorganized to take the next step in organization even when repeatedly faced with the Roman threat. A similar failure occurs in Ionia in the same period when the city states assembled at Priene ignored Thales's advice that they unite against the threat posed by Cyrus the Great. Wittgenstein would say that the word "Etruscan" meant something slightly different in each of the cities, yet each iteration carried enough similar connotations to constitute a family relationship with an underlying commonality. In the larger historical picture this is more than just a question of semantics if we recall that for Hegel a stateless nation can't be considered a part of history. The fluid archaic nature of the overall political order probably accounts for the lack of a traditional Etruscan founding date of the kind that we have for Carthage (814 BCE), Greece (776 BCE) and Rome (753 BCE). Also lacking is a strong creation myth, an epic, a chronicle, history, and numerous stories of heroes, all of which help to establish a national identity.

More generally the Etruscans are remembered as a commercial empire on sea and land that reached its zenith between the eighth and fifth centuries, when they began to be gradually conquered and assimilated. There is a consensus that the defeat in 474 BCE of the Etruscan fleet off Cumae by Hieron of Syracuse marked the collapse of Etruscan power in central Italy. The event is the climax of two novels, Mika Waltari's *The Etruscan* (1955) and Sybille Haynes's *The Augur's Daughter* (1981). Until the sixth century most of the cities were ruled by lucumones (Etruscan: *lauchme*, meaning king) supported by an aristocracy. There was also a large slave population. From 616 to 509 BCE (the dates are traditional) Etruscan kings ruled Rome, though, as Cornell argues, this did not imply Roman political subservience to Etruria: "The ethnic diversity of archaic Rome, together with the fact that all the Roman kings were in some sense outsiders, suggests that the Etruscan origin of the Tarquins was incidental, at least in the

16 Spengler, *The Decline of the West*, 245.

sense that it did not necessarily have any far-reaching political or cultural implications."[17] In other words, the Romans deposed Tarquin not because he was an Etruscan but because he was a tyrant.

If we turn to gender politics, Etruscan women were famous (or notorious) for enjoying liberties and rights unavailable to women in almost all other Mediterranean societies. Inscribed bronze mirrors suggest women were as literate as men. That they also had property rights is suggested by an inscription on an Orvieto tomb that a woman owned it. Unlike Athenian women, they not only attended games but dined with their husbands at banquets, a custom reviled by Greek and Roman writers as immoral and uncivilized. Unlike Roman women, who were known as their father's daughter or their husband's wife, they kept their first names, and their full names were recorded on sarcophagi. In the absence of a male heir, the inheritance passed to the female line. The long-lived Diodorus Siculus (60 BCE–30 CE) was repeating a slur already tired by the Augustan era when he claimed that Etruscan power had declined because of their "life of drunkenness and effeminate sloth" which had cost them their ancestral glory in war.[18] Early Christians faced a similar slur from the second-century Greek philosopher Celsus who mocked them because of the prominence of women in the Gospels. If you think traditional values are being forgotten and society is in decline, point the finger at the usual suspects – oriental luxury (see Horace, "Persicos odi, puer, apparatus," *Odes* 1.38) or women. As late as Constantine, Gibbon tells us, the emperor was accused of "Asiatic pomp" and assuming "an air of softness and effeminacy" inappropriate for an emperor or a military veteran.[19]

Those who were convinced that the Etruscans were inherently immoral would have had a difficult time reconciling this view with Livy's comment that the "Etruscan communities, deeply learned as they were in sacred lore of all kinds, were more concerned than any other nation with religious matters" (5.1.6). Seneca made the same point slightly differently: "they attribute everything to god" (2.32.2).[20] As prominent as it was, Etruscan religion was never fixed or unitary, and it changed significantly with later Hellenization and the gradual standardizing of the divine

---

17 Cornell, *The Beginnings of Rome*, 158.

18 Quoted in Macfarlane, "'*Tyrrhena Regum Progenies*,'" 256n4.

19 Gibbon, *The History of the Decline and Fall of the Roman Empire*, 1:646.

20 Seneca, *Naturales Questiones*.

pantheon. There is also general agreement that the various cities had differing religious beliefs, traditions, and rituals. Like most belief systems, the religion altered over the centuries: for instance, the gods mentioned in seventh-century inscriptions are few and rarely correspond with their better-known successors; the early vision of a joyful afterlife changed during the catastrophic fourth century to something closer to what we associate with Hades and Hell. The religion's early phase featured non-anthropomorphic deities like Usil, the sun god, Tiv, the moon god, and Cel, the earth goddess. At least seven of the later divinities are referred to in both genders. Velthumna (Latin: Vertumnus), for instance, is a sexually ambiguous shape-shifter within a pantheistic cosmos, and he has been variously described as a national god, a god of war, or a divinity of vegetation; he was probably all three. Pallottino memorably commented that "the Etruscan conception of supernatural beings was permeated by a certain vagueness as to numbers, sex, attributes and appearance."[21] The influence of Greek myth can be seen in the increased anthropomorphism of the gods, though the Etruscan originals continued to retain their traditional names and local characteristics. Beyond the pantheon were higher gods who advised Tinia (Zeus) when to hurl his most powerful thunderbolt and eight further gods also involved in lightning strikes. As in Greece and Rome there were also countless local deities, like Selvans, a god of boundaries and the wild, who anticipates the Roman Silvanus but has no Greek ancestor. Sybille Haynes lists thirty-four gods in her *Etruscan Civilization: A Cultural History*.

Etruscan religion, unlike Judaism and Christianity but like Roman state religion, did not possess a formalized theology or dogma; the emphasis was on myths, rites of worship (including the cult of heroes and ancestors), prayers, and divination. Daniele F. Maras writes that the Greek and Latin sources suggest that "Etruscan religion was based on revelation handed down in writing, not unlike Judaism and Christianity. Nevertheless, the comparison does not look appropriate, since Etruscan Libri were not as all-embracing as the Hebrew and Christian Bibles, nor were they at the same time a collection of laws or a collective historical memory."[22] There were two prophetic figures, Tarchies (Latin: Tages), an aged boy ("puer senex"), and Lasa Vecuvia

---

21 Quoted in de Grummond, *Etruscan Myth, Sacred History, and Legend*, 21.
22 Maras, "Religion," 279.

(Latin: Vegoia), a nymph. Tages sprang from the earth when the ploughshare of Tarchunus (Latin: Tarchon) went deeper than usual. This is probably a late etiological myth intended to suggest the autochthonous origins of the Etruscans while simultaneously providing a mythical charter in a series of revelations copied down by Tarchon, the founder-hero, after whom Tarquinia was probably named. It has the whiff of a primordial historical myth – embedded in reality by the plough and oxen – without quite providing one. It is worth noting that the original boundaries of Rome were established in the Etruscan manner by a plough covered with bronze and yoked to a bull and a cow. Tages brought various divinatory rituals that facilitated communication with the omnipotent gods, for which the Etruscans became famous, instructions on how to lay out a city using a plough, and how to succeed in agriculture. The revelations were copied down by Tarchon and later collected together with the *Libri Rituales, Libri Haruspicini,* and *Libri Fulgurales* in a book the Romans called the *Etrusca Disciplina*.[23] Lasa Vecuvia was said to have revealed in the *Libri Vegoici* that Tinia was responsible for both the order of the cosmos and the rules for setting earthly boundaries.[24] During the period of assimilation the corpus of Etruscan books continued to play an important role in Roman religion and divination long after almost everything else about the Etruscans had been forgotten. If either Tages or Vecuvia offered an original vision of the cosmos, a new philosophy of life, a vision of the afterlife, or what we would recognize as scriptures, these haven't survived. It is worth repeating that we have all this information from non-Etruscan sources. The titles of Etruscan books survive but we have only Latinized fragments of their contents. That most contemporary writers refer to Tarchies and Lasa Vecuvia by their Latin names indicates how dependent our knowledge is on the nation that absorbed them. Latin names have an almost familial quality for us because they are embedded in the major European languages and therefore easy to remember and pronounce. In contrast, Etruscan names sometimes sound as foreign as Klingon: Elcsntre (Alexander), Phulphsna (Polyxena?), Natinusnai,

---

23 The best-known autochthonous peoples in the Mediterranean were the Athenians, Thebans, Arcadians, and Carians. The Arcadians had the best claim to priority since their Arcado-Cypriot dialect was earlier than the others.

24 Other titles: *Etrusca scripta, Etruscae disciplinae voluminae, Tusci libelli, Tyrrhena carmina, Libri Vegoici, Libri Tagetici.*

Phersipnei (Persephone), Arnth Velcha. My occasional use of Rasenna and original names instead of the more familiar Latin is a small gesture of protest against a historical onomastic wrong, however inevitable.

Not surprisingly the Etruscans became and remained famous into the next millennium for their detailed systems of divining the will of the gods. This had various branches: a haruspex (*netśvis* in Etruscan) was more narrowly someone who examined animal entrails (extiscipy), especially the liver; a fulgurator was skilled in reading lightning; and an augur interpreted bird flight. The degree of detail in these can be gauged from Nancy Thomson de Grummond's comment that in the books on auspicious birds (*auspicium*) "there were even illustrations to identify each bird that was being observed." They also practised the casting of lots, divination by gazing into a bowl, and divination with mirrors.[25] Those who, like Hegel, were not impressed by divination tended to describe the Etruscans as superstitious and trapped within a fatalistic world view. Imagine trying to plan the battle order of a modern army but having to wait for an interpretation of the flight of an eagle or of an animal's liver.

The Etruscan language, though indebted to the Greek alphabet, was unique and presented problems to translators into the twentieth century. Almost everything we know about it is based on inscriptions, many of which follow a formulaic system. The earliest were modelled on "talking inscriptions" as in "I am the jar of Squria, beauty of a beauty." Mortuary inscriptions usually just name the individual and the family. Not one inscription is as full of life as this Greek one by Simonides (556–468 BCE): "Drinker, glutton supreme, / Supreme defamer of men / I, Timokreon / Of Rhodes, now lie down here."[26] No evidence of a secular literature has been found and whether there was one remains an open question, part of the large evidential void. Marcus Terentius Varro, described by Quintilian as "the most learned of Romans," mentions a *Tuscae Historiae*, dealing with the Etruscan domination of Italy, and Volnius, an Etruscan tragedian.[27] The most important historical fact is that the Etruscans lost more battles on land and sea than they won. Against the neighbouring Romans, their hereditary enemy, they were perennial losers, and it was not a gentle age. By the

25 de Grummond, "Haruspicy and Augury," 543.
26 In Peter Jay, ed., *The Greek Anthology*, 41.
27 Heurgon, *Daily Life of the Etruscans*, 241.

middle of the fourth century the Romans had a better-trained and bigger army.[28] Looking back from the early fifteenth century, the Florentine Leonardo Bruni thought that "if all the Etruscans had waged war with a unified strategy, they might have defended themselves long and magnificently. Whether it was the presence of the Gauls as a permanent threat on their borders, or discord among themselves, or the Fates now favoring the Roman side, or a combination of all these, they didn't go to war with a common plan. It was certainly this that gave the Romans the upper hand."[29] Some ancient historians attributed their decline to a widespread moral and social decadence. Instead of decadence, Tim Cornell suggests "fossilisation," the failure to match Roman economic, social, and political development.

What I am suggesting is that in the archaic period Rome, although different in language, and probably also in self-conscious ethnic identity, from the Etruscan cities, was nevertheless comparable to them in material culture, social structure, and institutions. But during the course of the first three centuries of the Republic their paths diverged; Roman society and culture were transformed, first by the internal political changes that gave power to the plebs, secondly by conquests which revolutionised Rome's economy and brought it into direct contact with other civilisations, and third by a continuing open-door policy which changed the composition of the citizen body. The Etruscan cities experienced none of this; on the contrary, they remained largely static and comparatively isolated, so that in the age of the Punic Wars, perhaps even down to the time of the Social War (91 BCE), they retained an archaic culture and a fossilised social system similar to that which had obtained at Rome before the emancipation of the plebs.[30]

Like Waltari and Haynes, Cornell sees the defeat of the Etruscan fleet in 474 BCE at Cumae as a harbinger of their final collapse.

Etruscan disappeared as a living language over the two or three centuries after the loss of political autonomy in 265 BCE. As W.D. Whitney put it in the nineteenth century, "When the Etruscans were Latinized, their speech passed out of all reach of knowledge."[31] Rome

28 Cornell, *The Beginnings of Rome*, 165.
29 Bruni, *History of the Florentine People*, 45.
30 Cornell, *The Beginnings of Rome*, 365.
31 Whitney, *The Life and Growth of Language*, 42.

granted citizenship in 89 BCE, and in 27 BCE Etruria became an administrative division of Roman Italy. As Etruria became part of Rome, Etruscan began to slip out of common usage even as it appeared increasingly on bilingual inscriptions. In his attempt to revive ancient institutions, Augustus revived the Etruscan League and the title of "praetor Etruriae," but there are no signs that this led to an Etruscan revival. The religious festival of the Fanum Voltumnae, where the cities of the confederacy gathered annually, survived into the reign of Constantine (306–37). Divination survived longest, still mentioned, as I said, as late as the beginning of the fifth century of our era.

Discussing Carthage, Serge Ancel addresses the question of what constitutes a nation's disappearance as follows: "Besides its institutions and laws, three orders of reality on very different planes have always constituted a state, especially in Antiquity: its walls and the material expression of its urban existence; its temples and cults; its language and the written traces of its history and past. Walls may fall, temples disappear, books be carried away or destroyed; but that immaterial content formed by its language and its religion can escape and survive destruction or be reborn."[32] For the Etruscans, conquest entailed the disappearance of everything from their social and political institutions to their language and religion, though, as I point out below, aspects of all of these found their way into Latin and into Roman customs to a degree that would mislead later commentators like Gibbon and Roger Fry to attribute much of what was most civilized about Rome to Etruria.

II

Assimilation

It is possible that Thucydides, for example, contains a fact of prime importance that will not be noticed until a hundred years from now.

                                                            Jacob Burckhardt[33]

The Etruscans had the mixed good fortune of having Titus Livius (59 BCE–17 CE) as their default historian. Not that he (or they) would have thought of him that way, but his history contains the longest and

32 Lancel, *Carthage: A History*, 428.
33 Quoted in Canetti, *The Secret Heart of the Clock*, 5.

most detailed account we have of Etruscan civilization, including significant figures, social and religious customs, and their relations with the Romans. Inevitably the Etruscans appear as an adjunct to a patriotic history of Rome that emphasizes the virtues Romans believed constituted their character, including the patriotism that bound them. The Etruscans and the Carthaginians lacked precisely what the Romans possessed, what Ibn Khaldun, in another culture, called "*asabiyya*," the sense of bonding and unanimity of a tribe. Not even in wars against Rome could one Etruscan city count on the support of the others. Only at the annual religious meeting did they show some unanimity of purpose that reflected their common language, culture, religion, and ethnicity. War was another matter. Perhaps the Etruscans also lacked *kleos*, the Homeric heroic obsession with the perpetuation of one's name by a glorious accomplishment. Herodotus, it will be recalled, declares in his first paragraph that he wrote his history "in the hope of thereby preserving from decay the remembrance of what men have done, and of preventing the great and wonderful actions of the Greeks and the Barbarians from losing their due meed of glory."[34] The Romans celebrated by Livy and Plutarch exhibited it in abundance. Did the Etruscans also lack the bards to express and communicate it, since the word carries the implication of "what others hear about you"? Imagine Greek athletes without Pindar's *Odes*: without Nemean VII the feats of young Sógenes of Aigina would "have a great darkness" instead of immortality. There are no remembered acts in history without Clio, its muse, and the sisters responsible for poetic kinds. Of the Etruscan "heroes" whose names survive, the Vipinas brothers are shown on mirrors capturing Cacu the seer, and Macstrna was probably another name for Servius Tullius. Of the scenes of violence on the ash urns and sarcophagi, none celebrate Etruscan military heroes. Except for Lars Porsena, it's a forgettable (and forgotten) list. R.S. Conway sums up Etruscan history as follows in the 1911 edition of the *Encyclopedia Britannica*: "The authentic history of Etruria is very meagre and consists mainly in the story of its relations with Carthage, Greece, and Rome."[35] And in these "relations" the Etruscans are almost anonymous. Pericles's well-known claim in the "Funeral Oration" that "the whole world is the

34 Herodotus, *The Histories of Herodotus*, 1.1.
35 Conway, "Etruria," in the *Encyclopedia Britannica*, 854.

sepulcher of famous men" doesn't apply to the Etruscans (Thucydides, 2.43). I cite R.S. Conway not as a contemporary authority but to indicate the view at the turn of the twentieth century at a time when Edgar Degas, Anatole France, Marcel Proust, and Aldous Huxley were incorporating the Etruscans into their work.

As Livy tells it, the decline is slow but definite. Between the expulsion of the Tarquins from Rome in 509 BCE and the third century, the Etruscans lost all the important battles against Rome. By the Second Punic War, the Etruscans supported Rome against Hannibal with supplies. In 89 BCE they were granted full citizenship under the Lex Julia. If they didn't quite disappear, they assimilated, to become less obviously present. One writer even suggests that "since the days when Etruscan kings ruled the city on the Tiber, Romans had had such a strong admixture of Etruscan blood that it is impossible to distinguish Etruscans and Romans from each other."[36] Livy's account may be partial in both senses of the word, but without his books about early Rome what we know about the Etruscans would be sparse indeed. His version has not lacked pro-Etruscan critics. Two historians begin their account with a "spoiler alert": "It is the intention of this book to reject the value of the Roman historians as sources for Etruscan history" and to replace them with the evidence of archaeology.[37] Others have expressed similar reservations. This is in every sense a rearguard battle. The Greek and Roman historians remain our primary resource, and it is in their languages that we encounter the Rasenna. To be fair to Livy, his endorsement of Roman hegemony is no different from Hegel's and Leopold von Ranke's insistence that European history would culminate in the triumph of the German people, or the position taken by contemporary Americans like Francis Fukuyama, for whom the history of the immediate future will follow the American republican capitalist model.

The world historical story Livy tells is how Rome developed from a small settlement into a world power by overcoming other nations, beginning with the Etruscans. Not surprisingly, the narrative is airbrushed throughout to justify Roman conquest. The long reign (616–509 BCE) of Etruscan kings at Rome is an embarrassment to Roman historians who underemphasize their achievements to make the

36 Kähler, *The Art of Rome and Her Empire*, 36.
37 Spivey and Stoddart, *Etruscan Italy*, 14.

expulsion of Tarquinius Superbus in 509 and the coming of the Republic seem an inevitable Roman event. That he was driven out by nobles of Latin-Etruscan stock is closer to the truth. As several historians, including Ogilvie, have pointed out, the break was probably less decisive than indicated and Etruscans remained in positions of power in the so-called Republic. Overall, however, this is the Roman version of the Whig theory of history. Etruscan sea power is exaggerated to give the conflict drama and to justify Rome's aggression against the various Etruscan cities. In the larger canvas, Livy wants the reader to think of the wars between Rome and the never quite united Etruscan confederacy in the context of the Persian invasion of Greece and Rome's three wars with Carthage. In the Roman imagination these are wars of Roman republicanism against Oriental tyranny. Ronald Syme suggests that "as long as Livy had to recount the exploits of the Populus Romanus in its early troubles with the Volscian, the Etruscan, and the Samnite, he was content with the edifying contrast between valour and virtue on the one side, on the other perfidy, cruelty, or cowardice. Knowledge and sympathy are absent. Nor was he disposed to be just to the Carthaginian or the Macedonian in their dealings with the imperial Republic."[38] We might think of the post-Augustan near silence on the subject of the Etruscans as a way of dealing with past events that didn't fit the accepted official version. Any Etruscan reference would inevitably recall other peoples (Sabines, Oscans, etc.) who were sacrificed to the creation of Rome and the need for a triumphalist version of Roman history. In that account, the conquered, like their conquerors, are known by Latin names: they have been posthumously naturalized.[39] As J.N. Adams points out in *Bilingualism and the Latin Language*, conquest inevitably included the subordination of Etruscan to Latin. During the first century BCE "there were some families which were keen to give some sort of linguistic expression to their Etruscan roots while parading their Romanness, but the shift

---

38 Syme, *Tacitus*, 139. In his *Sallust*, Syme criticizes Varro: "the science of Varro served to propagate errors and foster the growth of sentimental romanticism about the Roman past" (233). Momigliano suggests in *The Classical Foundations of Modern Historiography* (99) that Greek and Roman historians drew on Etruscan sources.

39 Lancel makes a similar complaint about Livy's simplified onomastic transcription of the Carthaginians: everyone is called Hanno or Hannibal, Hamilcar or Mago (*Carthage*, 111).

to Latin that was in progress is much in evidence, in the imitation of a Latin formula in Etruscan, in the use of Latin alone to convey traditional Etruscan information, in the survival of numerous purely Latin epitaphs in the region of Etruria, and in the use of Latin script to write Etruscan ... The use of Etruscan script to write Latin ... is all but non-existent."[40]

To his credit, Livy acknowledges that Etruscan traditions continue after the conquest in Roman versions of Etruscan originals: the purple-fringed toga, fasces, consuls, throne of state (*sella curulis*), the "triumph" accorded a general, forms of divination, temple architecture, gladiatorial games, realistic portraiture, and many Latin words with Etruscan roots. "Rome" itself may be an Etruscan word. There were also many forms of behaviour, social and religious rules and rites, political customs, and relics of various kinds that survived late into the Republic and even into the Empire. We can recapture these from Roman writings and their plastic arts just as we understand what John Berger calls "the system of etiquette" for eighteenth-century Europe from its painting.[41] They are part of the full description of the past if the remains are substantial. We know, for instance, that a noble Roman often had his own haruspex: Herennius Siculus attended Gaius Gracchus (154–121 BCE); Caesar's was Spurinna, who is remembered for "Beware the Ides of March!"[42] A good example of an Etruscan-related tradition surviving far beyond its time is recorded in a description of the 62 BCE elections for the Centuriate Assembly (*Comitia centuriata*) held outside the city's sacred limits on the Campus Martius, where a red flag traditionally flew above the field on the Janiculum Hill to assure all that there was no Etruscan attack. Citizens could appear for the elections, as Cicero did, wearing defensive armour. Even though there had not been an Etruscan attack in two centuries and all Etruscans were Roman citizens, the tradition of the red flag was maintained.[43] To cite one

---

40 Adams, *Bilingualism and the Latin Language*, 175–6. Benelli points out that "the use of Latin in private epigraphy appears at different times in the different Etruscan cities. In the south, it seems to have followed immediately on the receipt of Roman citizenship and law in 89 BCE, while in the north (especially in inland cities like Chiusi and Perugia) it does not seem to have occurred before the mid first century BCE, and Etruscan survived occasionally into the reign of Augustus" (270).

41 John T. Hall, *Etruscan Italy*, 105.

42 Emeline Richardson, *The Etruscans*, 238.

43 Baron, *From Petrarch to Leonardo Bruni*, 8.

other example, Etruscan religion survived and prospered in at least one important form, the interpretation of animal entrails, prodigies, bird flight, and lightning. Despite the established presence of Roman augurs, the Etruscans flourished and were eventually organized into a collegium under the empire. Just as Rome looked to Athens for its philosophy, in divination it turned to Etruria. Emperors had their own augurs or haruspices. De Grummond indicates that "long after [Etruscan] ceased being a living language, it was studied and spoken by priests in the Roman college of haruspices or soothsayers, much as Latin continued to be used into the twentieth century by priests of the Catholic church. As late as the reign of Julian the Apostate (360–363), there were still haruspices at court."[44] Latinization occurred most quickly in centres like Cerveteri (Etruscan: Caere), where it is predominant by the end of the second century BCE, and a few decades later in places in the interior like Chiusi.

Even earlier than the Augustan era, Etruscan must have seemed like a language doomed to extinction except in divination. The only Etruscan writers whose names survive wrote in Latin. The best known is Cicero's friend, the prolific scholar Nigidius Figulus, who died in 45 BCE.[45] In the next generation, Gaius Musonius Rufus was famous enough as a philosopher to influence Epictetus and to attract the notice of Tacitus as the foremost Stoic of his day. Had either he or Nigidius Figulus written in Etruscan they would have felt as lonely as contemporary Gaelic and Kashubian writers. There were still families like those of Propertius or Maecenas that celebrated their Etruscan origin, and Ovid lists among his rivals, in *Epistles from Pontus* (4.16), at least three poets with Etruscan names. Had Maecenas not been Augustus's right hand and the patron of the major poets, no doubt there would be far fewer references to Etruscans in the period's poetry. The several poems addressed to Maecenas are a case in point. Take Horace's invitation (*Odes* 3.29) to Maecenas, the "scion of Tuscan kings," to join him for a "jar of mellow wine." These Latin poems are sprinkled with occasional Etruscan references, like those to Lars Porsena and Tarquin the Proud, but these represent decorative

---

44 de Grummond, "Rediscovery," 19.

45 Figulus is described in Lucan's *Pharsalia* as one "whose study it was to know the gods and the secrets of the sky" (1.638–9). A modern scholar called him "a living encyclopedia of errors" (*Pharsalia*, 48).

detail: the real show is elsewhere. Maecenas is said to have written a
Prometheus and a *Dialogue.* There is no suggestion that either he or the
Etruscan poets mentioned by Ovid wrote in Etruscan. On the evidence
of the poetry, Horace had the closest relationship with Maecenas.
Several poems are addressed to him in a tone that implies intimacy,
and the first volume of the *Odes* begins with his name and descent:
"Maecenas atavis edite regibus" ("Maecenas, sprung from royal stock").
But perhaps the clearest sign of the intimate degree of the friendship
comes in the *Satires,* where 1.6 opens with a respectful address pointing
out that "in Tuscan lands none is of nobler birth than you" and that
"grandsires of yours, on your mother's and father's side alike, com-
manded mighty legions in days of old." Having established Maecenas's
impressive descent, Horace then praises him for befriending a man
like himself "of unknown birth, a freedman's son." That they are friends
seems confirmed by the subject matter and tone of the book's ninth
poem, which mocks an irksome poetaster who keeps trying to insinu-
ate himself into Horace's circle. In the next satire he even takes the
liberty of mocking a bad poet named Cassius Etruscus, probably
fictional, whose style is both turgid and violent and who was rumoured
to have been burned on a funeral pyre of his books. There is no question that, whether real or a figure of Horace's imagination, Cassius
Etruscus wrote in Latin. Only a poet secure in his relationship with a
powerful friend from an Etruscan family would take such liberties.
When William Blake satirized an ideologue named "Etruscan Column" –
see below – he didn't have to worry about a powerful Etruscan patron.

Robert Macfarlane suggests that Horace is playing a variation on the
traditional description of Etruscan decadence that goes back as far as
Theopompus in the fourth century, who was dismissed by Cornelius
Nepos as "maledicentissimus" or "the wickedest tongue in all literature."[46]
According to the Greek historian, Etruscan women were promiscuous,
exercised undressed, drank with the men at dinner, were bisexual, and

46 Heurgon, *Daily Life of the Etruscans,* 34. Some modern scholars have suggested
that the banquet scenes with men and women in the tomb paintings represent pleasures of drink, music, dancing, and company that will be available in the afterlife. As
late as the reign of Tiberius, Valerius Maximus's *Epitome* repeats Livy's claim that the
Etruscans in Volsinii "degenerated with luxury" and "fell into an abyss of outrage and
turpitude ending in subjection to the insolent rule of slaves." Valerius Maximus,
Memorable Doings and Sayings, 2:9.303.

couldn't be sure who were the fathers of their children.[47] Catullus's one Etruscan glance seems to play with this commonplace when he mocks a character as an "obesus Etruscus" (39.11), while Virgil, whose last name Maro is cognate with the Etruscan *mar* – a priest and/or magistrate – shows a "pinguis Tyrrhenus" ("a fat, stout, or puff-cheeked" Tyrrhenian) playing "an ivory pipe" in the *Georgics* (2.193). Were the accusations of obesity just another slur directed at the Etruscans of the period of decline, or were they really stout or fat? M.I. Finley is willing to consider the latter possibility. Pointing to sarcophagi of stout men, Finley suggests that "The Etruscans were unlikely to have chosen the coffin as the proper locale for poking fun at its occupant."[48] It is worth keeping in mind that notions of masculinity and male beauty vary. In Lady Murasaki's eleventh century *Tale of Genji* the aristocratic hero is plump, is easily provoked to tears, writes brief love poems, and prides himself on his skill in making perfumes. In the Heian period (950–1050) the males at the court lived for beauty and pleasure. Genji's statue on a sarcophagus would resemble Cai Cutu's in Perugia (see figure 0.1).

Would Maecenas have laughed at Catullus's "obesus" and Virgil's "pinguis" in the way that Greek youths mock a chubby youth on a fifth-century vase Kenneth Clark discusses in *The Nude*?[49] Unfortunately, none of the fragments of his writings indicate that Maecenas had any interest in his Etruscan heritage. He is silent about his people. Or, at least, his surviving work is. Francis Cairns suggests, however, that "Maecenas seems to have been a dedicated Etruscan. His un-Roman personal behaviour, dress, actions, and literary style, which attracted the criticism of Seneca, can best be seen as ostentatious expressions of his background in Etruria."[50]

Maecenas's active encouragement of his circle of poets did more to keep an Etruscan presence alive in Augustan poetry than anything he

---

47 Haynes, *Etruscan Civilization*, 256–7. A more recent example of this sort of vilification of the "other" occurs in George Orwell's *Animal Farm*. Once the farmers learn that the animals have taken over Jones's farm, "It was given out that the animals there practiced cannibalism, tortured one another with red-hot horseshoes, and had their females in common" (33).

48 Finley, "Etruscheria," *Aspects of Antiquity*, 109. I wonder how the rotund figures in the paintings of Fernanado Botero and Lucian Freud will be viewed by future generations.

49 Clark, *The Nude*, 23.

50 Cairns, *Sextus Propertius, the Augustan Elegist*, 271.

0.1 Tomb of Arnth Cai Cutu.

might have written himself. The appearance of his name is an instant metonymic summary of everything Etruscan, even when the poem intends nothing beyond an onomastic reference. In the opening poem of Propertius's second book, we see the poet, whose family is as Etruscan as that of his patron, separating Etruria's past from the Augustan present while at the same time twice using Maecenas's name to obliquely bring that past before the reader. The poem is simultaneously a justification of his commitment to love poetry and a probably insincere apology for not writing about the regime's accomplishments. This is troubled momentarily, however, by the mention of "eversosque focos antiquae gentis Etruscae" ("the ruined hearths of Etruria's ancient race"). The primary reference is to recent civil wars, but the image also suggests troubling earlier wars in which Romans vanquished Etruscans. As if sensing the ambiguity and ambivalence, the poet emphasizes Maecenas's loyalty by praising it twice. He then repeats that his lyric talent, like that of Callimachus, is inadequate to the larger themes and landscapes Augustus and Maecenas deserve. The only wars appropriate to the poet's talent are love's skirmishes. Virgil died in 19 BCE, and it is probable Propertius knew about *The Aeneid* when he confessed his inability to be the poet of war and empire. His 3.9 returns to the theme by reminding Maecenas that "Huge sails are not suited to my little boat."

Propertius's 4.2 isn't quite a historical poem though tectonic historical change is implicit in its antiquarian subject. The unexpected speaker is the Etruscan divinity Vertumnus, who is often identified with the Etruscan god Tinia, a bisexual Jupiter. Varro describes Vertumnus as principal deity of Etruria,[51] and he exists in both male and female (Vertumna) forms. Vertumnus claims that his name is Etruscan, though G.P. Gould, Propertius's translator, suggests that the name's roots are Latin. Vertumnus recalls how Rome welcomed both him and the Etruscans, though his memory doesn't extend to the bloodletting and destruction of at least two centuries of war. Instead, he mentions the defeat of the Sabines by the Romans and their Etruscan allies. Maecenas isn't mentioned, but his presence may be felt in the fact that Propertius's book of poems on the theme of the state begins with a blessing from an Etruscan god. Both are poems of loss and change that encompass this knowledge within an optimistic vision of the future. Ovid resurrects Vertumnus in the *Metamorphoses* (14.623–771) for a mythical narrative about the god's love for the nymph Pomona. The god's wooing involves various disguises, including changing age and gender. In the end he reveals himself as a young god "as when the sun / triumphs in glory through the clouds and rain" and she accepts him. If one is looking for some vestige of the Augustan ideology of unity here it might be in the union of Etruscan and Roman gods.

Virgil's *Aeneid*, despite its reputation as the most propagandistic of the Augustan poems, deals extensively and sensitively with Etruscan material, placing Etruscans among Aeneas's allies and enemies. The most complex and fully realized of them is Mezentius, a historical Etruscan king from the seventh century who in one tradition survives Aeneas and in another, followed by Virgil, is slain by him. He is

---

51 Macfarlane, "'*Tyrrhena Regum Progenies*,'" 262. Macfarlane also traces the influence of Propertius's treatment in Ovid (*Metamorphoses* 14.623), Tibullus (3.8.13), and Horace (*Satires* 2.7.14). De Grummond unravels some of the complications of the Tinia-Vortumnus relationship in *Etruscan Myth, Sacred History, and Legend*, an indispensable book, richly illustrated, with a CD of Etruscan mirrors, 61.

mentioned by Livy, Cato the Elder, and Dionysius of Halicarnassus. His name was found recently in the Louvre on a seventh-century vase of unknown provenance. Virgil departs from the tradition to make him a cruel monarch who has been banished by his subjects. Accompanied by his son Lausus, he joins Turnus in his war against Aeneas's invading Trojans. However, the Etruscan people, now led by Tarchon – also the name of the Etruscan founder-hero – are allied with the Trojans. Mezentius, whatever his faults as a monarch, is an exemplary warrior who would not have been out of place in the *Iliad*. His contempt of the gods, however, makes him the perfect antithesis to *pius* Aeneas. In battle he is strong, indomitable, and fearless, and his warrior's code prevents him from striking a foe from behind. Though wounded, he nevertheless rides against Aeneas, who killed his son, knowing that he is going to his death. He confronts his fate with a resolution worthy of a Homeric warrior. The encounter prepares the reader for the book's final battle between Turnus and Aeneas, just as the images of Lars Porsena and Horatio Cocles on Aeneas's shield anticipate this fight. Two thousand years later, Aeneas's triumphs over Mezentius and Turnus continue to trouble readers because he refuses them the clemency and justice we heard in his father's speech in Hades. With Mezentius, there is a further complication. Aeneas avoids attacking him directly as a warrior should: instead, he wounds his horse with a javelin with the result that its fall traps the rider underneath. What follows is an execution, not a combat. The trapped Etruscan refuses to show deference to the gods and displays an indomitable courage and pride. Before offering his throat to the sword, he asks only to be buried with his son. The mixture of heroism and pathos is profound and surprising: that accounts in large part for its dramatic and emotional power. The villain unexpectedly rises to the epic occasion and achieves almost heroic stature at the same moment that the triumphant hero is less than truly heroic. It is one of those numinous moments when Virgil writes beyond whatever ideologically inflected script we may have assumed he was following. There are other important Etruscan references, but Mezentius stands apart because he is such a fully realized human figure who, compared to other secondary characters, stands like a life-sized statue in the round next to smaller ones in high or low relief. Together with Dido and Turnus, he gives Virgil room to develop a moral complexity at the heart of acts of conquest or colonialization that claim the sanction of gods. Virgil fulfills the terms of his contract with Maecenas and Augustus with his story of a Trojan-Etruscan alliance that both reflects "the Etruscan support of Augustus" and provides mythological precedent for an Italy in which Aeneas (a Trojan becoming a Roman) and Tarchon (a "good" Etruscan) labour in tandem to ensure the establishment of a new civilization.[52] But he simultaneously fulfills his obligation to life and art with his fully human portrait of the godless, renegade Etruscan whom a later epic poet might have considered as a model for his fallen angels.

Robert Macfarlane's summary provides a finely balanced perspective on the Augustan poets' situation vis-à-vis their emperor's politics. "The Augustan poets produced what material they did on Etruscan themes in agreement, it seems, with their patron's vision of developing a national literature with themes of greatness that survived the decline of ancient Etruria and the coming of Rome. The mature works of Virgil, Horace, and Propertius illuminate this vision. The experiment was not long-lived. And by the time Augustus died, the vision was gone."[53] He might have added that each of the poets has a moment when he resists the emperor's vision even as he affirms it, as Virgil does memorably with Mezentius. In the next generation, however, the satirist Persius (34–62), of Etruscan descent, seems intent on ignoring the Etruscans when he asks, sarcastically, "is it appropriate to burst your lungs with pride because you draw your roots over a thousand generations from an Etruscan stock" (3.27)? As Macfarlane reminds us, neither Maecenas nor Persius "made as much of his Etruscan ancestry as others anticipated he should."[54] Another way of putting this would be to say that Persius reminds us that the Etruscans had their last hurrah in Latin writing with Horace, Virgil, Propertius, and Ovid, though for all the poets, as Francis Cairns points out, the Tiber remained an Etruscan river.[55]

---

52 Macfarlane quoting Hall in "'*Tyrrhena Regum Progenies*,'" 249. Virgil's use of Maecenas in the *Georgics* shows the poet paying homage to his patron while subtly weaving him into the rural and social themes. The opening of the fourth poem links Maecenas to the story of the bees. The allegory would seem to point to the bees as proto-Romans, but the concern with their periodic disappearance seems a wink at the "tiny world" of Etruscan history to which poet and patron both belong. For a full treatment of Maecenas's life and times, see Peter Mountford's *Maecenas*.

53 Macfarlane, "'*Tyrrhena Regum Progenies*,'" 255–6.

54 Ibid., 255.

55 Cairns, *Sextus Propertius, The Augustan Elegist*, 280.

If we turn to Augustan prose for residual evidence of the Etruscans, there is little of importance that doesn't derive from Livy. And as Nigel Spivey and Simon Stoddard remind us, "Livy's task was to remind his contemporaries what it meant to be Roman. There was nothing in his brief about doing justice to the first victims of Roman expansion."[56] Cicero discusses the Etruscans in *De Divinatione*, a dialogue on superstition and various forms of divination. His point of departure is the foundational story of the miraculous appearance of Tages, which he tells only to immediately offer a rational refutation, as if he were David Strauss or Ernst Renan dealing with the New Testament.

Who in the world is stupid enough to believe that anybody ever ploughed up – which shall I say – a god or a man? If a god, why did he, contrary to his nature, hide himself in the ground to be uncovered and brought to the light of day by a plough? Could not this so-called god have delivered this art to mankind from a more exalted station? But if this fellow Tages was a man, pray, how could he have lived covered with earth? Finally, where had he himself learned the things he taught others? But really in spending so much time in refuting such stuff I am more absurd than the people who believe it. (*De Divinatione* 2.23–24)[57]

The participants in the dialogue must have known that Cicero was an augur of the state and that one of his best friends, the Volterran Aulus Caecina, had written a now lost *De Etrusca disciplina*. So why does he take on the role of the doubter and hand over the role of believer to his brother Quintus, who reminds the participants that the Stoics have accepted divination as a valid form of knowledge? Roman superstition was a fact of life in all classes. The emperor Claudius revived the ancient college of the haruspices in 47 CE. Tacitus records Vespasian's reliance on prophecies, horoscopes, and astrology when deciding whether to accept the crown (*Histories*, 2.78.2).[58] Three centuries later, the Emperor Theodosius tried to put a stop to pagan divination in 391 with a formal ban.

56 Macfarlane, "'*Tyrrhena Regum Progenies*,'" 14.

57 For another view of Tages see Ovid, *Metamorphoses*, 15.558.

58 See also Suetonius: "his belief in astrology having persuaded him that the world was wholly ruled by fate." "Tiberius," 69.

Most other references to the Etruscans in prose are brief: Varro, Pliny the Elder, Vitruvius (on the Tuscan order), Diodorus Siculus, Strabo, and Quintilian, and a well-known paragraph in Suetonius's life of Claudius: "At last he even wrote historical works in Greek, twenty books of Etruscan History and eight of Carthaginian. Because of these works there was added to the old Museum at Alexandria a new one called after his name, and it was provided that in the one his Etruscan History should be read each year from beginning to end, and in the other his Carthaginian, by various readers in turn, in the manner of public recitations" (42). The passage is the basis of scenes in Robert Graves's *I, Claudius* and *Claudius the God* (both 1934) and Mika Waltari's *The Roman* (1964). Of lost books, I can't think of one whose rediscovery would excite me as much as that of Claudius's Etruscan history. Tacitus describes Claudius's efforts to restore the college of haruspices and in passing implies a connection between the Etruscan alphabet and the Latin (*Annals* 2.14). But the Etruscans of history lie outside his subject. When he wrote at the beginning of the second century, Etruscans had long been irrelevant to Roman history.

Not surprisingly the farther we move into the Empire the fewer the Etruscan references. In the *Chronicon* (380) Eusebius calls them the Tyrreni or Tyranni and lists them among the descendants of Noah's son Japeth in the catalogue of peoples and Roman emperors, while Jerome adds that "Tarquin the Proud contrived chains, leather whips, clubs, shackles, quarry-chains, prisons, exiles and mines."[59] By the time of *Lives of the Later Caesars* (probably c. 395–405)[60] and Augustine's *City of God* (412–27) Etruscans don't even warrant a reference, though the first informs us that "the deified Aurelian" (270–75) planned to give the profits from the sale of Etrurian wine to the people of Rome."[61] After the diviner's attempt to call down thunderbolts against the Visigoths for King Alaric's army in 408 CE, Etruscan civilization entered a cryonic phase without a date of return.

---

59 Jerome, *Chronicon*, Part II, 182.

60 This is a contested date. For a clear account of the problems involved, see Birley's "Introduction" to *Lives of the Later Caesars*.

61 *Lives of the Later Caesars*, 441.

III

Return

The trail remains cold for nearly a millennium though there are a few signs and references. The irrepressibly curious Isidore of Seville (560–636) finds a place in his *Etymologiae* or *Origines* (c. 600–625) for the story of Tages's autochthonous birth. William of Malmesbury (c. 1090–c. 1143) relates in *The Chronicles of the Kings of England* two marvellous stories about concealed treasure that may or may not be about Etruscan tombs. The second story involves Pope Sylvester II (946–1003) and ends in an underground room (an Etruscan tomb?) where the ancient statues come to life and threaten the explorers. The later discovery of tombs is confirmed by the evidence of Renaissance works that show an affinity with Etruscan paintings. Giotto's Judas and Satan resemble the demonic Charu in the Tomba dell'Orco. The form of the reclining Virgin in Pisa's Baptistery by Nicola Pisano (1225–1284) seems taken from a sarcophagus. The hero's pose in Benvenuto Cellini's "Perseus with the Head of Medusa" (1545–54) recalls that of Odysseus on an engraved Tuscan mirror. Other sightings, and this is a partial list, occur in Masaccio, Donatello, Michelangelo, Cellini, and Sansovino. Perhaps the most publicized Etruscan event of the sixteenth century was the discovery, described in detail by Vasari, of the Arezzo Chimaera in 1553. He identified it as Etruscan by the Etruscan inscription on its right foreleg: "TINSCVIL" ("offering belonging to Tinia," the Etruscan Jupiter). Like the Laocoön discovered in Rome in 1506 it would become essential to the discussion of ancient sculpture. An Etruscan Minerva had been found a few years earlier, and the Orator or Aule Meteli, later praised by Winckelmann and Hegel, would be found near Perugia in 1566.[62]

The growing interest in Etruscan art was co-extensive with the interest during the early Renaissance in the origins of the major Italian cities. Boccaccio, for instance, set in motion the idea that Corneto was the Etruscan city Corythus mentioned in the *Aeneid* as Trojan. A century later a prominent citizen wrote a poem describing in detail the ruins of the ancient city which he had supposedly seen under modern

---

62 This section is indebted to de Grummond's "Rediscovery," 18–46.

Corneto. The whole thing was a false scent since, as Petrarch had suggested in the previous century, Corneto was really the ancient Tarquinia. Leonardo Bruni, carrying on the work of his teacher Coluccio Salutati, described Florence's Etruscan origins in his *Historia Florentina* (written 1405–15) and praised the Etruscan's republican system of government in an effort to establish the dynastic claims of the Medici. The search for familial and communal roots was part of a larger wave of interest in things Etruscan by antiquarians, linguists, historians, and treasure hunters. Some of these must have seen themselves as carrying on the work of Pliny the Elder, Aulus Gellius, and Pausanias. They didn't know it, but they were creating a movement that by the eighteenth century would develop into a full-scale *etruscheria.*

Among these early proto-Etruscologists three very different figures stand out. The first and most notorious is the Dominican friar Annius da Viterbo (1432–1502) who may have been the first to claim he could read Etruscan. He also insisted it derived from Hebrew, a false lead that would be repeated by others. A few even took seriously his view that the Etruscans were the direct descendants of Osiris and, in turn, of Noah, supposedly known in Italy as Janus by the Latins and as Vertumnus by the Etruscans. His Latin was sufficiently proficient to allow him to pass off a forged history of Rome, supposedly by Fabius Pictor (c. 275–203 BCE), the earliest Roman historian. Annius was also an excavator but is best remembered today for digs in which he planted forged objects. He had a successor, Curzio Inghirami (1614–1655), who took advantage of the growing obsession with ancestry to forge Latin and Etruscan documents for those eager to prove or improve their ancestry. Using mud and hair, he made capsules for the documents and then claimed to have found them near Scornello. Since no one could read Etruscan, no questions were raised about authenticity. Annius and Curzio began a tradition of Etruscan forgery that continues today. It too is part of the beginnings of the Etruscan return.[63] Two more substantial figures close out this section.

Thomas Dempster (1579–1625) is a more serious figure. He was an itinerant Scots scholar with an uncertain temper, which led to duels and brushes with the law that, in the end, exiled him to Italy. This was

63 For Inghirami, see Rowland's informative and entertaining *The Scarith of Scornello.* Wellard devotes six lively pages to Annius da Viterbo in *The Search for the Etruscans,* 40–5.

a better fate than his equally quarrelsome brother found in France, where he was tried for murder, hanged, and quartered. A brilliant scholar, Dempster found success in Italy, first as a professor of law at Pisa and then as professor of humanities at Bologna. He also found favour with the Grand Duke Cosimo II of Tuscany who commissioned a book that would show the Etruscan roots of the Medici regime. He submitted the Latin manuscript sometime before his death in 1625, but the duke had died in 1621 and interest had waned. It remained unpublished for a century until discovered and bought by Thomas Coke (1697–1759) during a Grand Tour that included a visit to Florence. Coke, a generous man, paid to have the original Latin text published in a two-volume edition (1723–24) updated by the archaeologist Filippo Buonarroti and illustrated with engravings from various collections. Buonarroti had established a solid reputation with his systematic surveys of tombs at Civita Castellani and his attempts to date antiquities and monuments. Dempster, by contrast, had concentrated on textual sources to provide a comprehensive study of origins, religion, kings (most of whom he invented), cities, and a systematic history of the Medici family legitimizing their power.[64] The book became an unexpected success. Although Dempster had seen few of the Etruscan places and his imagination sometimes filled lacunae, his book can be regarded as one of the founding texts for the study of the Etruscans. Its flaws are of its time. His strengths are the following: he read the available classical texts; he attempted to gather everything known about the Etruscans; he offered a comprehensive interpretation of Etruscan culture; he understood that the Etruscan language was different from the other languages of the Italian peninsula, though he couldn't resist suggesting a link to Hebrew; and he was also the first modern figure to suggest that the Romans had inherited the fasces, the military triumph, the trumpet, the toga, and the gladiatorial games from the Etruscans.

The flood of Etruscan interest in the first half of the eighteenth century would have astounded earlier scholars like Dempster or the Jesuit polymath Athanasius Kircher (1602–1680), who wrote a guidebook to Latium in 1669 and left behind an early description of Etruscan tombs near Bomarzo. Massimo Pallottino, who is not given to

---

64 See de Angelis, "The Reception of Etruscan Culture," 130–5.

overstatement, has suggested that "Just as the sixteenth was the century of the rediscovery of Rome, and the nineteenth that of the discovery of Greece, so the eighteenth may certainly be called the century of the discovery of Etruria."[65] The founding of the Accademia Etrusca in Cortona in 1727 is one of the signs of that discovery (and the institution is still active). After a dormant millennium and a half, the Etruscans were about to be reborn, though in a very different way than predicted by the dark exigency of their cyclical theory of history that predicted eight or ten one-hundred-year cycles followed by a catastrophe. It isn't in the Etruscan script, but they returned into history decisively and permanently through the cumulative efforts of antiquarians, archaeologists, art historians, collectors of vases and scarabs, linguists, and historians, few, if any, of whom could have been aware of the scale of the recuperative project they were involved in as a group.[66] Three of the key figures in this movement are Johann Joachim Winckelmann, for his influential *History of the Art of Antiquity* (1764), Sir William Hamilton, whose collection of vases popularized Etruscan and Greek antiquities, and Josiah Wedgwood, who sold Europe on the idea of what he branded "Etruscan ware." Hamilton and Wedgwood were the links between commerce, art history, scholarship, antiquarianism, and the aristocracy. They set in motion what might be called a repurposing of the Etruscans as they imposed new ways of seeing and thinking about them and secured their place in discussions of art, style, and taste.

During the same period, the study of all things Etruscan became a field within the overlapping disciplines of ancient history, art history,

---

65 Pallottino, *The Etruscans*, 24.

66 Robert Graves's *I, Claudius* summarizes the theory as follows: "A cycle is a period reckoned by the longest life: that is to say, a cycle does not close until the death of everyone who was alive at the festival celebrating the close of the previous cycle. A cycle averages a little over one hundred years. Well, this was the last cycle and it would end with the total disappearance of Etruscan as a spoken language" (251). The Romans also had a "faint tradition" that "one hundred years was a span in the life of the world" (Ogilvie, *The Romans and Their Gods*, 117) but theirs was more optimistic. The Secular Games of 17 BCE reflected both general optimism and various prophecies, including those in Virgil's Fourth Eclogue and *Aeneid* (6.789.), that Augustus had inaugurated a golden age. The tradition was followed by some of his successors, notably Trajan. Horace's "Carmen Saeculare" was written for public performance in 17 BCE. For a clear overview of the Etruscans on time and *saecula* see de Grummond's *Etruscan Myth, Sacred History, and Legend*, 42–4.

the study of myths, ethnography, linguistics, and archaeology. Except for the few minor figures who sketched Etruscan sites and tombs, most creative artists were slow to incorporate Etruscan images, motifs, and themes. In the period between Nicolas Poussin and J.M.W. Turner the Etruscans are absent from the canvases of major painters. We must go back to Titian to find an Etruscan-themed painting. He painted two, both featuring Lucretia: *Lucretia and Her Husband* (1515) – in which Tarquin's presence is implied – and *Tarquin and Lucretia* (1571). In the more famous later painting, as in Shakespeare's almost contemporary *The Rape of Lucrece* (1594), the Etruscans are represented by their least attractive figure, a royal rapist. Another indication of how far they had to come before they could enter Europe's artistic imagination can be gauged by their absence from popular eighteenth-century genres like drama and opera. In these we find Persians, Egyptians, Greeks, Jews, and Romans with always the same rotating cast: Cleopatra, Alexander, Julius Caesar, Samson, Scaevola, Scipio, Xerxes, Sulla, Agrippina, Bajazet, Aurangzeb, Nero, Darius, Cato, and Cloelia, to name just a few. Cloelia, to take one example, is the subject of a very long romance by the very popular Madeleine de Scudéry in 1661 and of three operas – based on Pietro Metastasio's libretto – written in the eighteenth century by Johann Adolf Hasse (1762), Christoph Willibald von Gluck (1763), and Josef Mysliveček (1767). Lars Porsena, the most famous Etruscan hero, has a major part but the opera remains a Roman story and a Roman opera.

Despite their absence from the arts in the late eighteenth century, the Rasenna began to move from the twilight zone between myth and history into historical time as a serious subject for ancient studies; an exotic area for art historians, connoisseurs, and collectors; a potential source of themes and images for artists and writers; and a novel but recognizable "brand" from the ancient past. I need to be careful not to claim too much for them since some of their new fame came through association with their better-known neighbours. The discovery of Herculaneum in 1709 and the beginning of excavations at Pompeii in 1748 stimulated a more general interest in ancient ruins. The Etruscans were not and never will be on history's celebrity list with the Egyptians, Jews, Greeks, and Romans, but they separated themselves from Hittites, Carthaginians, Parthians, Gauls, Oscans, etc. We shouldn't underestimate the role of the allure of novelty in people's interest, which extended to Persians (Montesquieu's *Persian Letters*) and Chinese

(Gluck's *Le Cinesi*).[67] Part of the Etruscan appeal was the ambiguous relationship between their culture and those of the Greeks and Romans: there was a clear family relationship, yet they were sufficiently different to attract attention as something new and literally mysterious. Its "gold had [not] been tarnished from knocking about too much in the rude world," to adapt Claude Debussy's words about certain musical chords that had become "cheapened by use in mass-produced music" and had "lost their symbolic values at the same time."[68] They also joined the list of nations remembered by a name they did not use when referring to themselves: they returned not as Ras, Rasna, or Rasenna but the Etruscans. The Mexicans suffered the same fate when renamed Aztecs by their conquerors.

By 1764, the year of the publication of Winckelmann's great book, the Etruscans had begun to move out of what Norman Davies calls the shadow world of "half-forgotten" Europe.[69] *The Etruscans in the Modern Imagination* traces the remaining phases of that journey through the works of roughly fifty representative creative artists and intellectuals, among them, Winckelmann, Wedgwood, Blake, Niebuhr, Mérimée, Stendhal, Bachofen, Emerson, Hawthorne, Degas, France, Freud, Proust, Huxley, Lawrence, Queneau, Alberto Giacometti, Pablo Picasso, Zbigniew Herbert, Wisława Szymborska, and Carson. Overall, there is at least one figure from each decade since Winckelmann. The works vary in intellectual scope and artistic intensity; a few are even of the first rank. But all show the Etruscans appearing in works of art and discourses of various kinds to a degree not seen since the Roman poets.

Rediscovery inevitably entails reinterpretation, and the following chapters show different Etruscans. Etruscans as a synonym for "Orientalism"; Etruscans as proto-feminists; Etruscans as a link between Greek and Roman art; Etruscans as the "non-Romans" or "anti-Romans";

67 The following are just a few of the books that show the period taste for the foreign and exotic: Montesquieu, *Persian Letters* (1721); George Lyttleton, *Letters from a Persian in England* (1735); Horace Walpole, *Letter from Xo Ho, a Chinese Philosopher to his Friend Lien Chi at Peking* (1757); Samuel Johnson, *The History of Rasselas, Prince of Abissinia [sic]* (1759); Oliver Goldsmith, *The Citizen of the World, or, Letters from a Chinese Philosopher* (1762).

68 Debussy, *Debussy Letters*, to Ernest Chausson, 3 September 1893, 51–2.

69 Davies defines vanished kingdoms as "poorly remembered or half-forgotten, or completely derelict" (*Vanished Kingdoms*, 9). The year 1764 was also when London's Society of Dilettanti sent a mission to explore the sites of ancient Ionia.

Stendhal's republican Etruscans; mysterious Etruscans; New Age Etruscans; the anti-modern, life-affirming Lawrentian Etruscans living in harmony with the cosmos before the disenchantment of the world; the Etruscans who symbolize all small nations threatened by new empires; and zombie Etruscans. Unlike the Romans, however, they could never be a model for modern European nations with imperial aspirations: the British in the eighteenth century, the French under Napoleon, Bismarck's Germany, and the United States after 1900. As Eric Hobsbawm suggests, when Theodore Mommsen was writing about the Roman Empire, behind his Julius Caesar "we discern the shadow of Bismarck."[70] Lars Porsena was not Caesar and, after all, they had been defeated by Rome. They arc also that rare thing among civilizations, a people with relatively clean hands: no Etruscan leader left an inscription resembling that of Sennacherib the Assyrian bragging that he had taken over 200,000 Jews into captivity; none wrote, like Julius Caesar, that he had killed hundreds of thousands of Gauls and enslaved an equal number.[71] Michael Kulikowski describes Caesar as "the first *génocidaire* in European history" and suggests that while the number of Gauls "he left in his wake is of course unknowable ... a million, give or take, would not be hyperbolic."[72] The sentence should make all of us pause. In Tacitus's unforgettable summary: "Solitudinem faciunt pacem appellant" ("They make a wilderness and call it peace," *Agricola*, 30). The most egregious blot on the Etruscan record is the sacrifice of 307 Roman prisoners in 356 BCE; the Romans retaliated by killing 358. On the slaughter bench of history these are acceptable

70 Hobsbawm, *On History*, 228.

71 Fagan, *Returning to Babylon*, 124. The King's braggart bas-reliefs were dug up by Austin Henry Layard in 1848. A biblical account of the siege of Lachish appears in 2 Kings 18:13. Sennacherib's sons murdered him in a temple in Nineveh after the Judean campaign. Albert Camus reminds us that in our time "We have preferred the power that apes greatness – Alexander first of all, and then the Roman conquerors, whom our school history books, in *an incomparable vulgarity of soul* [my italics], teach us to admire." *Lyrical and Critical Essays*, 150.

72 Kulikowski, "A Very Bad Man," 15–16. Thomas Campbell (1777–1844), a very popular poet, makes a similar point in *The Pleasures of Hope* (1799): "What millions died – that Caesar might be great" (2.375). See also Pliny the Elder's *Natural History* (6:43): "Owing to a curious disease of the human mind we are pleased to enshrine in history records of bloodshed and slaughter, so that persons ignorant of the acts of the world may be acquainted with the crimes of mankind."

numbers. And in our century, in which the two dominant totalitarianisms turned to the ancients for an aesthetic style, Etruscan art, though often violent in subject matter, attracted little attention, even in Italy.

In this book I present them as the resilient Etruscans who came back from the dead after two millennia. For modern students they represent the challenge of putting together what the sociologists call a thick description of a people contemporaneous with the Greeks and Romans but who left elusive materials and few written traces of their existence – we might say that they wrote their deaths but not their lives, and none more memorably than the predicted catastrophe that would end their world. The individuals I focus on reinsert this fascinating and historically significant civilization into Western art and thought. They had been denied what Aby Warburg memorably called, though with a different emphasis, "das Nachleben der Antike" ("the afterlife of antiquity"). Winckelmann's century set in motion the undoing of this historical wrong with contributions from antiquarians, archaeologists, collectors (especially of gems and vases), a potter, and an "Etruscomania."

PART TWO

Creating a Taste for the Etruscans

It is so interesting to discover a whole civilization of which one was ignorant and which has had an enormous effect on the course of modern civilization through the great plagiarists of the world, the Romans.

Roger Fry[1]

1   Fry, *Letters of Roger Fry*, 1.132.

1

Johann Joachim Winckelmann: *The Etruscan Chapter in* The History of the Art of Antiquity *(1764)*

[Winckelmann] is like Columbus, when he had not yet discovered
the new world but had a presentiment of it in his mind.

Goethe[1]

Winckelmann's *History of the Art of Antiquity* is generally remembered as
a classic of art history that combines historical knowledge, classical
scholarship, antiquarian interests, connoisseurship, and a developmental
aesthetic theory. Its insistence on the unique greatness of Greek art – its
noble simplicity and quiet grandeur – was instrumental in the neoclassical revival. But it has led a less-well-known second life in Etruscan
studies where its importance lies in the brief third chapter, "Art of the
Etruscans and Their Neighbours." Had Winckelmann (1717–1768)
omitted the Etruscans from his book few would have noticed, and those
who did – with the exception of Etruscan antiquarians – would not have
been surprised. His emphasis, after all, was on establishing the primacy
of Greek art within the art of antiquity and to illustrate how the arts of
Egypt, Etruria, and Rome fell short of the Greek ideal. Despite the

---

1 In Johann Peter Eckermann, *Conversations with Goethe*, 16 February 1827, 173.
See also Hegel: "Winckelmann was inspired by his contemplation of the ideals of the
ancients to impart a new meaning to the contemplation of art, which wrested art away
from views dictated by common aims and mere imitation of nature and set up a
powerful stimulus to discover the [true] idea of art in artworks and in the history of
art. For Winckelmann is to be regarded as one of those men who managed to open
up in the field of art a new medium and a whole new way of looking at things for the
human spirit." Quoted in Potts, "Introduction" to *The History of the Art of Antiquity*, 30.
All references will be to this text.

fashion for *etruscheria* when he arrived in Italy in 1755, only collectors could identify, however tentatively, Etruscan bronzes, mirrors, and engraved gems; fewer could confidently distinguish Greek from Etruscan vases. How could one be certain about a red-figured volute krater from Vulci, with Etruscan inscriptions, showing Alcsti (Alkestis) offering to die in place of her husband Atmite (Admetos)? The Greek couple stand between two Etruscan figures: the demonic Tuchulcha, and Charu(n), of whom there are more representations than any other supernatural being.[2] Was it made by an Etruscan or by a Greek artisan living in Vulci? Most judgments were based on guesswork supported by shaky scholarship. Etruscans, let's not forget, despite the period's interest in them, would continue to be relatively small change in the culture wars of the ancient world for at least another century.

Winckelmann's path-breaking chapter described the history of Etruscan art and the state of the field and, incidentally, created wider interest in a dimly remembered culture. It is worth recalling that the Etruscans were just one of several civilizations that Winckelmann's century declared the fashion of the day. Though I tend to emphasize Winckelmann's seminal role in the Etruscan return, in his era his book was read, at least by anyone interested in the Etruscans, in the context of many others. Almost every decade of the century produced a publication. The 1720s saw the publication, delayed by a century, of Dempster's *De Etruria regali*. Between 1737 and 1743, Antonio Gori, inspired by Filippo Buonarroti to survey tombs at Volterra, published his *Museum Etruscum*, a three-volume survey of antiquities. Equally notable were the Comte de Caylus's *Receuil d'antiquités égyptiennes, étrusques, romaines et gauloises* (1752–62) and Luigi Lanzi's *Saggio di lingua etrusca e di altre antiche d'Italia* (1789). Lanzi (1732–1810), highly regarded by Pallottino, offered an overview of current knowledge of Etruria and the Etruscan language, and produced an almost "completely definitive decipherment of the Etruscan alphabet and an initial sketch of phonetics and grammar."[3] In a later work he established a basis for distinguishing Greek from Etruscan vases. He also introduced more accurate methods of research for future epigraphists. No small achievement.

2 de Grummond, *Etruscan Myth, Sacred History, and Legend,* 214.
3 Della Fina, "History of Etruscology," 62. In the same passage, Della Fina describes Lanzi as "the father of scientific Etruscology."

The Comte de Caylus's interest in the Etruscans, like Winckelmann's, was a very small part of a more comprehensive study of the evolution of ancient art based on stylistic analysis of visual evidence. Both were serious students of Etruscan gemstones. Like the influential Earl of Shaftesbury, Montesquieu, and Winckelmann, de Caylus believed that the quality of a society's art was influenced by climate and by the degree of freedom available in it. Again, like Winckelmann, he thought a people's art might reveal their character, the eighteenth century's version of what the Annales school calls a *mentalité*. De Caylus's analyses were limited in scope, however, because he had never been to Rome. He worked, as did Winckelmann at the beginning of his career, primarily with coins and engraved gems because these were numerous and often reliably dated. De Caylus, however, showed no interest in an overall theory or periodization of ancient art. Winckelmann, by contrast, emphasized that "the history of art should inform us about the historical origin, growth, change, and fall of art" (71). For the Greeks this sequence took the following forms: "archaic crudeness and simplicity," "an early classical austere phase" in the fifth century, "a later classical graceful and beautiful period" in the fourth, and decline through "imitation, overelaboration."[4] In addition to the idea of a sequence followed by the art of all nations, Winckelmann also introduced "the idea of evolution from the austere and useful to the beautiful and superfluous."[5] Inseparable from this was a clear hierarchy of subject matter.

Almost all the art Winckelmann discusses he saw in Rome.[6] Like most of his contemporaries who wrote about art, he never travelled to Greece. On very slim evidence he grants that the Etruscans had three phases of creativity: "from the simple forms of their earliest period to the blossoming of their art, which at long last was improved, it is very likely,

4 Potts, "Introduction," 3.

5 Ibid., 47. For Potts these are "the two main paradigms underpinning Winckelmann's schema."

6 Montesquieu had advised "le grand et le simple" in *Considération sur les causes de la grandeur des Romains et de leur décadence* (1734). Katherine Harloe confirms that "Winckelmann's reading of both *L'Esprit des lois* (1748) and the earlier *Considération sur les causes de la grandeur des Romains et de leur décadence* (1734) is securely documented" and she discusses their methodological affinities in *Winckelmann and the Invention of Antiquity* (115). It is unlikely that Winckelmann had read or even heard of Giovanni Battista Vico (1668–1744) whose *New Science* (1744) developed a theory of the recurring cyclical development of history.

by the imitation of Greek works and assumed a form quite different from that of earlier periods" (169). For our purposes it is the Etruscan second style that is interesting. Winckelmann labels it "*mannered,* which means here the use of a uniform character for all figures. Apollo, Mars, Herakles, and Vulcan, for instance, are not rendered differently in Etruscan works." But this style also refers to "strained and violent" figures that he interpreted as indicating a national Etruscan psychology characterized by a sense of jealously guarded freedom (hence their federalism) and violent melancholy (defeat by Rome). He then attributes these traits to modern Tuscans when he leaps across eighteen centuries to claim, a bit rashly, that "the style of the ancient [Etruscan] artists can still be seen in the works of their descendants, and the impartial and discerning eye will find it in the drawing of Michelangelo, the greatest of them all" (173). A comparison to "the greatest of them all" isn't quite the compliment it seems since ultimate praise is reserved for the painter who in the lightness of his figures most resembles the Greeks, Raphael. Winckelmann sees Etruscan melancholy, however, in the "overpowering force … achieved at the expense of grace and beauty" in Michelangelo's work (160). It's a moot point whether Winckelmann attributes melancholy to Etruscan art because he looks at it with the knowledge of their demise and disappearance.

His highest praise for an Etruscan work is for the life-sized bronze usually called The Orator (also Aule Meteli, or in Latin Aulus Metellus). Though Winckelmann is as opposed to the realism of the Romans as he is to the mannerism he sees in the Etruscans, The Orator impresses him, though he doesn't explain why. His praise of the sculpture doesn't carry over to Roman portraiture, which is today seen as marking an original development in realism in European sculpture. As I discuss below, it is precisely this new art in which we can see "nature in its prosaic actuality" – what we call realism – that makes late Etruscan art and subsequent Roman art distinctive. Winckelmann's low view of portraiture left him blind to not only the Romans but, in his own time, Bernini. His advice to Bernini would have been identical to his judgment on the Etruscans: you should have imitated the Greeks.[7] Almost exactly a century later Matthew Arnold would be saying much the same thing.

7 This had already been the argument of Winckelmann's essay "Reflections on the Imitation of Greek Works in Painting and Sculpture" (1756).

Both were Greek utopians nostalgic for a culture grounded in what they saw as permanent normative Greek values. Friedrich Nietzsche's *Birth of Tragedy* and Lawrence's *Etruscan Places*, though they have little else in common, are both reactions against Winckelmann's idealization of the Greeks, which continues to form a part of our collective blinkered historical consciousness.[8] We may know that Greek statues were painted, but we still prefer them white.

But Winckelmann's misjudgments are much less important than the simple fact of his immediate and long-lasting influence, and what artists, connoisseurs, and writers took from him, even when, like Giovanni Battista Piranesi, they disagreed. For instance, Piranesi's *Diverse manière d'adornare i cammini ed ogni altra parte degli edifizi* (1769) argued, on the basis of his studies of Etruscan monuments, which he attributed to King Tarquin, that the Etruscans were the sole progenitors of Roman architecture and civilization, and that the severity of Etruscan architecture could be seen in the Roman emphasis on utilitarian engineering.[9] During his stay in Rome Winckelmann saw few genuine Etruscan and Greek sculptures, and he was taken in by two fake Etruscan paintings done by Casanova, probably with the help of Anton Rafael Mengs. He knew that "the insufficiency of our knowledge ... does not always allow us to tell the Etruscan apart from the archaic Greek." Yet it is worth emphasizing that Winckelmann saw more Egyptian, Etruscan, and Graeco-Roman works than anyone who had written on art before him. His argument was guided by his view that a normative aesthetic of the beautiful was embodied in the finest Greek sculpture, like the Laocoön and the Praying Boy. The neoclassical revival began with his insistence that "the only way for us to become great, and, if possible inimitable, lies in imitation of the Greeks."[10] Any art without "noble simplicity and quiet grandeur" is inadequate because, by definition, it can't be

8 Leppmann, *Winckelmann*, 117.

9 Hyde Minor, "G.B. Piranesi's *Diverse manière* and the Natural History of Ancient Art," 326. Piranesi's most original insight traces the forms of Etruscan vases to seashells, a suggestion that has a predecessor in Vitruvius's linking of seashells and architectural ornament (*De Architectura*, 4.2). Piranesi also encouraged artists and architects to combine Egyptian, Greek, and Etruscan decorative motifs. He didn't realize, however, that of the 114 architectural elements and cultural artifacts he calls Etruscan on a plate in *Diverse manière* only 6 are Etruscan (Hyde Minor, 337).

10 Winckelmann, "Reflections on the Imitation of Greek Works in Painting and Sculpture," quoted in Leppmann, *Winckelmann*, 116.

beautiful. Beauty is the focus of art and its highest aim. Johann Gottfried Herder understood that Winckelmann's book was as much a "historical metaphysics of beauty, abstracted from the Greeks" as a history of art.[11] He anticipated Kant and Hegel in seeing that Winckelmann "helped form the growing preoccupation with the aesthetic as a domain that merited serious investigation in its own right, alongside the ethical and the rational."[12] But as Alex Potts points out, "While these thinkers still considered the ideals embodied by Greek art as in some sense exemplary, they also saw those ideals as historically unique and hence as inherently at odds with the norms of modern European society."[13] Herder was enough of a historicist to know that modern classicism would inevitably differ from ancient. Winckelmann didn't.

Two and a half centuries later, Winckelmann's discussion of the Etruscans and their art is as dated as D.H. Lawrence's in *Etruscan Places*, though Lawrence saw far more Etruscan sites and genuine Etruscan artifacts. Both idealized the past even as they realized that our knowledge of it was partial. Extolling ancient freedom, for instance, Winckelmann overlooked Athenian slavery and the tragic fate of Melos in the Peloponnesian War. Discussing the purity of Greek art, he ignored the predominance of draped statues over nude ones and the use of paint. There's also little doubt that the acceptance of homoeroticism in Greek society probably influenced his preference for the nude. That so little was known about the Etruscans allowed him to misinterpret their socio-political structure as fostering a sense of freedom enjoyed under a ruler who, he supposed, was more a combination of spiritual leader and commander than an arbitrary monarch. "This freedom, which is the nursemaid of the arts, and the Etruscans' extensive trade by land and water, which preoccupied and nourished them, must have awakened in them the desire to emulate the artists of other peoples, especially as in every free state, the artist has more true honour to hope for and achieve" (159). It is fair to say however that, despite their freedom, Winckelmann, because he was blind to realism, judges the Etruscans as not having realized their potential as artists. He gives two

11 Winckelmann, quoted in ibid., 296.
12 Potts, "Introduction," 30. Hegel gave a metaphysical extension to Winckelmann's view of Beauty as the goal or achievement of the greatest art when he insisted that art's purpose is the creation of beautiful objects that give sensuous expression to freedom.
13 Ibid., 29.

reasons: they "did not prosper long enough to overcome their nature and its influence on art" and their series of wars with Rome brought their evolution as a nation to an end. Etruscans became Romans before their art could achieve its apogee. Looking back, perhaps we might say that the missing final stage in the evolution of their art lay in the two millennia it took to discover and identify it and then describe its proper place in history. Hegel would help.

As I suggested earlier, in the long view, it really made no difference whether Winckelmann praised or dismissed Etruscan art, or that he didn't realize that *Etruscan* was not always Etruscan art. More important was the simple fact that he had secured publicity for it by placing it among the arts of Egypt, Greece, and Rome in an ambitious organic theory of the history of art. His book was read throughout Europe and influenced thinkers like Lessing – who wrote his *Laokoön* (1766) in response – Herder, Goethe, Madame de Staël, and Hegel. These are figures who shaped the artistic and intellectual climate of the Romantic era. Their discussions of civilizations and their arts had to go through Winckelmann's great book, even when they disagreed. I can't help seeing something of Adam Smith's "invisible hand" or perhaps of Hegel's "cunning of history" in all this: Winckelmann wasn't enthusiastic about Etruscans, yet he helped create both greater scholarly interest in them and a fashion for things Etruscans. Together with Sir William Hamilton, Pierre-François Hugues d'Hancarville, and Josiah Wedgwood, Winckelmann brought the Etruscans a degree of popularity they had not enjoyed since the Medici, with the important difference that this time they were the talk of Naples, Rome, Florence, Paris, London, and even Russia, where Lady Jane Cathcart, Josiah Wedgwood's sister, introduced Wedgwood's neo-Etruscan vases and "creamware" to Catherine the Great. Winckelmann's brief is responsible, moreover, for Hegel's interest in the Etruscans both in *The Philosophy of History* and in *Aesthetics: Lectures on Fine Art*. Winckelmann is cited more often in the latter than any other writer.

Half a century after Winckelmann's death, Hegel (1770–1831), a more historically minded thinker, warns his students against the era's nostalgia for the world of the Greeks even as he evokes it in emotionally charged prose.[14] He admires the greatest works of Greek sculpture as much as Winckelmann, but he notes that although a Greek sculpture

14 Hegel, *Aesthetics*, 2:719.

may be "artistically perfect ... it cannot contain the inner complexity of human experience as the nineteenth century knows it. The romantic arts of painting, music, and poetry far exceed sculpture's capacities"[15] to do so. One might say that Greek sculpture was perfect, but its perfection was of its time and inevitably less perfect, because less comprehensive, than that of the Romantic poetry that benefited from more than a millennium of Christianity's emphasis on subjectivity and spirit.

For Hegel, Etruscans have a walk-on role in helping bring about the necessary dissolution of Greek perfection with what he calls "the extreme prose of the Spirit" in *The Philosophy of History* and "prosaic actuality" in *Aesthetics*.[16] We can sense the shift away from the Greeks in Hegel's comments on The Orator (see figure 1.1), the life-sized bronze statue of Aule Meteli, which Winckelmann had discussed. Dated to 90 BCE, the statue was found in Lake Trasimene, north of Perugia, in 1566.

The Etruscan works of art which are testified as genuine by inscriptions show just the same imitation of nature [as the ones from Aegina], though in a still higher degree, but the posture and facial expressions are free, and some of these works are very nearly portraits. So, for instance, Winckelmann speaks (iii, ch. 2, p. 189) of a male statue which seems to be wholly a portrait, though emanating from the art of a later period. It is a life-size figure of a man, apparently a sort of orator, a magisterial and dignified person, presented with great and unforced naturalness and with no vagueness of posture or expression. It would be noticeable and significant if what was at home on Roman soil from the start was not the ideal but nature in its prosaic actuality.[17]

We need to keep in mind that neither Winckelmann nor Hegel saw The Orator whereas we can find it in a moment online. They looked at drawings or etchings. Winckelmann relied on an etching in the 1723 edition of Dempster's *De Etruria regali*; Hegel relied on Winckelmann. The statue's arm is raised in a manner that seems prophetic ("the art of a later period"), more free and more expressive than earlier sculpture. The figure is Etruscan, but all the details of the portrait are Roman, from the senatorial ring and boots to the toga. These suggest the degree

15 Ibid., 2:357.
16 *Philosophy of History*, 287–8; *Aesthetics*, 2:787.
17 Hegel, *Aesthetics*, 2:787. The Orator is currently in Florence's Museo Archeologico.

1.1 The Orator, or Aule Meteli, c. 90 BCE.

of Etruscan assimilation – Aule Meteli's name is Etruscan, but his statue is that of a Roman senator named Aulus Metellus. It comes from a period when some Etruscan inscriptions appear in a bilingual format with Latin.

With hindsight we follow Hegel in imagining the statue as sounding the trump for the end of Greece and the beginning of Rome, Christianity, and what Hegel calls romantic art. The words "prosaic actuality" are expanded significantly in *The Philosophy of History* where Hegel defines the Roman spirit as follows: "This extreme prose of the Spirit we find in Etruscan art, which though technically perfect and so far true to nature, has nothing of Greek Ideality and Beauty: we also observe it in the development of Roman Law and in the Roman religion."[18] Roman law made the Roman state possible, and the latter was the seedbed and permanent home of Christianity, without which Hegel's philosophy, history, and aesthetics would have no telos.

These ideas were half a century distant when Winckelmann was murderered in Trieste on 8 June 1768. He was only fifty, but his influence would be felt in the vases Sir William Hamilton imported to England and the "pottery" created by Josiah Wedgwood.

18 There are twenty-six pages on the Etruscans in Winckelmann and six in John Boardman's *The Oxford History of Classical Art,* buried at the end of a chapter on "The Later Roman Empire." Hegel, who never saw an Etruscan sculpture, devotes a medium-length paragraph.

2

Sir William Hamilton and Josiah Wedgwood:
The Indispensable Connoisseur and
the Potter Who Made the Etruscans Visible,
Fashionable, and Popular

[Wedgwood was] the greatest man who ever, in any age or country,
applied himself to the important work of uniting art with industry.

William Gladstone

He also drew on his own experience to commission what became
a very famous jasperware medallion depicting a chained male slave in a
half-kneeling position with the inscription, "Am I not a Man and a Brother?"

Keith Thomas[1]

At the time of Winckelmann's murder, Sir William Hamilton
(1730–1803) had been planning to involve him in the publication of
the second volume of his four-volume *Collection of Etruscan, Greek, and
Roman Antiquities* (1766–77).[2] The collaboration would have brought
the art historian back to Etruscan matters. The dedication plate to the
book is dominated by Etruscan motifs including "a fragment of Tuscan
architectural entablature [that] indicates one of the principal discoveries of the Etruscans, a people formerly celebrated for their strength
and for their taste in the arts." Hamilton's editor was Pierre-François
Hugues d'Hancarville, and the esteem in which the two men held
Winckelmann can be seen in the frontispiece to the second volume.
It depicts an imaginary tomb, a miniature Pantheon, with the great
scholar's sarcophagus in the centre carrying a valedictory inscription

---

1 In Dolan, *Wedgwood*, 339; Thomas, "Success on a Plate," 8, 9.
2 The title page of the first volume is dated 1766.

from d'Hancarville that ends "PET. DHANCARVILLE / DOLENS FECIT."[3] D'Hancarville's text agrees with Winckelmann that the vases excavated in their period were mostly the work of Greek not Etruscan artists. He errs, however, when he asserts that the Etruscans preceded the Greeks in achieving complete success in the arts. He also wrote that he had been to the then not well-known temples at Paestum and had discovered the ruins of an Etruscan temple older than the Greek which, in his opinion, the Greek architects had copied. D'Hancarville subsequently published his own eccentric magnum opus, *Recherches Sur L'Origine, L'Esprit et Les Progrès Des Arts De La Grèce; Sur Leur Connections Avec Les Arts Et La Religion Des Plus Anciens Peuples Connus.* Combining his interest in art with his recent research in Eastern religions, his book is closer in spirit to J.G. Frazer's *The Golden Bough* and comparative mythology than to Winckelmann's magnum opus. His argument that sexuality and the creative urge are the source of religion would have caught Freud's attention. As for the Etruscans, he lost interest in them after completing his work for Hamilton.

Sir William gradually began to realize that the vases he had imagined Etruscan were Greek, a suspicion confirmed by Luigi Lanzi in 1806. The Etruscans disappear from the title of his second publication, *Collection of Engravings from Ancient Vases mostly of Pure Greek Workmanship* (1791–95). He acknowledges in the book that most of the vases in both publications were of "Grecian, and not of an Etruscan origin."[4] The distinction between the two kinds of vases would remain porous. Only the distinctive black bucchero pottery discovered in Etruria was definitely Etruscan. The discussion would become more complicated in the twentieth century when it was realized that not only had Etruria imported Greek vases, but Greek craftsmen had been working in Etruria and Italy. Having established a taste for Etruscan and Greek vases and gemstones, Hamilton turned his attention to volcanology. In the decade after the appearance of the catalogue's last volume he published three volumes of letters and three of etchings (by Pietro Fabris) about

---

3 "Pierre D'Hancarville, grieving, made this." D'Hancarville's writing adds some energy and colour to any narrative. He published two pornographic books set in Ancient Rome: *Lives of the Twelve Caesars* (1780) and *Monumens du culte secret des dames romaines* (1787). Each carries the fictional imprint "Rome: De l'Imprimerie du Vatican." Pius VI would not have been amused.

4 Quoted in Brian Fothergill, *Sir William Hamilton: Envoy Extraordinary*, 235.

his observations of volcanoes. The letters had been sent regularly to the Royal Society, where they were well received. His first four-volume collection of vases was twice reprinted, first in Paris (1785–88) and then in Florence (1801–08). A second new collection of engravings of vases appeared in Naples (1791–95) and was reprinted in Florence, Paris, and twice in London between 1800 and 1814. Hamilton was the kind of collector who gave the pastime a good name, the very opposite of the suspect antiquary William Blake satirizes – see below – as "Etruscan Column the Antiquary" in "An Island in the Moon." Hamilton had unknowingly helped prepare the ground for the next boom in everything Etruscan that would follow the discovery in the 1820s of undisturbed tombs on Lucien Bonaparte's estate at Vulci in Lazio. These tombs weren't quite Pompeii but they were much more widely discussed than the ones Buonarroti had excavated a century earlier.

When Hamilton returned to England from Naples he didn't know Josiah Wedgwood (1730–1795). Fortunately for the Etruscan return, his sister, Lady Cathcart, did, and in 1768 she had shown Wedgwood a copy of the first volume of Hamilton and d'Hancarville's catalogue. The potter, always on the lookout for a new style, was in search of something to succeed his very popular line of "creamware" or "Queen's Ware," which had begun as a tea service for Queen Charlotte in 1765.[5] It was his first major success and marked a turning point in his fortunes. Robin Reilly calls it his "most influential achievement."[6] He was named Queen's Potter in 1765. His second success followed quickly and, in the words of a Wedgwood scholar, "Wedgwood's debt to Hamilton as a source of designs is scarcely calculable."[7] In return Wedgwood helped popularize Hamilton's collection, which enhanced his reputation as an antiquarian and a man of taste. The engravings fascinated Wedgwood both with their beauty and with the possibilities they presented for creating vases that would be purely ornamental. He realized that the potter need no longer be just an artisan, he could become an artist creating original works for display. To this point Wedgwood had been a successful factory owner, businessman, and chemist. He excelled in all three roles. Almost all the materials produced in his workshops were

5 This has since disappeared.
6 Reilly, *Wedgwood*, 123. He distinguishes between creamware and "jasper" which he calls "Wedgwood's greatest invention."
7 Ibid.

the result of his experiments with glazes and clays, five thousand of which were conducted just for the creamware of 1760. In 1769 he built a model factory, with housing for the workers, which he called "Etruria." As a craftsman-artist-industrialist he became as influential as anyone in the period in changing the nature of the industry and styles in ornament and decoration. He also made the Etruscans popular, and synonymous with the Wedgwood brand.

Hamilton's first volume had helped introduce the Etruscans to England in 1767. Five years later Parliament approved the purchase of his antiquities for display in the British Museum. But without Wedgwood and his "Etruscans," as he sometimes referred to his employees, few outside the aristocracy would have heard of the Etruscans, much less have owned an Etruscan vase or what passed for one in England at the time. Without Wedgwood's "Etruria," there would be no Etruscan rooms designed by Robert Adam at Osterley Park (1775–78) or in the palace of Leopold III of Anhalt-Dessau.[8] Of course, the fashionable Etruscan style, including Wedgwood's, was not something the Etruscans would have recognized as their own. The closest Wedgwood came to the genuine article was with his "black basaltes" vases that remind us of the *bucchero nero* vases with moulded or incised ornament. Wedgwood had developed a black basalt body for his vases in 1768. And in August he sent his partner William Bentley two of these so-called Etruscan vases that had also been bronzed. He soon decided to reserve the name "Etruscan" for pieces decorated with red paint like that on ancient red-figure vases. It is worth emphasizing that although he drew the shapes of his vases from many models, Hamilton's engravings were his primary source.

Wedgwood's Etruscan vases have a solid black body made with a material known as "Egyptian black," common in Staffordshire since early in the century. He refined the coarseness of the composition, improved the colour, and hardened it. In 1769 he patented a matte enamel, inaccurately called "encaustic," developed in imitation of the painting on Hamilton's vases. This was applied to the black vases. The turning point of Wedgwood's career as a potter came on 13 June 1769 when he held the ceremony opening "Etruria." He had chosen the name to call

8 Jenkins, "Contemporary Minds: Sir William Hamilton's Affair with Antiquity," in Jenkins and Sloan, *Vases & Volcanoes*, 60. For examples of Angelica Kauffmann's involvement with Etruscan decoration see Rosenblum's *Transformations in Late Eighteenth Century Art*.

attention to the new kinds of wares he would be making and to emphasize his agreement with Hamilton's call for a revival of the ancient arts
in the artwork, materials, and techniques involved. Staffordshire had a
geological advantage over other areas. Brian Dolan describes the geological formation as follows: "Epochs of land submergence and elevation
had worn down the grit and limestone rocks to form clay, while the coal
and ironstone seams that appeared in strata in hillsides mixed with the
presence of different ores and minerals, particularly iron oxide, to
render a unique composition and colour to the clays. The red clays so
striking within the Staffordshire landscape came from a geological
formation now called the Etruria Formation that lies immediately above
the coal measures. It is a formation unique to the English Midlands."[9]
Wedgwood gave a brief speech and then:

he and [Thomas] Bentley, his partner, put on a show that would become
legendary. He donned the potter's "slops," the leather apron and cap, and
formed one mound of clay after another into elegant Etruscan vases, while
Bentley cranked the shaft to spin the wheel. Josiah threw six vases in black
basalts, fashioned after Hamilton's Etruscan Antiquities, which his artist
David Rhodes painted with red figures depicting "Hercules in the Garden of
the Hesperides," with the inscription

June XIII M.DCC LXIX
One of the First Day's Productions
At
Etruria Staffordshire
By
Wedgwood & Bentley
Artes Etruriae Renascuntur

The last line of the inscription says it all: "The arts of Etruria are reborn."
[See figure 2.1.]

Wedgwood had invented a special pigment, "a chemical concoction
including bronze powder, vitriol of iron, crude antinomy, and specific
proportions of other chemicals."[10] He immediately patented it, but that
did not prevent a nearby potter from producing similar antique vases

9 Dolan, *Wedgwood*, 25.
10 Ibid., 189, 227.

2.1 Josiah Wedgwood, First Day's Vase, 13 June 1769.

within a few months. It was no consolation that this kind of copying was
a form of compliment and dissemination. Wedgwood and Bentley set
the trend with each new style. After these Etruscan vases, Wedgwood
and his workers became more secretive. From now on the first day of
their London show was by invitation. Guests came to the showrooms to
inspect objects released in a limited quantity. So far as we know,
Wedgwood never read Adam Smith's contemporary *Inquiry into the*

Nature and Causes of the Wealth of Nations (1776), but if he had he would have recognized himself in Smith's description of the modern market and of like-minded entrepreneurs who created it and factories like "Etruria." A social and political radical, Wedgwood was also a consummate capitalist. Wedgwood was becoming a brand name in the modern sense, and the company's clientele was international. His status as potter to Queen Charlotte and supplier to the Empress Catherine of Russia had secured his reputation. In 1773, the latter had bought Wedgwood's now famous Green Frog Service of 994 pieces each painted with an English scene and a green frog.

To cap his career, he copied the Portland Vase (formerly the Barberini Vase, sold in 1780 by Donna Cornelia Barberini-Colonna, Princess of Palestrina, to settle gambling debts).[11] Wedgwood thought the original vase slightly flawed – he was not impressed by the ancient potter – and he asked Hamilton whether he would mind if he improved it. The great antiquarian thought it best to be accurate and hinted that perhaps a copy was a better idea? It would be Wedgwood's last hurrah, a *punctum* to mark his retirement. Hamilton, Joshua Reynolds, and Joseph Banks all praised Wedgwood's copy, and the popular historical painter Benjamin West placed it in his crowded painting *Genius calling forth the Fine Arts to adorn Manufactures and Commerce and recording the names of eminent men in these pursuits* (1791) to illustrate the theme of "Etruria."

When he died in 1795 Wedgwood had no competitors, not in England or Europe or the United States, which had been one of his first foreign markets. He knew that while Italians were buying his "Etruscan" wares and ornamental pieces, Italian potteries were simultaneously imitating them. His china was being exported to the Chinese. Of his main European competitors, the Delft and Sèvres companies had closed, while Meissen would avoid bankruptcy during the Napoleonic wars only by producing *Wedgwoodarbeit*, "Wedgwood-work." He had changed the

---

11 It had long been thought that the vase had been found in the sixteenth century in a sarcophagus containing the remains of Emperor Alexander Severus and Julia Mamaea, his mother, both of whom died in a revolt in 235 CE. Robin Reilly writes in *Wedgwood: The New Illustrated Dictionary* that the earlier account has been challenged, though there seems to be agreement about the sarcophagus itself, if not about its occupants. Ian Jenkins and Kim Sloan suggest the vase is a product of the first century of this era (187 CE). They also indicate that Piranesi engraved the tomb, sarcophagus, and the vase for his *Antichità Romane* (1756, plates 31–5).

profession, and his ornamental creations had contributed, along with Hamilton's work, to the spread of neoclassicism, which had already begun before the publication of Sir William's volumes or the opening of "Etruria." Nevertheless, they were part of the movement's history. Wedgwood would have been pleased but not surprised by two orders in the twentieth century: in 1903 Theodore Roosevelt ordered a presidential service for 1,300 people, and in 1995, the Russian government ordered one of 47,000 pieces. Not least, Wedgwood made "Etruscan" if not a household word, then at least one that was much more widely recognized than before the opening of "Etruria." At the beginning of the eighteenth century, one might still find the words "Hetrurian" and "Hetrurians" in use. After Wedgwood, the usage is standardized to "Etruria" and "Etruscans."[12] Wedgwood, unlike Hamilton, seems to have had little interest in the historical Etruscans: they were just a brand to sell ware, pottery, and vases.

His factory is celebrated by his close friend Erasmus Darwin in *The Botanic Garden* (1791):

Etruria! Next beneath thy magic hands
Glides the quick wheel, the plastic clay expands,
Nerved with fine touch, thy fingers (as it turns)
Mark the nice bounds of vases, ewers, and urns;
Round each fair form in lines immortal trace
Uncopied Beauty, and ideal Grace. (291–6)

The passage comes with Darwin's lengthy historical footnote about Italian Etruria, Wedgwood, D'Hancarville, and Hamilton. I quote it at some length because it also suggests what passed for common knowledge about the Etruscans in the last decade of the eighteenth century:

Etruria may perhaps vie with China itself in the antiquity of its arts. The times of its greatest splendour were prior to the foundations of Rome, and the reign of one of its best princes, Janus, was the oldest epoch the Romans knew. The earliest historians speak of the Etruscans as being then of high antiquity, most probably a colony from Phoenicia, to which a Pelasgian colony acceded, and was united soon after Deucalion's flood … It is supposed

12 The *OED* gives "Hetrurians" in 1623 and "the Hetrurian inscription" in 1706.

that the principal manufactories were about Nola, at the foot of Vesuvius; for it is in that neighbourhood that the greatest quantities of antique vases have been found; and it is said that the general taste of the inhabitants is apparently influenced by them; insomuch that strangers coming to Naples, are commonly struck with the diversity and elegance even of the most ordinary vases for common uses. See D'Hancarville's preliminary discourses to the magnificent collection of Etruscan vases, published by Sir William Hamilton.[13]

As I wrote earlier, the vases Darwin mentions were made in Etruscan cities or areas of influence, but most were not Etruscan. We know that nearly 80 percent of all Greek vases in museums are from Etruria. Everything Darwin treats as part of the Etruscan historical record would be jettisoned with the publication of Giuseppe Micali's *L'Italia avanti il dominio dei Romani* (1810, 1822) and Barthold Niebuhr's very influential *The History of Rome*, the first two volumes of which appeared in 1812.

In the late 1840s the Swansea industrialist Lewis Llewelyn Dillwyn paid Wedgwood a tribute, perhaps close to the great potter's heart, by "producing inexpensive ceramics on ancient Greek models (a sort of diffusion line of Wedgwood, sold for between two and four shillings) in the hope of 'carrying into the more humble homesteads of England forms of beauty in combination with useful ends, and in placing in the hands of all, ornaments of a high character at a cheap rate.'" These were inscribed "DILLWYN'S ETRUSCAN WARE."[14] Wedgwood left an estate of £600,000. Had he been alive he could have afforded to smile in admiration at Dillwyn's cheek.[15]

Winckelmann, Hamilton, and Wedgwood had created a rising tide of European interest in the Etruscans that extended from dinner

13 Darwin, *The Botanic Garden*, 85.

14 Vout, *Classical Art*, 215.

15 By the time Dillwyn went into the Etruscan market, writers, historians, and philosophers had begun to pay serious attention to the Rasenna. And books were being written about them by serious ethnographers. In addition to Lanzi and Micali, mentioned earlier, two should be noted. Karl Otfried Müller (1797–1840) was both an active archeologist and a prolific scholar whose *Die Etrusker* (1828) remains a respected work of scholarship in our time. Friedrich Wilhelm Eduard Gerhard (1795–1867) has a least four claims to fame, including a multi-volume *Etruskische Spiegel* (Etruscan Mirrors, 1840–67) in which he presented a systematic approach to the field. For a full account see Pallottino's chapter "A Short History of Etruscan Studies" in *The Etruscans*. For Lanzi see 23–4.

settings in palaces to relatively inexpensive ware used at home; from antiquarians to scholars and philosophers; and from travellers to artists in whose works the Etruscans were beginning to appear. After Waterloo, English and French tours of Italy began to stop at Etruscan sites. The great return had begun. Its next notable impetus would come in 1828 when Napoleon's brother, Lucien the Prince of Canino, discovered Etruscan tombs on his Italian estate and flooded the antiquities market with Etruscan ware.

3

William Blake:
What Is an "Etruscan" Doing in
"An Island in the Moon" (1784–85)?

[The Artist] knows that what he does is not inferior
to the grandest Antiques.

William Blake

Time, which antiquates antiquities, and hath an art to make dust
of all things, hath yet spared these minor monuments.

Sir Thomas Browne[1]

William Blake (1757–1827) is not mentioned in Brian Dolan's biography
of Wedgwood, though he was probably introduced to Wedgwood by the
painter John Flaxman, who worked with the potter for many years. That
there was a connection is not in doubt; there is some disagreement,
however, about the nature and extent of Blake's work for Wedgwood
on his house and ware. Robin Reilly writes that "Blake is said to have
painted the ceiling of Etruria Hall, but the evidence is inconclusive and
no trace of any such work has survived."[2] G.E. Bentley, Jr, corrects this
in *The Stranger from Paradise: A Biography of William Blake*. He suggests
that "in 1784 Flaxman made a series of 'Drawings for Ceiling' for
Wedgwood's new house called Etruria Hall in Staffordshire, for which
he was paid £4.6.6. The design represented an elaborate allegory outlined in the centre, 'like paintings on the Etruscan vases,' with heads
of divinities in the corners. Flaxman evidently obtained the commission

---

1 Blake, "A Descriptive Catalogue," in *Complete Writings*, 179; Browne, *Religio
Medici, Hydriotaphia, and The Gardens of Cyrus*, 126.
2 Reilly, *Wedgwood*, 69.

for his friend 'Blake for painting on Ceiling Pictures.' Probably Blake's copies of Flaxman's designs were on canvas shipped to Staffordshire, as Flaxman's sketches on paper had been. Blake's fee, £3.17.0, was paid by Wedgwood to Flaxman who gave it to Blake."[3] That Wedgwood also gave Flaxman another £5.5.0 for "his own work," which may have been another design for Etruria Hall, suggests that Blake had done two different sorts of work for the house. Blake's life would have been significantly happier, at least from a financial point of view, had he continued to work for the Wedgwoods as regularly as Flaxman did. Bentley has found evidence that in 1815 Flaxman persuaded Josiah Wedgwood II "to employ Blake to engrave for the firm's catalogues 'The Designs of the Pottery … made by Mr. Flaxman.' Wedgwood would send Blake the soup terrine or bedpan to be represented, and Blake would draw it and send the drawing to Wedgwood, who would despatch another piece of pottery. When all the drawings were completed, Wedgwood directed how they should be arranged on the copperplates. Blake worked on the Wedgwood drawings all autumn, and in the new year he began his engravings. Eventually he engraved 189 pieces of earthenware and porcelain on eighteen copperplates and was paid £30 for his work on 11 November 1816, a very modest fee."[4]

These connections with the works at Etruria and an Etruscan subject matter interest me, both because they indicate the continuing diffusion of interest in the Etruscans and because Blake refers indirectly to them in "An Island in the Moon," an early minor piece of satire dated by Geoffrey Keynes to 1784–85 and never published or produced. "Etruscan Column" is the name of one of the many characters involved in this intellectual dialogue. The Etruscans return twenty-five years later, for a final unexpected appearance in Blake's work, in the *Descriptive Catalogue* of 1809 where he uses an earlier spelling, "Hetrurians."[5] The reference comes in the most tendentious part of Blake's argument where he tries

   3 Bentley, *The Stranger from Paradise*, 86. The full documentation is in Bentley's *Blake Records* (2), second edition, which incorporates the earlier editions of 1969 and 1988.

   4 Bentley, *The Stranger from Paradise*, 358.

   5 Milton uses this form in his Latin poem "In Quintum Novembris": "Dextra veneficiis infamis Hetruria" (line 51) ("to his right Etruria notorious for its sorceries"). *Paradise Lost* has the well-known lines about Galileo, "Through optic glass the Tuscan artist views" (1.287) and "the brooks / In Vallombrosa, where the Etrurian shades / High overarched imbower;" (1.302–4). The author of *Milton* would have known them.

to justify his paintings of Nelson and Pitt: "*The spiritual form of Nelson guiding Leviathan, in whose wreathings are infolded the Nations of the Earth*" and "*The spiritual form of Pitt, guiding Behemoth.*" He continues, "The two pictures of Nelson and Pitt are compositions of a mythological cast, similar to those Apotheoses of Persian, Hindoo, and Egyptian Antiquity, which are still preserved on rude monuments, being copies from some stupendous originals now lost or perhaps buried till some happier age." It was from these that the "Greeks and Hetrurians copied Hercules Farnese, Venus of Medicis, Apollo Belvedere, and all grand works of art."[6] The pieces of sculpture were among the most famous examples at the time of ancient "grand works of art." Blake first encountered them when he bought a copy of Henry Fuseli's 1765 translation of Winckelmann's *Reflections on the Painting and Sculpture of the Greeks.*

I suggest Plutarch's dialogue "Concerning the Face which Appears in the Orb of the Moon" as a possible source for Blake's early dialogue, primarily because the historian is mentioned three times in "An Island in the Moon" and discusses the moon's composition, purpose (it contributes to the life cycle of souls), and various philosophical systems. Why else would Blake refer to Plutarch except to indicate the connection? Martha W. England offers another source closer to London. She suggests that "An Island in the Moon" is a *jeu d'esprit* modelled on a satirical allegory by Samuel Foote titled *Tea in the Haymarket.* It shows Blake's awareness of the conventions of the vaudeville-like Little Theatre in Haymarket and needs to be understood in the context of what she terms the multi-generic "antiplays" of the period.[7] Bentley suggests that the Haymarket pieces were "deliberately formless and unscripted so that they could be performed outside the licensed theatres. Blake called it a 'piece' and it might equally well be called a 'farrago.'" Bentley goes on to describe it as "something between a burlesque and a satire and a comic vignette of a self-important society in which everybody talks but nobody listens."[8] England offers a much more positive response: "The text as it stands is essentially complete, a unified whole, the parts arranged with tact, the style appropriate to the intention. The sense of a show under the complete control of one man is present. The stock

6 Blake, *Complete Writings*, 564–5. References to Blake's works will be to this edition.

7 England, "Apprenticeship at the Haymarket?," 8.

8 Bentley, *The Stranger from Paradise*, 81.

jokes are there and are handled so as to come through with novelty and freshness."9 My own impression is that the intellectual frame of reference and the humour are so period specific that the modern reader remains tone deaf to it, unless of course he or she is a specialist in the period. Other than Karen Mulhallen, no one has mentioned a possible link with the Lunar Society, a discussion group active from 1765 to 1813 whose shifting membership included, among many others, Wedgwood, Joseph Priestley, Erasmus Darwin, James Watt, and William Withering.10 In this context Blake's burlesque can be read as a satire on Enlightenment figures and ideas.

The piece begins by indicating that the setting is "a certain Island near by a mighty continent" in the moon. The symbolic characters resemble humans and speak English. Each is a distorted portrait of one of the following: Blake (Quid the Cynic), his brother John (Suction the Epicurean), John Flaxman (Sipsop the Lawgiver), and Joseph Priestley (Inflammable Gass). The antiquarian Thomas Astle is probably the original of "Etruscan Column the Antiquarian," though the Reverend John Brand (1744–1806), author of the popular *Observations on Popular Antiquities,* has also been suggested. The antiquarian was an established "type" in English satire. Though at first "Etruscan" may seem onomastically out of place, a sort of category error, its presence side by side with Epicurean and Cynic suggests Blake's confidence that the audience will understand it as a reference to the classical world. Only an architect, however, would recognize the nod to Vitruvius, who first described "Etruscan columns" and the "Ordo Tuscanus" in *De Architectura* (4.7.2–3). The Roman did not, however, include them among the three canonical orders. The Etruscan order was generally considered an older, primitive, pre-Greek architectural form with relatively simple unfluted columns and round capitals.

The first scene promises a philosophical discussion but meanders in casual and often nonsensical chatter about Voltaire, Chatterton, Locke, and various topics like dangerous scientific experiments, kings, and gods. Every character, including Quid the Cynic, is treated roughly, even mocked. "Cynicism" is as suspect as any other system of thought or group or trade. If Astle is the source for "Etruscan Column the

9 England, "Apprenticeship at the Haymarket?," 27.
10 Personal communication to the author.

Antiquarian" – and I agree with David V. Erdman that he is – then Blake is assuming that at least some of his audience will know what is intended by "he read old documents not for the meanings of the words but for the shapes of the letters" and that "he pored over pictures of the 'monuments of the Etruscans' to make out 'the Pelasgian language and characters.'"[11] The internal quotations are from Astle's *Origins and Progress of Writing,* published in London in 1784 and reprinted in 1803. Erdman points out that the illustrations for Astle's book were published in the shop of James Basire, with whom Blake was apprenticed from 1772 to 1779. Blake describes Etruscan Column as a pedant who produces "an abundance of Enquiries to no purpose" (44) and this may be his general view, despite the work he did for the London Society of Antiquaries, of most antiquarian studies of the remote past. As for the meaning and connotations of "Etruscan" in the name "Etruscan Column," Martha W. England suggests that the word is associated with "those modern and native 'imported antiquities' staged for many years by [Samuel] Foote and auctioned off by [David] Garrick. The name suggests about as awkward and obvious a fake as one can imagine."[12] Winckelmann's relatively low estimate of Etruscan art must have been generally known. And Wedgwood's "Etruscan" products, however popular, couldn't dispel the uncertainty about Hamilton's Etruscan vases: if they were genuine then they were inferior when compared to Greek ones, and if they were adjudged excellent, they were reclassified as Greek. Blake's later dismissal of "Hetrurian" art in *Descriptive Catalogue* may indicate a downward revaluation of the so-called Etruscan art of his youth.

"An Island in the Moon" is ephemeral Blake and would probably be neglected if not for the presence in it of three of the *Songs of Innocence* among its twenty-one songs. The work suggests, however, the extent to which Etruscan and its cognates had entered contemporary consciousness by the 1770s and '80s: the sale of Etruscan ware in London showrooms; passing references in the letters of Horace Walpole; the Etruscan rooms at Etruria Hall; Robert Adam's 1777 design, based on his drawings at Herculaneum, for the "Etruscan Room" at 20 Portman Square, London, and his Etruscan dressing room at Apsley House;

11 Erdman, *Blake,* 31. Reverend Brand was a more serious student of the past than Astle.

12 England, "Apprenticeship at the Haymarket?," 10.

Thomas Astle's speculations about the Etruscan language; and a reference in a piece of doggerel in 1787 by George Keate to the fall of an "Etruscan ceiling: / The ground with beauteous figures strewing, / Spreading a dusty cloud of ruin."[13] Keate and Blake counted on name recognition among a very unsophisticated audience. Without it, Blake's "Etruscan Column" and his humour would be white noise.[14]

---

13 George Keate (1729–1797), "Distressed Poet."

14 Byron in the same general period uses "Tuscan" and "Etruscan" conservatively as synonymous with Tuscany or Italy. In "Hints from Horace" he refers to "eunuchs from Etruscan schools" (317) in admitting that he loathes "an opera worse than Dennis did" (296). *Childe Harold's Pilgrimage* (Canto 4) refers to Dante, Petrarch, and Boccaccio as "the all Etruscan three" and describes the last as having formed "the Tuscan's siren tongue" (Cantos 56, 58). And in Beppo he rhymes "Tuscan" and "Etruscan" (treated as synonyms) in praising a count who speaks Italian properly. Overall, Byron and the other major Romantics show little interest in the ancient Etruscans or Etruria.

4

Barthold Georg Niebuhr:
The Return of the Etruscans in The History
of Rome *(1812)*

"Imagination is often truer than fact," said Gwendolen, decisively,
though she could no more have explained these glib words than if they
had been Coptic or Etruscan.

George Eliot[1]

First published in 1812, Barthold Niebuhr's *The History of Rome* was a
popular and critical success that established him as the most important
classical historian since Gibbon. G.P. Gooch refers to him as "the first
commanding figure in modern historiography, the scholar who raised
history from a subordinate place to the dignity of an independent
science." And Theodore Mommsen suggests that "all historians,
so far as they are worthy of the name, are Niebuhr's pupils."[2] Niebuhr
(1776–1831) combined a command of languages, wide erudition, source

---

1 Eliot, *Daniel Deronda*, 37. The words are spoken by the heroine Gwendolen
Harleth. George Eliot has two connections with Etruscan jewellery: Gwendolen owns
an Etruscan necklace (11, 234–5) and Eliot and George Henry Lewes, when visiting
Rome, chose the jewellers C. and E. Tombini to mount a cameo of a Bacchante they
had acquired. In his diary for 18 April 1860 Lewes wrote: "The Bacchante we took to
a goldsmith and there chose an Etruscan mounting" (see Yale University Library GEN
MSS 818 for the cameo in its Tombini gold mount).

2 Quoted in Gooch, *History and Historians in the Nineteenth Century*, 23. We can
also gauge Niebuhr's stature and reputation from Edgar Allan Poe's book review in
1836 of Francis Lieber's *Reminiscences of an Intercourse with Mr. Niebuhr, the Historian,
during a Residence with him in Rome*. Poe suggests that "Mr. Niebuhr has exercised a very
powerful influence on the spirit of his age" and mentions having read his *Roman
History* and the *Life of His Father*. The review article appeared in the *Southern Literary
Messenger* 2, no. 2 (January 1836): 126–7. We also know that Walt Whitman read and

criticism, and what came to be called (with Leopold von Ranke) a "scientific" approach (*wissenschaft*). He regarded ancient civilizations as living organisms. More controversial was his "divinatory method." This is most obvious in his intuitive interpretation of often fragmentary sources like myths and legends, surviving scraps of early verse, and reported traditions. Like an editor working on a problematic ancient manuscript, he made educated guesses about gaps in the record. They were guesses informed by his wide knowledge and by available evidence, but they were still guesses. Not even his admirers were comfortable with this aspect of his methodology. He justified himself in a letter to a friend: "I am an historian ... for I can make a complete picture from separate fragments, and I know where the parts are missing and how to fill them up. No one believes how much of what seems to be lost can be restored."[3] As we shall see below, Johann Jakob Bachofen also relied on intuition and imagination to fill the lacunae in the prehistory of ancient civilizations, and even the more philosophical Wilhelm Dilthey relied on *erlebnis*, by which the historian relives the past in himself by means of the available historical evidence. Even the scientific Pallottino occasionally lets his imagination roam. Writing about the beauty of "the rock necropoleis of inland southern Etruria" he slips from describing "the chromatic contrast between the vegetation and the vivid reds and warm greys of the tufa" to having "the impression of fantastic mirages of the ancient cities which seem to rise up among the *macchia* from the thickening shapes of the carved tombs."[4] Anyone who has spent an afternoon among the looming, distressed hillside tombs at Norchia will know what he means.

The History of Rome was sufficiently popular that an expanded edition came out in 1828, and a third volume, taking the narrative to the First Punic War, appeared posthumously in 1832. Ten substantial chapters on the pre-Roman peoples of the peninsula, all of whom disappeared when absorbed into the Roman Empire, distinguish this book from earlier histories of Rome. The exception to this is Micali's *L'Italia avanti*

annotated a review article in the *Western Review* of the 1844 edition of Niebuhr's *The History of Rome* and the 1842–4 edition of Thomas Arnold's *History of Rome. Western Review* 1 (April 1846): 211–72.

3 Gooch, *History and Historians in the Nineteenth Century*, 19.

4 Quoted in Steingräber, "Etruscan Rock-Cut Tombs: Origins, Characteristics, Local and Foreign Elements," in *Etruscan by Definition*, 64.

il dominio dei Romani (1810), which would have the distinction of being discussed by Thomas Jefferson in an 1817 letter to John Adams: "Micali has given the counterpart of the Roman history for the nations over which they extended their domination. For this he has gleaned up matter from every quarter, and furnished materials for reflection and digestion to those who thinking as they read, have percieved [*sic*] there was a great deal of matter behind the curtain, could that be fully withdrawn. He certainly gives new views of a nation whose splendor has masked and palliated their barbarous ambition."[5]

Working with the same scant evidence available to Micali, Niebuhr tries to do justice to the Oenotrians, Pelasgians, Opicans, Ausonians, Aborigenes, Latins, Sabines, Sabellians, Tuscans or Etruscans (he insists on a distinction), Umbrians, Iapygians, Ligurians, and Venetians. These aren't all the peoples absorbed into the empire – others are mentioned in passing, even "a few nameless races in the south" – but Niebuhr devotes nearly two hundred pages to them, an essential monograph in itself. I think of this as done in the spirit of Walter Benjamin's judgment that "it is more difficult to honour the memory of the anonymous than it is to honour the memory of the famous."[6] The peoples on Niebuhr's list aren't nameless but they are recognized only by scholars. And though he devotes more space to the Etruscans than to any other group, he emphasizes that "there is no traditional ground for the opinion entertained by the moderns, that, independently of the extensive empire they once held, they were one of the most remarkable nations of antiquity." Despite the qualification, his admiration of Etruscan civilization is obvious. Niebuhr emphasizes that "no other part of literature relating to ancient history contains so much that is irrational, hasty, and unprofitable, as may be found, along with much that is dishonest, in what has been written on the Etruscan language and history since Annius of Viterbo."[7] Niebuhr's chapter attempts to take the Etruscans out of myth, legend, and dishonesty to make them a historical subject. This is a

5 Jefferson, Letter to John Adams, 5 May 1817.

6 The sentence is followed a few lines later by Benjamin's famous assertion that "there is no document of culture which is not at the same time a document of barbarism." "Paralipomena to 'On the Concept of History,'" 406–7. A version of the sentence quoted above is engraved on the memorial of Benjamin's grave at Portbou Municipal Cemetery, Spain.

7 Niebuhr, *The History of Rome*, 109–10. All references will be to this edition.

turning point in Etruscan historiography, as important in its way as the
countless vases and antiquities with which Lucien Bonaparte flooded
the European antiquities market in the 1820s and '30s. If we look back
from Niebuhr, we can see him as marking both the end of the often
too-speculative methodologies of eighteenth-century Etruscan antiquarians and historians and the beginning of what Pallottino calls "the
general progress in scientific method and knowledge" in figures like
Karl Otfried Müller and Eduard Gerhard and their successors into the
twentieth century.[8]

    The historian wastes no time clearing the ground by arguing with
predecessors except when they are ancient writers whose work is without
value but is part of the established record. Not surprisingly, chief among
these is the Greek historian Theopompus, who told "stories ... of the
shameless profligacy of the Etruscans." Niebhur suggests that "we may
join the modern Italians in rejecting [Theopompus's stories] altogether.
His credulity and his fondness for scandalous tales were well known to
the ancients." Niebuhr adds for good measure, "there are no licentious
representations on any Etruscan works of art" (141–2), a view that is
wrong though it is probable that the historian was not aware of any. He
also warns that Roman accounts of events are just that, "Roman" versions.
A story about slaves ruling "Vulsinii [*sic*]" while "the citizens ... abandon
themselves without interruption to voluptuous indulgences ... had been
fabulously exaggerated by Greek writers; and their fictions were fool-
ishly adopted by the Romans. Moreover, it was necessary that those,
for whose extermination Rome took up arms, should be represented
as extremely criminal. Nor was the virulence of party-spirit without its
influence" (123). Niebuhr warns repeatedly about posterity's temptation to read the past from the viewpoint of the victors because the only
surviving sources are theirs. He is our contemporary in his insistence
that a critical history needs to read the past suspiciously. Were the

---

    8 Pallottino, *The Etruscans*, 25. Cornell offers a recent assessment of Müller:
"Müller identified and organised what was best in etruscheria and created the modern study of the Etruscans as we know it today. The updated second edition of his
book by W. Deecke is still required reading, and all subsequent books of any seriousness on 'the Etruscans' are basically new versions of Muller. The most important feature of his work, however, was its strong emphasis on the deep influence of the
Etruscans on the political and religious life of Rome. The notion of Etruscan Rome,
so prevalent in modern work on archaic Italy, goes back essentially to Muller." Cornell,
The Beginnings of Rome, 151.

Phoenicians and the Etruscans really pirates, or did Greek and Roman historians use the pejorative term of anyone sailing a non-Greek or non-Roman ship? Should we be as impressed as the Romans were that Julius Caesar's armies killed nearly countless Gauls? On the evidence of his *Life of Agricola*, the skeptical Tacitus would have offered a more balanced view. Tacitus doesn't hesitate to remind his readers that what defeated Britons (and we might add Etruscans) were taught to call "humanitas" or civilization was also "pars servitutis," part of their enslavement.

Niebuhr's larger question is: What do we really know about the Etruscans, and on what basis do we know it? His answer is that we know relatively little that is not obscure since the Etruscans left no written record and many of the Greek and Roman sources are unreliable. Still, the ancient texts are inevitably Niebuhr's primary resources, especially Livy, Pliny the Elder, and Marcus Aurelius's mentor Festus, even if he must often read them against themselves. Except for a few vases, he makes no references to antiquarian and archaeological materials. Also missing are discussions of specific figures or historical events such as battles. The Etruscans left "no national heroic story" (134), though there are strong epic possibilities in Herodotus's story of a plague in Lydia that compelled the king's son Tyrrhenus to lead half the population to resettle in Umbria (1.94). Other than Lars Porsena and the Tarquins, there are no individuals of a stature to warrant a short biography on the model of Plutarch's. Acknowledging this lack, Niebuhr focuses on four areas of interest: the origin story; political organization; architecture and art; and religion and divination. The discussion of the last two contains a remarkably detailed account of the Etruscan belief in historical cycles.

On the much-debated issue of Etruscan origins he holds a theory that in some respects anticipates Pallottino's well-known compromise. Niebuhr suggests that the people we have come to call Etruscans need to be thought of as an amalgam of two distinct groups: Tyrrhenians, who were native to Italy, and Etruscans, who were immigrants, probably Pelasgian or pre-Greek in origin. He attributes the founding myth and the long tradition of divination to the original inhabitants. The only evidence he adduces is onomastic: the Greeks confusingly called several peoples Tyrrhenians, hence Herodotus's mistaken theory – "one of his less fortunate moments" (111) – of a Lydian origin. It is not a promising start to an otherwise thoughtful essay. Niebuhr agrees, however, with the Greek historian's assertion "that the language spoken by the Etruscans was one entirely peculiar to themselves and bore no affinity to any other" (111). He also agrees that the alphabet originated in Phoenician and Greek, and he confirms with a quotation from Lucretius that they wrote from right to left. He brings the contemporary Italian scholar Giuseppe Micali into the discussion by mentioning that the latter hears the rough sound of ancient Etruscan in the modern Tuscan dialect. It is worth noting that he retracted in 1828 the claim he made in 1811 that Rome began as an Etruscan colony. He also denied that the Tarquins were Etruscans.

Turning to art, he anticipates Ruskin's suggestions about continuities between Etruscan art and the painting of the early Renaissance, though he probably saw even less Etruscan art than Ruskin did: "One thing that strikes us, as though it were a national characteristic, is the exceeding accuracy of their drawing, though often without any regard to grace; exactly like what we see in the Tuscan painters at the revival of art in the middle ages" (134). He offers examples in a footnote referring to engravings in Micali's book. He also offers a periodization of Etruscan art that places its peak in the fifth century BCE, with "the she-wolf of the Capitol" as one of the finest works. He postulates a following period between the Romanization of Etruria (c. 300 BCE) and the age of Sulla (c. 90 BCE) in which the art "is in a tamer, more delicate, and softer style" (134). Without more examples we can't evaluate his aesthetic judgments.

His comments on Greek influence on a native tradition of vase making are generally sound. And he is conventional in following Winckelmann in praising the Greeks to whom "alone was that idea revealed, by which the human body is fashioned into life and beauty. From their spirit proceeded the spark, by which genial natures have been kindled in every genial people. Hence the subjects of the most beautiful Etruscan works of art often belong to Greek mythology: but, having once been enlightened, the Tuscans were also able to treat their own conceptions in the spirit of Greeks" (134). The last clause introduces a distinction important for future discussions of Etruscan art. His praise extends as well to the practical art of architecture where he prefers the Etruscan public buildings to the Egyptian temples and tombs because the former were built "without taskmasters and bondmen" (129) and were for public use. (Hegel and Ruskin would have nodded in agreement.) This is a tradition he sees continued by the Romans of the middle Republic – small temples, yes, but no ostentatious pyramids or tombs. He takes a moment to challenge the tradition, recorded by Varro and Pliny the Elder, that an enormous tomb was built for Lars Porsena: "Pliny's expressions show that no trace of it can have been visible in his time: yet so colossal an edifice must have lasted undamaged down to this day: so that it can be nothing but a dream. Indeed, a building like the one described by Varro is absolutely impossible and belongs to the Arabian Nights" (130). Until the recent discovery of the Fanum Voltumnae, the sanctuary that was the site of pan-Etruscan meetings, I would have agreed with this view.[9]

Though he says little about political organization, Niebuhr is impressed by the flexibility of the twelve-city confederation in which the different Etruscan groups were united "loosely and transiently" (126). He also praises their resistance to hereditary kingship while choosing a single leader for all twelve cities in times of crisis. He is as troubled as Cicero in *De Divinatione*, however, by the fact that the Etruscans were "a priest-ridden people" (117). He is confident that "a free expansion of the intellect in poetry and science could never take place among a people whose pride and chief study lay in divination and ritual observances" (129). Unlike Cicero, Niebuhr doesn't reject the practices of the soothsayers because they are fraudulent. Instead, he offers a political reason that would resonate with a nineteenth-century reader and declares that this sort of religion abets tyranny: "In the East and in Italy the soothsayer was a tyrant, and the abetter of the ruling powers: he always tried to keep the people in chains. Of this yoke the stirring spirit of the Greeks soon eased itself" (139). The emphasis on the importance of freedom recalls Winckelmann and Hegel. However, we need to resist the temptation to read this as a call to revolution in Europe. Niebuhr was a good citizen of Prussia, a faithful government servant, and an admirer of Britain's orderly political development since the revolution of 1688 established it as a constitutional monarchy. He admired Edmund Burke and despised Jean-Jacques Rousseau and the French Revolution. The elusive Etruscans fascinated him but, in the larger picture, they were ultimately just a prelude to the well-documented and far greater history of Rome. For Niebuhr they are less

9 There is a drawing based on Varro's description in Wellard's *The Search for the Etruscans*, 200.

a mysterious people than one about which we would like to have more historical materials, like texts, coins, scarabs, tombs, and ruins. Having neither these nor descriptions of the Etruscans' social and political structures, he gives as complete an account as he can.

The History of Rome marks an important moment in the return of the Etruscans into historiography. In 1828, the year of the publication of Niebuhr's second edition, the people who called themselves Rasenna made a more dramatic reappearance at Canino, the estate of Lucien Bonaparte, 64 kilometres northwest of Rome: the ground collapsed under the hooves of a pair of bulls ploughing the fields to reveal Etruscan vases. More than one scholar at the time must have thought of the myth of Tages. Where Hamilton had introduced Etruscan antiquities to select groups like the nobility and the Society of the Dilettanti, of which he was a member, Bonaparte would make them available to anyone who could afford them.

5

Lucien Bonaparte, Prince of Canino:
Selling Out the Etruscans

Lucien Bonaparte, Prince of Canino, removed a staggering number of Greek vases from his personal estate, setting the tone for the plundering of Etruscan tombs for vases that persists to the present.

Nancy Thomson de Grummond[1]

Like the other members of the Bonaparte family, Lucien (1775–1840) followed his older brother to France from Corsica. He worked for him in Paris and was instrumental in his putsch in Thermidor (27 July 1794). Lucien broke with Napoleon, however, over his insistence that Lucien abandon his wife to make a political marriage. He also strongly opposed Napoleon's intention to be crowned emperor; Lucien's own political sympathies were more republican. Eventually Lucien went into self-imposed exile in Rome. When Napoleon escaped from Elba, however, he joined him for the one hundred days. He was proscribed at the Restoration, but the allies allowed him to remain prince of Canino. Historians describe him as the most able and the most politically astute of Napoleon's brothers, though that may not be as high a compliment as it seems.

At Canino, Lucien and his enterprising second wife, Alexandrine – she bore them ten children – became amateur archaeologists, mainly because of their precarious financial situation. They had bought the principality of Canino from Pope Pius VII in 1814. After Napoleon's fall they depended on loans and the generosity of the family to remain solvent. Their financial situation changed with the unexpected discovery of Etruscan tombs in 1828 during ploughing. Within a year over two thousand vases had been excavated. Though by no means

---

1 de Grummond, *An Encyclopedia of the History of Classical Archaeology*, 409.

comparable in drama or significance to Champollion's decipherment of Egyptian hieroglyphics (1822–24), the discovery of Etruscan tombs caused a stir. The excavations at Canino provided a steady flow of Etruscan antiquities for the next three decades.

Unlike Sir William Hamilton, the prince didn't depend on dealers. His land, a small part of which had been owned by Cicero, made him the primary source of things Etruscan being sold around Europe until his death in 1840. I can't help thinking that the prince missed an opportunity to put the Etruscans decisively on the archaeological, cultural, and historical maps. The time was propitious. Publication of the multi-volume *Description de l'Égypte* (1809–29), about the loot Napoleon had brought back in 1801, was completed in 1829. And the same period saw the reappearance of Pompeii with the publication between 1817 and 1832 of Sir William Gell's *Pompeiana: The Typography, Edifices and Ornaments of Pompeii.* We can imagine someone in Bonaparte's position recognizing possibilities beyond personal gain in the discovery of new tombs. At roughly the same time, the enterprising and visionary John Lloyd Stephens, along with Stephen Frederick Catherwood, his artist, discovered Mayan cities unknown except to locals, and Stephens published two best-selling books that helped found Mayan archaeology.[2]

The discovery at Canino spurred other property owners in the area to begin excavations. As George Dennis points out with justifiable irritation in *The Cities and Cemeteries of Etruria* – the most detailed description we have of the sites – almost as much of the pottery was destroyed as made available for sale: the black bucchero vases, for instance, were smashed because they might flood the market and bring down the price of painted items. Armed overseers also ensured that the diggers and peasants stole nothing. At Veii and Vulci, between 1842 and 1847, Dennis witnessed wanton destruction of anything not considered valuable. By then, Bonaparte was dead and his widow, the princess, was in charge.

I find it difficult to bring the prince into focus. On the one hand, his interest in the excavation was driven by understandable commercial motives: his French biographer suggests that "on the advice of his wife" Lucien began to sell a greater part of his collection to deal with "the

2 John Lloyd Stephens, *Incidents of Travel in Central America, Chiapas, and Yucatan* (1841) and *Incidents of Travel in Yucatan* (1843). Neither Stephens nor Catherwood had any previous experience in Mayan archaeology.

disastrous financial situation."[3] On the other hand, he was a serious antiquarian, and Giuseppe M. Della Fina even praises his "successful excavations" as carried out "with innovative methods for the time." He invited Eduard Gerhard, a scholar of some stature, to make a record of the vases before they left the estate. He corresponded with scholars like August-Aubin Millin, curator of medals at the Royal Library in Paris, who had written a book about antique vases, and he hired others with greater expertise than himself to help catalogue his holdings. Lucien had originally thought – based on a misinterpretation of Pliny the Elder – that his excavations at the hill of Cucumella were at the ancient Etruscan city of Vetulonia. But Gerhard, a German archaeologist with a long-standing interest in Etruscans, showed in 1832 that Lucien had discovered ancient Velch (or Vulci). Had Lucien known more about Greek vases he would have realized that most of his were Greek, not Etruscan, of the sixth, fifth, and fourth centuries. Nevertheless he "continued to maintain the Etruscan origin of the Greek vases he discovered and the supremacy of Etruscan art." His loyalty to the Rasenna probably owed much to his adherence to "Philo-Italic" theories.[4] Of the roughly five thousand vases found at Vulci most are now in the collections of the Vatican, the Louvre, and the British Museum. By the time the prince and princess were finished, their finds were scattered all over Europe and across the Atlantic: Bavaria, Rome, Berlin, Copenhagen, London, St Petersburg, Brussels, Boston, Philadelphia, Naples, and Florence. It is possible that the prince made available more Etruscan artifacts than anyone else in the nineteenth century, both in private collections and museums. Thanks to these sales Lucien could undertake the renovation of his palace, today the Palace Valadier.

The Etruscans made Napoleon's brother rich and unexpectedly famous. This time, however, he was famous not as the emperor's brother, but as the man who had excavated Etruscan tombs and discovered artifacts of value. People came to visit him because of the Etruscans and not just to hear anecdotes about *L'Empereur*. They included Stendhal, George Dennis, a traveller who became an Etruscologist, and the irrepressibly curious Mrs Hamilton Gray, who will stand in for all those on the Grand Tour who had done some homework, hoped to find the

3 Ibid., 273. My translation.
4 Della Fina, "History of Etruscology," 62–3.

prince of Canino at home when they called, and were on the lookout for vases. He didn't invent the post-Napoleonic Grand Tour, but he gave it an Etruscan option between Florence and Rome. From now on the cities and cemeteries of Etruria would tempt travellers into detours from what was already a crowded tourist highway. Most of the subjects in this book who come after Bonaparte will travel it.

6

Thomas Babington Macaulay: Lays of Ancient Rome (1842), a Poem of Empire

The Etruscans' territory extended roughly south to this river
where the hero Horatius stopped them at the bridge.

Question on Jeopardy!

[Patrick] O'Brian couldn't fathom his son's inability to memorise Macaulay's
"Horatius" ... and sometimes whacked him with a Malacca cane.

Christopher Tayler[1]

In 1927 Robert Graves, not yet famous as the author of the anti-war
memoir *Good-bye to All That*, published *Lars Porsena or the Future of Swearing
and Improper Language*. It is a book that owes the Etruscan part of its title
to Thomas Babington Macaulay's popular and hugely influential
Victorian poem "Horatius," based on Livy's heroic Roman story of how
the soldier Horatius Cocles defended a bridge against Lars Porsena's
Etruscan army and saved Rome. But Graves is less interested in the story
than in the poem's first verse: "Lars Porsena of Clusium / By the Nine
Gods he swore / That the great house of Tarquin / Should suffer wrong
no more." Porsena's oath, "By the Nine [Etruscan] Gods" who send
thunderbolts, is Graves's point of departure for a lament on the decline
of swearing and strong language in English. Notice that he takes it for
granted that his readers will understand the connection between Porsena
and "Swearing." Not only had Macaulay's *Lays of Ancient Rome* been a
best-seller, but the poem "Horatius" had been studied and memorized

---

1 Tayler, "For Want of a Dinner Jacket," *London Review of Books*, 37. For *Jeopardy*,
see episode 6510, first aired 28 December 2012.

for over a century in schools. Discussing the Etruscan monarchs in his
Outline of History (1920), H.G. Wells, one of the most popular writers
of the time, calls the *Lays of Ancient Rome* "familiar to every schoolboy."[2]
One can go further and say that it is the most popular work of art in
which the Etruscans play a prominent and significant role. The poem's
opening couplet was once as famous as anything by Shakespeare or
Wordsworth. It is ironic, however, that Macaulay's celebration of Roman
(and English) virtues begins with thirteen stanzas about the invading
Etruscan army of Lars Porsena of Clusium, described by George Dennis
as "the greatest Etruscan prince and hero whom history commemorates."[3]
The Etruscan plays a supporting role to the story's hero, a Roman soldier. He's not a villain, however: he is the "non-Roman" leading a foreign
army trying to restore the deposed Tarquinius Superbus to his throne.
Readers of Livy remember that the Romans replaced the Tarquins with a
republic, though this transition didn't happen as quickly or as smoothly
as the historian suggests.

Macaulay informs his readers that "what is called the history of the
Kings and the early Consuls of Rome is to a great extent fabulous" since
the early records had been lost or destroyed.[4] But he believed that there
had existed an early Latin ballad-poetry, now completely lost, in which
Livy's stories of early Rome had first been told. Among them he lists
the familiar stories of the she-wolf, Romulus and Remus, the rape of the
Sabine women, Scaevola putting his hand in the flame, Coriolanus, and
countless others. Like later investigators of myths, he postulates a core
of fact hidden deep in the myth or legend. Having made the decision
to revive these in poems for the modern age, he "borrowed ... from our
own old ballads and more from Sir Walter Scott, the great restorer of
our ballad-poetry." He confidently cross-pollinated these with
echoes of the *Iliad* "because there is reason to believe that some of the
old Latin minstrels really had recourse to that inexhaustible store of

---

2 Wells, *The Outline of History*, 384.
3 Dennis, *The Cities and Cemeteries of Etruria*, 2:347.
4 Macaulay, *Lays of Ancient Rome*, 3. All quotations will be from this edition.
Macaulay cites James Perizonius as the first critic to recognize a poetic element in
Rome's early history. He goes on acknowledge that the theory "was revived in the
present generation by Niebuhr, a man who would have been the first writer of his time,
if his talent for communicating truths had borne any proportion to his talent for inves-
tigating them" (5). In other words, Macaulay doesn't think much of Niebuhr's style.

poetic images" (52). The combination of Scott, Homer, the ballad measure, Thomas Gray's "The Bard," and Macaulay's pulsing hortatory style resulted in a book that remained popular for over a century, not least because its Roman values were synonymous with those of his English audience. Reading the poems, they could hear two empires marching in step. Macaulay, a noted liberal and soon to be a famous historian of England, versifies and "Englishes" Livy in the service of the British Empire. But he can't tell the story of triumphant Rome without giving the Etruscans and their two most famous figures prominent roles.[5]

Though Lars Porsena was a more significant historical figure than Horatius, he and the Etruscans are cast in a supporting role in a story about the beginning of the hostilities that would lead over the next two centuries to Rome's dominion over the Etruscans. "Horatius" is another instalment in a long saga in which the Romans are presented as more important than the Etruscans, even when the latter are more historically significant at the time. There is a later example of this in Dante's *Paradiso* (4.84) in which Gaius Mucius Scaevola is named while Lars Porsena, whom he attempted to assassinate, isn't. The date of Horatius's story is traditionally given as 510 BCE, though Livy is probably closer to the historical mark with 507. R.M. Ogilvie suggests that the first date was originally chosen to align the expulsion of Tarquinius Superbus with the expulsion in 510 of the Peisistratids, the tyrants of Athens.[6] We tend to forget that Lars Porsena had the unenviable task of restoring an unpopular monarch. The story exists in two versions: Livy ends it, like Macaulay, with the hero swimming to safety when the Romans succeed in destroying the bridge separating Rome and the invading and about to be triumphant Etruscan army. Polybius, writing a century earlier, ends the narrative with Horatius drowning. Before going any further, it might be useful to have a brief historical account of the characters and events celebrated by the poem. According to

5 Macaulay's appropriation of Livy in his nationalistic poem in support of the British empire needs to be seen in the context of various nationalistic works in a variety of genres in his time throughout Europe. A well-known example is Elias Lönnrot's restoration of the fragments of myths that he titled *Kalevala*; published in 1849, it was an even greater imaginative reconstruction or "intuitive welding" of the past into an ideological construct with its eyes on the present. The phrase is Geoffrey O'Brien's in "Magic Sayings by the Thousands," *New York Review of Books*, 34.

6 Ogilvie, "Introduction to Livy," *The Early History of Rome*, 18.

tradition, Porsena was summoned by the exiled king of Rome to lay siege to the city to restore him to the throne. In the campaign that followed occurred the feats of Horatius Cocles, Scaevola, and Cloelia, the heroic Roman hostage. Repulsed in his attack, Porsena made peace with Rome. One tradition suggests, however, that Porsena became master of the city.[7] According to Ogilvie, Livy followed the Roman version that Porsena "failed to conquer Rome but the truth seems to have survived in a few sources despite the official version. Lars Porsena did capture Rome and may well have decided to set up a puppet government."[8] In other words, the Etruscan kings may have been replaced in the short term by an Etruscan leader and not by a republic. Whatever the case, it is a fact that between 509 and 493 BCE seventeen of the twenty-six consuls had Etruscan names, as did three of the four dictators. So much for Livy's neat separation of Etruscans and Romans, monarchy and republic.

One detail that would surely have been mentioned had Porsena been a Roman hero is the astonishingly large tomb, referred to earlier, built for him in Clusium (Chiusi). It is described by Marcus Terentius Varro (116–27 BCE) as two hundred metres high: "The base of Porsena's sepulchre was three hundred feet square and fifty feet high, inside which was built a labyrinth … On top of this base stood five pyramids, one at each corner and one in the centre of the square, all of them a hundred and fifty feet high." There were two further layers of pyramids. Rumoured to be under Chiusi's Cathedral of San Secondiano, the sepulchre has never been found, perhaps because Sulla razed the town in 89.[9] If Varro was, as Quintilian wrote, "the most learned of Romans" it's difficult to believe that either he or Pliny the Elder, who records this from Varro, could have credited the size of the sepulchre. Though they couldn't have known this, the Pyramid of Cheops, the highest of the Egyptian pyramids, is 147 metres. Porsena's tomb would have been almost two hundred feet higher at 200 metres. If ever found, it will be the greatest discovery in Etruscan archaeology. That is, if it exists. Incidentally, Pliny the Elder was outraged by the size of the tomb and attributed its construction to "vesana dementia" or crazed frenzy (*Natural*

7 Howatson, *The Oxford Companion to Classical Literature*, 457.
8 Ogilvie, "Introduction to Livy," *The Early History of Rome*, 19.
9 Wellard, *The Search for the Etruscans*, 201–2. For Pliny the Elder, see *Natural History: A Selection*, 91.

History, 36.19). In other words, it was not the sort of the thing the rational, sober Romans would have built.

In Macaulay's Whiggish view of European history, the Etruscans are the first of many obstacles Rome must overcome in its fated march to empire. His intention is as didactic as Virgil's, Livy's, and Plutarch's, and his readers understood that Rome was synonymous with England in the poem's symbolism, and the Etruscans perhaps with France or any other obstacle. The Roman virtues celebrated in *Lays of Ancient of Rome* were still relevant in the nineteenth century. Horatius could be celebrated as an exemplary figure, the courageous and self-sacrificing sort of Roman responsible for Rome's success. For Macaulay, as for Thucydides and Aristotle, actions are signs of character and heroes do not suffer from doubt: they understand the right thing to do and act on that understanding. They are exemplary figures.

To Macaulay's credit he reminds readers that Sextus Tarquinius, the king's son who raped Lucretia, does not speak for Etruscans when he curses Horatius and wants to see him drown. The catalogue of Etruscan heroes shows Macaulay taking an onomastic pleasure in introducing a worthy enemy impressed by Horatius's death-defying leap on his horse into the turbulent Tiber and his survival: "And when above the surges / They saw his crest appear, / All Rome sent forth a rapturous cry, / And even the ranks of Tuscany / Could scarce forbear to cheer" (60.6–10). The poem ends with an assurance that Horatius's heroism continues to be remembered in the poem's present: "And wives still pray to Juno / For boys with hearts as bold / As his who kept the bridge so well / In the brave days of old" (67.5–8). The present tense collapses the historical distance between Rome and England as Romans and Englishmen cheer for the brave soldier willing to sacrifice himself for his country. It will be almost a century before other writers find a political use for the Etruscans: the Frenchman Raymond Queneau, the Hungarian Antal Szerb, the Finn Mika Waltari, the Pole Zbigniew Herbert, and the Italian Giorgio Bassani.

7

Mrs Hamilton Gray and George Dennis:
English Travellers

A man who has not been to Italy is always conscious of an inferiority.

Samuel Johnson[1]

The year 1839 was a good one for Etruscan matters. The prince of Canino continued his well-publicized excavations. *The North American Review* published a very long review-article about two books by Giuseppe Micali: *Storia degli antichi popoli Italiani* and a companion volume of illustrations, *Monumenti per servire alla Storia degli antichi popoli Italiani.*[2] Micali's established reputation had already withstood an attack, later retracted, by the formidable Barthold Georg Niebuhr.[3] The anonymous American reviewer treated Micali's books respectfully as a major contribution to the field. The Countess of Blessington published *The Idler in Italy: Journal of a Tour* in which she noted that on the route "to Bracciano, Sir William Gell proposed our stopping to see Galeria, a village occupying the site of a citadel of an ancient Etruscan town of some importance."[4] But that is all we hear of the site near Rome. If we stretch the year into 1840, we can include Eduard Gerhard, who began the three-decade-long publication of his monumental *Etruskische Spiegel*, a systematic classification of Etruscan mirrors. Earlier he had written an account of Lucien Bonaparte's excavations at Vulci. It was also in 1839 that Mrs Hamilton Gray (1800–1887) and her husband, the Reverend John Hamilton Gray, made their second tour of Italy. They had been inspired by Vincenzo Campanari's popular exhibition of

---

1 Quoted in Jenkyns, *The Victorians and Ancient Greece*, 4.
2 Both published in 1832.
3 Quoted in Della Finna, *Etruscology*, 62–3.
4 Dennis, *The Cities and Cemeteries of Etruria*, 2:322.

Etruscan art in London's Pall Mall in January 1837.[5] On show were eleven reconstructed Etruscan tombs with watercolour paintings, actual sarcophagi, and grave goods. The Grays visited eight Etruscan places, including Tarquinia, Vulci, Cerveteri, and Chiusi. They also viewed several major collections of antiques and art, including the Museo Gregoriano Etrusco that Pope Gregory VI had opened in 1837 in response to Campanari's suggestion that Rome needed an Etruscan museum. *Tour to the Sepulchres of Etruria, in 1839*, Mrs Hamilton Gray's long and very informative account of the second journey, was published in 1840 and was popular enough to have two further editions.[6] She followed it with a history of Etruria which included a translation of parts of Müller's highly regarded *Die Etrusker* of 1827. She wrote three further books on ancient Italian history.

By any standard, Mrs Hamilton Gray was a serious student and traveller though she was typically reluctant, as Dennis tactfully points out, to mention sexual paintings or objects. Referring to a banqueting scene in the Querciola Tomb in which a young woman throws her arms around a young man's neck, Dennis writes that "Mrs Gray, with a praiseworthy tenderness for her sex, is blind to the evident amorous abandon of the fair Etruscan and can see in her only 'an afflicted mother consoled by her remaining son.'"[7] She went to the Etruscan sites better equipped than almost any English person but George Dennis, and he set a very high standard as we shall see. Before going to Italy, she met Micali, who wrote introductions for her. She was fluent in German and Italian and had a genuine intellectual curiosity about the ancient civilizations of the Mediterranean. Among her preparations was a visit to Sir William Richard Hamilton (not Emma's husband), a secretary of the Dilettanti Society and a trustee of the British Museum. She must have impressed him because they met several times and, according to her account, "he recommended to me several historical and critical works, all German, and all of which he lent me. This he continued to do for a series of years,

---

5 When the show closed, the British Museum bought most of the articles exhibited. These became the nucleus of the museum's Etruscan collection. Campanari is a key figure behind the collections of the British Museum and the Museo Gregoriano Etrusco founded in the year of his Pall Mall exhibition.

6 A full account with a portrait in old age is in Dyfri Williams, "The Hamilton Gray Vase," 10–20.

7 Dennis, *The Cities and Cemeteries of Etruria*, 1:323n3.

placing his rich library at my disposal."[8] Unlike D.H. Lawrence and most other interested amateurs, Mrs Hamilton Gray did more than her fair share of homework. She was definitely a traveller, not a tourist.

Her still very readable memoir is written in a lively conversational style that makes her an engaging, informed, and thoughtful guide.[9] Less impatient, opinionated, and irascible than Lawrence, she would probably be a more easygoing companion. They might have conversed as equals about the history of the Mediterranean, but he would have had to listen attentively to what she knew about ancient coins. She had also prepared herself by reading Bonaparte's account of his excavations, Müller's *Die Etrusker*, Micali's *Storia degli antichi popoli Italiani* (1832), and Gell's *Topography of Rome and Its Vicinity* (1834). Gell's was the first detailed account in English of the newly discovered painted tombs at Tarquinia. Mrs Gray paid enough attention to the current scholarship to be able to note that "in Etruscan sepulchral inscriptions, the name of the mother occurs, at least as frequently as that of the father, and always in conjunction with the patronymic" (488). Like many more scholarly and equally rash travellers she couldn't resist attempting to translate Etruscan inscriptions, though she is typically modest about the results. Across two centuries, I admire her preparation, determination, and sense of adventure. She deserves respect rather than condescension from posterity. If I sound slightly defensive on her behalf, it is in anticipation of Dennis's mixed response to her book in a letter and two reviews, which I discuss below. He seems worried that she might diminish the market for his own book still six years in the future. Could he have known he was about to write a masterpiece, no doubt he would have shown more patience.

Unlike most travellers, Mrs Hamilton Gray had what might pass for a theory of historical development, though she wouldn't call it that: she postulates either "the common origin of nations, or that the civilization of Greece and Asia Minor did really come from Egypt" (129). The Etruscan tombs and relics suggest to her that "long before the people of the ancient world were bound together under the leaden yoke of universal empire, very distant lands were intimately united by colonization, commerce and political alliance" (269). I suspect she

8 Quoted in Williams, "The Hamilton Gray Vase," 11.
9 Gray, *Tour to the Sepulchres of Etruria, in 1839*. All page references will be to this edition. It is worth noting that William Betham's *Etruria-Celtica* was published in 1842.

would have enjoyed Fernand Braudel's *The Mediterranean in the Ancient World* (2001) for its transnational perspective on Mediterranean cultures. In her more conventional judgments, she follows her Christian faith and period opinion and falls back too often on comparisons to Egyptian and Old Testament precedents: Etruscan sarcophagi remind her of "the Valley of the Kings," and Castel d'Asso somehow recalls Abraham, Job, Petra, etc. (411). Her reflection on the melancholy pleasure of ruins is a Romantic period commonplace and for that reason worth quoting: "It would almost seem as if the Etruscans had a presentiment that in distant times their name and race were destined to be rescued from oblivion by their tombs, for they have not only left subterranean traces of their existence for miles round the site of their principal cities, but have erected lofty monuments whose ruins now fill the beholder with wonder, differing as they do from all others in their architectural shape" (412). This is Shelley's "Ozymandias," but without the merciless irony.[10] But it is also a perceptive guess about the central role to be played by mortuary remains and ruins in the resurrection of the Etruscans then and now. The Etruscans certainly had a "presentiment" in their theory of cycles that their civilization would end, but Mrs Hamilton Gray didn't know that. No more than Dennis could know that his optimistic prediction that the history of the Etruscans "promises, ere long, to be as distinct and palpable as that of Egypt, Greece, or Rome" would never be quite fulfilled.[11]

Like most of us she tries to understand a new experience within the matrix of what is familiar. But in describing the ruins at Castel d'Asso she sounds an unexpected note about the fate of all empires by including Britain's. It is one of her finer set pieces about ruins and is worth quoting in full.

We had seen at Castel d'Asso the very rocks not able to preserve the dead committed to them; and the words graven upon those rocks, though not indeed obliterated, have in many instances been moved out of their place, and in all have ceased to tell their tale. Let us not, then, sentimentally and

---

10 Shelley wrote his sonnet in competition with Horace Smith who produced "On a Stupendous Leg of Granite, Discovered Standing by Itself in the Deserts of Egypt." His second stanza anticipates Mrs Hamilton Gray in envisioning London as a ruin. Both poems were published in 1818 in *The Examiner of London*.

11 Finley, "The Etruscans and Early Rome," 112.

uselessly lament the appointed lot of everything in this world, whether in flesh
or stone; let us not weep that all which lives must die, "all that's bright must
fade," all that exists must perish; but let *us*, who look upon their vacant places,
and either eulogize the day when they flourished, or give a sigh to their
decay – let us, who know that the time is coming when our own country also
may be laid as low – that even England may become a theme "to paint [*sic*] a
moral, or adorn a tale;" let us ask ourselves, Have we any reason to believe that
we are the possessors of better things; have we, with our full light, secured to
ourselves that which every Christian is entitled to account his own, a more
enduring habitation, a more lasting memorial, and a glory which passeth not
away?[12] (423)

At Castel d'Asso the choice is between Peter's "rock" and the weathered
tufa of the empty Etruscan outdoor tombs. More interesting and
disturbing, at least to her readers, must have been the unexpected
suggestion that even England is not exempt from the fate of other now
fallen empires. If Egypt, Greece, Etruria, and Rome have fallen, *why
not England?* This can't be a possibility that occurred often to people
of her class. As if the inevitable fall of the empire was not enough of a
worry, she also asks the reader to consider the state of his or her soul.
The Victorians were serious about these matters.

George Dennis's description of Castel d'Asso and its tomb-filled
glens is equally moving and of its time. Both the Romantics and Victorians
would have understood the writer's generic intentions. Like Mrs
Hamilton Gray, Dennis presses the site for its potential for sublimity –
"the loneliness, seclusion, and utter stillness of the scene ... nothing but
the ruined and picturesque castle on the opposite precipice" – but he
stops short of a brief moral summary. He lets the scene speak for itself,
as he usually does.[13] Despite Mrs Hamilton Gray's best efforts, however,
she can't escape the fact that Etruscan ruins, other than the hillside

---

12 "All that's bright must fade, – / The brightest and the fleetest; / All that's sweet
was made / But to be lost when sweetest." This is the first verse of a once popular lyric
or "Indian Air" (1823) by Thomas Moore. The second quotation is from Samuel
Johnson's translation of Juvenal's Tenth Satire, "The Vanity of Human Wishes," which
Mrs Hamilton Gray misremembers: "To point a moral, or adorn a tale."

13 Dennis, *The Cities and Cemeteries of Etruria*, 1: 74–5. Facing Egyptian ruins almost
daily during his tour of 1849–50, Flaubert can't resist mocking "the elevated thoughts
one should have in the presence of ruins" and landscapes, though, of course, he often
has them. *Flaubert in Egypt*, 74.

tombs, are too ruined, too paltry, almost totally lacking in the sort of architectural and sculptural detail that travellers expect. They also lack all sacred materiality. Orvieto is a case in point. It has the remnants of eight temples but the best that can be said of them is that the Belvedere Temple, mentioned earlier, has a good view. (See figure 7.1.)

None quite measure up to Susan Stewart's optimistic suggestion that "a ruin is the alter ego of a culture. An anomaly in the landscape of the present positing a question, requiring an explanation, asking to be used. By standing purposeless since their original purpose has been lost, they have the singularity of an autotelic object, an artwork."[14] The Belvedere Temple may provoke some questions, but it answers only fitfully. And whatever singularity it may have gained by losing not only its "original purpose" but almost all its material being, the result has not been the creation of an autotelic art object. Even its name alerts us to the view (*bel vedere*) instead of reminding us of its original function. The Belvedere Temple is no longer even sufficiently pictur-esque to provide a setting for the traditional painting of a writer sitting and reflecting on the ruins of the past. I'm thinking of Johann Heinrich Wilhelm Tischbein's *Goethe in the Roman Campagna* (1786–87) or Charles Lock Eastlake's *Lord Byron's "Dream"* (1827). Faced only by Etruscan remains, Piranesi would have been at a loss for a subject. Despite his loyalty to the Etruscans, Piranesi's "queste parlante ruine" referred to the ruins of ancient Rome. His *Study of Etruscan Friezes at Chiusi* owes more to his imagination than to Etruscan remains. As I wrote, the only Etruscan ruins that continue to amaze are the tomb sites, as we sense from Gray's and Dennis's descriptions.

That Mrs Hamilton Gray is a less determined traveller, a less evoca-tive and precise writer, and a less attentive observer than George Dennis (1814–1898) goes without saying. But Nancy Thomson de Grummond offers a balanced view of the relationship between their two books when she suggests that, together with the Campanari show, Mrs Hamilton Gray's book "created a favorable climate for the Etruscans that led directly to the publication of James Byres's *Hypogaei, Or Sepulchral Caverns of Tarquinia* (1842), some eighty years after his drawings were made, and to the investigations of George Dennis, who wrote the Etruscan classic of the century in *The Cities and Cemeteries of Etruria*

14 Stewart, *The Ruins Lesson*, xiv.

7.1 Belvedere Temple, Orvieto, c. 500 BCE.

in 1848."[15] It is no exaggeration to suggest that Dennis's book is as important to the story of the Etruscan return as Winckelmann's chapter and Lawrence's *Etruscan Places*.

In scholarly and historical value, it is in its own class. Dennis's is the only volume about the Etruscans published in the nineteenth century to remain in print except for Müller's, which has survived in an edition revised in 1877 by Wilhelm Deecke. There's something very pre-modern, perhaps just Victorian, in the fact that two of the more informative Etruscan books in the period were produced by the wife of a minister and a man whose parents took him out of school to work as a clerk. His impressive learning, like Mrs Hamilton Gray's or Austin Henry Layard's, was acquired on his own. Before he was done, Dennis had taught himself Greek, Latin, and at least four of the modern European languages, and he made careers in the Excise Office and the Colonial

15 de Grummond, *Encyclopedia of the History of Classical Archaeology*, 275.

Office. He also found time to make contributions to archaeology in Etruria, Sicily, and Turkey. It was Etruria, of course, that was his ticket to fame. No one else in the nineteenth century saw and recorded as much of the Etruscan world, or suffered as much serious discomfort and illness in the process. And, one might add, for as little personal or financial profit. His most tangible reward was his book, which was reprinted in an updated edition in 1878 and again in the Everyman's Library in 1907. There was also some recognition from his peers: he knew Layard; he was awarded an honorary doctorate by Oxford in 1885, the year of Lawrence's birth; and he is mentioned with high praise in Etruscan scholarship and travel writing to our day.[16] The great book was recently published in a new, abbreviated edition.

Dennis travelled to Etruria three times with the artist Samuel Ainsley, in 1842 and 1843. I mentioned that 1842 had seen the posthumous publication of Byres's *Hypogaei, Or Sepulchral Caverns of Tarquinia.* It's worth pausing to give a brief account of Byres (1733–1817), whose belated publication makes him a figure of the nineteenth-century history of the Etruscans. A Scot, he trained as an architect but quickly moved to Italy and became interested in art and archaeology. He sold the Portland Vase to Sir William Hamilton and the first series of Poussin's *Seven Sacraments* to the Duke of Rutland. He was aware of Thomas Jenkins's 1761 excavations at Tarquinia and hoped to reach the public first with a book with engraved illustrations of the antiquities. Unable to raise enough capital, he abandoned the project. Decades later Frank Howard resurrected the original plates by Christopher Norton and published the book in the same decade as Gray's and Dennis's volumes.[17] It is worth noting that the plates were based on watercolours by the Polish painter Franciszek Smuglewicz, some of which are the only records we have of caves that were later filled and disappeared from the record. Byres seems not to have written the text. Dennis's chapter on "Lost Tombs Delineated by Byres"[18] shows him using his predecessor as a guide, though he could no longer find some of the tombs.

16 See Mary Lovett Cameron's *Old Etruria and Modern Tuscany* (1909), Frederick Seymour's *Up Hill and Down Dale in Ancient Etruria* (1910), and Lawrence's *Etruscan Places* (1932).

17 Ridgway writes that Winckelmann knew of Byres's plans. "James Byres," *An Encyclopedia of the History of Classical Archaeology*, 211.

18 Dennis, *The Cities and Cemeteries of Etruria*, 1:398.

That Dennis also knew Gray's *Tour to the Sepulchres of Etruria, in 1839* is clear from a sour letter to John Murray I referred to above in which he says that one of the reasons he was writing his book was "to put a full stop to [Mrs Hamilton Gray's] erroneous progeny."[19] He is more polite in two tepid but informative 1844 reviews of her book, one in *The Dublin Review* and another signed "GD" in the *Westminster Review*. In the latter, Dennis pays his respects to her work and then goes his own way, describing the current state of knowledge in the field. "[The works] of Mrs Gray are perhaps most accessible to the reader, and this lady has the merit of having rendered the subject familiar to the British public by details of the highest interest" (146). Having tipped his hat in her direction, he writes an essay that wouldn't be out of place in today's *New York Review of Books* – the book is left behind as the reviewer offers his view of the subject. There is no evidence that Mrs Hamilton Gray responded to his criticism, but a sentence from the preface to her *History of Etruria* (1843) would serve: "I have found the field unoccupied, and mine has been the first plough to break the fallow ground. May more skilful hands cultivate it richly and reap a golden harvest."[20] Between her book and the publication of Dennis's, John Murray published in 1843 Octavian Blewett's *Central Italy Including the Papal States, Rome, and the Cities of Etruria*. The last three words may have stuck in Dennis's mind when he chose his title.

Dennis's two dense, long volumes are an archive of Etruscan information and learning. He describes monuments and ruins, hydraulics, sewers (inevitably the Cloaca Maxima), roads, art, politics, and the relationship with Rome. With the last topic his sympathy leans decisively in the Etruscan direction: "That Rome did not fully acknowledge the debt she owed to Etruria is a fact which may be attributed to several causes. 1. To national hatred. The Etruscans were her hereditary foes. 2. To jealousy. She must have felt Etruria to be the most formidable of the neighbouring nations, and the most capable of crushing her rising power. 3. To pride."[21] His near disdain for warlike Rome recurs throughout this book in, among others, Stendhal, Lawrence, Mika Waltari, Raymond Queneau, and Zbigniew Herbert. Looking back to the eighteenth century a similar viewpoint is already present in Montesquieu and Gibbon, as well as in

19 Quoted in Williams, "The Hamilton Gray Vase," 11.
20 Ibid.
21 *Westminster Review* 41 (March–June, 1844): 173.

the notes for a "History of Etruria" left by Byres.[22] Dennis's sympathy echoes Gibbon's and anticipates Lawrence's and is one of the reasons behind his book's enduring appeal: he cares deeply about the Etruscans and worries about the fate of their ruins and their memory.

The Cities and Cemeteries of Etruria deserves its classic status. It has aged better than most classics in the genre because Dennis is a travel writer who knows his subject, observes closely, and writes with passion and with as few prejudices as possible.[23] He engages the reader in a plain but vigorous style that keeps its eye on the object in descriptions of Etruria's different landscapes; offers historically resonant reflections on ruins; comments on works of art that continue to fascinate after two millennia; and presents engaging portraits of Italians of all classes – from the local nobility to peasants met on the road. That he is a master of the topographical sublime I suggested earlier in the quotation of his description of Castel d'Asso and of the cliffside necropolis at Norchia. I also want to quote a passage with a very different content and style. It is the description of a wall painting from what Dennis calls the "Grotta Francesca" at Tarquinia, known today as the Tomb of Francesca Giustiniani, who was present at its opening in 1833. One can feel his enthusiasm for the art in the speed of the description, the tone, and the ending's anticipation of remorse. There is something immediate and almost contemporary here. It could pass for a found poem. The female figure is brought momentarily into our time by the gentle opening imperative and the present tense throughout.

Turn to the right-hand wall. What spirit, what life, what nature, in this dancing-girl! Her gown of gauze or muslin floats around her in airy folds; the broad blue ribbon which binds her bonny brown hair, and the red scarf

22 Byres goes on as follows: "Fearing that posterity should receive any account of their actions other than the one they chose to give themselves, or envious of the high antiquity of some of these nations in comparison with their own, they endeavoured to bury them in oblivion. Such maxims are not uncommon among illiterate and barbarous nations, such as the Romans were at that time." Quoted in David Ridgway, "James Byres and the Definition of the Etruscans," 6.

23 The second edition of 1878 was reprinted in 1883. The first edition (1848) was reprinted in 1907. This was then reprinted in 1968 by an Italian publisher. Princeton University Press brought out in 1985 an indispensable abridgment of the second edition by Pamela Hemphill which doubles as a travel guide to the sites. She points out that Orvieto's L'Aquila Bianca on via Garibaldi, where Dennis stayed, is still open.

hanging from one shoulder across her bosom, stream behind her with the rapidity of her movements; while she droops her face and raises her arms to give expression to her steps. Her other arm is akimbo, so that you might declare she was dancing the *salterella*. For spirit, ease, and grace she has no rival among the *ballerine* of Tarquinii. Her dress is peculiar – I remember nothing like it on the painted wall or vase. It is as modern as that of her neighbours. In truth there is nothing antiquated about her; it is hard to believe she has been dancing in this tomb for some two or three and twenty centuries. She has now unfortunately but a short time to live; she will soon take her last step from the wall. Her partner in the dance is almost obliterated, though enough remains to mark his attitude as easy and graceful. Next to him are some fragments of another female; but everything else on this wall is utterly effaced.[24]

Dennis maintains the present tense even to the final clause, which properly might have employed the past perfect. He reminds us that Winckelmann suggested that "the colours lost their freshness by exposure to their atmosphere, though [Francesco Scipione] Maffei disagrees."[25] The references to Winckelmann and Maffei are followed in Dennis's account by a reference to Mrs Hamilton Gray, whose maternal interpretation of the relationship between a young man and woman at a banquet – "blind to the evident amorous *abandon* of this fair Etruscan" – is questioned politely by Dennis, as mentioned above.[26] Stephan Steingräber, a recent scholar, describes the wall as "largely destroyed; on the left, traces of a female dancer in pale, flowered robe with sash and hanging ribbons in her hair; in the center remains of two more dancers."[27] Dennis's prose evocation of the painting finds a perfect ekphrastic echo in Fellini's *Roma* (1973) where long-buried non-Etruscan frescoes begin to disappear within hours of discovery. As their solemn faces fade into nothingness, the sad eyes continue to look at us in a melancholy farewell. Wisława Szymborska misremembered the fading paintings in *Roma* as Etruscan in a slip of memory that brings

24 Dennis, *The Cities and Cemeteries of Etruria,* 1:364.

25 Ibid., 1:323. Francesco Scipione Maffei (1675–1755) was a reputable classical scholar interested in the Etruscans even before the publication of Thomas Dempster's *De Etruria regali* in 1723–24.

26 Dennis, *The Cities and Cemeteries of Etruria.*

27 Steingräber, *Etruscan Painting,* 305.

her interest closer to my own. (More on her Etruscan poem will follow in a later chapter.) It's worth recalling here the quotation from Ruskin's *Modern Painters* that serves as an epigraph to the volume: "Like the corpses of the Etruscan kings ready to sink into ashes at the first unbarring of the door of the sepulchre." Dennis records a similar story told by Carlo Avvolta, a Tarquinian magistrate, who discovered a tomb with a man in full armour lying on a rock with a sword and a crown of gold. As he watched, "the body became agitated with a sort of trembling, heaving motion (which lasted a few minutes) and then quickly disappeared, dissolved by contact with the air."[28]

Dennis is one of those travellers who seem incapable of boredom. Something always catches his attention. "Two miles beyond La Storta brought us to the Osteria del Fosso, a lonely wayside inn, which has nothing remarkable, save an hostess, who, if rumour is to be credited, like the celebrated white sow of Lavinium, has been the mother of thirty children."[29] Dennis must have smiled when the comparison of the hostess to the white sow of the *Aeneid* (3.390) occurred to him based on nothing more than the rumoured fertility of the mother. In Virgil, a priest prophesies to Aeneas that his travels in Italy will end when he sees a white sow with thirty piglets and builds a city on that spot. In Dennis's work, the scene carries no significance whatsoever beyond the unbalanced comparison of something mythic from the heroic past with something demotic, though in its own way heroic (thirty children!), in the present. Like the best travel writers, he is as open to the tavern's occupants as he is to everything about the Etruscans and his predecessors in Etruscan studies. He is never less than generous to writers like Thomas Dempster, Giuseppe Micali, and Francesco Inghirami who share his enthusiasm.[30] When he finds himself having to mediate between the last two on the issue of whether it is indecent for Etruscan wives to dine at banquets with their husbands, we can sense his bemusement at Micali and Inghirami's dispute (the former sees nothing untoward, the latter is indignant at "so licentious a custom"). His

28 Dennis, *The Cities and Cemeteries of Etruria*, 1:388.

29 Ibid., 1:145.

30 Ibid., 1:324. Inghirami should not be confused with Curzio Inghirami, the sixteenth-century forger-prankster from Scornello and Volterra, who belongs to the same family and was discussed in the opening chapter. Francesco is remembered for his multi-volume *Monumenti Etruschi* (1821–26).

footnote reminds us that the dispute goes back to Herodotus, Aristotle, and Theopompus who are predictable in preferring only *hetaerae* at dinners. Countless footnotes of this sort confirm the depth and extent of his scholarship and incidentally provide information for possible field trips described in the body of the work for the use of future travellers.

Some of his more topical notes on subjects like "Etruscan modesty," "The superiority of the Etruscans to the Greeks in their treatment of the fair sex," and the delightful "Chaplets in Etruscan Tombs" (the last is a cultural history of garlands) transport us unexpectedly into a history of adornment. Put simply, there is no better or more comprehensive introduction, before the modern era, to all aspects of Etruscan life and history. In all areas Dennis is thorough to a fault. Even today one comes away after reading him confident of a good knowledge of the basic Etruscan facts. On offer as well is a history of Etruscology from classical times to his.[31] As is inevitable in any scholarly field, Dennis has been superseded, just as art history has gone beyond Winckelmann. But Dennis continues to repay attention because he is a very fine travel writer closely attentive to life in the present even as he searches it for signs of the past. We will continue to return to him because he was the last to visit, describe, and sketch in accurate detail many sites before they deteriorated further or disappeared. For him, as for the nineteenth-century fathers of archaeology, authentic knowledge comes from antiquities that carry their dirt with them. Only if we can trace them back to where the ancients used and left them can we appreciate what these artifacts meant and did and "give them back their agency."[32] Dennis continues to help us see Etruscan sites that have disappeared since his time and to imagine historical contexts for almost forgotten events and antiquities now accessible only in museum display cases. *The Cities and Cemeteries of Etruria* is that rare thing, a volume that made an enduring contribution to its field and continues to be relevant and a pleasure to read.

31 His research in publications since the Renaissance is evident in footnote quotations like the one from Monaldo Monaldeschi's *Historical Commentaries on Orvieto* (1584). Surely the scholars who have consulted this document can be counted on one hand (1:534).

32 Vout, *Classical Art*, 1.

PART THREE

Etruscans in Basel, Rome, Massachusetts, Paris, London, and Vienna

8

Johann Jakob Bachofen:
Das Mutterrecht *(1861)*, The Saga of Tanaquil
(1870), and an Etruscan Queen

There was proclaimed a new mental attitude for all mankind …
It expressed itself an irrationalistic throwback, placing the conception
of life at the centre of thought … It set up for homage as the true
inwardness of life, the Mother-Chthonic, the darkness of the soul, the holy
procreative underworld.

Thomas Mann

Dig down beneath the sources and you find the Mothers.

Anthony Grafton[1]

Johann Jakob Bachofen (1815–1887) is remembered today primarily in relation to his more famous contemporaries in Basel, the cultural historian Jacob Burckhardt and the philosopher Friedrich Nietzsche. Bachofen and Burckhardt were born in the city and spent most of their lives there; Nietzsche spent a decade, from 1869 to 1878, as professor of classical philology at the university. In Lionel Gossman's *Basel in the Age of Burckhardt*, a lengthy study of Bachofen's life and work rides on Burckhardt's coattails. After a brief career as a judge and a professor at Basel, he withdrew to become an independent scholar with a focus on the constitutive role of myths and religions in the development of

---

1 Mann, *Reflections of a Nonpolitical Man*, quoted in Mark Lilla, "The Writer Apart," 20; Grafton, "A Passion for the Past," 50. Grafton's article is an excellent introduction to Bachofen and Burckhardt. The latter rejected, before Nietzsche, the nineteenth-century idealization of Greek culture. In his agonal view of Greek life, the Greeks are pessimistic, earthly, non-religious, and fascinated by suicide. His view of modern civilization was as tragic as Max Weber's.

civilizations. Never a declared Hegelian, Bachofen nevertheless followed the philosopher in his teleological view of history. He never made it into the first rank of thinkers, and *Das Mutterrecht* (*Mother Right*, 1861), his once influential masterpiece about matriarchy, sits on the same shelf of neglected masterworks as Eduard von Hartmann's *Philosophy of the Unconscious*, published at the end of the same decade.[2]

He is remembered primarily by two groups. Etruscan scholars, like Larissa Bonfante, mention Bachofen's *The Saga of Tanaquil* (1870), which treats the Etruscan-Roman queen as an exemplary matriarchal figure. This is not to say that Bonfante agrees with his interpretation of Etruscan women: "The case was over-stated – the 'tyranny of women' never happened. Bachofen's 'matriarchy' must be carefully distinguished from equality."[3] Feminist scholars and Joseph Campbell remember Bachofen for introducing the idea that early societies were matriarchal, and that even after its decline women were often influential in determining the succession in a kingdom, an important theme in *The Saga of Tanaquil.* There is a very good chance that he and Campbell are responsible for the presence of the ancient "mothers" in Frank Herbert's wildly popular *Dune* (1965). In Herbert's novel, the Bene Gesserit is a secret, ancient matriarchal order whose members train to acquire supernatural powers to exert social, religious, and political force in their universe. Those who complete their training are known as the Reverend Mothers. One of them is the Lady Jessica, the mother of Paul, who helps him to escape the annihilation of their world and prepare for his sovereignty. Later his half-sister Alia acts as regent after his death until his son, Leto Atreides II, can take over. Livy would have noticed the resemblance to the Etruscan Tanaquil who put two Etruscans on the Roman throne. But I anticipate.

Bachofen's first encounter with the Rasenna was most probably in Winckelmann's *History of the Art of Antiquity*, which he describes in an

2 Von Hartmann's book was by far the greater success of the two. It went through eight editions by 1879 and was noticed by Nietzsche and Freud. Yet Bachofen's reputation, however etiolated, has surpassed his.

3 For Campbell, see his *Goddesses: Mysteries of the Feminine*, where Bachofen appears briefly in the appendix, 265–6. Bonfante's dismissive judgment appears in "The Women of Etruria," 91. Rosemary Ruether offers a summary of his work and its influence on Jane Harrison, Arthur Evans, Friedrich Engels, and Karl Marx in *Goddesses and the Divine Feminine*, 23–8, 228–34, 241.

autobiographical essay as a book that changed the course of his intellectual life during his time at university. He describes reading Winckelmann's works as "one of the greatest pleasures of my whole life" and as spurring him to examine his own studies "for their relation to the supreme truths ... to the eternal meaning of things."[4] Bachofen's studies in the mythology, religion, and symbolism of ancient Mediterranean societies – especially eastern ones – convinced him that the earliest societies were matriarchal. As much as Herder and von Ranke, with whom he studied at Berlin, he assumed that a fundamental spiritual idea underlay each culture. In the Mediterranean it was a religious knowledge, derived from myths, that had achieved a communicable symbolic form. And it was only by studying symbols that one could grasp this version of *Volksgeist*. In studying the past Bachofen preferred to approach a historical situation – Rome's Etruscan kings – through its mythic or legendary residue because this preserved what he called the collective memory. He believed that research in the field of mythology could proceed with a method that privileged imagination and intuition over reason, and he stressed religion's importance in the development of cultural and social forms. It is worth recalling that Niebuhr's "scientific" methodology also had room for imagination. In an essay on Bachofen, the left-leaning Walter Benjamin describes this as "scientific prophecy" rather than "scientific prediction."[5] For Bachofen the evidence for his theory was everywhere, not least in ancient tombs and mortuary symbolism that revealed the belief in an ontological continuity between life and death, creation and destruction. Again, from the autobiographical essay: "In my wandering through the museums of Italy my attention was soon attracted to one aspect of all their vast treasures, namely mortuary art, a field in which antiquity shows us some of its greatest beauties ...At first we may regard the study of tombs as a specialized field of archaeology, but ultimately we find ourselves in the midst of a truly [religious] doctrine."[6] A nearly mystic strain

---

4 Bachofen, *Myth, Religion, and Mother Right,* 15. The essay was written in September 1854.

5 Benjamin, "Johann Jakob Bachofen," 11. Benjamin praises Bachofen for his multidisciplinary approach and his avoidance of positivism, and places him among the class of "lordly scholars ... with disdain for the conventional demarcations among the sciences." One can do far worse than be remembered as a "lordly scholar" by Benjamin.

6 Bachofen, *Myth, Religion, and Mother Right,* 10–11.

runs through his thinking: "Sometimes it seems to me that something of the divine, eternal meaning of human ideas will be revealed to me at the end of this road ... Abundance of information is not everything, it is not even the essential" (16). In other words, Rankean positivism has its limits and *Wissenschaft* must have room for sympathy and imagination. How else could a scholar fill the countless gaps?

More important than facts and ruins were the ancient myths that left him with the impression that, earlier than the Egyptian, Greek, Etruscan, and Roman pantheons of gods, there had been religions based on the power of one divinity, a primal goddess identified with life and the earth. The goddess gave life in the form of birth and agriculture. She was the key not only to the myths and religious beliefs of her society but even to its social and political structure. At a prelapsarian time when "the human race had not yet, as it has today, departed from its harmony with creation and the transcendent creator," matriarchy offered a ground of love, peace, equality, and unity. There's something of her in Rhea Silvia, the mother of Romulus and Remus. A century before Bachofen, the Reverend Joseph-François Lafitau had found evidence of matrilineal development among the North American First Nations, but he had not made it part of a more general theory of social and historical development.[7] For a variety of reasons, matriarchal or gynocentric societies inevitably gave way to patriarchal ones, a shift Bachofen describes as "the most important turning point in the history of the relations between the sexes,"[8] though he might also have called it the most important turning point in history itself. One set of sexual practices and legal and social structures replaced another, thus turning history in a different direction. In Bachofen's terms, the Occidental (patriarchy) overwhelmed and subsumed the Oriental (matriarchy). Looking at the same critical moment from another perspective, Erich Fromm suggests that Oedipus, allied with Demeter and the Erinyes, stands on the frontier between the matriarchal and patriarchal orders. By killing and replacing his father, Oedipus steps into the new world of patriarchy and is punished for it by the female Erinyes/Furies. There may even be a hint of the earlier matriarchal order in *Oedipus at Colonus* in the blind king's comment that in Egypt "the men / Sit indoors all day long, weaving; /

7 Joseph François Lafitau, *Moeurs des sauvages Amériquains comparés aux moeurs des premiers temps* (Paris, 1724).

8 Bachofen, *Myth, Religion, and Mother Right,* 109.

The women go out and attend to business" (337).[9] The image doesn't quite make it as a clear matriarchal marker, but it does suggest a late, superseded matriarchal form of social organization.

The Saga of Tanaquil argues that mother right never quite disappears. In later patriarchies, like Greece and Rome, one finds vestiges in residual myths and in Olympian goddesses like Hera, Aphrodite, and Demeter whose aura, power, and religious importance are in excess of their subordinate position in the pantheon. Secret chthonic rites are another hint of earlier matriarchal goddesses and powers that have literally gone underground to survive. Even in our predominantly rational and scientific age people continue to be prone to magical and mythical thinking. Bachofen's key example comes from Etruria by way of Livy. Tanaquil is a historical Etrusco-Roman queen who became a kingmaker in the late sixth century when Etruscan kings ruled Rome. Bachofen suggests that the presence of a powerful female of this kind is a residual sign of an earlier Oriental matriarchy, the record of which survives only in the displaced form of later stories of influential women, powers behind the throne. Our fullest account survives in Livy, who, like Bachofen, relies on myth, legend, and some history. As Ogilvie points out in his discussion of Tanaquil, "the name is Etruscan ... and the person real, but her character as a *femme fatale* is largely modelled on Greek prototypes ... in particular Medea."[10] When an eagle snatches off her husband's cap as they reach the Janiculum Hill, Tanaquil interprets it as a good omen: Livy writes, "like most Etruscans, she was well skilled in celestial prodigies" (1.34.9). This may be so, but some readers probably notice the strangeness of a woman filling the place of the expected male priestly interpreter. We get a clear sense of her strength of will in two speeches she gives on the eve of a battle, one to the king and one, in a different style, to the people. Her ambition helps elevate her Etruscan husband, named Lucumo, to the crown (the name, it is worth recalling, is an Etruscan title for a priest-king). He succeeds King Ancus and rules as Lucius Tarquinius Priscus who, we know from other sources, reigned from 616 to 578 BCE. In one version, Tanaquil later arranges for Servius, a talented son of a slave, to be taken into the royal household so that he can succeed her husband as Servius Tullius (578–534 BCE).

---

9 Quoted in Fromm, *The Forgotten Language*, 211.
10 Ogilvie, *A Commentary on Livy*, 143.

The popular Servius Tullius is succeeded by the son of Tarquinius, who gains the crown with the help of Servius's daughter, Tullia. In Bachofen's argument Tullia is a second Tanaquil, a strong woman who determines the succession. Her husband takes the name Tarquinius Superbus (534–509 BCE) and reigns until the Romans overthrow the monarchy.

Bachofen is less interested in the names, dates, and details of the story than in the repeated pattern of a strong or cunning woman – Tanaquil, Cleopatra, or Berenice – guiding royal power. For him this is a clear echo of the Aphrodite-Mylitta-Ishtar eastern archetype in which the goddess or her earthly representative (Dido, Cleopatra, or Zenobia) is more powerful than any male, or, in a diminished version, determines the succession. The myth is associated with what Bachofen calls primordial hetaeric values or sensual modes of being which were celebrated in various festivals in the ancient world and survived in a displaced form in Rome. One might say that Livy's account presents a sanitized version of prehistoric Orientalism acceptable to his Roman readers. After the fall of the monarchy, Tanaquil fulfills her ancient functions, but she does so as a proto–Roman goddess and matron later revered as a defender of maternal rights. As Bachofen puts it, she came "to embody the idea of ennobled love and self-sacrifice" and was "the champion of humanity in a society weighed down by the severity of the positive state order."[11] The inevitable Roman triumph over Etruria entailed the loss of something of value.

And indeed, who will deny that beside the cosmic world-spanning ideas of the … religion which gave rise to the notion of a woman commanding over life and throne, the humanized Tanaquil of the Roman tradition, adapted as she is to everyday life, seems an impoverished figure, scarcely comparable to *the colossal Oriental conception* [my italics]. And yet this regression contains the germ of a very important advance. For every step that liberates our spirit from the paralyzing fetters of a cosmic-physical view of life must be so regarded.[12]

"The cosmic-physical view" is another name for Bachofen, as it is for Lawrence, for "the older sensualistic civilizations" whose annihilation was tragic but necessary "for the [long-term] benefit of mankind" so

---

11 Bachofen, *Myth, Religion, and Mother Right*, 225.
12 Ibid., 236.

that it might "rise to a purer stage of life"[13] in which freedom and abstract ideas are possible. In other words, the story of Tanaquil occurs at the hinge of a world-historical paradigmatic shift in power from the Orient to Rome. Bachofen interprets it as revealing the deeper meaning of the relationship of Aeneas and Dido. Dido and Carthage are Asia, while Aeneas, who is in the process of shedding his eastern Trojan identity, is being guided toward a new vision of western nationhood based in Rome. Just as Aeneas abandons Dido, so Rome must destroy Carthage, whose defeat Bachofen calls the greatest turning point in the destiny of mankind. Rome, in turning its back on Etruria, Carthage, and the East, rejects the sensual and maternal and commits itself to patriarchy, spirit, reason, and civil law. This shift leaves it open to becoming the home of Christianity, the eventual religion of the West. This, however, could only happen with the further destruction of Jerusalem in 70 CE: "Flavian [Titus's] triumph ... meant the liberation of the religion of the future from Mosaic Orientalism and secured Rome's claim to the spiritual heritage of the Orient ... Rome took the place of Jerusalem. Christianity became Occidental, and through this assimilation Rome became so identified with the Occident that for the whole ensuing era all struggles against the Orient were waged by them in common."[14] In Bachofen's neo-Hegelian vision, the Etruscans and Carthaginians needed to be defeated and absorbed so that Rome might bring about the juncture of matriarchy and patriarchy, nature and law, and Orient and Occident, and, in a Hegelian move, lift these to a higher level. Tanaquil and the ancient "mothers" were sublimated and adapted to the new patriarchal world order whose religion would eventually be Christianity. In this historical scenario, Mary is the new Tanaquil.

Bachofen's reflections on matriarchy were noticed in his lifetime by a few like-minded intellectuals, particularly the Geneva sociologist Alexis Giraud-Teulon, who edited his posthumous study of funerary lamps, and Diomede Pantaleoni who acknowledged Bachofen's influence on his *Storia civile e costituzionale di Roma* (1881). More significant is Lewis H. Morgan's reference to *Das Mutterrecht* in *Ancient Society* (1877) during a discussion of descent in the female line in various ancient societies, including the Etruscan. Through Morgan's influence on Friedrich

13 Ibid., 231. For Lawrence on the Magna Mater or the "Great mothers of the cosmos" see *Apocalypse*, 77.

14 Lawrence, *Apocalypse*, 235.

Engels, Bachofen's ideas reached late-nineteenth-century Marxism in *The Origin of the Family, Private Property, and the State* (1884), a once very influential book. (It is worth noting that Claude Lévi-Strauss's *The Savage Mind* is dedicated to Morgan.) As I said earlier, Etruscan scholars rarely mention Bachofen, and when they do it is usually to correct him. In his *Daily Life of the Etruscans,* Jacques Heurgon makes the necessary distinctions about Etruscan matriarchy in his finely argued chapter "The Etruscan Family and the Role of Women." He thinks Bachofen overstates the case "in his ingenious – and inadmissible – *Sage von Tanaquil,* in which he defined Etruscan society as an example of *Mutterrecht* or matriarchy, surviving into historical times."[15] He suggests that although Etruscan society shows elements of both matriarchy and female influence, "if there was a form of *Mutterrecht* ... it existed in a very adulterated form."[16] His elegant conclusion finds a fine balance that might have satisfied even Theopompus and Romans kept awake at night by the thought of Etruscan dinners at which husbands sat with their wives. Heurgon stops far short of calling the Etruria of the seventh and sixth centuries feminist or matriarchal, but he is willing to grant that "in Etruscan society, the *pater familias* laid down the law, but the *mater familias* had her say also, and her word was often the last one."[17] If this wasn't true, it should have been.

As for Bachofen, he would be surprised to find that his place in intellectual history is among that small group who might be called the accidental fathers of the women's movement.

---

15 Heurgon, *Daily Life of the Etruscans,* 84–5. Heurgon (1903–1995) taught Latin Language and Literature at the University of Algiers from 1931 and Albert Camus was one of his students. Camus dedicated the essay "Summer in Algiers" to him. Heurgon finished his career at the Sorbonne.

16 Ibid., 85.

17 Ibid., 86.

9

Etruscan Vases:
Prosper Mérimée, Stendhal,
and Gustave Flaubert

ETRUSCAN All antique vases are Etruscan.

Gustave Flaubert[1]

I

Prosper Mérimée's "The Etruscan Vase" (1830)

[A] table of richly enameled and massive silver, upon which were a few
goblets fantastically stained, together with two large Etruscan vases, fashioned
in the same extraordinary model as that in the foreground of the portrait,
and filled with what I supposed to be Johannisberger.

Edgar Allan Poe[2]

A sign of the growing European awareness of the Etruscans in the nineteenth century is their presence, even if often ephemeral, in the works
of the best-known French novelists of the period between 1820 and
1920 – Prosper Mérimée, Honoré de Balzac, Stendhal, Victor Hugo,
Gustave Flaubert, Eugène Sue, Théophile Gautier, Anatole France,
and Marcel Proust. The present chapter will discuss Mérimée,
Stendhal, and Flaubert; a later one will deal with France and Proust.
A differently focused chapter might have included English novelists

---

1 Flaubert, *Bouvard and Pécuchet*, 304.
2 Poe, "The Assignation (The Visionary)," in *Complete Stories and Poems*, 147.

like Edward Bulwer-Lytton, Anthony Trollope, George Eliot, and Thomas Hardy.

For anyone interested in the Etruscans, Prosper Mérimée (1803–1870) seems at first glance to have possibilities, like an Italian field in which Etruscan tombs have previously been found. He lived during the period of Lucien Bonaparte's excavations; he was inspector-general of historic monuments for France from 1834 to 1860; he had a serious lifelong interest in the history of Ancient Rome and wrote an *Essay on the Social War* and *The Conspiracy of Catiline*; he wore a ring with a Greek inscription, "Remember to mistrust"; and the titles of two of his more famous stories, "The Etruscan Vase" (1830) and "The Venus of Ille" (1837), look back to the Mediterranean past. "Carmen" (1845), by far his most famous work, and perhaps the only one to escape Henry James's censure that the fiction is "not sympathetic,"[3] even begins with two lines in Greek by Palladas, a fifth century poet, and its narrator is in Spain to determine the disputed site of the battle in which Julius Caesar defeated the brothers Gnaeus and Sextus Pompeius on 17 March 45 BCE to end the Civil Wars. As his biography suggests, Mérimée found the past more interesting and pleasing than the present.

James's reviews still make the best case for the strengths and limitations of Mérimée's fiction, though it doesn't take long to notice that James, as he so often does, praises what he himself does best. Reviewing Mérimée's last stories, James writes condescendingly that "they remind us agreeably of the author's limited but singularly perfect talent" and suggests that a selection of the tales might be "presented to young narrators as a manual of their trade – a guide for the avoidance of prolixity" (562). James grants that Mérimée has talent but he insists that "decidedly [he] was not a man of rich genius" (573). Missing was the human dimension, call it sympathy, that Balzac, for all his sins against style and form, showed in every character. By contrast, Mérimée couldn't free himself of an ironic view of life that led to creative dryness and sterility. The stories entertain but the characters fail to come to life.

"The Etruscan Vase" is representative.[4] It gains some historical depth from an ancient artifact and some thematic and emotional resonance

3 Henry James, *Literary Criticism*, 566. All quotations from James will be from this edition and references will be in the text.
4 Worth noting here is Franz Liszt's "Orpheus," a symphonic poem of 1853, whose preface describes an Etruscan vase depicting Orpheus.

from references to Don Juan, Doña Juaña, and *Romeo and Juliet*. A more apposite Shakespeare play in this story of irrational jealousy would have been *Othello* or *Cymbeline* in both of which a wife is unjustly suspected of infidelity. The vase itself is described shortly before the story's end as "a rare piece [that] had never been catalogued. On it was depicted, in three colours, a combat between a Lapith and a Centaur."5 The story's hero, Auguste Saint-Clair, becomes obsessed with the vase when he learns that it was given to his mistress, the widowed Mathilde de Coursy, by Massigny, her rumoured former lover. In the story's fast-paced final pages he challenges the man who said Mathilde had been Massigny's mistress to a duel, learns from Mathilde that she had rejected Massigny's affection, and dies in the duel. Like Madame Marie de Tourvel in *Les Liaisons dangereuses*, Mathilde abandons society for her house in the country, sees no one for three years, and dies of "a chest infection brought on by domestic cares, according to Doctor M, who attended her" (115). I assume that "domestic cares" is an ironic euphemism for a broken heart.

In her scene of reconciliation with Saint-Clair she "seized the Etruscan vase and hurled it to the floor, shattering it into a thousand fragments" (114). But its image of a "combat between a Lapith and a Centaur" (114) survives to foreshadow the duel in which the jealous Saint-Clair plays the Lapith and Alphonse de Thémines the Centaur. In the myth the Lapiths had invited the neighbouring Centaurs to the wedding feast of their king, Pirithous, and his bride, Hippodamia. The Centaurs tried to carry off the women before being routed in a fight. Though the story of the Centaurs disrupting the Lapith wedding is well known, there is a very strong possibility that the vase Mérimée describes as Etruscan was Greek. Is it possible to establish a topos of this kind of misidentified object – a vase in Matisse's "Interior with Etruscan Vase," a character in William Gibson's *Idoru*, or even Braque's sometimes misidentified Louvre Etruscan ceiling? Misattributions also play their part, as do forgeries, in the Etruscan return.

The Etruscans do not figure in Mérimée's story except for the symbolic vase, which, together with another character's longish account of a trip to Egypt that divides the narrative in two, provides a continuing note of exoticism and good taste that distinguishes Mathilde de

5 Mérimée, *Carmen and Other Stories*, 114. All references will be to this edition.

Coursy. Because the story's characters treat sex and love lightly, as a diversion to pass the time, they lack psychological depth or human interest and have the insubstantiality of figures in Rococo paintings. Their suffering and death seem to belong to the demands of the narrative and not to life. I find it difficult not to think, again, of *Les Liaisons dangereuses* and the similar fate of Madame de Tourvel, whose death of a fever disturbs the reader, and Cécile's resigned return to the convent. These events have a moral weight and human significance that are lacking in Mérimée's story.[6] Laclos's characters remind us of a modern novelist's suggestion that "more die of heartbreak than anything else." No character in "The Etruscan Vase" seems quite as convincingly shattered as the Etruscan vase that, perhaps, really isn't Etruscan. At the time few could tell the difference.

II

Stendhal's Italian Etruscans

[Les Romains] ont détruit les aimables républiques de l'Étrurie.

Stendhal[7]

The only reference to the Etruscans in Stendhal's fiction occurs in the unfinished *Lucien Leuwen*, written between 1834 and 1836 and published posthumously in 1894: "There was a collection of Roman antiquities found at Lillebonne. Our men were wasting their time arguing with the keeper about the age of an Etruscan chimaera so green with age that its shape had all but vanished. After consulting his library, the keeper had just dated it as two thousand seven hundred

---

6 Mérimée makes slightly more use of the Etruscan motif than Thomas Mann does in his early story "Gerfallen" ("Fallen"), where the Etruscan vases are just part of a heterogeneous assortment of non-German decorative pieces signalling that the scene is set in a Bohemian atelier. Here the naive young hero meets his friends in a room "crammed full of a jarring mixture of Etruscan and Japanese vases, Spanish fans and daggers, Chinese parasols, Italian mandolins, and thick oriental rugs" (Brennan, *Thomas Mann's World*, 48). Except for a reference to an Etruscan exhibition in Switzerland in a letter to Herman Hesse (10 June 1955), Mann never mentions the Etruscans again.

7 Stendhal, *Voyages en Italie*, 508.

years old, when our travelers were greeted by a most polite personage."[8]
The polite personage is the general's valet summoning the soldiers.
With his appearance the Etruscans vanish from the novel having
provided an insignificant distraction. They are far more prominent,
however, in Stendhal's travel writings and letters, usually as part of his
very positive response to Italy, a country with all the qualities and values
he found lacking in France and England. It is well known that the
encounter with Italy was the most memorable of his life. His first
three publications were on Italian subjects: *History of Painting in Italy*
(1817), *Rome, Naples and Florence* (1817), and *The Life of Rossini* (1824).
The first offers a theory of painting, the second a theory of life, and
the third a theory of music. His *Life of Napoleon*, written in 1817–18
though not published until 1929, offers a theory of politics based on
the life of a man in whose army Stendhal served for over a decade and
to whose memory he remained faithful until his own death. Unlike
most of the European artists and intellectuals enthusiastic about
Napoleon, Stendhal (1783–1842) had served under him – most notably
on the disastrous Russian campaign – and had met him.[9] Though he
continued after Waterloo to prefer Napoleon to his successors, there
is no doubt that his attitude became ambivalent over the years. He was
often severely critical of the emperor (and Rome), but to turn his back
on Napoleon would have been to renounce his own youth and
republican idealism. Stendhal's ambivalent view of the Etruscans
(usually positive) and the ancient Romans (less so) reflects his mature
ambivalence not only toward France but also to the dominant figure
of his era.

Stendhal first travelled to Italy between 1800 and 1815 – the
Napoleonic years when there were few tourists on the Grand Tour. By
1821, however, France had 20,000 English visitors annually. Stendhal's
first visit came in May 1800 when he accompanied Napoleon's army
south. He was seventeen and still a civilian though about to wear a
uniform. At Ivrea, with time on his hands, he went to a third-rate opera
house with a mediocre orchestra to hear Domenico Cimarosa's *Il
Matrimonio Segreto*. Afterwards he wrote to his sister that he had experienced a divine happiness. The music, the women, the emotional

---

8 Stendhal, *Lucien Leuwen*, 484.
9 Among the emperor's fans were Hegel, Byron, Shelley, Goethe, Heine, Hazlitt,
Emerson, Manzoni, and Nietzsche.

spontaneity, the manners, the climate, the nearness of the ancient past – Italy was an entire way of life that he had been denied in his unhappy, restricted childhood in gloomy Grenoble. He found even Paris lacking by comparison: the French had manners, the Italians life. In *Italian Chronicles,* the Renaissance stories he wrote in the 1830s, he emphasizes the form this way of life takes as the "Italian passion ... that unbridled passion which one finds in the Italy of the sixteenth and seventeenth centuries. In our day, that fine passion is dead, entirely dead, at least among those classes who have let themselves become tainted by French customs and the way things are done in Paris or London."[10] Quoting Byron, he reviles his era as an "age of cant."[11] Stendhal had met Byron in 1816 in Milan and admired him. Each thought hypocrisy (with its Christian counterpart religiosity) was one of the defining sins of post-Napoleonic society.[12] Stendhal sees it in Ann Radcliffe giving "Italian names and grand passions to the characters of her celebrated novel *The Italian; or, The Confessional of the Black Penitents,*" because she feels "forbidden to write about 'hatred' and 'love' in that island of hers."[13] Another way of putting this might be that "Gothic" fiction allowed English readers to let themselves go, at least while reading.

Some degree of the idealization of Italy is found in most visitors from the eighteenth century on; Goethe, the Brownings, and Lawrence are among the most famous. For Stendhal, as for Lawrence, it also colours his view of the Etruscans, for whom he shows a slightly guilty preference over the more "Napoleonic" Romans. Travelling between Buon-Convento and Torinieri late into the night of 3 February 1817 he sees the following landscape and has a revealing, wavering response.

10 Stendhal, "The Duchess of Palliano," *Italian Chronicles,* 100.

11 Stendhal, "The Cenci," *Italian Chronicles,* 63.

12 A decade earlier, however, Stendhal wrote in a footnote that "Lord Byron, le Rousseau des Anglais, était tour à tour *dandy,* fou et grand poète." ("Lord Byron, the English Rousseau, was by turns a dandy, mad, and a great poet.") *Voyages en Italie,* 495.

13 Stendhal, "The Duchess of Palliano," *Italian Chronicles,* 102–3. A page earlier he wrote: "Thus, that Italian passion is no longer to be found, nor has it been for over a century now, in the better society of this country." Emerson, passing through Palermo, a few years later, asked in his *Journal,* "Has the South European more animal spirits than we, that he is so joyous a companion?" (*Emerson in His Journals,* 101).

In the distance, by the light of a lustrous moon, [the young Italian priest] pointed out to me the ruins of several of those cities of ancient Etruria ... and I felt my heart within me swell (let the reader weigh well the full absurdity of this confession) in a fury of indignation against the Romans, who rose up, with no sounder justification than the ferocity of their own courage, to overturn the very foundations of those antique Etruscan commonwealths, so infinitely superior to themselves in art, in prosperity and in the secret skills of happiness. And yet, despite so many grievances, my heart still sides with Rome. These old republics of Etruria, these Gaulish customs which were bastions of freedom – *I* see them not. On the other hand, in every page of history, I behold the deeds and see the life of Rome; and what the eye cannot see, the heart cannot love.[14]

This is wonderfully honest. Stendhal's head tells him that he should love the freedom-loving Etruscan commonwealths, but his heart belongs to Rome, *whose symbolic identity is Napoleon,* who, to complicate the issue, posed as a champion of revolution and freedom but eventually came out as a tyrannical emperor. Stendhal's unfinished biography of Napoleon compares him to Julius Caesar, Alexander the Great, and Frederick the Great, sullied or tainted ("entaché") by the vices indispensable to a conqueror but nevertheless assured of everlasting glory. The three million or so dead soldiers of the Napoleonic wars go with the job description, like the countless Gauls slaughtered by Romans in their civilizing mission. Stendhal finds even Napoleon's behaviour in exile exemplary, insisting against all the evidence that "Perhaps nothing in modern times recalls Plutarch's heroes more than this."[15] There are more references to Napoleon in Stendhal's collected works, including his letters, than to any other historical figure. Robert Alter's summary catches what he calls the novelist's "bioptic vision" where Napoleon is concerned: "having observed the great man firsthand, together with the ambiguous consequences of the Emperor's actions, he eventually would engage the Napoleonic phenomenon in his fiction with a peculiar and forceful conjunction of acute judgment and impassioned

14 Both quotations are from Stendhal, *Rome, Naples and Florence*, 335–6 and 345–6.
15 "C'est peut-être la chose dans les temps modernes qui rappelle le plus les héros de Plutarque." ("Perhaps in modern times it is what most brings to mind Plutarch's heroes.") Stendhal, *Napoléon*, 190.

sympathy."[16] At some deep level, Stendhal knew that to abandon Napoleon would be simultaneously to reject his own youth and career as a soldier. Instead, he abandons the Etruscans.

Stendhal's ambivalence toward the emperor was shared by Goethe, the greatest European figure of the time, who, for the sake of peace, accepted the Napoleonic status quo as the norm and saw him as a guarantor of European order. Unlike Stendhal, Goethe had no personal investment in Napoleon, yet, in a Hegel-like gesture, called him "the highest phenomenon possible in history." Napoleon reciprocated by famously greeting him, after a performance of *Britannicus* on 30 September 1808, with "Voilà un homme!" and later awarding him the Légion d'honneur. Seven years earlier Hegel wrote one of his most passionate letters after watching "the Emperor – this world-soul – riding out of the city on reconnaissance. It is indeed a wonderful sensation to see such an individual, who, concentrated here at a single point, astride a horse, reaches out over the world and masters it ... this extraordinary man, whom it is impossible not to admire."[17] Later, in *The Philosophy of History*, he describes history as "a slaughter bench," but his view of one of the great masters of slaughter remained unchanged. He justifies his view of the bloodied "world-historical individual" by granting that "so mighty a form must trample down many an innocent flower, crush to pieces many an object in its path."[18] Among those flowers had been his brother Georg Ludwig who died on the Russian campaign in 1812.

Stendhal spent two decades at Civitavecchia, a provincial backwater in the Papal States, as a customs official. Apart from expeditions to Etruscan and Roman ruins and conversations with a handful of liberals, he found little to amuse him. Tarquinia, then called Corneto, is just to the north, and the Etruscan tombs at Cerveteri are only thirty-three kilometres distant. He visits both tomb sites. He also travels to Canino. Here Stendhal's remarks disappoint. He sees frescoes and guesses wildly that a few date from the period of the Trojan War while the majority are probably from the time of Tarquin. He notes that, beginning with Romulus, the Romans borrowed freely "from their neighbours, the Etruscans, a very civilized people among whom real

16 Alter, *A Lion for Love*, 124.
17 Pinkard, *Hegel*, 228.
18 Hegel, *The Philosophy of History*, 21, 32.

power had been taken over by the priests." At the same time, he notes that after the conquest the Romans allowed the Etruscans to retain their religion and customs. Discussing the Etruscan priests, however, he can't decide whether they are a force for good because they represent the amelioration of "la force brutale" by spirit or whether they are an early incarnation of "les jésuites," always a red flag in his writing, memorably so in *The Red and the Black* (1830).[19]

Although Stendhal took his *nom de plume* from Winckelmann's home-town of Stendal, his few explicit references to the art historian are not flattering. I think, for instance, there is a glance at Winckelmann in his comments on gallery-going in Milan, where he distinguishes between himself as a traveller and the tourists ("les nigauds" or "bird-wits") among whom he finds himself. "The secret of invulnerability – as other travellers have all too readily discovered – is to stick to plain figures. How many pictures in *this gallery*? How many columns in *that* portico? And if, in addition, the traveller should cultivate a handy talent for chopping up this kind of statistical inventory into palatable hunks by means of adolescent text-book platitudes couched in reverberating academic periods, concerning the origins and subsequent history of divers notable buildings, not forgetting the *evolutionary transition* from Egypt to Etruria and from Etruria to Rome ... then no more is needed, and the bird-wits will pronounce it *admirable*" (30 October 1816).[20] Two passages are explicitly critical of Winckelmann's methodology. The first dismisses him: "Poor W, who could be very scholarly, doesn't reason at all. One is continually astonished by how he arrives at his conclusions" (20 January 1812)."[21] The second extends this into an attack on his methodology: "Winckelmann also seems to me to have this defect: he doesn't regard nature first and the Greeks afterward, but the Greeks and then nature, which he finds admirable only in the points that are imitated, adopted, by the Greek statue makers."[22] And in a letter he refers to him as both "un savant" (not intended as praise)

19 Stendhal, *Rome, Naples and Florence*, 920.
20 Ibid., 47–8.
21 "Ce pauvre W[inckelmann], qui pouvait être très savant ne raisonne pas du tout. On est sans cesse étonné de sa manière de tirer des consequences," (20 January 1812). Stendhal, *Oeuvres intimes* 1:818.
22 Stendhal, *The Private Diaries of Stendhal*, 446.

and "un cuistre" (a priggish pedant).[23] In an ideal world, Stendhal would have simply pointed out that Winckelmann represented classicism while he stood for Romanticism (which he did and didn't), and he would have gone on to discuss the Etruscan chapter in *History of the Art of Antiquity*. But to our loss he is silent about it.

III

Gustave Flaubert Casts a Glance at Etruria

On the tessellated doorstep the word *Ave*, in Latin and Etruscan lettering, greeted the guest with its hospitable salutation.

Théophile Gautier[24]

Though his knowledge of the classical world was impressive, Flaubert (1821–1880) never shared the general enthusiasm for things Etruscan, some of which he had seen in 1851 in Naples on his way back to France after two years in the Middle East. On 28 September of that year, he wrote Louise Colet from London, "We have just been to Highgate Cemetery. All that Egyptian and Etruscan architecture. So spick-and-span and orderly."[25] The dismissive tone tells us that English mortuary taste has been judged and placed: Etruscan antiquities were so common that, for Flaubert at least, they were a boring subject, a fad whose time had passed. One also senses this in *The Sentimental Education* (1869), *Bouvard and Pécuchet* (1881), and *The Dictionary of Received Ideas* (1881). The last two are a final settling of accounts with the French bourgeoisie and much else. In *The Sentimental Education* we meet the Etruscans in the pottery factory of the husband of Mme Arnoux, Frédéric Moreau's great love. As the two walk around the factory they see "specimens hanging on the walls or arranged on shelves [that] bore testimony to Arnoux's efforts and his successive infatuations. After searching for the copper-red of the Chinese he had tried to produce ... Etruscan and Oriental pottery, and had finally attempted some of the improvements of the later eras ... but his intelligence was neither great enough to attain to art nor mediocre enough to think

23 Stendhal, *Correspondance de Stendhal*, 2:386.
24 Gautier, *My Fantoms*, 120.
25 "Flaubert to Louise Colet," 136.

of nothing but profits, so that he was ruining himself without pleasing anybody."[26] M. Arnoux is without talent and he tries to make ends meet by cashing in on contemporary fads and fashions. Like Bouvard and Pécuchet, he is a man limited by "received ideas."

In their novel, the two friends stumble from one failed project to another in a test of Flaubert's research and inventiveness and the reader's patience. Trying out different ideas for their garden, "they had sacrificed the asparagus to build in its place an Etruscan tomb, a six-foot-high black plaster quadrilateral resembling a dog kennel. Four dwarf firs flanked this monument at its corners, and it was to be surmounted by an urn and embellished with an inscription ... At the top of the vine-clad mount, six squared trees supported a tin hat with turned up points, and the whole thing represented a Chinese pagoda."[27] The "dog kennel" and "a tin hat" ensure that even the least attentive reader gets the satiric point, the contemptuous dismissal. If Bouvard and Pécuchet are the French bourgeoisie, then that class's taste is very dated. The point is restated in *The Dictionary of Received Ideas* with the sentence that is this chapter's epigraph: "ETRUSCAN All antique vases are Etruscan." In other words, this is what everybody says and knows – and therefore it must wrong. Going back to the Etruscan tomb in the garden, is it possible that behind this silly construction is a memory of the description of Lars Porsena's equally misconceived gargantuan tomb? Before we dismiss the possibility, let's keep in mind Flaubert's lifelong interest in the classical world and his voluminous research for *Salammbô* (1862), his novel about the end of the First Punic War. He had told friends that his next novel would be about Thermopylae.

Salammbô presents the Etruscans positively as part of the unpaid polyglot mercenary army rebelling against the Carthaginians at war's end. Polybius describes the conflict between the mercenaries and the Carthaginians as "distinguished by far greater savagery and disregard for convention than any other war in human history."[28] The mercenaries' last stand is heroic and has something of the grandeur of Thermopylae. As Flaubert reminded his critics, the book was meticulously researched. It is often as shimmeringly and exotically beautiful as a painting by Odilon Redon or Gaston Bussière. And there's no

26 Flaubert, *The Sentimental Education*, 191.
27 Flaubert, *Bouvard and Pécuchet*, 57.
28 Polybius, *The Histories*, 76.

denying that the military scenes are as vivid as any of the century's enormous historical paintings, with the added benefit that they are dramatic and have the authority of Polybius. But the private scenes lack drama and human interest, and the heroine remains more a sensuous portrait or tableau than a living character. Her aura as a priestess is all surface effects. In Charles Augustin Sainte-Beuve's backhanded compliment, "[M. Flaubert] enjoys the esteem of learned archeologists and semitic scholars ... and of eminent minds."[29] For once, the critic who misjudged *Madame Bovary* and the work of Stendhal, Balzac, and Baudelaire was right.

29 Brown, *Flaubert*, 367.

10

Etruscans in America:
Ralph Waldo Emerson's Dream (1862),
Nathaniel Hawthorne's The Marble Faun
(1860), and Emily Dickinson's Etruscan Triptych

I

Emerson's Etruscan Dream of 9 January 1862

The text of our life is accompanied all along by this commentary
or gloss of dreams ...

Their double consciousness, their sub- & ob-jectiveness is the wonder.

Emerson[1]

It is widely known that nineteenth-century Americans were interested
in Egyptian, Greek, and Roman antiquity. John T. Irwin's *American Hieroglyphics: The Symbol of the Egyptian Hieroglyphics in the American Renaissance*
tells part of that story. This chapter focuses on three major writers of
the period who mention the Etruscans. Along for the ride are Edgar
Allan Poe, who mentions them in passing, and Walt Whitman. Sometime
in 1846 or 1847 Whitman read and annotated a long article in the
Western Review looking at the 1844 edition of Niebuhr's *The History*

---

1 Emerson, *Emerson in His Journals*, 9 January 1862 (322) and 20 April 1838
(185). Unless otherwise indicated, all references to the journals will be to this text.

of Rome, which, as I mentioned earlier, begins with a lengthy section about the Etruscans and the early history of the Italian peninsula. And, as is indicated by the epigraph to the section on Emily Dickinson, Whitman is buried in what struck William Sloan Kennedy as "an Etruscan-like tomb." I take these references as markers of the dissemination of knowledge about the Etruscans not only among the writers discussed but among their readers and the literate population at large.

Emerson mentions the Etruscans only three times, but one of these references emerges in one of his most self-revealing dreams, where it gleams like an Etruscan carnelian gem. But to get to it I must test the reader's patience and digress about Emerson's interest in the classics and his theory of dreams. This is also the approach I will take later with Freud, who admired Emerson, and who also had a lifelong interest in antiquity, the Etruscans, and dream interpretation. But I anticipate.

On the evidence of his several journals, Ralph Waldo Emerson (1803–1882) dreamed often and was fascinated by dreams, by their endless stratigraphy of beauty and meaning, their sheer unpredictability and contradictoriness, and their dramatic, often chaotic nature. An inveterate and skilful interpreter, he thought of dreams as mysterious self-generated texts that might be read as commentaries on what he calls "the text of our life." He anticipated Freud in understanding that however poetic, symbolic, and chaotic dreams might seem, they "are more logical sometimes than waking thought."[2] Like an Etruscan's or Blake's, Emerson's universe was filled with signs, correspondences, and symbols, all as much in need of translation as Egyptian hieroglyphics, which had fascinated him since childhood. Trained in biblical exegesis, he extended his hermeneutic energies to the volatile book of the inner world. It is appropriate that one of his dream fragments shows him troubled even in his sleep with codes and symbols: "Struggled hard last night in a dream to repeat & save a thought or sentence spoken in the dream; but it eluded me at last: only came out of the pulling, with this rag, 'his the deeper problem, but mine the better ciphered'" (1 September 1867, 545). The striking epigrammatic concision of what he calls "this rag" also shows the pleasure Emerson takes in the often aleatory process of interpreting.

2 Emerson, *Journals of Ralph Waldo Emerson*, Vol. 16, 12 October 1866, 48. See also Fromm's comment, "A dream which is not understood is like a letter which is not opened." *The Forgotten Language,* 2.

Emerson anticipates Freud's view that "dreams are completely egoistical."[3] He understood that the characters in a dream are avatars of the self, especially if there are only two, engaged in disagreement (543). He thinks of these antithetical dreams as often offering "completion" (282) or a "balancing of the self" as in the dream of an acquaintance who though an "honest man" dreamed he was a "drudge, a miser, and a footman, by night." Emerson sums this dream up as revealing the "civil war in our atoms, mutiny of the sub-daemons not yet subdued" (396). He has no illusions about the complex nature of the "sub-daemons" and in a later entry suggests that "if in dreams you see loose & luxurious pictures, an inevitable tie drags in the sequel of cruelty & malignity" (1857, 479). Even writing for himself, Emerson can't be more explicit, but "loose" and "luxurious" both carry the pressure of an irresistible sexual intimation that energizes the sadism latent in the last two nouns.

He justifies nightmares – always a problem for dream theory – as valuable because compensatory for individuals whose lives are so "safe & regular that we hardly know the emotion of terror ... And yet dreams acquaint us with what the day omits ... you may, in the course of an hour or two, have this neglected part of your education in some measure supplied." That Emerson's view of "the visions of the Night" tends toward the cathartic is indicated by the close of the passage where, having described his own nightmare, he ends, "After I woke and recalled the impressions, my brain tingled with repeated vibrations of terror – and yet was the sensation pleasing, as it was a sort of rehearsal of a Tragedy" (282). Note the view of the dream as a "rehearsal" – like a tragic play – for the terrors of life not yet experienced, especially death. Emerson's dreams dispel once and for all the image of the great transcendentalist as a naive, trusting innocent walking around Concord in a blissed-out state of contentment. That image may fit Bronson Alcott and sometimes even Whitman, but not the tough-minded Emerson, who would recognize his voice in William James, especially when James insists that "evil facts ... are a genuine portion of reality, and they may after all be the best key to life's significance, and possibly the only

3 Freud, *The Interpretation of Dreams*, 358.

openers of our eyes to the deepest levels of truth."[4] Two generations later Emerson might have been an outstanding psychoanalyst.

Emerson's only Etruscan dream occurred on 9 September 1861 when he was fifty-eight years old. Though the Etruscans are mentioned only twice more in his writing – a reference to "Etruscan barbarism" and an "Etruscan vase" – references to other ancient civilizations are scattered throughout his work. Egypt appears most frequently but Assyria, Babylon, Greece, and the Phoenicians are also mentioned, as are figures like Jean-François Champollion and the famous adventurer and archaeologist Giovanni Belzoni (1778–1823) who published a popular account of his Egyptian travels in 1820. The intellectual journals Emerson followed, like the *London Quarterly*, *The Edinburgh Review*, and *The North American Review*, regularly published articles about antiquity. For instance, the last published in 1831 an essay on "Hieroglyphics" and in 1839 a sixty-page review of Micali's Italian study of the Etruscans.[5] Champollion, to take just one name, appears in Emerson's "History," Poe's *Eureka*, Thoreau's *Walden*, and Herman Melville's *Mardi* and *Moby-Dick*. Napoleon's disastrous invasion of Egypt in 1798 had initiated a period of intense interest not only in Egyptology but in all things ancient in the Mediterranean area. As early as 1823 a merchant named van Lennep presented Boston with an Egyptian sarcophagus, and in 1832 Colonel Mendes Cohen established the first private collection of Egyptian artifacts in America. In 1842 the former vice-consul in Cairo gave a series of lectures on antiquities in Boston before touring the country for two years. He often attracted audiences of two thousand. The Etruscans were one of the novelties of the century, often in the press because of books about them and the excavations at Canino and elsewhere. The period was fascinated by archaeology, and awareness of the Etruscans was disseminated by this perennial interest. Since Emerson often refers to archaeology, it is evident he took it for granted that both his audience and his "ideal" reader would understand references to ancient characters, events, and places. They were as constitutive a part of the period's cultural hum and buzz as are references to local and

    4 William James, "The Sick Soul" from *The Varieties of Religious Experience* in *Writings 1902–1910*, 152.

    5 Emerson read the quarterlies critically: "When I read the *North American Review*, or the *London Quarterly*, I seem to hear the snore of the muses." *Selected Journals 1820–1842*, 609.

contemporary figures and events completely forgotten today. Emerson's classical references reflect this. A good example is his casual use of an Etruscan vase in an almost homiletic diary entry addressed to his imagined neighbours: "You admire your Etruscan vase, and with reason, but I also have a cup and cover that pleases me better, to wit, the Earth and the Sky."[6] The irony in the first clause recalls Flaubert's. Both express a doubt about the taste for Etruscan vases.

For Emerson, the ancient civilizations – Egypt is the outstanding example because of hieroglyphs – are potentially closer to a primal unity between body and spirit, man and god, and word and world. It was a transcendental truism that Nature speaks in natural signs. Dreams, therefore, fascinate Emerson because they seem an obvious portal to the spirit and are as enigmatic and elusive as ancient languages. When I consider Emerson's overall lack of interest in the Etruscans as opposed to the Egyptians, the following dream, rich in narrative, emotion, and detail, is a surprising document. Why is the dream's focal image an Etruscan vase and not a Greek one or an Egyptian statuette? Emerson didn't know, and neither can we since, as Freud taught us, we can go only so far in interpretating a dream without the dreamer and his or her memories of the residue of the previous days.

Sept. 9, 1861 Last night a pictorial dream fit for Dante.[7] I read a discourse somewhere to an assembly, & rallied in the course of it to find that I had nearly or quite fallen sleep. Then presently I went into what seemed a new house the inside wall of which had many shelves let into the wall on which great & costly Vases of Etruscan & other richly adorned pottery stood. The wall itself was unfinished, & I presently noticed great clefts, intended to be filled with mortar or brickwork, but not yet filled, & the wall which held all these costly vases, threatening to fall. Then I noticed in the centre shelf or

---

6 Emerson, *The Journals and Miscellaneous Notebooks*, 29. From the same period, see also Alexander Dumas's casual reference in *The Black Tulip* to "Tarquin the elder, who grew poppies at Gabii" (*The Black Tulip*, 91).

7 Emerson's comments a few years later about Dante are worth noting. "But Dante still appears to me, as ever, an exceptional mind, a prodigy of imaginative function, executive rather than contemplative or wise ... not like Shakespeare, or Socrates, or Goethe, a beneficent humanity, would not desire such for friends & contemporaries. Abnormal throughout like Swedenborg. But at a frightful cost these obtain their fame. A man to put in a museum, but not in your house. Indeed I never read him, nor regret that I do not." (*Emerson in His Journals*, July–August 1867, 545.)

alcove of the wall a man asleep, whom I understood to be the architect of the house. I called to my brother William who was near me, & pointed to this sleeper as the architect, when the man turned, & partly arose, & muttered something about a plot to expose him.

When I fairly woke, & considered the picture, & the connection of the two dreams – what could I think of the purpose of Jove who sends the dreams?[8]

Stumped by the dream and hoping for some biographical residue to help with interpretation, I sent it to Neal Dolan, colleague at the University of Toronto and author of *Emerson's Liberalism*. His response:

I read the dream, perhaps not surprisingly, as a compressed retelling of the foundational crisis of Emerson's vocation – the break from the Unitarian ministry in favor of a career of secular-symbolic cultural exhortation of essentially Enlightenment values. With an apparently incidental framing reference to Dante – a great religious-symbolic exhorter – he relates the dream as a story of himself falling asleep in the midst of his own public discourse – the slipping away of his own commitment to Christian symbology – only to find himself awakened amidst a vast "new house" with "many shelves," some of which are occupied by Etruscan and other richly adorned pottery, but some of which are empty. This new house is the framework of the secular symbolic orientation that must take the place of the old Biblical structure, but which has not yet been fully furnished. It is Emerson's task, still somewhat uncertainly performed, to try to fill the empty shelves perhaps with his own books, his new revelations. The significance of the Etruscan pottery, I would suggest, is its status as secular-historical-symbolic material. It is at once pre-Christian and extra-classical, not exactly Latin-Roman and thus not as yet fully claimed and assimilated into a new modern symbolic system that must reach both forward and backward in time beyond both Christianity and Classical culture as hitherto understood. In the dream Emerson thinks the somewhat ghostly architect is his brother William – the brother, not incidentally, who in letters from Germany first introduced young Waldo to the secular "higher" criticism of the bible which began the unraveling of his belief. But, of course, William is also here an image of himself in his second vocation – and secular scholars like ourselves – which entails establishing a new account, or accounts, of our origins, which includes understanding the Etruscans. Fascinating journal entry.

8 Emerson, *The Journals of Ralph Waldo Emerson*, ed. Robert N. Linscott, 417.

More generally, I would add that the Etruscan reference indicates the degree to which the Rasenna had become a relatively common presence in the minds of New England intellectuals. Here, they are an alternative to everything offered by Emerson's family, society, and education – a relatively novel figure and symbol behind which Emerson hides even as he reveals himself in the dream. Egyptians, Greeks, and Romans were too compromised by long usage to be useful to a man turning his back on Christianity to offer a new vision.

II

Nathaniel Hawthorne's The Marble Faun *(1860) and the Last of the Etruscans*

That granite soil which produced the essential flavour of Hawthorne is just as inevitably the environment which stunted him.

T.S. Eliot[9]

Between 1835 and 1900 the number of American tourists visiting Europe increased from 300 annually to 30,000. When the Hawthorne family arrived in Rome in 1858 to visit the usual sites and the recently popular Etruscan ones, including Canino, there were enough American artists and tourists (Hawthorne's word) to make the writer complain about the crowds of Americans. Forty years later Henry James, grumpy and classist, would grouse that Venice had become the "vomitorium of Boston" and that "the bark of Chicago disturbs the siesta."[10] None of the visitors – then, as now – who complain of tourists ever include themselves among the offenders. Among Americans, Hawthorne (1804–1864) had been preceded to Italy by Washington Irving, James Fenimore Cooper, William Cullen Bryant, Thomas Cole, Joel Tyler Headley, Horace Bushnell, Margaret Fuller, and Henry Adams, among many others. Most left some written account of the tour. In the century since Winckelmann, the Etruscans had become, if not an essential part of the Grand Tour, then at least a well-known detour on it. Margaret Fuller, for instance, visited a tomb in Perugia and wrote that its female

9 Quoted in Craft, *Present Perspectives*, 206.
10 Quoted in Nathaniel Hawthorne, *The Marble Faun: Or, The Romance of Monte Beni*, from the "Introduction" by Broadhead, xiv.

figures were "dignified and calm." William Cullen Bryant made a close study of the Etruscan remains in out-of-the-way Volterra. The clergyman Joel Tyler Headley was saddened by not being able to read the inscriptions on the tombs. He also noted that he felt "strange sensations" when he realized that the Etruscans predated the Romans and that they were an aging civilization when Rome was young. The painter Thomas Cole had a similar sense of "desolate sublimity" and the centuries of historical time that he had been unaware of in America.[11] Just to complete the record, it is worth noting that Henry James, who visited Italy fourteen times and spent more time there than most, somehow missed the Etruscans, even though he spent a week in Perugia, which he found memorable primarily for the view from the ramparts and the still-standing Etruscan gate. (The Perugian ramparts will reappear with Anne Carson in the final chapter.)

Hawthorne and Sophia, his wife, say surprisingly little of interest in their journals about works of art, buildings, landscapes, or history. They stop at the expected sites and record mostly conventional responses. As James was probably the first to notice, Hawthorne's "Note-Books are chiefly taken up with descriptions of the regular sights and 'objects of interest,' which we often feel to be rather perfunctory and a little in the style of the traditional tourist's diary. They abound in charming touches, and every reader of *Transformation* [*The Marble Faun*'s English title] will remember the delightful colouring of the numerous pages in that novel, which are devoted to the pictorial aspects of Rome."[12] James's praise of "the delightful colouring" of Hawthorne's descriptions of Rome doesn't extend, however to the novel. He mentions that it is among Hawthorne's most popular, but he is certain it is an artistic failure. He is unconvinced by the combination of romance and realism – "this is the trouble with Donatello [the hero] himself" – and finds "the art of narration … more at fault than in the author's other novels. The story straggles and wanders, is

---

11 Baker, *The Fortunate Pilgrims*, 148, 210.
12 James, "Nathaniel Hawthorne," in *Literary Criticism: Essays on Literature*, 445. James was also not impressed by Roman architecture: "I discovered in [Pont du Gard and the arena at Nîmes] a certain stupidity, a vague brutality. That element is rarely absent from great Roman work … I suppose a race which could do nothing small is as defective as a race which can do nothing great." Quoted in Finley, *Aspects of Antiquity*, 143.

dropped and taken up again, and towards the close lapses into an almost fatal vagueness."[13] James, who understood belatedness almost better than any writer, recognized that Hawthorne had come to Italy too late to be influenced by it or to make full imaginative use of the Italian material for a novel. This is particularly disappointing for *The Etruscans in the Modern Imagination* because no other writer in the century gives an Etruscan character as central a role in a novel. Donatello is one of the four people, closely related by plot, who will undergo to different degrees the transformation of the English title. The novel collapses around him because the limitations of romance prevent Hawthorne from developing him beyond a sketched symbol of meridional instinct and repressed or attenuated sensuality. He remains a blurred photograph from beginning to end.

Where Emerson's journals show a man insatiable in his interest in what travel throws his way, Hawthorne's reveal a more provincial sensibility circumscribed by American moral and cultural assumptions like the ones Lambert Strether sets aside successfully, if temporarily, in the Paris of James's *The Ambassadors*. There is little in the Hawthornes' journals to suggest the Etruscans impressed them, and certainly not enough to create any expectation of their appearance in his next novel. The travel book they relied on – George Stillman Hillard's *Six Months in Italy* (1853) – notices the Etruscans once: Hillard stops at a hillside tomb three miles outside Perugia, describes it in six unevocative lines, gets back into his carriage, and drives off to Assisi.[14] Sophia's *Notes in England and Italy*, published in 1869, notices Etruscan tombs outside Viterbo, ruins in Bolsena, and the Janus Quadrifons (the Arch of Janus) in Rome, whose "blocks of marble are enormous. It is no doubt Etruscan [it isn't]. The Etruscans, and the race they were of, easily moved mountains about, it is plain to see."[15] Hawthorne is equally sparing in his notice of the Etruscans, which makes even more surprising the appearance of an Etruscan hero – he is "the marble faun" – and Etruscan motifs at important points of thematic development in the novel written in 1858 and 1859 during the stay in Rome.

13 James, *Literary Criticism: Essays on Literature*, 447.
14 Hillard, *Six Months in Italy*, 475.
15 Sophia Peabody Hawthorne, *Notes in England and Italy*, 523.

Hawthorne's last novel is set predominantly in the city, which the author describes in the "Preface" as "chiefly valuable ... as affording a sort of poetic or fairy precinct, where actualities would not be so terribly insisted upon, as they are and must needs be in America. No author, without a trial, can conceive of the difficulty of writing a Romance about a country where there is no shadow, no antiquity, no mystery, no picturesque and gloomy wrong."[16] The story involves two couples: Kenyon and Hilda, the Americans; and Miriam and Donatello, an American, who has perhaps stayed abroad too long, and an Italian of Etruscan descent. The Americans are art students from New England; Donatello does little beyond being mysterious and following the black-haired Miriam around like a tame faun. The others nickname him "the marble faun" because of a resemblance to a statue known as the Faun of Praxiteles (actually, the *Resting Satyr*) which the foursome sees in the novel's opening scene "in the sculpture gallery in the Capitol" (1.13). At the heart of the story is the loss of innocence for Hilda, a blond New England Puritan, and Donatello. Despite his Etruscan heritage, Donatello seems to be an almost prelapsarian creature until he falls for Miriam, whose chafed past is represented by a sinister figure who shadows her until Donatello kills him. Miriam is another in the line of sensual women in Hawthorne's novels, a sister to Hester Prynne (*The Scarlet Letter*) and Zenobia (*The Blithedale Romance*), but the hint of sexuality between her and Donatello is so understated that it almost doesn't exist. Hawthorne tells us that Miriam is passionate and sensual, and Miriam repeatedly hints at an unspeakable sin, but these aspects of her character remain disembodied rumours, never achieving the vividness of a single appearance by Hester Prynne.

The "faun" is at the heart of the novel's romance-generated unconvincing "perplexities" and mysteries, what T.S. Eliot describes as "all its Walter Scott–*Mysteries of Udolpho* upholstery."[17] He exists somewhere between an animal and a man, and Hawthorne does little with the "Etruscan" aspect of his character. If not quite without speech, Donatello remains uncomfortable and slightly awkward conversing with the others. The two women repeat the tired romance formula Hawthorne used previously in *The Blithedale Romance*: one an innocent blonde, the other

---

16 Nathaniel Hawthorne, *The Marble Faun*, vi. All references will be to this text.
17 Matthiessen, *American Renaissance*, 312.

exotic, dark-haired, and with a mysteriously blemished past. After the murder, both pairs of lovers walk in the shadow of *Paradise Lost* as the allegorical element is foregrounded. The knowledge they gain is at the expense of Donatello and Hilda's innocence. Donatello's fall into knowledge of good and evil distances him from the instinctive faun-like mode of being that was supposedly his charm. He seems doomed to return to his ancestral country home, which is compared to "an Etruscan tomb, being paved and walled with heavy blocks of stone, and vaulted almost as massively overhead" (24.162). Hilda is as helpless as Donatello when confronted by moral complexities, though we sense her struggle to reconcile her affection for Miriam and Donatello with her suspicion that they have behaved immorally. When, close to the novel's end, Kenyon plays what might be called the "*felix culpa*" card and suggests that "sin has educated Donatello and elevated him" and wonders "Did Adam fall, that we might ultimately rise to a far loftier Paradise than his?" Hilda responds that his creed makes a mockery "not only of all religious sentiment, but of moral law, and … it annuls and obliterates whatever precepts of Heaven are written deepest within us." Hoping to marry her, Kenyon retreats from his essentially conventional theological argument and pleads unconvincingly, "Forgive me, Hilda! … I never did believe it!" For a moment it appears as if Kenyon is giving up his humanism for what might be called Hildaism. But when he begs her to be his counsellor and to guide him home, her response offers hope of some sort of compromise: "We are both lonely; both far from home! … I am a poor, weak girl, and have no such wisdom as you fancy in me" (50.329). As if Hilda doesn't have enough to worry about, an old German artist advises her to return home because "the [Roman] air has been breathed too often, in so many thousand years, and is not wholesome for a little foreign flower like you, my child, a delicate wood anemone from the western forest land" (37.241).[18] I find that "anemone" almost chimes with "faun," and even the latter can't survive in the Roman miasma. One of the novel's unresolved moral confusions is how Donatello remains innocent in his gloomy villa – which foreshadows the prison that is his fate – or in Rome's fetid air.

---

18 From our vantage point we read the scene backwards through *The Sun Also Rises* and *The Ambassadors*, among many novels and films, as examples of "the complex fate" of Americans in Europe.

Before Hilda and Kenyon leave for America, Miriam sends Hilda a gift – a wedding bracelet of seven red gems – which foregrounds the novel's Etruscan motif. The gift retrieves and magnifies an Etruscan image introduced earlier – a solitary red gem – and invests it with a cumulative though vague symbolic significance Etruscan in origin. The gems are probably carnelian, whose etymology from the Latin for flesh (*caro*) subtly calls to mind Miriam's sensuality and sin and Hilda's lack thereof. Kenyon had noticed the gem when Miriam returned to Rome after the murder. Not quite able to account for his impression that she has changed, he wonders whether it "was partly owing to a gem which she had on her bosom; not a diamond, but something that glimmered with a clear, red lustre, like the stars in a southern sky. Somehow or other, this coloured light seemed an emanation of herself, as if all that was passionate and glowing, in her native disposition, had crystallized upon her breast, and were just now scintillating more brilliantly than ever, in sympathy with some emotion of her heart" (48.285). In a manner of speaking the Etruscan gem is Miriam's scarlet letter. Kenyon notices the gem, but he completely misses the deep change Miriam has undergone: "passionate and glowing" doesn't quite do it justice. Whatever is really at stake emotionally and symbolically here is lost in Hawthorne's avoidance of sex (Miriam and Donatello's) and violence (the murder). Almost as if sensing his failure with the original scene with one red Etruscan gem, Hawthorne tries again at the novel's end when he expands the stone's significance with the Etruscan bracelet Miriam gives Hilda as a wedding present.

Before they quitted Rome, a bridal gift was laid on Hilda's table. It was a bracelet, evidently of great cost, being composed of seven ancient Etruscan gems, dug out of seven sepulchers, and each one of them the signet of some princely personage, who had lived an immemorial time ago … It had been Miriam's; and once, with the exuberance of fancy that distinguished her, she had amused herself with telling a mythical and magic legend for each gem, comprising the imaginary adventures and catastrophe of its former wearer. Thus, the Etruscan bracelet became the connecting bond of a series of seven wondrous tales, all of which, as they were dug out of seven sepulchres, were characterized by a sevenfold sepulchral gloom; such as Miriam's imagination, shadowed by her own misfortunes, was wont to fling over its most sportive flights. (50.330)

The description once again goes through the motions of oblique hints about Miriam's supposedly mysterious life – the passage features three sepulchres, a catastrophe, and gloom – but we are no nearer to understanding Miriam. More troubling is the fact that neither the characters nor Hawthorne think the blood-red bracelet with gems found in Etruscan graves an inappropriate wedding gift for the innocent Hilda. If each gem is associated with the "catastrophe" that met its "former wearer," surely the bracelet is closer to a curse than to a gift. What is going on in Hawthorne's mind? I wonder whether he and Sophia saw the gems and the bracelet at C. and E. Tombini's jewellery shop in Rome, where George Eliot and George Henry Lewes bought an Etruscan mounting for a cameo of a Bacchante on 18 April 1860.

Donatello eludes Hawthorne as well as he shifts from the gloom of his ancestral house to the even greater gloom of a prison. Did Hawthorne decide to make Donatello an Etruscan simply because he had read that the Etruscans were gloomy, mysterious, and doomed and would therefore automatically introduce an element of Gothic "mystery" constitutive for a romance in the way that Jesuits carry evil into a Gothic novel? Since we can't be sure how much Hawthorne knew about the Etruscans, we can't know whether the reference to the symbolism of the red gems and their "sepulchral gloom" includes a specific Etruscan dimension or resonance – divination, warrior princes, pagan religion, conquest, and extinction. How much moral weight is the bracelet intended to carry? For Hawthorne's readers it probably suggested sexuality, luxury, and perhaps a Gothic connection at the same time as it hinted at the seven cardinal sins, of which Miriam commits at least three – pride, lust, and wrath – while Donatello is guilty of the last two. His paradoxical prelapsarian condition – his ancient estate makes for a melancholy garden – failed to protect him once he stepped outside and fell in love with Miriam. The gems, like much concealed within the generic machinery of the romance, would only realize their full symbolic and historical potential after Freud, or more precisely after Frederick Crews's Freudian *The Sins of the Fathers* (1966).

When I think back to the novel, I imagine poor Donatello, the absent presence at the heart of his own novel, as the last of the Etruscans, unknown from beginning to end. Perhaps his character is somewhere behind the Etruscan who gasps "Ah … " in Anne Carson's "Canicula di Anna" as he falls from the parapet on Perugia's city wall.

III

Emily Dickinson's Etruscan Triptych: "Etruscan Invitation,"
"Etruscan Argument," "Etruscan Experiment"

There the tomb stands today, Etruscan-like in its granite simplicity,
with the words WALT WHITMAN carved on the pediment.

William Sloane Kennedy[19]

Emily Dickinson does more with the Etruscan inheritance in a briefer
compass than anyone in this book except perhaps Anne Carson. Her
use is confident, creative, compact, and challenging. She knows enough
about the Etruscans to make references to them the hinges of meaning
in two cryptic poems and a well-known letter.[20] Not only does she use
Etruscan material, she uses it figuratively, which indicates a confidence
in her readers' familiarity (or at least acquaintance) with it as well.

Etruscans first appear in 1861 in "Unto like Story – Trouble has
enticed me –" (poem 295), a dark, elegiac poem with a litany of implicitly
historical deaths and martyrdoms that occur in the shadow of "God's
full time." These provide a context for the interconnected questions
tacit in the different suggested narratives: Why do we die? For what
cause? Am I brave enough to be a martyr?

Unto like story – Trouble has enticed me –
How Kinsmen fell –
Brothers and Sister – who preferred the Glory –
And their young will
Bent to the Scaffold, or in Dungeons – chanted –

---

19 The full quotation is "Christmas Day of 1890 was spent by Walt Whitman in
giving himself and all his family a Christmas present for eternity. He went out to
Harleigh Cemetery, suburbs of Camden, to select a site for a tomb; chose a place on
a woody, laurelled hillside, bird-haunted, with living water near by. There the tomb
stands to-day, Etruscan-like in its granite simplicity, with the words WALT WHITMAN
carved on the pediment. His father and mother, and brothers and sisters, will sleep
beside him. When asked why he chose this spot, he said, 'I would rather go in the
woods.'" Kennedy, *Reminiscences of Walt Whitman*, Walt Whitman Archive: Whitman
Archive ID: med. 00567.

20 "Life is death we're lengthy at, death the hinge to life." Letter to Louise and
Frances Norcross, late May 1863. Dickinson, *Selected Letters*, 183.

Till God's full time –
When they let go the ignominy – smiling –
And Shame went still –

Unto guessed Crests, my morning fancy, leads me,
Worn fair
By Heads rejected – in the lower country –
Of honors there
Such spirit makes her perpetual mention,
That I – grown bold –
Step martial – at my Crucifixion –
As Trumpets – rolled –

Feet, small as mine – have marched in Revolution
Firm to the Drum –
Hands – not so stout – hoisted them – in witness –
When Speech went numb –
Let me not shame their sublime deportments –
Drilled bright –
Beckoning – Etruscan invitation –
Toward Light –

The references to "Crucifixion" and "Light" introduce the comforting Christian eschatology but it sits uneasily next to the implied contradictory Etruscan one, which is as grim as that of the Maya, who had been in the American news since the publication in the early 1840s of John Lloyd Stephens's two best-selling books. The third stanza begins "Feet, small as mine – have marched in Revolution / Firm to the Drum –." Looking back at the dead, she imagines her own "Crucifixion" before seeing her predecessors "Beckoning – Etruscan invitation – / Toward Light –." The Etruscans are the last dead mentioned and the ones closest to, perhaps even within, the "Light." Dickinson takes the chance that if the reader fails to understand the "Etruscan invitation" the lyric will remain a cipher unresolved. The key to the poem depends on what is figured by "Etruscan invitation." The adjective may have attracted Dickinson because of the subtle chime between "Etruscan" and "invitation." But the implied metaphor must depend on an association of the Etruscans with martyrdom in a losing cause when even their "Speech went numb" – which I take as a reference to the disappearance of the language and the undecipherability of their inscriptions. The "Light" promises no more than the event horizon of a Black Hole. The emphasis is on showing up to fight even if in a hopeless struggle. The Etruscans died fighting the Romans, and we all lose to death. Written either just before or at the start of the Civil War, this poem that resists dejection and resurrection ends with an allusion to a dead people from the heart of the Italian peninsula who lost a lengthy war – one might call it a civil war – in which one side didn't just suffer defeat but disappeared. The poem is permeated by a dream of dying for a great and perhaps hopeless cause which remains unnamed though implied. The reader decides what is meant by the "Light." The reader in 1861, had Dickinson published the poem, would also have brought the armies of the Civil War into the poem's symbolic possibilities. Is it possible to read the poem's sympathy as extended to *whoever* will lose and play the Etruscan part?

The Etruscans return twenty years later in poem 1528 (c. 1881), where the path to the poem's meanings passes through an Etruscan metaphor that depends on the reader's awareness of the importance of divination in Etruria. Dickinson never suggested that reading her was for the faint-hearted or those nurtured on Longfellow.

The Moon upon her fluent Route
Defiant of a Road –
The Star's Etruscan Argument
Substantiate a God –

If Aims impel these Astral Ones
The ones allowed to know
Know that which makes them as forgot
As Dawn forgets them – now –

The "Etruscan Argument" (or use of divination) helps "The ones allowed to know" (seers) to chart the heavens and interpret the will of the gods. The second stanza, however, undermines these efforts: even if they manage to "Substantiate" – one of the more worried words in Christian theology – or to prove the existence of "a God" and read the future, they will only see their own eventual complete oblivion, an event as natural as the next "Dawn," which I take as a trope for the cycle of time. There is an almost Lucretian pessimism here: to know is to know that we will disappear like the Etruscans and be forgotten as completely as the Etruscans. The "Astral Ones," whoever they might be, pay no attention to the "ones" below. Dickinson had few readers, but on the evidence of this poem she expected her implied reader to know something about the Etruscans. Without that first step, a reader can't begin to figure the poem's thematic possibilities.

We notice a similar confidence on Dickinson's part in a letter from mid-October 1885 to her cousin Eugenia Hall on her wedding day: "Will the sweet cousin who is about to make the Etruscan Experiment, accept a smile which will last a life, if ripened in the Sun?" The "Etruscan Experiment" suggests two connected possibilities. It makes sense if we think of a sarcophagus with a married couple each smiling a "smile which will last a lifetime." It may also be the poet's cryptic allusion to the fact that Etruscan women, unlike their modern New England counterparts, had an unusual degree of freedom in marriage and therefore a valid reason for smiling.

While Dickinson was writing her Etruscan texts, Ralph Waldo Emerson was dreaming Etruscan dreams and recording them in his journals. He wasn't writing for publication, but he also refers to Etruscans with a confidence implying that they were familiar at least among people of his social stratum, which was also that of the Dickinson family. Both the prophet and the poet show brilliantly how much can be done with a diminished thing like the recently rediscovered Etruscan inheritance. On their pages, "Etruscan" flickers into life as part of a cultural tradition. No one is surprised by Dickinson's allusions to Greek antiquity; Thermopylae, for instance, appears in four poems and two letters. But the Etruscan appearances are something like a warm late-November day. What was it about the Etruscans, the poor relations at the classical table, that caught her attention, when the Egyptians, Greeks, and Romans couldn't? "Egyptian Argument," "Egyptian invitation," and "Egyptian Experiment" would be as euphonic as their Etruscan counterparts, so it couldn't just be the verbal music of chimes, echoes, and slant rhymes. There must be specific associations Dickinson was working to evoke, but without unveiling the mystery. It was precisely the mystery associated with the mysterious Etruscans that she wanted. Even if just for herself. In this she resembles no one as much as Anne Carson, another poet at once meticulous in her penchant for figurative compacted "argument." Neither poet gives anything away. In a manner of speaking, their readers must dance for their suppers.

Edgar Degas, Mary Cassatt, and Edith Reveley:

The Sarcophagus of the Married Couple

The dust of great persons' graves is speechlesse too,
it sayes nothing, it distinguishes nothing.

John Donne[1]

The Sarcophagus of the Married Couple is among the best known and most admired of Etruscan sculptures (see figure 11.1). In popularity it has traditionally been in the same class as the tomb paintings, the Chimaera of Arezzo, and the Orator in Florence. Recently, however, it has entered the world of popular culture with an appearance as a question on the very popular game show *Jeopardy!*: "The terracotta Sarcophagus of the Spouses reclines at Rome's National Museum of these darn ancient people." (I wonder what would have happened to the contestant who insisted that it wasn't in "Rome's National Museum" but in the "Museo Etrusco di Villa Giulia"?) If we were doing public relations for the Etruscans, we might be tempted to use this television appearance as evidence that they have arrived, though Flaubert and Adorno would judge it an example of the commodification of the Etruscans by mass culture.

There are two original versions of the sarcophagus: one at the Louvre, discovered in 1845 and purchased by Napoleon III in 1861, and one at the Villa Giulia. Both are from the same period, 530–520 BCE. There is also a forgery in the British Museum. It is worth noting that the Louvre sarcophagus has been heavily restored, and the one in Rome was

1 Donne, "At Whitehall, 1st Friday in Lent, 8 March 1621–2," *The Complete Poetry and Selected Prose,* 486.

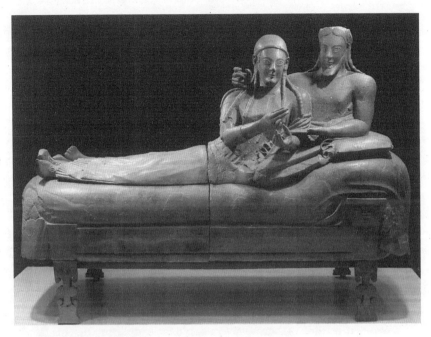

11.1 Sarcophagus of the Married Couple, 540–520 BCE.

reassembled from over four hundred pieces. Sybille Haynes suggests that "if not made by the same master, the sarcophagi are certainly works of a single atelier."[2] The couple are represented reclining as if at a banquet, though Haynes suggests that "the position of their fingers rules out" that they were holding "the drinking cups usually shown in banqueting scenes."[3] She describes it as a funerary banquet whose main concern is an anointing rite. Following the Etruscan custom, the wife accompanies her husband. According to the Louvre's description, they recline "on cushions in the form of wineskins, a reference to the sharing of wine, a ceremony that was part of the ritual. Tenderly clasped by her husband, the deceased woman is pouring a few drops of perfume into his hand, probably from an alabastron; in so doing, she is making the gesture of offering perfume, another essential component of funerary ritual. In her left hand she is holding a small, round object,

2 Haynes, *Etruscan Civilization*, 215.
3 Ibid., 217.

possibly a pomegranate, a symbol of immortality."[4] The sarcophagus is distinguished from more common large cinerary sarcophagi with a reclining figure or figures by the absence of a closely framed tableau in relief showing a scene from mythology: Achilles killing Troilus, the Calydonian Boar hunt, and Philoctetes on Lemnos were popular. Interpretations have varied from the typological (a killing shows the work of fate) to the local (the dead Etruscan is shown in relation to the implied heroic tradition of his family). There are later Roman sarcophagi, such as the sarcophagus of Alexander Severus in the Capitoline Museum, that combine the reclining couple and the tableau of Achilles and the Greek heroes.

The scope of the fame of the Sarcophagus of the Married Couple can be gauged by Seamus Heaney's use of it in his memoir of Czesław Miłosz, "In Gratitude for All the Gifts."

… a mighty terracotta sculpture of a married couple, reclining on their elbows. The woman is positioned on the man's left side, couched close and parallel, both of them at their ease and gazing intently ahead at something that, by all the rules of perspective, should be visible in the man's out-stretched right hand. But there is nothing to be seen there. Was it a bird that has flown? A flower that has been snapped away? A bird that is approaching? Nothing is shown, yet their gaze is full of realization.[5]

Heaney's interpretation is attractive in the same way as some of Lawrence's intuitive responses to things Etruscan. But it is misleading and in one detail wrong. Nigel Spivey's response – he begins with the version in the Villa Giulia – brings us back closer to Haynes.

It comes from a tomb, and though we do not know whether it actually once contained the joint remains of husband and wife (which is unlikely), it has been taken as emblematic of nuptial bliss. A second example of the same type of sculpture has been preserved (now in the Louvre), suggesting that we should not be looking for "portraits" as such, and a number of earlier and smaller types establish a pattern of gestures whose eloquence has faded.[6]

---

4 Collection of the Louvre Museum, https://www.louvre.fr/explore#collections. Accessed 26 May 2018.
5 Haven, *The Invisible Rope*, 209.
6 Spivey, *Etruscan Art*, 92.

Spivey's suggestion that it is unlikely that the sarcophagus contained the remains of a married couple is a useful reminder that away from its original context a work of art can give rise to influential unintended meanings. In this case, the couple is perhaps not a "couple," and the portraits are perhaps not individualized "portraits." Spivey adds to the controversy by suggesting that the perfume flask may be an aphrodisiac device, as it often is in Greek lyric. Whether the sculpture of the couple is intended as retrospective (as if the couple were alive) or prospective (as dead) is an open question, though most of us respond to both possibilities with funerary sculpture. This was Lawrence's view in *Etruscan Places*: "And death, to the Etruscan, was a pleasant continuance of life, with jewels and wine and flutes playing for the dance. It was neither an ecstasy of bliss, a heaven, nor a purgatory of torment. It was just a natural continuance of the fulness of life. Everything was in terms of life, of living."[7] The couple recall for us all the lounging Etruscans in the tomb paintings celebrating life either in the here and now or in the afterlife.

The works by Edgar Degas (1834–1917) and Edith Reveley (1930–?) offer two very different responses. The work of neither is as distinguished, in artistic terms, as the sarcophagus, but each shows an artist putting the past at the service of the present and, in the process, bringing it back to life. Seen thousands of times a day in Paris and Rome, the sarcophagus is now an object within modern culture. It is also the only Etruscan object to appear in Degas's body of work. It occurs in a handful of small and, with one exception, undistinguished works the painter devoted to Mary Cassatt between 1879 and 1884. These continue to attract attention primarily because we can't be certain of the exact nature of the relationship between the two painters: friends? passionate friends? discreet lovers? an elective affinity? Most commentators settle for some version of "intimate friends" and leave the impression that neither was strongly drawn to sex or marriage. Few seem to credit the comment of Forbes Watson, an American critic, that he heard Degas remark, "I would have married her, but I could never have made love to her." Ian Dunlop quotes the the American critic only to add, "Although there has been some speculation of an affair between them, it hardly seems likely."[8] Degas is undoubtedly the larger figure of the

7 Lawrence, *Sketches of Etruscan Places*, 19.
8 Dunlop, *Degas*, 168.

two, and his artistic achievement would have been the same had they never met. The works in which Cassatt is represented add little to his reputation: *At the Louvre: The Etruscan Sarcophagus* (c. 1879), graphite drawing; *At the Louvre: Mary Cassatt in the Picture Gallery* (1879–80), pastel and etching; *At the Louvre: Mary Cassatt in the Etruscan Gallery* (1879–80), etching; *Mary Cassatt* (1880–84), an unfinished oil; and *Young Woman Tying her Bonnet (Mary Cassatt)* (c. 1882), pastel and charcoal. For Cassatt, writes Griselda Pollock, the meeting with Degas "was decisive and productive, for in him she found an artistic alter ego who, by introducing her to experimental printmaking, prepared the way for her radical modernization of a challenging subject: women and children."[9] Though only eleven years separated them, he was clearly the master who had little to learn from an apprentice during the years they worked together.

The two etchings of Cassatt at the Louvre show her from behind. In one she stands looking directly at paintings, in the other at the Sarcophagus of the Married Couple. In both, her seated sister Lydia holds what is assumed to be a handbook open high enough to screen part of her face, surely at Degas's suggestion. In the second etching, Cassatt's pose, in which she leans on an umbrella, reveals almost nothing about her except that she visited the Louvre and didn't use a handbook. The more interesting question for this study is why Degas chose to position Cassatt in front of the famous terracotta sarcophagus, a funerary receptacle carved in the shape of a sofa with a smiling, graceful couple – slightly smaller than life – reclining in the attitude of banqueters. He had already done two preparatory drawings of the sarcophagus by itself, one of which has disappeared. Cassatt turns her back on everything to concentrate her attention on the sarcophagus: she needs no introduction, handbook, or intermediary. That is also why she stands alone, though sponsored, so to speak, by Degas, who, as the artist, is behind her. It is not a stretch to suggest that each painter is aware of the challenge posed to all artists by an anonymous work that survived two millennia and has found a distinguished place in the Louvre. If nothing else, it is an artistic challenge and a *memento mori*. But I can't shake off the thought that Degas, notoriously reticent with his emotions, is also using the etching to communicate something about the relationship with Cassatt. If indeed, as is most likely, they were never more than

9 Pollock, *Mary Cassatt*, 8.

respectful colleagues and intimate friends, is he also reminding Cassatt and himself of what each perhaps occasionally (often?) longed for – something as simple yet unachievable as the sensual, emotional, and perhaps spiritual happiness of the smiling Etruscans embodied in terracotta? The ancient couple remind the painters that they will never lie together like that – in life or death. This is what they sacrificed for a life devoted to painting.

Six years after the etching of the Etruscan sarcophagus, Degas recasts the topos of a woman looking at an ancient work of art in *Hélène Rouart in Her Father's Study*. The oil painting shows the young woman looking at a glass case with three Egyptian objects, most prominently an ushabti of Ptah-Seker-Osiris, a composite figure representing creation, stability, and death that is buried with the corpse to act as a helper in the afterlife. Behind her are Jean-François Millet's drawing *A Peasant Woman Seated against a Haystack* and Jean-Baptiste-Camille Corot's *Naples and the Castello dell'Ovo*. She leans on her father's large empty chair and, with an expressionless face, seems insignificant, disconnected from his room and his things, which seem more vividly colourful and present than she is. There were four sons in the family, and maybe that was Degas's point. The chair is empty, the father somewhere else: she knows she doesn't belong here and feels unwanted. Degas was a master at revealing separation in his portraits. Think of the mother's black dress in the early *Family Portrait*, also called *The Bellelli Family* (1858–67), or the grim *Duchessa di Montejasi with Her Daughters* (c. 1876). Little in the portraits indicate that these people meant anything to Degas except as models for his art.

Did Cassatt sense something of this detachment, not just in the Etruscan etchings but also in the well-known sombre portrait (1880–84) Degas painted of her, seated leaning forward, distracted, and holding some cards in her hands? Although she owned the painting, Cassatt wrote to the art dealer Durand-Ruel just before the war asking him to sell it for her: "I do not want to leave it with my family as being of me. It has some qualities as art, but it is so painful and represents me as such a repugnant person, that I would not want it known that I posed for it."[10] Taken together with her burning of his letters, this fierce rejection of a portrait that embodies the intimate connection between them suggests a depth of clenched feeling unjustified by any surviving

10 Meyers, *Impressionist Quartet*, 277.

evidence. Did she suspect that the stark, potentially cruel portrait had meant nothing to Degas beyond what it represented as a work of art? No one looking at it would think she meant anything more to the painter than the Bellelli family, which included his aunt Laura and two nieces, Giovanna and Giulia.

I I

Edith Reveley's "The Etruscan Couple" (1976):
The Judgment of a Sarcophagus

Calvin removed himself to the floor, where he reclined in the position
of an Etruscan lying on his tomb. Calvin was a tall man, with pale eyes whose
colour no one could ever remember.

Iris Murdoch, *The Flight from the Enchanter*[11]

In Edith Reveley's story "The Etruscan Couple" (1976), she does much more with Etruscan material than Mérimée, Flaubert, or Degas. It tells the story of Vera's trip (her first name is as resonant as Isabel Archer's) with her brother Calvin to Italy. She is a middle-aged woman with "few real resources" who is recovering from a nineteen-year marriage to an insensitive man who had used sex "too often and too cruelly against her."[12] Calvin planned the trip for her, and the story focuses on their last day in Rome and a visit to the "Villa Giulia where they would next go to give the Etruscans their due" (10). The title, unlike Mérimée's, does some work by introducing the possibility that the well-known terracotta sarcophagus of an Etruscan couple will have some thematic significance in the story: "Etruscan couple" is casual enough to suggest a "modern couple" in counterpoint. Another nudge to the reader occurs when Calvin reads to her over lunch "from Lawrence's book on the Etruscans" (12). Though he admits that "usually I can't abide Lawrence," the English writer's ghost and his well-known view of Etruscans and Italians hovers over the story. One can sense it in Vera's reflection about the Italians she sees around her in the café: "She amused herself by watching the Italians at the nearby tables lounging over their espressos and ices, so enviably secure in the sense of their

11 Murdoch, *The Flight from the Enchanter,* 15.
12 Reveley, *The Etruscan Couple and Other Stories,* 18. All references will be to this text.

own desirability, potency and God-given right to waste time. Time was a public luxury here like the water that sprang, leaped, bubbled and cascaded all over the city. But for people like Calvin and herself it was measured out in pure and tepid draughts according to reasonable need" (21). There is a Lawrentian echo, this time from his famous poem "The Snake," in the description of a Contessa, who takes Vera shopping, as uncoiling "herself from [her car] like a long elegant snake" (15). There is also something of Henry James when the so-called Contessa takes Vera to a glove shop and persuades her to buy. Vera senses that "the Contessa was getting a percentage, she had been gulled. She felt a sick thud of embarrassment and hurt and also a certain wonder that her aristocratic friend should deign to chisel on so small a scale. Then she recalled what a well-travelled acquaintance had told her on the eve of her departure. 'Beware the professional European, Vera'" (20). Life in Makepeace, Maine, had not prepared her for the moral sinuosities of the Contessa any more than life in Albany, New York, had prepared Isabel Archer for Gilbert Osmond and Madame Merle. Her brother's name is a tacit reminder of the religious climate of her American world. Reveley's names deliver.

The "gulling" is her second shock of the day. She had woken out of a troubling dream "about [her husband] Hal and the virulence of his power over her" (9), and this cast a pall. The disillusionment with the Contessa deepens this to the point that she is on the verge of cutting short the tour of the Villa Giulia. The guide's insistence and Calvin's enthusiasm – "It's the sarcophagus of an Etruscan couple, Vera, evidently quite famous" (22) – convince her to go on to what will be the story's moment of revelation, which will evolve and deepen in significance over four scenes. Reveley's accurate description of the Etruscan couple from Vera's point of view is worth quoting in full.

They had come to a small light rotunda. The sarcophagus occupied a pedestal in the centre. The figures, nearly life-size, were half reclining, each supported on an elbow, the husband behind the wife. Their lips were curved in archaic smiles and their faces, gently rounded, gazed at a point beyond the viewer with an affability, a mild benignity that was incredibly attractive. Contiguous and yet independent – the wife didn't quite lean against the supporting shoulder of the husband – their positioning suggested an unconscious and habitual embrace like that of sleepers in a union that was serene and perfectly complete. (22–3)

Although Vera and Calvin are only mildly interested in the Etruscans, the sarcophagus surprises them, not by what one of Vera's college professors called "a valid aesthetic experience" but by a direct Lawrentian appeal to their lives – art for life's sake. This is made explicit in Vera's case and left implied in Calvin's – "his expression was quite beatific."

Although Vera tries to limit the significance of the relationship depicted to love between a man and a woman, Calvin, a homosexual, understands its deeper potential, that "it happens to be a portrait of a marriage, if you like, but as an expression of a valid relationship it transcends the particular nature of the subject" (24). Tellingly, Vera resists this attempt to extend the meaning. In a manner of speaking, at that moment the couple are too important to her – they have revealed too much about her life – to be shared with anyone. Everything she didn't have in two decades with Hal is suddenly present in a terracotta sculpture 2,500 years old: "Calvin ... couldn't possibly know how beautiful they were in the manifest wisdom and bliss of their union" (24). She wants to keep them within her memory-charged orbit for a little bit longer. A slighter story would have ended here, but Reveley, in a Jamesian swerve, shows Vera (the name has grown in importance) slowly realizing that this unexpected vision of an ideal union has made her aware of a previously unsuspected aspect of her marriage. When Calvin leaves for the *gabinetto*, she "tips the guard to be rid of him" and stands "alone with the Etruscan couple in the rotunda, quiet as the nave of a chapel, stark as a tomb" (24). She acknowledges her "possessive jealousy" of the sarcophagus and regrets having sniped at Calvin "in a way that reminded her most unpleasantly of Hal's baleful persecution" (25). Again, Reveley might have chosen to make a segue to a reconciliation with Calvin on his return as a preparation for the ending, but she uses Hal to allow Vera to come to terms with her past and the continuing profound suffering from her marriage. Despite the advice of friends, there are things one doesn't get over.

Why did Hal love hurting me so? she wondered suddenly and with real anguish for the first time in years, for the first time, in fact, since she had believed the doctors when they told her that sick as she was Hal was much much sicker. But sick or not, she had experienced something out of the ordinary. She had suffered long and hard, she had loved a man literally beyond human reason and that was enough ... But the smiling faces in front of her were so plainly something else again. To have had something like that, she thought. Her sorrow freshened from a deeply hidden spring. (25)

There's no doubt in her mind (or the reader's) which "out of the ordinary" relationship is preferable, but she finds a way of coming to terms with her regret (or is it remorse?) without falsifying the past. When Calvin returns, she conceals her ambivalent tears from him and says, "I'm glad I saw the statues" (25). The conciliatory brother gets the last word: "Actually, funerary statuary is apt to be pretty idealized" (26). He's right, but even idealized the sarcophagus has helped Vera to a richer understanding of love, even when it is one-sided and ultimately fails a relationship. A comment by F.R. Leavis seems apposite here: "The work that commands the reader's most deeply engaged ... attention asks at a deep level: 'What, at bottom, do men live *for*?' And in work that strikes us as great art we are aware of a potent normative suggestion: '*These* are the possibilities and inevitablenesses, and, in the face of them, *this* is the valid and the wise (or the sane) attitude.'" Vera wouldn't use those words, but she would understand what the great critic is suggesting.[13]

The Etruscans do not return in any of Reveley's other stories or her two novels, *A Pause for Breath* (1979) and *In Good Faith* (1985), even though the latter is set in part in Italy. Nor does Lawrence. She had written her small masterpiece on the subject. There was no need to return to it.

13 Leavis, *The Critic as Anti-Philosopher*, 193.

12

Anatole France's The Red Lily (1894), a Glance at Marcel Proust, and Etruscan Humour

"We must go back to classical antiquity. David is designing beds and armchairs in the style of Etruscan vases and the paintings at Herculaneum."

Anatole France, *The Gods Will Have Blood*[1]

I

The Nobel Prize for Literature, which Anatole France (1844–1924) received in 1921, has often been a tombstone (or sarcophagus) for writers with careers in free fall. It is sometimes a definitive *memento mori* about the fragility of even the greatest reputations. Prior to the First World War, France was the most famous living French author. That his reputation early in the century extended across Europe is casually indicated in Zbigniew Herbert's early poem "My Father": "My father liked Anatole France / and smoked Macedonian tobacco." Aldous Huxley remembered in an interview in the early 1960s having been "fond [at Oxford] of a novelist who is now very much out-of-date ... Anatole France." Claude Lévi-Strauss records a meeting in a village in the Brazilian interior in the 1930s in which "an old man overcome by emotion had exclaimed, 'Ah Monsieur, you are French! Ah, France!

---

1 France, *The Gods Will Have Blood*, 23. This is said by Évariste Gamelin, a second-rate painter devoted to Robespierre and the revolution. The more extreme his views, the more obvious it becomes that he will be one of those to be devoured by the violence. Some consider the novel France's masterpiece. The French title is less violent, *Les dieux ont soif.* It was published in 1912. The thirst of the gods was about to be satisfied by the bloodiest war in history, at least to that point.

Anatole, Anatole!' as he clasped me in his arms."[2] A year after the Nobel, almost as if in a panicked reaction, the Vatican put his works on the *Index Librorum Prohibitorum*. *The Red Lily* (*Le lys rouge*, 1894), a novel with a small though entertaining comic interest in the Etruscans, is one of the few to have escaped the downward spiral. The collected works rest in that plush mausoleum called a Pléiade edition, and there is also the immortality of being the model for Proust's novelist Bergotte in *À la recherche du temps perdu*.

Despite his fall from favour, France's writing has two qualities we expect from a major writer: a style and a voice that distinguishes him from his contemporaries – think of Gabriel García Márquez – and a vision of humanity, society, and perhaps history. France had a lifelong interest in the classical world, though he always found the Greeks and their comprehensive vision of life far more attractive than the tough-minded Romans. France had no religion, but he worshipped Greek humanity and beauty as the supreme achievement of the human race. He admired the sensuality at the heart of Hellenism but rejected the rationalism and asceticism in its later development in Stoicism, Skepticism, and Epicureanism. In idealizing the past, however, he also ignored the suicidal internecine wars, the slaughter and enslavement of entire populations, and the importance of slavery to the survival of various states. In a manner of speaking, France's vision, like Winckelmann's, Hegel's, and Arnold's, depends on an airbrushing of the ending of the fifth book of Thucydides: "the Melians surrendered at discretion to the Athenians, who put to death all the grown men whom they took, and sold the women and children for slaves, and subsequently sent out five hundred colonists and settled the place themselves" (5.116).

Though Greeks play no role in *The Red Lily*, many of the qualities France attributed to them can be found in the novel's aestheticism, obsession with style and beauty, discussions of the arts, and eroticism and sensuality, and in the surprising references to the Etruscans, particularly their language and cultural artifacts. The novel is the closest France came to a conventional novel of romance. Today we also have the option of reading it autobiographically as his farewell to a long,

---

2 Herbert, *The Collected Poems*, 13; Huxley, "Aldous Huxley, Interview," 207; Lévi-Strauss, *Tristes Tropiques*, 31.

passionate, and troubled love affair with Mme de Caillavet. Marie-Claire Bancquart, his Pléiade editor, writes that "this masochistic and sadistic love affair" was the basis for the central relationship in the novel.[3]

The novel's story has the following trajectory: Thérèse Martin, a married woman of a certain social status, takes a lover, abandons him, takes a new, very jealous lover, and is in turn abandoned by him. Though Thérèse is more reflective than Emma Bovary, and has better taste in clothes, art, and men, there is nevertheless an element of Bovarysme in her vanity, her continuing melancholy, and her desire for a life of intense passion. France anticipates her aestheticized milieu and its values in a fine, slowly moving opening paragraph – the narrator's eye pans like a camera around her in her elegant reception room, whose decor is an extension of her stylishness and aestheticism: she is what she sees.

She looked round at the arm-chairs in front of the fire, at the tea-table with its tea-things glittering like shadows, at the big bunches of delicately coloured flowers in Chinese vases. Lightly she touched the sprays of guilder roses and toyed with their silver buds. Then she gazed gravely in the glass. Standing sideways and looking over her shoulder, she followed the outline of her fine figure in its sheath of black satin, on which floated a thin drapery, sown with beads and scintillating with lights of flame. Curious to examine that day's countenance, she approached the mirror. Tranquilly and approvingly it returned her glance as if the charming woman it was reflecting lived a life devoid of intense joy and profound sadness. On the walls of the great empty silent drawing-room, the tapestry figures at their ancient games, vague in the shadow, grew pale with dying grace. Like them, the terra cotta statuettes on pedestals, the groups of old Dresden china, the painting on Sèvres, displayed in glass cases, spoke of things past. On a stand decorated with precious bronzes the marble bust of some royal princess, disguised as Diana, with irregular features and prominent breast, escaped from her troubled drapery, whilst on the ceiling a Night, powdered like a marquise and surrounded by Cupids, scattered flowers. Everything was slumbering, and there was heard only the crackling of the fire and the slight rustling of beads on gauze.[4]

3 France, *Oeuvres* 2:1196. The relationship's turmoil and violent end are suggested by the title France first considered for it, "La Terre des morts." The translation is mine.

4 France, *The Red Lily*, 5. All quotations will be from this edition.

The fashionable setting and the fashionably dressed woman mirror each other and are as stylish and self-conscious as the writing. When not looking at her surroundings she looks at herself in the mirror only to see it reflecting a life devoid of any intensities. The remainder of the novel will dramatize her attempt to escape from the room and the mirror image into an intense and passionate life. That she may be too late (or incapable of it) is the novel's final irony.

The conventional works of art on show anticipate many scenes in which painting, sculpture, and writing will be discussed at some length. The poems of her friend Vivian Bell will be read by the poet to those visiting her house outside Florence. The Etruscans play a small, mostly comic part in this cultural array by way of Mme Marmet, the dull widow of an equally dull academic – a one-trick pony – devoted to Etruscan studies, especially the language. He is that stock traditional figure, the specialist who recognizes only one topic of interest, his specialty. A contemporary example would be the academic dinner guest unable to discuss anything except semiotics. There is a slight echo in Marmet of Jules Martha (1853–1932), one of the best-known Etruscologists of the period. In the seven years before the publication of *Le lys rouge,* he published three books on Etruscan topics, including *Manuel d'archéologie étrusque et romaine* (1884) and *L'Art étrusque* (1889). A closer candidate, however, might be Nietzsche's teacher Wilhelm Corssen (1820–1875) whose book *Ueber die Sprache der Etrusker* (1874) was attacked so mercilessly by William Deecke (1831–1897) in *Corssen and the Language of the Etruscans* (1875) that his "untimely death at the age of fifty-three was rumoured to have been caused by his colleague's derision."[5] After his death, Professor Marmet is remembered chiefly for his feud with Joseph Schmoll, a fellow intellectual with an interest in the ancients. The novelist Paul Vence describes the academic feud's thin substance to Thérèse before a dinner at her home.

"Can it be possible, Madame, that you have never heard of this erudite and bitter quarrel?

"The Etruscan language was its cause. Marmet devoted his life to the study of Etruscans. He was nicknamed 'Marmet the Etruscan.' Neither he nor anyone else knew a single word of that completely lost language. Schmoll used

5 Wellard, *The Search for the Etruscans*, 178. Deeke later adopted his rival's theories and was similarly derided.

to be always saying to Marmet: 'You know that you don't know Etruscan, my dear brother; that's why you are so greatly honoured as a scholar and a wit.' Piqued by such ironical praise, Marmet determined to know something of the Etruscan. He read his brother Academicians a paper on the use of inflexions in the ancient Etruscan idiom …

"Be content to know that in this paper poor Marmet quoted Latin texts and quoted them incorrectly. Now Schmoll is an accomplished Latin scholar, who, after Mommsen, knows more than anyone about inscriptions.

"He reproached his young brother (Marmet was not quite fifty) with knowing too much Etruscan and not enough Latin. From that moment he never let Marmet alone." (14)[6]

Schmoll's mockery hastens Marmet's death by reducing him to a caricature – the dull pedant. Ronald Firbank revives the type two decades later in his novel *Vainglory* (1915) with Professor Inglepin, famous for having discovered a line of Sappho's poetry which he recites as often as possible: "Could not, for the fury of her feet."[7] France treats Marmet's obsession as a joke; the Etruscans are reduced to a trope for the absurd. Here, Edgar Allan Poe anticipates France in a minor piece titled "Mellonta Tauta," a letter written by a madman. At one point he exclaims "Tempora mutantur," and adds, "excuse me for quoting the Etruscan."[8] It doesn't help Marmet that his name is close in sound to the following words, none of which is flattering: marmite, marmiton, marmot, marmotte, marmotter (to mumble, mutter), marmouset (a quaint or grotesque figure). The text mocks him by euphonic association every time he is named, even posthumously.

Marmet's hapless but loyal widow becomes the keeper of the sputtering flame. The two early pages devoted to Marmet's interest in the Etruscans suggest misleadingly that they will play a significant role in the story. They don't, but they do have a few more walk-on appearances. It's as if France had considered giving them more prominence and then changed his mind. The second Etruscan appearance occurs

6 Later Mme Martin meets Lagrange, another dull academic specialist. She knows that scholars lack curiosity and that it is unwise to question them about anything not in their area of interest. "It is true that thunderbolts had made Lagrange's fortune in science. And that they had led him to the study of comets. But he was prudent. For twenty years his chief occupation had been dining out" (70).

7 Fairbank, *3 More Novels*, 26.

8 Poe, *Complete Stories*, 375.

about a quarter of the way through the novel. When Mme Marti visits the Marmet apartment she notices the presence on a bookshelf of "a skeleton in armour. It was strange to find established in the kind lady's home this Etruscan warrior, wearing on his skull a helmet of greenish bronze and on his disjointed body the rusty plates of his cuirass … Her friends had tried to induce [Mme Marmet] to get rid of it … But the good widow would not sell it. She imagined that if she were to part with the warrior in his helmet of tarnished bronze crowned with a wreath of gilded leaves, she would forfeit that name she bore with such dignity and cease to be known as the widow of Louis Marmet of the Academy of Inscriptions" (69). If this were a Gothic novel, we would later discover that the skeleton is her husband's. The image is a memorial both to Professor Marmet and to the Etruscans whom he failed to resurrect. To his widow's friends, the Etruscans are without interest, irrelevant.

The warrior is not mentioned again, but the Etruscans reappear twice – a visit to the Etruscan museum in Fiesole is mentioned, and Vivian Bell is described as drawing profiles of bearded Etruscans on canvas for a cushion for Mme Marmet. After that the Etruscans return to their half-life in the shadow of the Egyptians, Greeks, and Romans. They are part of the sumptuous artistic and cultural tapestry of references enriching the "habitus" (socially ingrained habits, skills, and dispositions) of the class to which the main characters belong. Though there are many discussions of politics, I don't have the impression that France is counterpointing the corrupt state of the society of the Third Republic to some idealized vision of the past. Scholl is alone in his insistence that modernity represents a decline, and even he is hard pressed to find a preferable past: "Israel's mission is to instruct the nations. It was Israel, who in the Middle Ages, introduced into Europe the wisdom of Asia … The Jews, who educated and civilised Europe, can alone today save her from that mischievous [socialist] propaganda which is preying upon her. But the Jews have failed to do their duty" (223). The professional politicians, aristocrats, and businessmen seem concerned with maintaining power against the true republicans and democrats. The art, history, and languages of the past are mostly decorative relics, reminders of other societies, values, and ways of life. Within the larger historical context, the Etruscan suit of armour suggests warriors and battles more heroic than the recent humiliating French defeat at the hands of the Germans at Sedan.

II

Proust is much less interested in the ancient past than his older friend and one-time mentor, France. One of his more extended references occurs in *Time Regained*. The speaker is Gilberte, the widow of Robert de Saint-Loup, who "maintains that we return always to the methods of the ancients. Well, do you realise that the Mesopotamian campaigns of this war … recall at every moment, almost without alteration, Xenophon's *Anabasis*? And that to get from the Tigris to the Euphrates the English command made use of the *bellam*, the long narrow boat – the gondola of the country – which was already being used by the Chaldeans at the very dawn of history."[9] Like Mme Marmet, Gilberte is a puppet mouthing her husband's questionable opinions. The listeners are too polite to disagree. Her comments give the narrator "a sense of that stagnation of the past through which in certain parts of the world, by virtue of a sort of specific gravity, it is indefinitely immobilized, so that it can be found after centuries exactly as it was."[10] The Etruscans have nothing to do with this sense of historical or temporal stagnation, but they offer a tenuous connection between Proust and France. Proust's earliest reference occurs in a lovely painterly riff in an 1888 letter to Robert Dreyfus describing a beautiful day in Paris before illustrating it with an imagined portrait of "a certain grand courtesan, for example, whose bared nape has just the charming roundness of those amphoras in which the patient Etruscans expressed their whole ideal, their whole consoling dream of grace, the corners of whose mouths are the same as in the naïve virgins of Luini (Bernadino) or Botticelli, which I very much prefer to those of Raphael."[11] It's a lush, slightly showy letter not untypical of its period or Proust's style at the time – he's eighteen, after all, and camping it up a bit – but it leaves some questions hanging: Can a nation express its "whole ideal" in the "charming roundness" of an amphora? Does it make sense to describe the Etruscans as "patient" when no one in the historical record has? (He may have known Ruskin's suggestion of a continuity between Etruscan faces and those of modern Tuscans.) Whatever the answer, my impression is that young Proust is writing to impress, as he will in his early essays and sometimes even in

9   Proust, *Time Regained*, trans. Andreas Mayor, 1030.
10   Ibid., 381.
11   Proust, *Selected Letters*, 10? September 1888, 19.

Jean Santeuil (1895–99), his first attempt at a long novel. One might say that he is writing to find himself while losing himself in a period style. The reference to the Etruscans here is part of an aesthetic vocabulary intended to establish the writer's credentials in the arts. The marginal "Etruscans" were a cultural card one might play to surprise and impress those to whom they were just an exotic name. Some in Paris were doing something similar at century's end with purchases of Japanese prints. Others would play a similar Etruscan card in conversations about style.

Anatole France was a presence in Proust's life and work from his late teens, and they remained close friends until a disagreement over Stendhal's style in 1920. France wrote the introduction to Proust's *Les plaisirs et les jours* (1896), and, as I said, Proust used him when creating the novelist Bergotte in *À la recherche du temps perdu* – many of Bergotte's sentences are borrowed and adapted from France. Jean-Yves Tadié suggests that "France's sentences hover watchfully at the very heart of Proust's work, and are so numerous that they cannot be listed here. In one page of *Du côté de chez Swann* there are enough to provide Bergotte with an anthology."[12] They were long-time friends and, also, Dreyfusards together. The letters indicate that Proust had read *The Red Lily* and that he also saw Gaston de Caillavet's adaptation for the stage in 1899.[13] What I'm wondering is whether Proust remembered Professor Marmet on the half dozen occasions he mentions the Etruscans in *À la recherche du temps perdu*. I can't shake the feeling that Proust's scattering – it is an almost decorative gesture in a nearly imperceptible pattern – of Etruscan references is an inadvertent trace of his reading of *The Red Lily*. However, if they magically disappeared overnight, I doubt anyone would notice. There is, for instance, something of Marmet's overspecialization in Mme de Villeparisis, who knew or knew people who knew Stendhal, Baudelaire, and Hugo. Her conversation reminds the narrator of people who are "mines of learning … when we get them upon *Egyptian paintings or Etruscan inscriptions* [my italics]" but who talk "tediously about modern works."[14] In other words, do they really know anything about the Etruscans? In fact, Mme Villeparisis knows as much or as little about

12 Tadié, *Proust: A Life*, 725.
13 See Proust, *Selected Letters*, to Robert Montesquiou, 18 September 1894 (79) and to Gaston de Caillavet, 2 or 3 March 1899 (193).
14 Proust, *Within a Budding Grove*, Part 2, trans. C.K. Scott Moncrieff, 9.

the Etruscans as the Princess de Parme when she hears the Duchess
of Guermantes use "Etruscan" to describe

"a complete card-room done in the Empire style which came to us from
Quiou-Quiou and is an absolute marvel! There was no room for it here,
though I think it would look better here than it does in his house. It's a thing
of sheer beauty, half Etruscan, half Egyptian."

"Egyptian?" queried the Princess de Parme, to whom the word Etruscan
conveyed little.

"Well, you know, a little of both. Swann told us that, he explained it all to
me, only you know I'm such a dunce. But then, Ma'am, what one has to bear
in mind is that the Egypt of the Empire cabinet-makers has nothing to do with
the historical Egypt, nor their Romans with the Romans nor their Etruria."[15]

This is a good example of Proust's often comic stage management of
the salon's artistic wars. Knowledge and taste are shaped by social
chatter – "Swann told us that, he explained it all to me" – and may or
may not be reliable. Swann's opinions on art, we know, can be trusted.
But this doesn't extend to those who report them.

The card-room returns in *Cities of the Plain* when Marcel walks into it
and describes it as aesthetically as France's narrator describes Mme
Martin's in the first paragraph of *The Red Lily*:

[T]he card, or smoking-room, with its pictorial floor, its tripods, its figures of
gods and animals that gazed at you, the sphinxes stretched out along the
arms of the chairs, and most of all the huge table, of marble or enamelled
mosaic, covered with symbolical signs more or less imitated from *Etruscan
and Egyptian art*, gave me an impression of a magician's cell. And, on a chair
drawn up to the glittering, *augural table*, M. de Charlus, in person, never
touching a card, unconscious of what was going on round about him, incapable of observing that I had entered the room, seemed precisely a magician
applying all the force of his will and reason to drawing a horoscope. Not only
that, but, like the eyes of a Pythian at her tripod, his eyes were starting from
his head ...[16]

15 Proust, *The Guermantes Way*, Part 2, trans. C.K. Scott Moncrieff and Terence
Kilmartin, 541–2.

16 Proust, *Cities of the Plain*, trans. C. Scott Moncrieff, 123. The italics are mine.

Charlus sitting at the "augural table" like "a malign Pythia" recalls the second page of *Jean Santeuil* and Proust's first version of Bergotte, then described secretively as "C.," whom Jean and his friends regard as "the greatest of living writers." He is evoked against the landscape in a scene Hardy might have admired: "he arrived at the lighthouse-keeper's cottage which stood in a place where no one ever went. And there in that truly sublime spot he followed with his eyes the movement of the clouds, observed the flights of birds above the sea, listened to the wind, and scanned the sky like *an Augur of the ancient world* not so much to draw from these sights a presage of the future, as, so far as I could see, to find in them a memory of the past: Many a time did we watch him thus, my friend and I."[17]

Augur and Pythia catch my eye. Marcel, after all, is a social augur. He knows how to read signs. Charlus is a reader of inversion – a Pythia looking inward whose predictions are coloured by personal preference. Etruscan and Egyptian art remind the reader more explicitly, as in Emerson, that the world is made up of "symbolical signs" and signatures in need of deciphering just as much as the novel in which they appear demands interpretation, even if that interpretation will differ with each reader. For us, there is an added signification – we know that the character Marcel is Charlus closeted. His words must be put under more pressure than a century ago.

I will end with a glance back toward Anatole France's posthumous Marmet who, perhaps, lives on in his fellow student of signs, Dr Cottard. Cottard has made a lifelong study of commonplace turns of phrase with which he bores other members of "le petit clan" at Mme Verdurin's dinners: "Cottard, who knew the ins and outs of them all, having himself laboriously acquired them, pointed out to the Marquis, who admitted his stupidity, that they meant nothing: 'Why "stupid as a cabbage"? Do you suppose cabbages are stupider than anything else? You say: "repeat the same thing thirty-six times." Why thirty-six? Why do you say: "sleep like a top"? Why "Thunder of Brest"? Why "play four hundred tricks?" [*les quatre cents coups*].'"[18]

The last word should go to Anatole France. His secretary recorded that in one of their last conversations, after his 1920 parting of the ways

17 Proust, *Jean Santeuil*, trans. Gerard Hopkins, 6. The italics are mine.

18 Proust, *Cities of the Plain*, C. Scott Moncrieff and Terence Kilmartin, 953. For the French, see Proust, *À la recherche du temps perdu*, 923.

with Proust, he summed up the relationship as follows: "I've tried to understand him, and I haven't succeeded. It's not his fault. It's mine."[19] This is thoughtful and typically generous. Equally so and more important than the misunderstanding over Stendhal and style that played out in the September and November issues of *La Revue de Paris* was the homage I mentioned earlier that Proust paid to his one-time master by borrowing so freely from his work for *À la recherche du temps perdu*. France must have known that Proust had learned how to write a new kind of society novel by close readings of *Le lys rouge*. In other words, whatever the state of his current reputation, Anatole France lives on in Proust. Did he notice the thin, connecting Etruscan thread?

19 Tadié, *Proust: A Life*, 725.

1 3

Sigmund Freud's The Interpretation of Dreams *(1900):*
Etruscan Dreams

Rome is still distant; do you know my Roman dreams?[1]

Sigmund Freud

Freud's small but significant interest in the Etruscans is inseparable from his lifelong interest in archaeology, particularly that of Rome, which he compared figuratively to the human mind when he thought of the analyst as an archaeologist. Writing about the "Wolf Man," "the psychoanalyst, like the archaeologist in his excavations, must uncover layer after layer of the patient's psyche, before coming to the deepest, most valuable treasures."[2] The most obvious manifestation of Freud's obsession with the ancient world's treasures was his remarkable collection of antiquities. He bought his first antique figure in December 1896, two months after his father's death, and he bought at least one item a week until his death in 1939. This is a staggering investment of time and money. He collected primarily Egyptian, Assyrian, Greek, Etruscan, and Roman antiquities, though there were also some Asian objects. By 1939 he had over two thousand items, either bought or given to him by friends and patients.[3] He had no illusions about the motivations behind his hobby. He knew

1 Freud, *The Complete Letters of Sigmund Freud to Wilhelm Fliess*, 346–7.

2 Quoted in Simmons, *Freud's Italian Journey*, 140. See also Gay, *Freud:* "Perhaps the most intriguing, certainly among the most poignant of the clues to his mind that Freud scattered through *The Interpretation of Dreams* is the theme of Rome, glittering in the distance as supreme prize and incomprehensible menace" (132). It is germane to this book's argument that Rome's deepest strata – think of them as its unconscious – are Etruscan, and that the Romans absorbed Etruscan culture and its DNA.

3 Burke, *The Sphinx on the Table*, 159. Burke puts the number at around 2,500.

that collecting of any kind was inseparable, at least in psychoanalytic theory, from early erotic pleasures. He also must have understood that a room filled with ancient objects would leave his patients with the impression of having entered a special precinct, even a kind of *sanctum*, with a timeless aura sheltering them from the world outside 19 Bergstrasse as they approached a secular priest (or lucumo). How aware was he that the statues represented his self-chosen gods and not the deity of his people, his wife, and his father? He knew that Exodus XX forbids sculptured images because of their association with polytheism and idolatry. Was he disappointed when a patient failed to bring a figure?

We are fortunate that before the Freud family left Vienna for London on 4 June 1938, a professional photographer named Edmund Engelman took photographs of the apartment as well as of Freud, his wife Martha, and his daughter Anna. In the memoir of the event Engelman describes the shoot in detail and pauses to comment on Freud's collection.

I had been aware that Freud was a collector of ancient art, for my closest friend was the son of a well-known antique dealer in Vienna. Once a week, Freud had made the rounds of the city's dealers. They, in turn, would know what he was looking for and saved items for him. Nevertheless, I was amazed by the unbelievable number of art objects. There was nothing of the popular Austrian Baroque or Biedermeier art; there were only antiques of great age – Roman, Egyptian, Assyrian, and Etruscan. Wherever one looked, there was a glimpse into the past. The view from Freud's chair, looking up at the elongated figures on the bookcase, was particularly dramatic … Torn by my excitement and eagerness to look closely at every piece of art and every memento, I had to pull myself together to live up to the purpose of my visit.[4]

Engelman also noted many books on archaeology. When the American writer Hilda Doolittle (H.D.) was analyzed by Freud in 1933 she was equally impressed by the collection and felt that "He is at home here. He is part and parcel of these treasures."[5] The penultimate photo is of Freud – very tired, very old, and justifiably very worried – looking down at the antiquities on his desk. The place of honour was usually occupied by a small 10.5-centimetre bronze statue of Athena, goddess of war,

---

4 Engelman, quoted in Scholz-Strasser, *Vienna IX, Bergstrasse 19*, 97.
5 Hilda Doolittle [H.D.], *Tribute to Freud*, 97.

patron of the arts, and personification of wisdom. It is a Roman copy of a Greek bronze. Freud told Doolittle in 1933, "She is perfect, only she has lost her spear."[6]

Freud owned a handful of Etruscan artifacts but his interest in the Etruscans was marginal, a fact that makes their appearance in three dreams, including a particularly rich one, surprising but also very suggestive, since the Etruscan level of Rome is deeper and earlier than that of Latin Rome. Keeping in mind Freud's analogy of the analyst as archaeologist, an Etruscan-themed dream promises to be more profound, in both senses of the word. The most prominent of the Etruscan figures, because it stood on his desk and can be seen in Max Pollak's 1914 etching, is an Etruscan warrior, a bronze dated circa 500–450 BCE and 20.3 centimetres in height.[7] "He wears a helmet with a long crest, its details finely incised, and with upturned cheekpieces that reveal his rather crude features – large nose and eyes, small mouth, firm chin. His short cuirass is incised with decorative patterns; below is the skirt of his tunic, too short to cover his genitals."[8] The Freud Museum in London has an Etruscan bronze mirror incised on the back with "two naked women bathing at a basin on a plinth. One figure is standing with right hand on hip and left hand on basin. The other is in the act of discarding her mantle. The scene is framed around the edge of the disc with decoration of ivy (?) leaves, topped by stylised palmette design. The palmette design is repeated on the handle flange on the front. It is dated c. 350–250."[9] The naked woman is Turan (the Etruscan Aphrodite). At one point Freud had a drawerful of Etruscan mirrors. Also on his desk was a small Etruscan third-century two-faced bronze polychrome balsamarium; one side shows the face of a satyr, the other of a maenad, both votaries of Dionysus. One face looked toward Freud, the other across the room. The 8.25-centimetre container for perfumes may have appealed to Freud because of his

---

6 Quoted in Scholz-Strasse in *Vienna IX, Bergstrasse 19*, 7.

7 He is described as Umbrian or Etruscan, but I have adopted him for the sake of neatness. A nineteenth-century forgery was owned by Richard Payne Knight (1751–1824), the great English collector whom Sir William Hamilton's associate, Pierre-François Hugues d'Hancarville, had instructed in the value of coins as history and art.

8 Gamwell and Wells, *Sigmund Freud and Art*, 106.

9 Description of the item in the collection of the Freud Museum (London, England), https://freud.org.uk/2018/07/23/self-reflection-mirrors-in-sigmund-freuds-collection/.

interest in the various dualisms that ran through his thought: Eros/
Thanatos, human bisexuality, the pleasure principle and the reality
principle, reversal or the turning of a thing into its opposite in dream
work, the antithetical meanings of primitive words, and so on.

Freud often gave pieces away. An early acquisition that disappeared
in this way is an Etruscan funerary urn of which we would have no record
had it not found its way into a dream Freud analyzed in *The Interpretation
of Dreams* to illustrate the wish-fulfillment element. He labels this a
"comfort dream."

Recently, the same dream [about slaking one's thirst] underwent slight
modification. This time I felt thirsty before falling asleep, and I drank the
whole glass of water that stood on the little cupboard by my bed. Some
hours later, during the night, I had a fresh attack of thirst – with awkward
results. To obtain water I should have had to get out of bed and go and
fetch the glass that stood on my wife's bedside table. So I dreamed (appropriately enough) that my wife was giving me a drink from a particular vessel;
this was an Etruscan cinerary urn that I had brought back from a trip to
Italy and since given away. However, the water in it tasted so salty (obviously
from the ashes) that I had to wake up. Notice how conveniently a dream
manages to arrange things; wish-fulfilment being its sole purpose, it can be
totally selfish.[10]

This is among the simplest dreams of the forty-six in the volume, but
Freud's interpretation leaves me wondering whether he goes far enough
in his interrogation. Should he have paused longer over the salt taste
of the water? It's unlikely that the urn he owned still held the original
ashes. And if it is the dreamer who provides the ashes of a cremated
body, whose ashes are they, and why does he do so? Can we avoid the
suggestion that the dream uses thirst, the loss of an Etruscan funerary
urn, and the taste of ashes to bring Freud's recently dead father back
to life? If Freud had a patient on the sofa, wouldn't he have lingered
more on the meaning of "thirst" (*durst* in German), eating a father's
ashes (*asche*), and the taste of ashes in one's mouth? I'm troubled here
and in similar instances throughout by the gap between his interpretation and his comment that "a dream might be described as *a substitute*

10 Freud, *Interpreting Dreams*, 137–8.

for an infantile scene modified by being transferred on to a recent experience. The infantile scene is unable to bring about its own revival and must be content returning as a dream" (Freud's italics).[11]

Freud also regularly swerves away from dream details related in some way to his marriage. His analysis of the second Roman dream – "A View of Rome in the Mist" – does nothing with the names of two Austrian towns associated with his life: Lübeck, the site of his honeymoon, and Gleichenberg, where Freud visited his sister-in-law's dying fiancé. As Laurence Simmons points out, "These family allusions may in fact point to the extra content that Freud says he was not prepared to detail."[12] Fair enough, but without these kinds of details and without any reference to "infantile material," the interpretation seems anodyne and the dream not particularly interesting. A full interpretation of Freud's self-interpreted dreams is of course impossible: we have no access to the dreamer, and his interpretation distorts our view of the dream work by selecting data he considers relevant. We are only given information he has chosen to make available. Can any dreamer be trusted to interpret his or her dreams ruthlessly, especially in print? Even with the best intentions, can a dreamer succeed in overcoming his or her own resistance when confronted with particularly troubling suggestions and revelations? Having said that, I doubt that few of us would push our dream interpretations to the limit in front of strangers.

Etruscan details occur in two other dreams, both from May 1898: the dream of "The Castle by the Sea" also known as the "Breakfast-Ship" dream, and the bizarre or macabre dream of "Dissecting my Own Pelvis" or the "Self-Dissection." Like the dream of the funerary urn they have their origins in his journeys to Italy. "Breakfast-Ship" is important because it shows Freud overcoming his reluctance to make his self-analysis public. "Dissecting my Own Pelvis" includes a memory of seeing two skeletons lying on stone beds in a tomb in the Orvieto Etruscan necropolis and a visit to the Etruscan Museum. It's possible that immersion in Etruscan artifacts reminded Freud of the Etruscan obsession with interpreting natural signs. The dream needs to be read in full.

11 Quoted in Simmons, *Freud's Italian Journey*, 126.
12 Quoted in ibid., 135.

Old Brücke must have set me some problem; STRANGELY ENOUGH *this has to do with dissecting my own underpinnings, my pelvis and legs, which I see before me in the dissecting room but without being aware of missing them on my body and without any feeling of horror. Louise N. is standing beside me, working with me. The pelvic girdle has been emptied of its contents, revealing now the view from above, now the view from below, all muddled up. There are thick, flesh-coloured lumps visible (which even in the dream remind me of piles). It was also necessary to pick something out with great care, something that lay over it and looked like tinfoil. Then I was once again in possession of my legs and making an excursion through the city, though (because of weariness) in a carriage. To my astonishment the carriage drove in through a house-door, which opened to allow it to pass along a passage that, having turned a corner, eventually carried on further into the open air. Eventually, I was hiking with an Alpine guide (who carried my things) through a shifting landscape. On one stretch (out of consideration for my weary legs) he carried me. The ground was swampy; we circled it; there were people sitting on the ground, a girl among them, like Red Indians or gypsies. Previously, I had made progress over the slippery ground myself, constantly amazed that, after the dissection, I am able to do this so well. At length we came to a small wooden hut that terminated in an open window. There the guide set me down and laid two planks, which stood there ready, on the windowsill in such a way as to bridge the abyss that needed to be negotiated from the window. I now felt really anxious about my legs. Instead of the anticipated crossing, however, I saw two grown men, lying on wooden benches against the wall of the hut and two children, as it were, sleeping beside them. As if not the planks but the children were to make the crossing possible. I wake up with mental fright.*[13]

Ernst Brücke was Freud's much-admired professor in physiology. He was a positivist who insisted that only common physical-chemical forces "are active in the organism."[14] The unidentified "Louise N." may be Minna Bernays, Freud's sister-in-law, who worked closely with him at this time. Several elements are at play in the dream: Freud's lengthy self-analysis is behind the self-dissection and the dangerous journey through unknown territory; the room that is simultaneously tomb and coffin recalls his father's death even as it marks Freud's rebirth as the father of psychoanalysis; Freud's explanation that some of the imagery is from Rider Haggard's *She* introduces an implicit troubling female image that is simultaneously the immortal mother

13 Freud, *Interpreting Dreams*, 466ff.
14 Gay, *Freud*, 34.

of her people (an echo of Bachofen's *Mutterrecht*) and a powerfully erotic and threatening figure who leaves the suggestion that the self-dissection is also a castration: a man un-manned by his father's death. The Etruscans aren't mentioned explicitly in the dream, but they might be represented by the "Red Indians," and they seem to appear when Freud explains that he had "been in a tomb, but it was an Etruscan tomb near Orvieto, one that had been emptied of its contents, a narrow chamber with two stone benches along the walls on which the skeletons of two adults had been laid. That is precisely how the interior of the hut in the dream looks, except that the stone has been replaced by wood. The dream seems to be saying, 'If you have to be in the tomb already, let it be the Etruscan tomb, and with this substitution it turns the saddest expectation into a highly desirable one.'" Is the image of the two men side by side Freud's wish to have died with his father, or a reminder that like him he too will die, or both? There must be more here than the preference for a stone tomb over a wooden coffin. Is Freud contrasting the Etruscan burial (his own, so to speak) with his father's Jewish one? I wonder whether at some level Freud remembered a scene in a cave in *She* where the travellers rest and drink "a fermented fluid, of by no means unpleasant taste, though apt to turn the stomach" from two-handled amphorae that "as in the case of Etruscan amphorae … were placed there for the spiritual use of the deceased."[15] Is there a suggestion of a death wish coupled with a fear of death – not an unusual pairing? Are the two unexpected boys lying side by side with the two men reminders of the presence of infantile sexual material?

Freud was too intelligent not to understand that there is no such thing as a completely explicated dream. In a remarkable passage near the end of *The Interpretation of Dreams* he reminds us that:

In the best-interpreted dreams, one often needs to leave a particular passage obscure, having become aware, during the work of interpretation, that a knot of dream-thoughts rises there that refuses to unravel but in fact made no further contribution to the dream-content. This then is the hub of the dream, the place where it squats on the unacknowledged. Most of the dream-thoughts that one comes across must of course remain unresolved and seep

15 Haggard, *She*, 97.

away in all directions into the web-like entanglement of the world of our thoughts. From a spot on this intricate web that is denser than the rest, the dream-wish then arises like a fungus from its mycelium.[16]

Simmons reads this as a Prospero moment: "Freud's final gesture in closing his volume should be read as an act of resistance to his own theoretical fictions and an acknowledgement of the figurative nature of his own explanations."[17] I would add that we might also see it as a great humanist's realistic acknowledgment of the inevitable limitations of his ambitious theory of interpretation: the mind will ultimately elude our efforts to understand it fully. It is worth comparing Freud's humility in the face of the limits inherent in our analyses of human nature with Jean-Paul Sartre's troubling self-confidence in describing his multi-volume biography of Flaubert: "The most important project in the *Flaubert* is to show that fundamentally everything can be communicated, that without being God, but simply as a man like any other, one can manage to understand another man perfectly, if one has access to all the necessary elements. I can deal with Flaubert, I know him; and that is my goal, to prove that every man is perfectly knowable as long as one uses the appropriate method and as long as the necessary documents are available." I can only account for Sartre's absurd self-confidence here by thinking that it is a rhetorical shield to distract the reader from the fallibility of his approach.[18] The challenges to his picture of Flaubert were many and the multi-volume biography remained unfinished. We have learned much about dream interpretation since the publication

---

16 Freud, *Interpreting Dreams*, 540. The Strachey translation is slightly different: "There is often a passage in even the most thoroughly interpreted dream which has to be left obscure; this is because we become aware during the work of interpretation that at that point there is a tangle of dream-thoughts which cannot be unravelled and which moreover adds nothing to our knowledge of the content of the dream. This is the dream's navel, the spot where it reaches down into the unknown. The dream-thoughts to which we are led by interpretation, cannot, from the nature of things have any definite endings; they are bound to branch out in every direction into the intricate network of our world of thought. It is at some point where this meshwork is particularly close that the dream-wish grows up, like a mushroom out of its mycelium." Freud, *The Interpretation of Dreams*, 561.

17 Simmons, *Freud's Italian Journey*, 134.

18 Sartre, "On *The Idiot of the Family*," *Life / Situations*, 123.

of Freud's great book, but his close readings and his musings about limits still repay attention.

Etruscan antiquities remained in Freud's collection throughout his life. But he doesn't mention them in his work after May 1898. Today they can be seen in London's Sigmund Freud Museum.

PART FOUR

The Etruscans
after Lawrence

Aldous Huxley's Etruscan Decade:
Those Barren Leaves (*1925*)
and *"After the Fireworks"* (*1930*),
with a Glance at Roger Fry

... wandering through the ripening wheat and popping down into
the rock-hewn chambers with their still gay paintings of hunting,
wrestling, dancing, even copulation and sodomy.

Aldous Huxley, in a letter to his son Matthew[1]

Though Lawrence visited the Etruscan places a few years later than
Huxley, I call this section "The Etruscans after Lawrence" because it was
Etruscan Places rather than Huxley's fiction of the 1920s that drew
attention to the Etruscans and which continued to be a magnet for
debate about their "mystery." It is also no exaggeration to say that,
for Huxley, Lawrence was a contemporary Etruscan. Both men were
surprised by their unlikely friendship. On the one side was the short
miner's son, a controversial novelist with a teaching degree from
Nottingham University; on the other, the tall, brilliant Oxonian with
roots in the English intellectual elite (the Huxleys were related to the
Arnolds and Darwins) and friends in Bloomsbury. But they had far more
in common as men, writers, and thinkers than was first apparent: both
were dedicated travellers, open to new cultures and unexpected experiences; each had to deal with a serious physical debility (Huxley blindness,
Lawrence tuberculosis); Huxley satirized the same society Lawrence
rejected, and each was looking for an alternative; and both loved Italy
and the Etruscans, spent long periods there, and wrote about them

---

1 Quoted in Bedford, *Aldous Huxley*, 553.

with a passion. The main hurdle they had to overcome to friendship was Lawrence's rejection of science, no matter how patiently Huxley approached scientific topics. Fortunately for the friendship Huxley recognized qualities in Lawrence – his passion, belief in spontaneity, and spirituality – that he knew he lacked but desired. He recognized that in some sense being with Lawrence completed him. It is no exaggeration to say that he saw the Etruscans through Lawrentian eyes. He sensed that Lawrence's vision of the self offered something he needed to achieve, what his fiction calls a complete self in which intuition, emotion, and reason function harmoniously. He was in sympathy with Lawrence's views and his faith in the Etruscans because his own religion was based on a post-Christian belief "in the profound and unfathomable mystery of life … which has a sort of divine quality about it."[2] The search for that "divine quality" and a life philosophy expressive of it would take him over four decades, from Lawrence and the Etruscans to Buddhism, mysticism, and in his later years to LSD and mescaline. Over the same period, he evolved from a satirist to a novelist of ideas and one of our first intellectual gurus.

The Etruscans first appear in Huxley's fiction in his Italian novel, *Those Barren Leaves* (1925), written during a year-long sojourn near Florence. The book is an entertaining Huxleyan mixture of travel writing, social comedy, romance, satire, and social ideas. The characters, but for the rogue Mr Cardan, don't quite come to life, but the book has an engaging nervous intellectual energy, an elastic plot, wit, and inventiveness. As in Anatole France's *The Red Lily*, the Etruscan material isn't essential to the story or the characterization but it provides some very exotic local colour and cultural and historical interest, not to mention humour at the expense of amateur "Etruscology" that might owe something to France's novel. As mentioned earlier, Huxley had read and admired France at Oxford.

The pages devoted to the Etruscans focus on a visit to the painted underground tombs at the Monterozzi necropolis near Tarquinia. The visit begins with a comical discussion between the freeloader Cardan and the young writer Chelifer about the Etruscan language. Cardan, pretending to some expertise, absurdly insists that

2 Ibid., 727.

"It's a great language ... It's the great dead language of the future."[3]
He even playfully envisions coming generations writing poetry and
history in it. The only solid fact he knows about the language is that
Fufluns is the Etruscan name for Dionysus. Having exhausted their
opinions, the party turns to the paintings in two tombs. The first
seems to draw visual details from the following: Tomb of Hunting
and Fishing, Tomb of the Augurs, Tomb of the Bulls, and Tomb of
the Anina. The description of the second tomb and the tourists'
responses are worth quoting at some length, not least because of
Huxley's ekphrastic intent in "painting" the paintings in words:

On one wall they were horse-racing and wrestling, hieratically, all in profile.
A goddess – or perhaps it was merely the Lady Mayoress of the city – wearing
that high bonnet-shaped coiffure which the Roman matrons were afterwards
to borrow from their neighbours, was distributing the prizes. On the other
walls they were feasting. The red-brown men, the white-skinned ladies
reclined along their couches. A musician stood by, playing on his double
flute, and a female dancer, dressed in what looked rather like a Persian
costume, was dancing a shawl dance for the diversion of the diners.

"They seem to have had simple tastes," said Mr. Cardan. "There's nothing
very sophisticated or *fin de siècle* here – no bull-baiting by naked female
acrobats, as at Cnossos; no gladiatorial fights, no wholesale butchering of
animals, no boxing matches with brass knuckle-dusters, as in the Roman
arena. A nice school-boyish sort of people it looks like to me. Not quite civilized enough to be *exigeant* about their pleasures." (310)

The athletes are from the Tomb of the Olympic Games, while the "Lady
Mayoress" and the "female dancer" are from the Tomb of the Jugglers,
but it is difficult to be certain. We should keep in mind that this was
written three years before Lawrence's *Etruscan Places*. If Huxley is echo-
ing Lawrence, it is his novels and his conversation, not *Etruscan Places*.

Cardan and Chelifer's condescending attitudes reflect the judgment
of the era, which can yet be heard in Roger Fry's last, still very rewarding
lectures at Cambridge from 1934. Fry is not blind to certain distinctive
qualities in Etruscan art setting it apart from the Greek and Roman. He
notes, for instance, "a real feeling for the significance of gesture, a sense
of movement and life, of something actually going on [in the tomb
paintings], which is altogether wanting in the frozen perfection of the

---

3 Huxley, *Those Barren Leaves*, 304. All references will be to this edition.

best Greek vases." He also allows that they had "certain instinctive apti-
tudes which the Greeks either lacked or which were suppressed by their
passion for geometric harmony." And his analysis of the Apollo of Veii
(see figure 14.1) shows him waffling between the formalist principles
which made him famous and his instinctive recognition of something
original and important in the statue that those principles can't account
for, and that impressed Huxley in "After the Fireworks."

This strange and ungracious conception of Apollo for instance, in which, as
you see, everything is borrowed from archaic Greek originals, has none the
less a certain ungainly energy and vitality. There is no evidence of that preoccupation with a balanced and perfectly understood pose, still less with the
Greek notion of a noble serenity and calm – Apollo trudges along exactly as
the artist had seen one of his contemporaries. And in his head there is the
same aggressive and crude vehemence of accent, which makes the archaic
smile a grim caricature. But what sensibility the artist possessed has not been
polished and obliterated, as it was in most Greek work, where you will look
in vain for any such expressive accents of modelling as you find here. Clearly
if we judge of art by the kind of life which it suggests to us, by its moral elevation or nobility of sentiment, all Etruscan art must be condemned; but
we are not concerned with such high matters in the present enquiry and we
have to note the evidences of vitality and sensibility which transpire even
through the crudities of Etruscan works.[4]

There are few pages in Fry's criticism that I like as much as these
slightly indecisive and wrong-headed remarks on the Etruscans. They
remind me of critics who begin by dismissing Lawrence and end by
granting that he has "life" and "genius." Fry recognizes that Etruscan
art lacks most of the qualities he has valued for several decades. And
yet when looking at the Apollo of Veii – among my favourite sculptures
(and he doesn't "trudge") – he knows as a painter and critic that it
possesses "energy and vitality" and therefore can't be ignored. His training and critical principles keep pulling him away ("*a certain ungainly
energy and vitality*") but even as he registers his qualifications he under-
cuts himself ("but we are not concerned with such high matters"). The
Apollo of Veii throws Fry off balance as much as it does Miles Fanning

4 Fry, *Last Lectures*, 210–11.

14.1 Apollo of Veii, late sixth century BCE.

in Huxley's novella "After the Fireworks," when he first sees it after the war ("the most beautiful statue in the world" [152]), and as, I suspect, it continues to do to a surprising number of visitors to the Villa Giulia, just as it did to me over four decades ago. Fry has reservations about it, but his instincts override them and tell him to keep looking. He probably felt the same way when he first saw a work of Cubism. This is one of those moments in criticism where much of the pleasure lies in seeing a first-rate critic struggling between his fixed opinions and the challenge of a new aesthetic experience.

Cardan and Chelifer do not have the authority of Bloomsbury behind their attempts to place the Etruscans as not quite civilized or perhaps not even "a nice school-boyish sort of people." Cardan's suggestion that they weren't "*exigeant* about their pleasures" leaves the impression that if only they had spoken Italian they might have been socially acceptable at the English table. The two men might have revised their opinions had they noticed the notorious scenes of copulation in the Tomb of the Bulls. That they were in the tomb is suggested by the following sentence: "Over the low, narrow door that led from the tomb into the ante-chamber there knelt a benevolent white bull" (306). Though Cardan comments that "You see them … hunting, drinking, playing, making love," he doesn't remark on the lovers. Or perhaps, and this is more likely, Huxley just didn't want to face his publisher's objections to a description that would certainly be censored.

The visit to the tombs is an interlude without any obvious influence on the lives of the visitors. No one walks away thinking they must change their life. Chelifer's response is representative. He prefers the Etruscans to the ancient Romans, but he stops there: "There's a freshness, as you say, Mr. Cardan, a certain jolly schoolboyishness about all the fun they represent. But I have no doubt, of course, that the impression is entirely fallacious. Their art has a certain archaic charm; but the artists were probably quite as sophisticated and quite as repulsive as their Roman successors." Cardan's only demurral is half-serious: "you forget that they called Bacchus Fufluns. Give them at least the credit that is due to them" (312). A few pages later the novel ends with Calamy, a minor character in search of life's meaning, watching the sunset from a cottage to which he has retreated to live alone and meditate for three months to understand himself. The other characters have dispersed from the house they lodged in. Nothing has changed except that Mrs Aldwinkle, their hostess, has died.

Huxley's most extensive fictional use of the Etruscans occurs in one of his most accomplished works, the novella "After the Fireworks," published in the volume *Brief Candles* in 1930. He explains in a letter to Floyd Starkey that the story is "an elaboration and emendation of an incident recorded in the letters of Chateaubriand. When he was sixty, a very young girl at a watering place came and threw herself at his head."[5] Huxley changes this into the story of Miles Fanning, a successful fifty-year-old English novelist, who responds to a fan letter from a young American woman named Pamela Tarn. The novella might have been titled "A Modern Pamela." They happen to meet, in a well-handled coincidence, in Rome. A May–October friendship in which Fanning completes her Italian education – Etruscans included – results in a credible love affair. However, within a few months the girl's love attenuates to an impatient affection, while the older man finds himself unexpectedly enamoured. The story ends with the disenchanted Pamela feeling trapped and sitting down to write a letter to Guy, a young English admirer: "'Dear Guy,' she began, 'I wonder if you're back in Rome yet'" (205). *La commedia è finita.*

Fanning is as conventional in life as in his writing. At best, he might be said to be unconventional in a conventional way. He fancies himself a bon vivant, a sensualist, a man open to all aspects of life. A corner of his self-image is perhaps suggested by the fact that he has written a book about Blake, a name which is almost code for Lawrence in Huxley's fiction. His charm, however, is undeniable. Articulate and knowledgeable, he is an ideal guide to Rome and all things Italian. He is also intelligent enough to understand that he is overly susceptible to women's charms, and that Pamela is much younger than he is. The plot is complicated by the fact that among his many lovers was Clare Tarn, Pamela's mother, who came to Italy hoping to have a love affair with a Sicilian peasant or a "gamekeeper … or a young farmer" (133). I take the "gamekeeper" as a nod in the direction of *Lady Chatterley's Lover*, the final third of which Huxley's wife Maria had typed for Lawrence in 1928. A self-centred man with a gift for storytelling, Fanning can't be Blake (or Lawrence) but he understands what differentiates them from other people. As part of Pamela's education, he takes her to Villa Giulia. For him, its showpiece is the sixth-century

5 Quoted in Bedford, *Aldous Huxley*, 240.

smiling Apollo of Veii about which he delivers a lengthy, impassioned lecture concerning its history and meaning. Put simply, the smile stands for an entire way of being fully open to life, as does the pure laughter of Homer's gods, untroubled and undistracted by memories or fears of human distress. In other words, it is laughter unshadowed by the possibility of suffering and death.

Fanning offers a version of T.S. Eliot's "dissociation of sensibility," but he places it not in the early seventeenth century but, like Nietzsche, Lawrence, and Heidegger, before Socrates and Plato: "'Homer lived before the split; life hadn't been broken when he wrote. They're complete, his men and women, complete and real; for he leaves nothing out, he shirks no issue even though there is no tragedy. He knows all about it – *all*.' He laid his hand again on the statue. 'And this god's his portrait. He's Homer, but with the Etruscan smile. Homer smiling at the sad, mysterious, beautiful absurdity of the world. The Greeks didn't see that divine absurdity as clearly as the Etruscans.'" According to Fanning, the Greeks "'followed Plato and Euripides. And Plato and Euripides handed them over to the Stoics and the Neo-Platonists. And these in turn handed humanity over to the Christians. And the Christians have handed us over to Henry Ford and the machines. So here we are'" (155–6). To his credit, Fanning understands that for him Apollo's smile is at best an enigmatic reminder of possibilities no longer available. He knows what the statue represents but he can't act on that knowledge "because the division, the splitness, has been worked right into my bones." One can't will belief in a past faith. When he admits having followed "after strange gods" – "mystical experiences and ecstasies and private universes" – his commitment to the Apollo of Veii begins to seem less like a life-changing revelation and more like an episode in a search for the meaning of life. When Pamela asks him whether he believes in God: he answers that "he believed in a great many gods, it depended on what he was doing, or being, or feeling at the moment. He said he believed in Apollo when he was working, and in Bacchus when he was drinking, and in Buddha when he felt depressed, and in Venus when he was making love, and in the Devil when he was afraid or angry, and in the Categorical Imperative when he had to do his duty" (169). There's a world of difference between this casual catalogue of beliefs adopted and shed – uncomfortably close to Huxley's life – and Lawrence's insistence on a "religion of life" which was a reality for the Etruscans and, in a different form, still a possibility in his time.

Despite Fanning's several attempts to keep the relationship platonic, Venus Anadyomene (as he calls her) triumphs, at least for a few months. Eventually the writer's illness and the young woman's boredom provide an inevitable answer to her earlier question, "why shouldn't it be fireworks all the time?" (174). The ending is predictable and comic: after having learned much about Rome and the Etruscans and even more about love, Pamela leaves Miles, as he knew she would. As for the novella's treatment of the Etruscans, Fanning's strong rhetorical and emotional response to the way of life he sees embodied in the Apollo of Veii survives his failure to live up to it. It stands above the world, untouched and untouchable. As in *Those Barren Leaves* the Etruscan smile suggests a way of being in the world preferable to modernity, even if its full significance eludes our understanding or is unrealizable in the present.

D.H. Lawrence's Etruscan Places (1932): The Invention of the Etruscans for the Twentieth Century and Margaret Drabble's Lawrentian The Dark Flood Rises (2016)

Whoever writes the as yet unwritten history of Etruscan art will
have to reckon with [Lawrence's] notations which, quite apart from
the brilliant play of paradox, have a much greater critical relevance,
and are much more richly stimulating, than many a weighty tome
brought out by distinguished archeologists.

Massimo Pallottino[1]

I

Pallottino's reference to Lawrence is a useful reminder that no other figure outside the profession is referred to as often in the literature about the Etruscans as he is. If we look more widely, there is no doubt that no writer has done more to create the century's dominant image of the Etruscans as a life-affirming people with a way of life far preferable not only to that of the conquest-obsessed Romans but to our own. He subsumed them within a primitivistic strain in his thought apparent as early as *Women in Love*, published in 1920 but written during the First World War. Rejecting the society based on capitalism, imperialism, and Christianity that made the war inevitable, Lawrence turned to a view of the self that emphasized elemental human needs, a pagan view of spiritual life, and a spontaneous instinctual life on the basis of which one might build an organic society without alienation or money-based values and classes. Had he been paying attention to contemporary

1 Pallottino, "In Search of Etruria," 27.

anthropology he might have noticed that Bronisław Malinowski found a roughly similar society among the Trobriand Islanders about whom he wrote, from a similarly pluralistic point of view, *Argonauts of the Western Pacific* (1922). The anthropologist describes them as a joyously sociable people with a refined poetic sensibility. If the Etruscans were a better match for Lawrence's needs it was precisely because they could no longer be studied as closely as Malinowski's islanders. Whatever information was lacking, Lawrence could supply with his imagination, like Niebuhr and Bachofen.

Lawrence first became aware of the Etruscans in September 1920 while staying in Fiesole, where he noticed the Etruscan walls nearby. His first published reference is in the poem "Cypresses," which appeared in *The Adelphi* (October 1923). But it wasn't until 1927, three years before his death, that he finally visited the heart of ancient Etruria. The epochal if astonishingly short journey to Etruscan places (5–11 April 1927) is the culmination of his search for a people with "a conception of the universe and man's place in the universe which made men live to the depth of their capacity."[2] I sometimes think of *Etruscan Places* as a recasting of his Mexican novel *The Plumed Serpent* (1926), but set in a distant almost prehistoric past. Each book is an episode in the period's fascination with primitivism and prelapsarian modes of being, a companion to Picasso's *Les Demoiselles d'Avignon* (1907), France's *Penguin Island* (1908), Freud's *Totem and Taboo* (1913), Igor Stravinsky's *Le Sacre du Printemps* (1913), and Malinowski's *Argonauts of the Western Pacific* (1922) and *Sex and Repression in Savage Society* (1927). Stravinsky had his own Etruscan moment in his opera *Oedipus Rex* in the same year Lawrence was touring Etruria: the work used Etruscan masks designed by Jean Cocteau.

Lawrence's health declined noticeably after the brief trip. The change in his condition may underlie his increasing concern with sensitivity, nature, reciprocity, and tenderness in relationships, and a turning away from the emphasis on power, violence, and political leadership that had marked his previous three novels. His fragile health during this period was much closer to that of Rupert Birkin during his severe illness in *Women and Love* (1920) than to Don Ramon's ostentatious health in *The*

2 Lawrence, *Sketches of Etruscan Places*, 56. All quotations, unless otherwise indicated, will be from *Sketches of Etruscan Places*, which is the text included in the *Cambridge Edition of the Letters and Works of D.H. Lawrence*. It was Lawrence's working title.

Plumed Serpent. Lawrence wrote to Witter Bynner that he had decided that "the hero is obsolete, and the leader of men is a back number. At the back of the hero is the militant ideal: and the militant ideal, or the ideal militant, seems to me also a cold egg ... And the new relationship will be some sort of tenderness, sensitive, between men and men and men and women, and not the one up one down, lead on I follow, *ich dien* [I serve] sort of business."[3]

   The Plumed Serpent, a historical romance about a violent revolution in modern Mexico, gives way to *Etruscan Places*, a pastoral of ancient Etruria, which avoids armies, politics, and wars. Both societies are hierarchical, with the difference that the Etruscan one seems natural and organic and is led by a spiritual leader. If Lawrence has a "late" period as an artist, it begins with the writing of the Etruscan sketches and continues with *The Escaped Cock*, its revised version *The Man Who Died*, the three versions of *Lady Chatterley's Lover*, the three volumes of poems published in 1929, and *Apocalypse*, finished in January 1930, two months before his death. The writing is more serene, less willed, less dogmatic, and shows a writer generally at peace with himself and the world. Having struggled and failed with political ideology, Lawrence finds shelter in his vision of the lost Etruscan world which gave him what he had wanted since the time during the war when he dreamed of setting up a commune on Frederick Delius's estate in Florida. He sums up the Etruscan way of life as follows: "To the Etruscan, all was alive: the whole universe lived: and the business of man was himself to live amid it all. He had to draw life into himself, out of the wandering huge vitalities of the world. The cosmos was alive, like a vast creature. The whole thing breathed and stirred ... The whole thing was alive, and had a great soul, or anima: and in spite of one great soul, there were myriad roving, lesser souls; every man, every creature and tree and lake and mountain and stream was animate, had its own peculiar consciousness. And has it today" (56–7). Interesting here is the lack of interest in language, as if thought for the Etruscans was pre-linguistic or, as in Heidegger, at a stage where ideas and things were identical with the words used to express them. No one could have predicted when Lawrence died on 2 March 1930 that his posthumously published

---

3 Lawrence, to Witter Bynner, 13 March 1928, *The Letters of D. H. Lawrence*, 6:321.

unfinished manuscript, tentatively titled "Sketches of Etruscan Places," would become over the next half century the most popular book about the Etruscans. It is referred to widely by travellers, general readers interested in the ancient world, and even Etruscan scholars. The seven sketches are based on a handful of books and a short trek through Etruscan country from Rome to Cerveteri, Tarquinia, Vulci, and Volterra. After completing the surviving sketches, Lawrence wrote his agent Martin Secker that he was planning a further series on Florence, Fiesole, Corneto (Tarquinia), Arezzo, Chiusi, Orvieto, and Perugia. As late as the autumn of 1928 he thought there was a possibility of returning with Huxley and his wife Maria, to whom he felt particularly close.[4] Tuberculosis made further travel impossible.

With a title chosen by his publisher, the book was published in the autumn of 1932. It was reviewed widely, as one would expect with a writer as well known and, with the banning of his paintings and *Lady Chatterley's Lover*, as controversial as Lawrence. The reviewers in the *New Statesman and Nation* and *The Bookman* noted that the book was unscholarly but praised Lawrence as "a born writer" whose imaginative style made the subject vivid and memorable. The *Times Literary Supplement* gave the book to a professional archaeologist who noted its slight scholarship but appreciated Lawrence's sketches for their ability to bring to life "memories of the desolate, primitive grandeur of the earth where life and all it meant to a great race of men are found only in its tombs."[5] Huxley and Max Plowman, both firmly in Lawrence's camp, praised the book almost without reservation. But perhaps the most perceptive comment was made a few years later by George Orwell who suggested that, considering how little was known about the Etruscans, a contemporary could make them a symbol of almost anything: "But what he is demanding is a movement away from our mechanized civilization, which is not going to happen, and which he knows is not going to happen. Therefore his exasperation with the present turns once more into idealization of the past, this time a safely mythical past, the Bronze Age. When Lawrence prefers the Etruscans (*his* Etruscans) to ourselves it is difficult not to agree with him, and yet, after all, it is a species of defeatism, because that is not the direction in which the world is moving."

4 For the chronology see Lawrence, *Sketches of Etruscan Places*, xxxiii–xxxv.
5 Quoted in Lawrence, *Sketches of Etruscan Places*, li–lii.

He continues, "[Lawrence] imagines – quite likely he is wrong – that savages or primitive peoples live more intensely than civilized men, and he builds up a mythical figure who is not far from being the Noble Savage over again. Finally, he projects these virtues on to the Etruscans, an ancient pre-Roman people who lived in northern Italy and about whom we don't, in fact, know anything."[6] Orwell admires Lawrence and places him among his twelve favourite writers, but is impatient with what he calls his "defeatism" and his retreat from the modern world. Orwell doesn't put it this way, but he is reminding his readers that the Etruscans will not help Europe to deal with industrialism, capitalism, and Hitler and Stalin.

Orwell agrees with other reviewers that *Etruscan Places* has Lawrence's unmistakable strengths. There is the usual quicksilver style that brings both the writer and various aspects of the subject to life. Much of the time one has the impression that Lawrence is writing a letter or speaking in the present as if, following his own guide, he is simultaneously guiding the reader looking over his shoulder. Describing the painted boats in the Tomb of Hunting and Fishing he points out that "the prow of the boat has a beautifully painted eye, so the vessel shall see where it is going. In Syracuse you will see many a two-eyed boat today come swimming in to the quay. One dolphin is diving down into the sea, one is leaping out. The birds fly, and the garlands hang from the border" (45). Though the colours have been damaged by damp, the painting shimmers both in Lawrence's memory and in his evocative writing: "It is all small and gay and quick with life, spontaneous as only young life can be. If only it were not so much damaged, one would be happy, because of the young liveliness of it. There is nothing impressive or grand. But through the paleness of time and the damage of men one still sees the quick ripple of life here, the eternity of the naive moment, which the Etruscans knew" (45). How do we know that they "knew?" Just look at the paintings. Lawrence's intimate idiolect introduces value judgments and shapes our response: small, gay, quick with life, spontaneous, young life, quick ripple of life, the eternity of the naive moment. He plays variations on these throughout the sketches, and some of the images gain a cumulative authority when we also recall

6 Orwell, *The Collected Essays, Journalism and Letters* 1:556; "The Rediscovery of Europe," 2:234.

them from stories and novels. Particularly important for him are the dancers who represent the creative spontaneity at the heart of life and a primal human activity.

My favourite non-Etruscan moment comes in the book's penultimate paragraph, drawn from the Volterra prison located in a fortress outside the walls. It has nothing to do with the Etruscans but everything with a traveller's attention to the world around him. Lawrence pauses to tell the story of "a man, an old man now, who has written an opera inside those walls. He had a passion for the piano: and for thirty years his wife nagged him when he played. So one day he silently and suddenly killed her. So, the nagging of thirty years silenced, he got thirty years in prison, and still is not allowed to play the piano. It is curious" (171). This is a masterpiece of minimalism, cousin to Raymond Carver, and to Hemingway's short interludes in *In Our Time*. There is a much longer story within this vignette that might have been told by Luigi Pirandello or Giovanni Verga (whom Lawrence had translated) and set in Sicily. I admire the rhythm of "So … So … and still … It is curious." Another brief prison anecdote follows – also with potential for a short story – and the book ends with the firing of the governor of the prison. Had Balzac or Stendhal known the anecdotes, we might have had a novel *The Prison House of Volterra*.

When Lawrence writes at a visionary pitch – however direct and simple the style may be – the vision is like a magnet organizing all the filings into the complex cosmic dance of his vision. Each "spirit of place" described and evoked is similar to but different from all the others. How? Just compare the flowers. As a literary florist Lawrence is in the same league as the Shakespeare of the fourth act of *The Winter's Tale* and John Clare. But I'll take my example from the essay "Flowery Tuscany," which Lawrence still sees as the land of the Etruscans.

But just as January draws towards February, these hellebores, these greenish Christmas roses become more assertive. Their pallid water-green becomes yellower, pale sulphur-yellow-green, and they rise up, they are in tufts, in throngs, in veritable bushes of greenish open flowers, assertive, bowing their faces with a hellebore assertiveness. In some places they throng among the bushes and above the water of the stream, giving the peculiar pale glimmer almost of primroses, as you walk among them. Almost of primroses, yet with a coarse hellebore leaf, and an uprearing hellebore assertiveness, like snakes of winter. (228)

It would take little effort to recast this as a free verse poem. In the second sentence you can feel the flower's "assertiveness" as it rises up, pushes, and spreads in a Darwinian assault on its patch of ground (think of Darwin's "entangled bank"). I admire the way the internal rhyme of "throng among" announces the shoving together of two words normally kept apart when rhyming. What would normally be a harmonious bell-like echo is a dissonant clangour that catches the growing flowers crowding and rubbing and bumping each other. Flowers are the distinctive signature of each region's countryside: they are similar yet unique, natural, spontaneous, vivid, and distinctly beautiful. Lawrence's words give us that.

The Etruscan scholars who have paid serious attention to the book have done so by seeing its importance in the context of the history of the modern reception of the rediscovery of the Etruscans. They can't ignore its popularity and influence. Another way of putting this: the Etruscans many of us imagine are in large part Lawrence's creation. He ventured into a neglected corner of antiquity and breathed enough life into it to evoke a convincing vision that continues to attract. The most astute account from within Etruscan studies – it combines criticism and appreciation – comes from Pallottino, the dean of the field in the twentieth century. He offers a balanced summary of the claims of knowledge (*wissenschaft*) and imagination. Writing for an audience of scholars in his classic study *The Etruscans*, he suggests reasons for the appearance of speculative and unhistorical accounts of ancient Etruria like Huxley's and Lawrence's.

Scholarly uncertainties and polemics on the interpretation of Etruscan inscriptions, on the classification of the language, on the problem of Etruscan origins gave birth to the notion of an "Etruscan mystery"; and this notion, rather than describing, more or less aptly, a scientific situation, developed into a sort of irrational belief, a truly aprioristic sentimental position deeply rooted in modern culture, a commonplace handed down over generations, regardless of what progress was in fact being made in Etruscan studies. The "Etruscan" theme has, for instance, inspired some lively passages in contemporary literature [in which] the ancient civilization of Etruria is symbolically transfigured into the myth of a "lost world," of a spontaneously natural human society, festive and sensuous, contrasting with the rational and moral orders of Graeco-Roman and Christian cultures. It is obvious that such suggestive literary fantasies have rested on the often unclear and uncertain picture of Etruscan civilization provided by archaeological and historical research – that is, by the positive data of science – which have contributed to keep prejudices and aberrations alive.[7]

Pallottino is more sympathetic to Lawrence's unscientific, subjective approach in his 1957 essay "In Search of Etruria: Science and the Imagination," later reprinted as the foreword to an edition of *Etruscan Places*. He praises, for instance, the sensitivity to image and symbol in Lawrence's evocative descriptions of paintings. Allowing that Lawrence is not a reliable historian, he nevertheless points out that his speculations about Etruscan origins were in line with those of modern scholars, including himself. Recognizing that Lawrence can be placed in the line of anti-Roman writers reassessing the early history of the peninsula, he mentions the nineteenth-century revisionist Giuseppe Micali whose "ingeniously erudite approach turns, in Lawrence, into the pattern of myth, into the incandescent matter of a symbolic historical drama."[8] And Lawrence's reliance on imagination becomes less of a problem when seen as resisting the arid empiricism of the young German scientist he meets when exploring the painted tombs of Tarquinia, whose response to everything he sees is "*Nicht viel Wert! – not much worth – doesn't amount to anything*" (119). Pallottino even ventures a Lawrentian description of the landscape he spent his professional life exploring and studying: "All of us even today, despite the tide of agricultural and industrial development which is invading the desolate silences of the Maremma, have experienced unique emotions in travelling along the ravines of Norchia, thick with brambles, among wild olives, mastic bushes, myrtles, along high banks of red volcanic tufa out of which innumerable tombs open their mouths and fantastic buildings are outlined, with perhaps a few rooks circling against the azure sky."[9] The scholar is stretching himself here to show that, despite his professional commitment, he can almost match Lawrence's imaginative response. His subjectivity is as surprising as Lawrence's occasional citation of a fact. A later sentence confirms one's sense that the professor has style: "One of the unique effects of

7 Pallottino, *The Etruscans*, 32. This is a revised and enlarged version of the 1942 Italian edition, *Etruscologia*. David Ridgway's introduction is excellent.

8 Lawrence, *Etruscan Places*, foreword by Massimo Pallottino, 20. No other edition has as generous a selection of period photographs.

9 Ibid., 15–16.

the Etruscan landscape is that of fusing together in one indissoluble impression of beauty both natural characteristics and the traces of human activity: rocks, plants, ancient and medieval ruins, present-day dwellings, almost as if the handiwork of history, under time's usury, had gradually reverted to nature's living womb."[10] He might almost be putting into words a painting by one of the Macchiaioli artists whose landscapes have been popular in Italy since the second half of the nineteenth century.

These sentences show Pallottino meeting Lawrence on his own ground. He can't follow Lawrence in his "wildest imaginings," but he appreciates the originality and authenticity of his encounter with the Etruscans. "It would not make sense to judge this experience by the yardstick of true or false ... For 'an experience' either exists or it does not: and this particular experience consists not so much in the discovery of the Etruscan as in the discovery of the writer's own mind, with his ideals, his sympathies, his passions, his rages. Etruria is a mere pretext for self-revelation."[11] The "mere" is a bit strong but it points in the right direction – the personal element in Lawrence's writing which includes a visionary approach to history. Pallottino might have mentioned that he and Lawrence are equally impatient with discussions of the Etruscan "mystery." While Pallottino emphasizes the many gaps in our knowledge, he is unwilling to fill them with some version of the myth of a lost prelapsarian society.[12] This is where he and Lawrence part. So far as I can tell, Pallottino subscribes to no obvious theory of history with a single teleological narrative, Christian, Hegelian, or Marxist. Lawrence, by contrast, belongs to the Romantics, for whom history has two eras divided by a fall into reason, a literate culture, and

10 Ibid., 17.

11 Ibid., 24. He adds, a page later, "But I wouldn't like anyone to extract from this talk of mine the moral that the reasons of the heart and the reasons of science are absolutely irreconcilable when it comes to speculating about the ancient civilizations of the Etruscans" (25). I take the plural "civilizations of the Etruscans" as indicating an awareness that the Etruscan cities were not identical in their social organization and religion and that the Etruscan world view changed over the centuries. There is no *one* Etruscan civilization.

12 I sometimes wonder whether *The Plumed Serpent* prevented Lawrence from venturing a historical story or novel about the Etruscans along the lines of *The Escaped Cock* (*The Man Who Died*) which shows Jesus turning his back on Christianity to choose paganism.

what Max Weber famously called "the disenchantment of the world."[13] Before this happened, participation between humans and the natural world was taken for granted by people who, as Anne Carson puts it, "had a different sensual deployment [and] a different way of conceiving [their] relations with their environment, a different conception of [their] bodies and a different conception of [their] self."[14]

To an admirable extent Pallottino writes against himself when he sympathizes with *Etruscan Places*. In part this reflects his realization that he and the novelist are both engaged in resurrecting and popularizing a nearly extinct culture. But I think there is also the possibility that Lawrence's example encouraged the great Etruscologist to write outside the limitations imposed by European scholarship without committing himself to Lawrence's animistic view of the Rasenna. Is Pallottino right that Lawrence, like Dennis, Giosuè Carducci, and Huxley before him, saw in the Etruscans his own "ideals, his sympathies, his passions, his rages"? In other words, did he see what he needed to see? Of course, he did, and parts of the historical record undermine his view. But as I said before, the sparseness of the remains is an invitation to the imagination as well as to scholarship. The same can be said about Tacitus's fanciful anthropology *Germania* or Ibn Khaldun's view of the Bedouin, in the *Muqaddimah*, as morally superior to city dwellers because of their primitive way of life, stark simplicity of character, and purity of faith. Niebuhr's interpretation of early Roman and Etruscan history is sometimes as imaginative as Lawrence's. Even a tragic thinker like Weber occasionally looked back to what had been lost when modernity disenchanted the world. And to pile one near paradox on another, there is no record that Lawrence, who admired the dancing of the Etruscans, ever danced: it was enough that he liked the idea of people dancing.

---

13 "The fate of our times is characterized by rationalization and intellectualization and, above all, by the 'disenchantment of the world.' Precisely the ultimate and most sublime values have retreated from public life either into the transcendental realm of mystic life or into the brotherliness of direct and personal human relations." Max Weber, "Science as a Vocation," in *From Max Weber*, 155.

14 Carson, *Eros the Bittersweet*, 43.

II

Those stones in the [Italian] sun, dislodged along the *strada bianca*; I know
that obscurely, below them, persist sources of the irrational, phantasms,
magic: *il buio*, that darkness, which conceals a whole peninsula history,
Etruscan, then Roman, and their traditions.

Yves Bonnefoy, The Arrière-pays[15]

Bonnefoy's almost unclassifiable book – I think of it as *pensées* on the
mystery in the aura and sublimity we find in unexpected sources – is
one of three important intertexts Margaret Drabble integrates into her
late masterpiece *The Dark Flood Rises* (2016), whose title comes from
Lawrence's late poem "The Ship of Death." The novel is the thematically
related but free-standing pendant to her trilogy of the Thatcher years:
The Radiant Way (1987), *A Natural Curiosity* (1989), and *The Gates of
Ivory* (1991). The two other intertexts are a fictitious art book about
the Etruscans and Lawrence's *Etruscan Places*. The musings of the
French symbolist poet-scholar pause briefly on the Etruscans, but I
think he's more important to Drabble's vision in providing a broader
spiritual context for Lawrence's Etruscan-based vision of life. Lawrence
doesn't figure in Drabble's earlier fiction, and he and the Rasenna
play a minor role in the trilogy. The latter are unmentioned in *A Natural
Curiosity* (1989) and *The Gates of Ivory* (1991); Lawrence is mentioned
in the first and *The Rainbow* in the second. Both the writer and the
Etruscans, however, are prominent at key moments in *The Dark Flood
Rises*. *Etruscan Places* is mentioned when the dying Teresa – a friend of
the novel's central character, Fran Stubbs – is given the large Etruscan
picture book. It reminds her that she "had read, long ago, D.H.
Lawrence's *Etruscan Places,* and is inclined to share his view that the
Etruscans were a happy breed, happy in life as in death, a view not
upheld by [the author] Massimo Vignoli who dismisses Lawrence,
not with contempt but with a scholarly compassion. As he puts it,
'Lawrence's views are out of date, but he couldn't, at that period have
known any better.'"[16] In the disagreement between the novelist and
the Etruscan scholar, the novel takes the writer's side. Readers who
noticed references in earlier novels, including two in the trilogy, to

---

15 Bonnefoy, *The Arrière-pays*, 150.
16 Drabble, *The Dark Flood Rises*, 237. All references will be in the text.

F.R. Leavis, the Cambridge critic who championed Lawrence, can't be surprised by the novel's Lawrentian and Etruscan sympathies.

Though *The Dark Flood Rises* sits comfortably as a continuation of the trilogy, only one of the major characters does an encore in it, the enigmatic art historian and Etruscan, by one degree of separation, Esther Breuer, now in a minor but significant role. Independent, brilliant, and sexy, she carries an air of mystery and has been casually associated with the Etruscans since *The Radiant Way* (1981), where she visits an Etruscan archaeological site in Tuscany with an acquaintance who studies them. It's not much, but together with her work authenticating a painting by Carlo Crivelli and her interest in a particular shade of green-blue in Renaissance painting it provides one of many threads of formal and thematic stitching in the tetralogy. Esther, Crivelli, and Bonnefoy's wide-ranging volume remind the reader not to forget that the novel is a work of art, as worked over as a Renaissance painting and as worthy of being examined closely. Esther's aura combines her Semitic features, secretive nature, ambiguous sexuality, and her suggestive names – Esther is star, Ishtar, and an Old Testament heroine, while Breuer points us toward *Studies in Hysteria* and Freud's early collaboration with Josef Breuer. Bachofen would have classed her with Zenobia, Dido, and Tanaquil as a living reminder of matriarchal power. That she is in touch with primal forces is suggested by her relationship with a scholar who believes in lycanthropy and the presence of a serial killer in a contiguous flat.

We don't learn in *The Dark Flood Rises* whether Esther authenticates the painting, but an art critic recalls reading "a colourful new book about a 1990s forgery/attribution scandal, involving impeccably trustworthy art historian Esther Breuer" (212). We learn nothing more about this alleged "forgery." It deepens the shadows around Esther. There is strong evidence that none of her friends can claim to know Esther, and I also have the impression that she is the one figure who remains opaque even to the narrator, who, in a deft narrative gambit, grows increasingly wary of her. If Esther were a cosmic phenomenon, she would be a black hole. The four novels circle around her and offer different perspectives, but she cannot be known – described and discussed, yes, but not understood. And the mystery surrounding Esther and the scandal surrounding the Crivelli painting is never cleared up. Neither is her connection to the Etruscans developed – the two remain a category that Bonnefoy would label "the never-captured, the half-glimpsed" (96). From another viewpoint, Esther is the sign of Drabble's increasingly free approach to the novel: one might say that she moves under the sign of "Etruria," a character about whom there are more rumours than facts.

Esther and the Etruscans occupy separate parts of the narrative, but they are related by subtle tendrils of implication. It wouldn't be too much to claim that for Drabble the dark-featured Esther is a Lawrentian figure, a sort of modern Etruscan, never quite at home in any of the social circles she inhabits or visits. Drabble's Lawrence is the writer in his last phase, writing the Etruscan sketches, *The Escaped Cock*, *Lady Chatterley's Lover*, and the influential late poems in which, suffering from tuberculosis, he prepares himself for death by imagining it in proleptic elegies like "The Ship of Death." The novel begins with an epigraph from the poem: "Piecemeal the body dies, and the timid soul / has her footing washed away, as the dark flood rises." It doesn't take the reader long to realize that the novel is an elegy for the generation that came to maturity during the Thatcher years of the trilogy. Esther's presence implicates the preceding novels in this one's resolution.

The book's final movement concentrates on the dying Teresa, who finds consolation both in Lawrence's view that the Etruscans were happy in life and death and in the pleasure she takes in the vision of their "little terracotta red-brown cinerary huts of the dead [that] are small and homely. Like doll's houses" (237). As the last simile deftly suggests, Lawrence's Etruscans help her to domesticate death. One of her dreams combines the images of an Etruscan sarcophagus and a little white Christian chapel, each cognate with the ship of death. Thinking about Teresa's death, Fran reflects that she and her friends gather most frequently now for funerals and memorial services and again recalls "The Ship of Death": "We are dying, we are dying, piecemeal our bodies are dying / and our strength leaves us / and our soul cowers naked in the dark rain over the flood, / cowering in the last branches of the tree of our life." Lawrence's tree of life returns in Teresa's richly figured last dream, whose meaning is more transparent than Emerson's or Freud's.

In the centre of the scene, the huge deep-rooted trunk of an ancient tree bears upwards in its forked branches a slab of stone like a sarcophagus. Far away, upon the background, upon the distant hillside, stands a little white chapel. The place is known and unknown, familiar and unfamiliar.
    When she wakes, she will recognise in this dream landscape an allusion to the Etruscan tombs, and to the saving of the virtuous heathen from antiquity,

and to a hand-coloured print given to her one year for Christmas by grateful parents ...

A heavy stone coffin, a flesh-eating sarcophagus, borne upwards in the living growing branches of a tree.

Her dream had married Jerusalem and Athens. She is pleased with the inventiveness of her dream life. (243)

If the Christian Theresa finally achieves a sense of wholeness in which body and soul, life and death seem reconciled, she does so also under the sign of Lawrence and the Etruscans, the latecomers in her education into life. Her last book of life is the richly illustrated Etruscan volume she received as a gift. It joins Etruria to Jerusalem and Athens and, in doing so, completes them.

16

Raymond Queneau:
How a Restless Surrealist and Future
Pataphysician Resurrected the Etruscans
in The Bark Tree *(1933)*

If this work seems so threatening, this is because it isn't simply eccentric
or strange, but competent, rigorously argued, and carrying conviction.

Jacques Derrida[1]

Raymond Queneau (1903–1976) is a master of narrative surprise: the
unexpected neologism or anachronism; the absurd twist in an already
unpredictable narrative; overdetermined names begging to be interpreted and sometimes frustrating the effort; and contingent details that
produce category errors, like guns loaded with macaroni:

Capua was the capital of the Etruscans; they'd just been informed of that by
the newspapers, which also explained that these people loaded their guns
with macaroni, and that that didn't hurt, and that their mandolins weren't
any match for French bombers. In short, the war wouldn't last long and they
weren't to worry. Not to mention that it was going to be good for industry ...
Now and then someone would yell: Long live France, and others would yell
back: Death to the Coches. The Coches, that was what they were beginning

---

1 Derrida, "Honoris Causa: 'This is Also Extremely Funny,'" in *Points* ..., 409. A
useful brief definition of "pataphysics" is an intricate and whimsical nonsense intended
as a parody of science. The term was first used by Alfred Jarry. *The American Heritage
Dictionary* defines it as "a branch of philosophy or science that examines imaginary
phenomena that exist in a world beyond metaphysics ... the science of imaginary solu-
tions." The Greek means "That what is above metaphysics."

to call the Etruscans, and in the paper they'd explained that it was an abbreviation for Etruscoche, which was slang for Etruscan.[2]

"Etruscoche" also rhymes with "Boches" which is slang for another traditional French enemy. But what is truly surprising in *The Bark Tree* (*Le Chiendent*) is the historical interest – however oblique and figural – at the heart of a novel by a former Surrealist whose work consistently resists mere realism, chronological narrative, and history with every artistic and philosophical device available. Language itself is the focus of his interest. Queneau's admirers suggest that *The Bark Tree* is among the most innovative and original novels of its time. Despite Queneau's early interest in Surrealism, the novel shows him turning toward what might be called a new kind of playful linguistic classicism infused with the spirit of François Rabelais, Alfred Jarry, Erik Satie, and James Joyce and more than a little interested in history. Its ludic vision is stretched on a rational lucidity destabilized by an encounter with Heidegger's essay "What Is Metaphysics?" At the same time, it is his farewell to Surrealism's insistence on the primacy of the unconscious, while its neo-Joycean parody of realism's conventions announces a new kind of fiction in Paris.

As in almost all this writer's work there is certainly much for readers and critics to worry. One can begin with the French title. *Le Chiendent* is a commonplace noun that looks as if it should have something to do with dogs and teeth but translates as "couch grass" or "quack grass … any of several grasses of the genus *Agropyron*, especially *Agropyron repens*, having long creeping roots." Claude Simonnet, a prominent Queneau scholar, suggests that "le chiendent is a sort of personal emblem, the weed that grows on the ground of marasmus." Simonnet adds that Queneau thinks of it as "a symbol of wisdom." Constantin Toloudis adds, "Nothing has been said or written to this date that offers a more plausible interpretation of the title."[3] That's not quite the answer one expects from tenured professors. How about something simple: since the novel focuses on very ordinary Parisians leading dull, monotonous, and even from their own viewpoint meaningless lives on the edge of non-being, perhaps the couch grass is an image of inconsequence, ordinariness,

2 Queneau, *The Bark Tree*, 255. All references will be to this edition.
3 See Simonnet, *Queneau déchiffré*, 18, and Toloudis, *Queneau and the Agony of Presence*, 103.

transience, and simple perdurability, worthy of Faulkner's "they endured" which ends *The Sound and the Fury* or Eugenio Montale's "cuttlefish bones"? There is a hint of this in "*la brosse en chiendent,*" a scrubbing brush, a utensil the French bourgeoisie and upper classes are only indirectly acquainted with – at one remove, so to speak. Whatever the meaning of the title, it does nothing to prepare the reader for the delayed or deferred appearance of the Etruscans, who, in their modern guise, are a key to the novel's politico-historical meaning.

The title is the first of many onomastic sinkholes in Queneau's experimental first novel, which undermines realism's conventions with a tip of the hat to *Ulysses* and whose circular form anticipates *Finnegans Wake.* Queneau returns to Joyce in 1947 when he uses names borrowed from *Ulysses* in *On est toujours trop bon avec les femmes,* published as a pulp paperback under the pseudonym Sally Mara. *The Bark Tree* reveals the Irish writer's presence most obviously in various kinds of narratives: among these are a dog's point of view (an anticipation of Leon Rooke's *Shakespeare's Dog*), dreams, soliloquies, stream of consciousness, letters, dialogues, catalogues, and newspapers. Proust joins the novel in casual allusions such as "the peasants from the Guermantes had slung him out of the window, into the rails" (255). Though most readers probably don't notice it, various philosophical viewpoints, especially Heidegger's, are also a ghostly presence behind characters incapable of serious thought, much less philosophy. The exception is Saturnin, the philosophical concierge, whose reflections on a lump of butter – "up to its eyes in the infinity of nonbeing" (244) – reveal his difference from his neighbours. According to one now legendary account, the novel began when Queneau gave up translating Descartes's *Discourse on Method* into spoken French during a trip to Greece.[4] Translation gave way to a novel, influenced more by Heidegger than Descartes, that shows the "coming-into-being through consciousness" of an ordinary character leading a literally two-dimensional life (like a character in a novel) until

---

4 The idea that *Le Discours de la Méthode* might provide the basis for a novel had been suggested earlier by Paul Valéry in a letter, 4 August 1894, to André Gide: "I recently reread *Le Discours de la Méthode,* which is indeed the modern novel as it might be written. It should be noted that subsequent philosophy rejected the autobiographical part. However, that is the point that should be revived, and one should thus write the life of a theory as one wrote, far too often, the life of a passion (in bed)." Gide, *Self-Portraits,* 127.

he glimpses a window display of plastic ducks floating in a waterproof hat. His attempt to decipher this enigmatic sight propels him into a full three-dimensionality as he trips or is thrust into being. (I visualized this scene with Buster Keaton as a protagonist being observed by Heidegger.) His gradual metamorphosis simultaneously transforms the world around him, making it a place of baffling complications and endless speculation.[5] Previously without a name, he is now identified as Étienne Marcel. He meets others and sets in motion an unstable narrative that involves, among countless mundane and forgettable affairs, a search for a nonexistent treasure supposedly hidden behind a blue door, and a war between France and Italy announced as a newspaper headline:

LES FRANÇAIS ET LES ÉTRUSQUES
SE DÉCLARERONT MUTUELLEMENT LA GUERRE
LE MERCREDI ONZE NOVEMBRE (253)

The war provides Queneau with an occasion to satirize French patriotism and militarism: "Old-gents-with-medals were weeping from the emotion caused by watching the men go by on their way there. Lucky guys, who're going to go boom-boom, thought the old-gents-with-medals, and: Long live France, they added, letting a surreptitious tear drop onto their shoulders. And once again French culture was going to be saved, French culture was even going to be nicely fertilized, with something very special – blood and corpses" (256). Press accounts predict an inevitable French victory over an enemy characterized as barbarians who play mandolins and eat macaroni. Official propaganda, anticipating Orwell, describes French retreats as attacks or repositioning. Stores selling macaroni or mandolins are vandalized by patriots. French women are praised for working in brothels. It's worth recalling that Queneau wrote the novel at a time when some photographs from the previous war were still barred from publication. The passing reference to "the bodies

---

5 Stump, *Naming & Unnaming*, 45. Was Queneau familiar with Hilaire de Barenton's *La Texte Étrusque de la Momie d'Agram* (Paris, 1929), in which the Capuchin friar suggests that, on the evidence of the writing on the linen wrap of the Zagreb mummy, Etruscan is an Egyptian dialect? For the connection to Heidegger I am indebted to Denis Hollier's "Plenty of Nothing," in Hollier, *A New History of French Literature.* Hollier points out the nod to Descartes's piece of wax in Saturnin's lump of butter.

[*les zoiziaux*] perched on the telegraph wires" (271) may be an oblique reference to these. Jean Renoir's *La Grande Illusion* would be banned in the late 1930s as unpatriotic. Across the ocean the release of Charlie Chaplin's *The Great Dictator* (1940) was delayed out of official concerns that it might offend Hitler. Governments have long memories for images that embarrass.

The puzzling current war – why is France (now also known as Gaul) fighting an ally (Italy) of the Great War? – recalls 1914 and anticipates 1939. When the foes are called Gaul and Étruscoche, we find ourselves in the ancient world, which suggests that nothing ever changes. The Étruscoche, or Coches, suggest onomastically the Boches of 1914, the Italians of the 1930s, and the Etruscans. The labile Madame Cloche undergoes an onomastic metamorphosis with the declaration of war into Miss Olini or Aulini, the Queen of Italy, which must be a thrust at the masculinity of the Italian dictator whom Chaplin would rename eight years later Benzino Napaloni, the dictator of Bacteria. The absurd war is propelled by the government, the media, rumours, and mass hysteria. According to one character, "none of this would have happened if there hadn't been an atheist government. This war is God's punishment" (274). If reason can't explain it, try one of the usual suspects. In France during the 1930s it was the left (always presumed atheist) when it wasn't the Jews.

Some decades later the few surviving characters decide to erase everything that has happened in the novel and to begin again with its first two sentences: "The silhouette of a man appeared in profile; so, simultaneously, did thousands. There really were thousands" (280). There is something of Joyce here but also of Nietzsche's theory of eternal recurrence in which, in the philosopher's unsparing version, everything will repeat itself. And a casual reference to Polish troops coming to help the Gauls reminds us that this is a novel of the 1930s, a decade in which Poland figured large in European awareness. But it also looks back to the most famous reference to Poland in French literature: Alfred Jarry's *Ubu Roi*. In his preliminary address to the audience Jarry declared that the play "takes place in Poland – that is to say, nowhere." Despite the presence of historical characters, Poland figures as little in Jarry's Ubu plays between 1896 and 1906, the year of his death, as it did in the minds of the French *before* the First World War and the Treaty of Versailles.

All of which still leaves me wondering about the presence of the Etruscans. The name is an inspired choice in a novel concerned with

the problematic nature of names, the relationship between the signifier and the signified, the mystery of identity, and the fate of nations.
We know that Queneau read Hegel during his time in the armed forces
between 1925 and 1927. In the mid-1930s he attended Alexandre
Kojève's legendary lectures on the philosopher, and he participated
a decade later in their publication. Did he read *The Philosophy of History*,
where Hegel mentions the Etruscans in his account of the rise of
Rome? Hegel notes, as mentioned earlier, the presence of an "extreme
prose of spirit … in Etruscan art, which though technically perfect and
so far true to nature, has nothing of Greek ideality and beauty" (289).
In *Aesthetics*, Hegel writes that Etruscan sculpture is "relatively spirit-
less" but adds that "the posture and facial expressions are free, and
some of these works are very nearly portraits."[6] I'm intrigued by the
possibility that Etruscans here can be traced back to Hegel, though
Queneau's interest in him is limited to using the deterministic theory
that culminates in Absolute Reason coming to self-consciousness
as a matrix for the novel's ludic vision of the hero developing a three-
dimensional consciousness.

But whether Queneau found the Etruscans in Hegel or not, they
remain an inspired choice for a novel that plays with names and with
several mystery stories. The Rasenna were much more of a mystery in
the early 1930s when *Etruscan Places* and *The Bark Tree* were published
than they are today. There is also, as I discussed earlier, their status as
what a character in *The Bark Tree* terms, in an apt phrase, one of "the
outworn races." This is an anonymous figure later identified as Pierre
"the Romany." He doesn't mention the Etruscans, but they are implicitly
present: "I have the Romany look, and the Romany despair. I am accompanying the outworn races toward their fatal dissolution. The Tasmanians.
The Dodos. The Aepyronithidae. The Thises. The Thats. Forgive me if
my erudition fails me" (205–6). I find it difficult not to add silently,
"and the Etruscans." After which, we reach for the dictionary
for "Aepyronithidae": these are not a people, but an extinct family of
flightless ratite birds also known as elephant birds that once lived on
Madagascar before disappearing between 1000 and 1200, most probably
because of humans.

6 Hegel, *Aesthetics,* 2:787.

In the closing paragraphs the speaker takes off a mask, which drifts into the novel's last lines, and suggests that he is perhaps an avatar of death – "the dead man," a speaker for all the dead and dying who have left being for non-being (the Etruscans?). In Queneau's imagination everyone in the novel is dead, if only in the very limited sense that his or her existence is purely linguistic. As we discover on the last page, the characters themselves are aware of this. They are no more truly alive than the extinct Etruscans or characters in a play by Pirandello. Dissatisfied with their lives, they decide "to rub it all out" and start all over again. As they separate, "A mask traversed the air, causing people of multiple and complex lives to disappear" (279) into non-being. Time and history are reduced to fictional categories that form matrices for names. In a manner of speaking, the characters are no more real or unreal than the Etruscans. Both have made an appearance – the characters in fiction, the Etruscans in history – and both have disappeared. One might also say that in Queneau's world the characters might reappear just as easily as did the Etruscans, or Etruscoche, in fiction, history, and Etruscology. Tyrsenoi, Tyrrhenoi, Ras or Rasenna, Etrusci, Etruscans, Étrusques, Étruscoche– the morphology or mask changes but the substance remains the same, whether in history or in this novel.

17

Mika Waltari's The Etruscan *(1955): Civilizations in Crisis and the Fate of Spirit*

The world changed, of course – they must have said to themselves –
it was no longer what it had once been, when Etruria, with its confederation
of free, aristocratic city-states, had dominated almost the whole peninsula.
Giorgio Bassani, The Garden of the Finzi-Continis[1]

Mika Waltari (1908–1979) is the most famous and most translated
Finnish writer. Some measure of his fame is indicated by two asteroids
being named after him: n:o 4266 Mika Waltari and n:o 4512 Sinuhe.
The only other writer I know immortalized in this way is Josef Škvorecký,
the Czech-Canadian novelist best known for *The Cowards*.[2] Waltari estab-
lished his reputation in Finland with realistic novels like his first success,
The Grand Illusion (1928). It is a Hemingway-influenced story of the
Lost Generation, not dissimilar to Antal Szerb's novel of the lost
Hungarian generation, *Journey by Moonlight*, published a decade later.
From the 1940s to the 1960s he wrote ten long historical novels, including *The Egyptian* and *The Etruscan*, most of which were translated into
the major western languages. It was a time when historical novels and
movies were internationally popular. *The Egyptian*, for instance, went
from being the most popular novel of 1949, when translated into
English, to a very successful Cecil B. DeMille film in 1954.

Of Waltari's ten historical novels, the most relevant for this study are
the Etruscan-themed *The Etruscan* (*Turms, kuolematon*, 1955) and, to a

---

1 Bassani, *The Garden of the Finzi-Continis*, 9.

2 Asteroid (26314) was discovered by J. Tichà and M. Tichý and named for the
Czech-Canadian writer, a hero in his homeland. I recently learned that the Russian
astronomer Nikolai Chernykh named a minor planet between Mars and Jupiter 2703
Rodari after Gianni Rodari, the Italian children's author, best known for *Telephone Tales*.

lesser extent, *The Roman* (*Ihmiskunnan viholliset*, 1964), which has a Roman hero of Etruscan ancestry who converts to Christianity. Though the latter has its moments, like the emperor Claudius discussing his multi-volume history of the Etruscans, I will focus on *The Etruscan* because it is set during the sixth and fifth centuries BCE just before the beginning of the decline of the Rasenna world, and it offers a greater historical density, including a wide variety of characters. These are novels of empires in transition and decline, as their traditional political structures and religions begin to be questioned. If not quite allegories of the twentieth century, they deal with issues we think of as modern, including the fall of empires, the disappearance of peoples, and religions in crisis. Read as a unit, Waltari's historical novels offer a panorama of civilizations from the time of Akhenaten in the fourteenth century BCE to the late Renaissance. Written in the spirit of Spengler, they dramatize the cycles through which empires inevitably pass, from birth to maturity to collapse. *The Etruscan* is not as reliable on social or historical detail as Sybille Haynes's closely researched *The Augur's Daughter* (1981) and its reach often exceeds its grasp, but it compensates with the traditional pleasures of historical fiction – fast-paced action in a dispersive narrative, a young hero with great expectations, exotic settings and peoples, historical figures and places, and variety. Waltari's democratic approach to narrative reminds me of Pieter Bruegel the Elder's large paintings in which every part of the canvas gets as much attention and space as the event announced in the title.

The Etruscan and *The Roman* have a flexible episodic form held together by a first-person narrator who moves through a broad international canvas crowded with characters, many of whom are types and caricatures, the staples of historical romances from the Renaissance to DeMille and *Game of Thrones*: the good-hearted hero, the frank and loyal soldier, the treacherous but irresistible vamp, the loyal virgin, the lost child, the faithful male and female servants, the ambitious courtier, the greedy man, the humanist stoic, and the ascetic sage. At the end of his life each narrator utters a version of Turms the Etruscan's "Farewell, my era. The century of the gods has ended and another has begun, new in deeds, new in customs, new in thoughts." Except for Turms, who is given to reflective turns of phrase and is as death-haunted as his people, the characters rarely speak or behave very differently from modern readers. Whatever Waltari's personal beliefs, these polyglot novels, with heroes as restless as Odysseus and Herodotus, explore various ideologies and ways of life in periods of confusing change. Together, the two "Etruscan" novels encompass half a millennium. The characters drift for the most part on the tides of historical events that determine the spirit of the age and its choice of great men. In Waltari's vision, a powerful and hegemonic system of belief can be supplanted only by one even more convincing and popular. But whatever the spirit of the age, fate (or plot) determines character, no matter how free his or her choice may seem.

Ancient history allowed Waltari to escape the inevitable provincialism of Finland and to see his country's problems from a historical perspective. We shouldn't underestimate the gain in historical fiction for a novelist writing in a minor language: historical Finnish characters, except for Jean Sibelius and Marshal Carl Gustav Mannerheim, had no purchase in the wider world during Waltari's lifetime. Akhenaten, the Etruscans, Claudius, Nero, and Vespasian are familiar – their names resonate among the historically minded – as is the history of monotheism and the birth of Christianity. These are the stuff of major history and myth. The characters and events have what Hegel saw as a world-historical gravitas, something rarely attained by or available to nations on the margins. The hero of a small nation is just that, his name rarely known internationally. When transposed symbolically or allegorically onto the world-historical stage, the local achieves an interest and a weight it is otherwise denied.

Waltari isn't the first historical novelist to use the past to comment on the present by making the local into the world-historical by transposing aspects of it onto a larger canvas with famous individuals. Though there are no overt allusions in his work to twentieth-century figures and events, I sense the pressure of modern history throughout. These are novels about authoritarian empires, shifts in ideology and spirit, and small nations caught between. Behind the past events one senses the Russian and German empires, the two elephants in Finland's recent history. Written in a century that saw two catastrophic world wars and in which life continued in the Cold War under the threat of nuclear disaster, Waltari's novels show the present in the past and the past in the present. He understands the point of Heraclitus's pessimistic – or is it just realistic? – aphorism "It is necessary to know that war is common, and right is strife and that all things happen by strife and necessity" (Fragment 80).[3] Waltari's lesson is that in the past as in the present,

3 Kirk and Raven, *The Presocratic Philosophers*, 95.

civilization, no matter what its religion, is always under threat. In the *longue durée* fascism and communism are just the two latest instances of gods that failed. The implication of Waltari's historical vision is clear: gods have died before – Aten, the Etruscan gods, the Graeco-Roman gods. No exception will be made for the Christian one.[4] Though Waltari's achievement falls short of the greatest historical novels, his ambition is the same: to illuminate his own era while simultaneously transcending it and encompassing it in a panoramic and teleological historical vision. The fiction in *The Etruscan* is grounded in history by a sprinkling of datable facts and historical figures: Lars Porsena's war on Rome; the burning of Sardis by the Ionian Greeks in 498 BCE; the capture and burning of Miletus by the Persians in 494 BCE; and the sea battle at Cumae in 474 BCE. Against this background, Turms ("Mercury" in Latin) writes his own story which includes, among many other historical figures, acquaintance with Heraclitus and people who have seen the Tarquins. Like Sinuhe, of the great Egyptian poem underlying *The Egyptian*, Turms writes his story as his tomb is being prepared. As he dies, he offers an ambiguous prophecy: he foresees the end of Etruscan civilization (or at least of this phase) and simultaneously predicts his own return, though the informed reader knows that if he does it will not be to an Etruscan world.

Waltari provides just enough historical information through conversations and descriptions to satisfy even a reader previously ignorant of things Etruscan. He restricts himself to dusting the style with occasional facts about language, dream interpretation, and known figures and events. He is particularly attentive to different forms of Etruscan divination. Missing, however, is a felt sense of how different the Etruscans must have been from us, how strange we would find their way of being in the world and they ours. The novel's history and minutiae of daily life differ from ours, but the people seem too familiar, insufficiently differentiated from us.

On a personal level, *The Etruscan* is a spiritual autobiography that begins in Ionia with the flight of Turms, an orphan, after he has taken

---

4 I'm reminded of Mencken's "Memorial Service," which gleefully lists once omnipotent gods whose shrines are untended and forgotten. "You may think I spoof. That I invent the names. I do not. They were gods of the highest standing and dignity – gods of civilized peoples – worshipped and believed in by millions. All were omnipotent, omniscient, and immortal. And all are dead." Mencken, *Prejudices*, 237.

part in the Ionian revolt against the Persians. His voyage across the Mediterranean is both an adventurous escape and a gradual discovery of his own past, the memory of which he lost when struck by lightning as a young man. As a result, the rest of the novel involves a form of gradual remembering, an *anamnesis* in which he gradually recuperates his Etruscan part. A later, similar event on the road to Delphi confirms his sense of a spiritual destiny: "Without realizing what I did I began to dance along the road to Delphi. My feet danced and my arms moved, not in a dance that I had learned from others, but in a dance that moved and lived in me ... Then it was that I knew myself for the first time. No evil could befall me, nothing could do me harm. As I danced the words of a strange language burst from my lips, words that I did not know."[5]

From the novel's title the reader knows that the language is Etruscan and that Etruria is the hero's destiny. Otherwise, what we learn about the Etruscans is co-extensive with Turms's discovery of his past. Our interest lies in the journey and what will happen at its end to the man we already know to be immortal. Turms's journey is as full of adventures as any picaresque novel or Hollywood film about the ancient world. He sails with a pirate; helps a Spartan friend to claim his patrimony; abducts a priestess of Aphrodite from a Sicilian temple; lives for several years with the reclusive Sicilian forest-people the Siccani; is imprisoned and threatened with death in Rome; and finally discovers that he is descended from the Etruscan leader Lars Porsena and is a lucumo, who is immortal. He also learns that his father sent him abroad as a child because he wanted Turms to discover his destiny on his own: "If my son is a true lucumo he must be able to find himself and his city as the lucumones did in former times. No one is a true Lucumo merely because of birth. Only at the age of forty can a Lucumo acknowledge himself and be acknowledged. That is why I must give up my son" (350). It's worth noting that there is no such requirement in the tradition as we know it. Waltari might well answer that, since the record is meagre, there might have once been some similar tradition. Like Niebuhr, Bachofen, and Lawrence, he fills the gaps in the record as required.

At each phase of his meandering return to Etruria, Turms recognizes signs and portents – white feathers, the flight of birds, lightning – that

5 Waltari, *The Etruscan*, 15. All references will be to this text.

17.1 "The dancer," Tomb of the Triclinium (Tarquinia), c. 470 BCE.

suggest a fated spiritual dimension to his journey. The novel proceeds by gathering the evidence for his destiny: he must come to remember what he already knows but does not know consciously. Moments of recall and unexpected bursts of revelation punctuate the narrative. In Veii, for instance, "With a catch of my breath I realized in a sudden flash of perception that once again I had previously lived that same moment of happiness. As in a dream I rose and turned a familiar corner. Before me rose a temple whose pillared front I recognized" (274). Waltari creates a polytheistic world in which angelic guardians, minor spirits, Olympian gods, and even an ultimate being mix with and communicate with humans. It is the pre-Socratic world idealized by Lawrence, Arthur Evans, and Heidegger. To paraphrase Max Weber, in such a myth-oriented and enchanted world one can still have recourse to magical means to master reality or implore the spirits.[6] A man like Turms can still summon the gods. The wall between matter and spirit is permeable,

6 Weber, *From Max Weber*, 139.

and the lucumones, of whom only a few survive, live on the border. Intimations of this appear earlier in the journey when Turms finds himself, like Prospero, able to rouse the winds to help propel a ship in flight or to prevent a fleet from advancing. Later he is even shown performing miracles – restoring sight, for instance – like the ones in the New Testament. Waltari suggests that if the early Christians believed in miracles and spirits, why wouldn't the famously religious Etruscans do so as well? His problem as a novelist is to make readers experience the felt pressure of the spiritual in the way that Doris Lessing makes them enter a man whose mind is in free fall in *Briefing for a Descent into Hell.* Lessing is more successful because she distresses and bends the language expressively. In Waltari there is no sharp break between descriptions of mundane events and spiritual crises. There is, of course, another factor: today's reader accepts more readily the reality of mental breakdown than its spiritual counterpart. Many have witnessed or experienced the first; fewer the second.

Turms gradually becomes aware that the Etruscan world is passing away, that small nations like that of the Etruscans are in danger of being absorbed by the larger empires of Persia, Greece, Carthage, and Rome. A sage warns him that far too many Etruscans, influenced by two centuries of trading with Greece, "already admire Greek culture and adopt the spirit of skepticism and derision that everywhere accompanies the Greeks. Only the inland cities are still sacred, for our seaports are unholy and poisoned" (334). And when the "veiled god" appears to the remaining lucumones during "the feast of the gods," one of them surmises, "It means the end of an era ... The veiled god has never before appeared during a feast of the gods." (376). The reader aware of ancient history knows that the old man is right. The Etruscans will disappear as surely, though not as completely, as the other peoples of Italy, who will all be absorbed into the "modernity" and progress of Rome. Diversity and difference will gradually become uniformity: languages, traditions, forms of dress, codes of gesture and behaviour, customs, literatures and arts, entire ways of life will be forgotten or assimilated.

Waltari is adept at presenting the circumstantial cultural facts of Etruscan life. He lingers over the details of temple architecture and furniture; the clothing of the priests; the rituals of worship; the tomb paintings. In one particularly memorable scene Turms enters a tomb outside Tarquinia where an artist named Aruns is in the process of painting the walls: "The painting on the right wall was already completed. There, reclining side by side on their left elbows on a cushioned couch, were both the future deceased in their festive garments and with wreathed heads. Eternally young, the man and his wife looked into each other's eyes with hands upraised while dolphins played below them in eternal waves" (280). The painting is probably from the Tomb of Hunting and Fishing. Though a few Etruscan vases bear an artist's name, no paintings do.[7] This is one of several ekphrastic scenes transposing paint into language. The emotions evoked by such scenes are double-sourced: from what we see on the page and, simultaneously, what we know from the paintings and vases. The joyful dancing and the smiling figures exist within the penumbra of the troubling knowledge that, as Turms puts it, "Nations also have their eras ... [and] the twelve Etruscan peoples and cities have been allotted ten cycles in which to live and die. We refer to them as lasting one thousand years because it is easy to say, but the length of a cycle may not necessarily be even one hundred years. It may be more or even less. We know only its beginning and its end from the unmistakable sign we receive" (13).[8] As he prepares for death, he realizes that Rome will eventually defeat the Etruscans and that "In the work of its artists my people and city will live even after its death" (380). *The Etruscan* and *The Etruscans in the Modern Imagination* are part of the confirmation of that prophecy of disappearance and resurrection. The last sentence – "Then someday I, Turms the immortal, will return" (381) – creates an interesting ambiguity. When I first read the novel twenty years ago, I pencilled in the margin, "Why? If the Etruscan millennium is ending as greater empires rise to dominance, what would an immortal Etruscan Lucumo return to?" The last historical event Turms mentions is the catastrophic

---

7 I'm surprised Waltari doesn't make some use of Vulca, the terracotta specialist from Veii who was hired to decorate the Temple of Jupiter Capitolinus. Spivey, *Etruscan Art*, 152.

8 Arruns Veltumnus announced during the Social War of 91–88 BCE that ten of the twelve Etruscan *saecula* had passed. Even then there was debate about the true length of a *saeculum*. Jacques Heurgon suggests that Arruns is probably responsible for the part of the "Prophecy of Lasa Vegoia" that defends land property from the new Roman allotment system in his time ("The Date of Vegoia's Prophecy," 41–2). Vegoia is the Latin form of Lasa Vecuvia, an elusive goddess with several names and one appearance as a male. "Lasa" is probably roughly equivalent to "nymph." Nancy Thomson de Grummond offers an informative account in *Etruscan Myth, Sacred History, and Legend*, 168–72.

sea battle of Cumae in 474 BCE in which the Etruscan fleet was defeated by Syracusan Greeks. This battle also ends Sybille Haynes's historically more accurate *The Augur's Daughter* (1987), a novel that takes place during the same period but tells it from the point of view of a woman. The next two centuries will see the decline of Etruscan military and economic power and the submission of major Etruscan cities to Rome. Yet it is worth noting that nearly three centuries later, at the time of the comet of 44 BCE, Octavian, later to be Augustus, is reported as saying that it betokened the beginning of the tenth saeculum.[9] This must have been received with polite applause and with not a few asking, "What's a saeculum?"

Unlike the Etruscans, Finns never vanished from the map, but for most of their history they appeared on it as subjects of a more powerful neighbour. From the twelfth century to 1809 Finland was part of Sweden. From that date to 1917, the country was a Russian duchy, which is why films are sometimes shot in Helsinki when the action is set in Leningrad/ St Petersburg – the nineteenth-century buildings are similar. Waltari was born a subject of the tsar. During the Second World War the country found itself in the impossible situation of having to choose between German fascism and Soviet communism. It chose the former. Defeated by the Soviet Union, it then had to sign the Moscow Peace Treaty of 12 March 1940 and cede 10 per cent of its eastern territory. Something of this must have been in Waltari's mind when he wrote *The Etruscan* just a decade after the war when his country's foreign policy was dictated from Moscow. Would Finland share Etruria's fate? Would it join the list of small countries that had disappeared or, like Lithuania, Latvia, and Estonia, were under threat of becoming Russified? When Waltari wrote *The Etruscan* at mid-century there were few optimistic nationalists in Finland or in Eastern Europe.

Today some of Waltari's novels stand on the library shelf at my university like ruins; the majority are in storage. The English first editions, printed on cheap stock, are faded, yellowed, worn, and dust-covered. None has been reprinted. *The Egyptian*, on DVD, is the exception, a digital survivor, still worth watching. Waltari's saeculum has come to an end.

9 Conway, "Etruria," *Encyclopedia Britannica*, 877.

18

Peggy Glanville-Hicks's Etruscan Concerto (*1954*):
Etruscan Music Imagined

For never are the ways of music moved without the greatest political
laws being moved.

Plato, *The Republic*[1]

Peggy Glanville-Hicks (1912–1990), the Australian-born composer,
wrote *Etruscan Concerto* in 1954, almost at the midpoint of a peripatetic
life that began in Melbourne and took her to England, France, Italy,
the United States, and Greece. Along the way she met and gained the
respect of most of the major composers of her generation – not an easy
thing for a woman in that era, as any historian of music will tell you.
During the 1930s she studied with Ralph Vaughan Williams at the Royal
College of Music and was introduced to French neoclassicism by Nadia
Boulanger, not known for her encouragement of female students.
On her arrival in New York in 1942 Glanville-Hicks would have described
herself as neoclassical in orientation but progressive in tendency – that
is, open to new ideas in music. She never found Arnold Schoenberg's
atonality (her term for both twelve-tone technique and serialism) attractive. She described it dismissively in later years as "not a musical form
but a mechanical gadget" that was "guaranteed to alienate the affections
of an audience."[2] And looking back at the neoclassicism of her early

---

1 IV, 424 E.

2 Glanville-Hicks, interview by Victoria Rogers, Australian Broadcasting
Corporation Radio, Perth, 19 August 1984, tape recording. Quoted in Victoria
Rogers, *The Music of Peggy Glanville-Hicks*, 88. Liner notes for *Sonata for Piano and
Percussion*, Columbia Records ML 4900 (New York, 1955).

compositions she wrote of it as "pushing around the rubble of the nineteenth century."[3] She thought of herself as thoroughly modern, far from Australian provincialism, and riding the wave of the new in the city that was challenging Paris for the title of the capital of contemporary classical music and art.

She knew most of the significant composers of her generation – among them, Leonard Bernstein, Benjamin Britten, Paul Bowles, John Cage, Aaron Copland, Henry Cowell, Lou Harrison, Henry Partch, Virgil Thomson – and many of the musicians who played their music. With her usual confidence she summarized the American scene in a 1950 article about new composers as follows:

America has a tiny minority of composers, often referred to as exotic, who are not content to make a new arrangement of the old sounds or a fresh version of the old forms. They want to change the whole sound and substance of the musical language and find new structural principles to govern their new materials.

The six composers, Edgar Varèse, John Cage, Colin McPhee, Alan Hovhaness, Paul Bowles, and Lou Harrison, have this in common despite a dazzling variety of ends and means: they each regard the rhythmic aspect of music as the basis of structure and form. They also realise the affinity this concept brings between their own and Eastern music systems. For most Far Eastern and Middle Eastern musical forms are based on a rhythm pattern. They are more like our jazz formulas, where a type of beat is the designing element, rather than a sonata form, a fugue, or some other convention as in our concert music.[4]

Anyone who read the article would be able to ask intelligent questions about the new music, name some of the prominent young composers, and even venture an opinion on the receptivity of the arts to foreign influences. Glanville-Hicks's high professional standing among these men is indicated by the fact that Leopold Stokowski, a star conductor in the period and remembered today primarily for his contribution to

3 Glanville-Hicks, interview by Charles Southwood, "Composer Profile: Peggy Glanville-Hicks," Sydney, n.d., tape recording, ABC Radio Tapes, Australia Music Centre Library, Sydney, Tape C2610, quoted in Rogers, *The Music of Peggy Glanville-Hicks*, 87. All quotations from Rogers will be cited in the text.

4 Glanville-Hicks, "Musical Explorers: Six Americans Who Are Changing the Musical Vocabulary," 112.

Fantasia (1940), premiered her *Letters from Morocco* in 1953 to a sold-out house at the Museum of Modern Art.

Anaïs Nin, a perceptive observer of the cultural scene, knew Glanville-Hicks well in the early 1950s and left a vivid portrait in her diary from the winter of 1950–51.

She is small, very slender, very quick, with eloquent hands designing patterns in space to illustrate her talk. She has a small, impish face, with innocent, sharp, focused eyes, a humorous uptilted nose, a dimpled smile. She is decisive, sharp-witted. She wears her hair short, like an adolescent, brushed upward. She is a witty polemicist. It does not appear at first like a battle. Her sword-play is invisible, it is done with a smile, but the accuracy of it is deadly. She mocks the composers and the critics who interfere with the development of a woman composer. She is asked to recommend, to bless, to support lesser composers, to introduce them, help them on their way. But this help is not returned. It was the first time I had heard a brilliant, effective woman demonstrate the obstacles which impaired her professional achievement because she was a woman.

I gave her all my books.[5]

The telling brief thrust of the penultimate sentence reminds us that Nin knew first-hand the obstacles her friend had overcome and continued to face.

Without New York's musical scene Glanville-Hicks probably wouldn't have discovered her new way of thinking about music. The English composers she knew were less experimental in seeking new systems of notation to replace the traditional Western scale and to stretch harmony to include discordant elements. The shift in thinking can be heard already in Debussy's whole-tone scales, Schoenberg's twelve-tone serialism, and Stravinsky's octatonic scales. Her work as an organizer with the League of Composers involved her in promoting the performance of new composers like herself. Not only did she know the new wave

5 Nin, *The Diary of Anaïs Nin*, 61–3. The friendship with Nin brought together two exceptionally independent modern women who admired Lawrence. Nin had published *D.H. Lawrence: An Unprofessional Study* (1932), a sympathetic reading of Lawrence's life and work. Henry Miller, Nin's sometime lover, saw himself as a disciple of the writer. His *The World of Lawrence: A Passionate Appreciation*, was published posthumously in 1985.

composers, she heard their music regularly, often as it was premiered. And, encouraged by the irascible Virgil Thomson, she reviewed from 1947 to 1958 for the *New York Herald Tribune*, while also freelancing for magazines like *Hi-Fi Music at Home* and popular magazines like *Vogue*. Her writing is a polygraph of her development as a composer.

Crucial to her development was her meeting with the multi-talented Paul Bowles in 1944. As much as any American composer, Bowles saw creative possibilities in the harmonic uncertainties of "Eastern music systems," particularly those of North Africa, that ignored European notions of harmony. Stimulated by their close relationship, Glanville-Hicks wrote works that look beyond the standard canon for their inspiration: *Profiles from China* (1944, five songs for mezzo-soprano and piano), *Letters from Morocco* (1952, song cycle for tenor and orchestra), *Sinfonia da Pacifica* (1952–53, for orchestra), *The Transposed Heads* (1953, opera), *Etruscan Concerto* (1954, piano and chamber orchestra), and *Pre-Columbian Prelude and Presto* (1957, for various instruments including pan pipes, whistles, maracas, conch).[6] The substantive change is on the level of musical structure. According to Virginia Rogers, the composer's "solution to the dilemma of Western art music ... was a musical structure based on melody and rhythm, and it drew extensively on the six musical explorers whom she so greatly admired" (91–2). Without abandoning harmony altogether, she reduced it to a decorative role in what is a "melodic-rhythmic structural procedure" (92). Today, she and artists like Bowles (interested in Morocco) and Colin McPhee (the gamelan music of Bali) would be described as post-Western and multicultural. Less generous critics might mention pastiche or appropriation.

It is not clear from Wendy Beckett's biography precisely when Glanville-Hicks became interested in the Etruscans, though it probably occurred when she took evening courses in classical history at Oxford. Beckett mentions a later collection of fine Etruscan vases, but it is doubtful she could have afforded these before the composition of the concerto written during her most productive and original period. There is no record of any comments by her about the Etruscans prior to the writing of the concerto in 1954, though she spent six weeks in Italy in 1937

---

6 The opera is based on Thomas Mann's story of the same title set in ancient India and involving a love triangle. Glanville-Hicks's score combined Indian folk elements with her melody-rhythm approach. The libretto closely followed Mann's story as translated by H.T. Lowe-Porter.

and returned there shortly after finishing the work. The comments on the cover of the MGM recording point to Lawrence as a source, perhaps the only one: "The three movements of this highly coloured work present evocations of the moods of the Etruscan tombs of Tarquinia and [have] quotations from D.H. Lawrence's *Etruscan Places*." These excerpts are not read during a live performance I have on CD. Without them, however, far too much depends on the adjective in the title to evoke an Etruscan mood or theme. The adjective can be nothing more than a general pointer to a relatively unknown culture whose musical sounds the listener must imagine before hearing the concerto. The same point applies to her *Pre-Columbian Prelude and Presto* three years later. Compare the two titles to *Slavonic Dances, The Pines of Rome, Karelia,* or *Warsaw Concerto,* all of which create expectations based on a known referent. My guess is that Glanville-Hicks was writing a musical palimpsest on Lawrence's *Etruscan Places* with each of the three sectional quotations evoking one aspect of his vision. Like many others she imagines the Rasenna by way of Lawrence, who, I imagine, would have been pleasantly surprised since he had little interest in music in general and no interest in modern music.

Virginia Rogers's account of the concerto, concise and musicologically informed, describes its sources as follows: "[T]he melodic sources in the *Etruscan Concerto* are, in whole or in part, non-Western … Glanville-Hicks herself pointed to the Indian derivation of the themes in the third movement … The six-note theme which opens the work, the pentatonicism of the second and fourth themes of the opening movement, and the decorative arabesques in the second movement all suggest non-Western sources of some kind. Exactly what those sources were is unclear; that the melodic material was derived from music of the Middle and/or Far East is suggested, however, by Glanville-Hicks's attraction to non-Western sources that can be linked broadly to a Eurasian cultural area (north African/Arab/Indian and later Greek)."

She closes with the judgment that "the work … is appealing in a timeless way" (167–70). I understand what Rogers means by "timeless" but have the impression that it is simultaneously very much of its time: in other words, this is what *timelessness* sounded like in the 1940s and 1950s. Today it is often evoked by electronic music. Unlike some reviewers, Rogers doesn't fall back on adjectives suggesting a vague Orientalism or exoticism, though these seem to me inevitable given the non-existence of an Etruscan connection. How Etruscan can a concerto be if the composer relies on melodic material derived from contemporary music of the Middle or Far East? Analogous questions could be posed about her ambitious and fascinating opera *Nausicaa* (1960) – with libretto by the composer and Robert Graves – described by Wendy Beckett as drawing "on musical idioms from regions as diverse as Epirus, the Peloponnese, Crete and the Dodecanese" (160).[7]

We know a great deal more about the music of classical Greece than about that of Etruria. Andrew Barker describes Greek music as "essential to the pattern and texture of Greek life at all social levels, providing a widely available means for the expression of communal identity and values, and a focus for controversy, judgement, and partisanship with which all citizens could enthusiastically engage."[8] Music's social importance is suggested by Homer's description of Achilles playing the lyre and singing in his tent (*Iliad*, 9.186–9). That one image establishes the essential difference between Greece and Rome, since no Roman epic hero sings or plays an instrument. Study of the lyre and pipes was part of the education of a young Greek but not of a young Roman. All forms of poetry, from epic to lyric, were accompanied by a lyre, and choruses in tragedies and comedies were accompanied by pipes, which also provided music at banquets, sacrifices, and funerals. A different indication of music's importance comes from Plato and Aristotle who assume that music helps express moral qualities and can shape character. Plato also suggests that only the positive Dorian and Phrygian musical modes be permitted because they give expression to courage and moderation respectively. Fragments of Greek music survive, and there is even a papyrus from 200 BCE with musical notation – perhaps by the dramatist – for Euripides's *Orestes*. So far as we know, "Greek music was almost entirely melodic, without harmonization," which was probably also true of Etruscan and Roman.[9] If I say little about music in Rome, it is because there is no doubt that, as with vases, Greece provided the decisive

---

7 *Time.* summarized the story as follows: "Princess Nausicaa hears a group of young noblemen, her suitors, planning to overthrow her father, King Alcinous. She plots against the suitors, sees them all killed, and asks only one thing as her reward: 'I demand that in future it will be / My version of a faithful Penelope / My story of the palace war / My account of the part women played that you will sing.'" It premiered at the Herodes Atticus theatre in Athens to an audience of 5,000 and was a hit. It has not been revived. See Beckett, *Peggy Glanville-Hicks*, 163–4.

8 Barker, "Music in Greek and Roman Life," 479.

9 Howatson, "Music," in *The Oxford Companion to Classical Literature*, 373–4.

influence on Etruscan music. Music played an important role in all
Roman secular and religious events, but no Latin writer claimed that it
was in any way original.

The Etruscan musical evidence is slighter. Tomb paintings and
inscribed mirrors with images of instruments, some surviving instruments, and a few scattered references give us an idea of what Etruscan
musicians looked like and what instruments they played. The player
with the double-tube reed *aulos* (Latin: *tibiae*) in the accompanying
image, from the Tomb of the Leopards (see figure 18.1), holds an
instrument that is a larger version of the one played in the Tomb of the
Triclinium. Add a lyre or two, and we can speculate that Etruscan music
(of which nothing survives) might have sounded like Greek or Roman.
Fredrik Tobin points out that "some scholars have gone so far as to
suggest that the music of Greece and Etruria were practically identical
in terms of rhythms, scales and melodic structures" but reminds us that
there is no evidence for this view. Still, it is a suggestive educated guess.
And though nothing is known about Etruscan musical notation or how
the music sounded, we do know "quite a lot about the way in which
music and instruments figured in Etruscan society."[10] Not surprisingly,
the instruments resemble wind, string, and percussion instruments
found around the Mediterranean. It is probable that Etruscans conducted sacrifices at altars to the accompaniment of an *aulos*, lyre, and
perhaps a *tympanon*, though Emiliano di Castro points out that "no
evidence of [the *tympanon*] exists in the archaeological record [and]
no surviving depictions in tomb paintings exist."[11] Other instruments
include the following: the *chelys lyra*; the *barbiton*, which resembles the
chelys lyra but has longer arms; the *kithara*, a flat-bottomed lyre with
elaborately constructed arms. Of lip reed instruments or trumpets there
are three general shapes: the *cornu*, which is curved; the *lituus*, which is
straight but ends with a short curve, rather like an elbow in a pipe; and
the *tuba* (Greek: *salpinx*) which is straight. Etruscan trumpets – *tyrsenike
salpinx* – are mentioned in Aeschylus (*Eumenides*, 567–8), Sophocles
(*Ajax*, 17), and Euripides (*Heracles*, 830, *Phoenician Women*, 1377–8, and
the still disputed *Rhesus*, 988). They were reserved for military and civic

10 Tobin, "Music and Musical Instruments in Etruria," 847, 841. This is an excellent
introduction to the topic, and I rely heavily on it in the following summary of music and
musical instruments.

11 Li Castro, "Musical Instruments," 517.

18.1 "The aulos player," Tomb of the Leopards (Tarquinia), c. 475 BCE.

events and, not surprisingly, are absent from banquet scenes. Strabo traces the use of trumpets in Rome to Etruscan sources, and we know that they were specifically used for rituals dealing with the dead. An engraved mirror now in the Museum of Fine Arts in Boston shows an athlete in mid-jump while a musician plays an *aulos* (a reed sometimes misidentified as a flute). Aelian, writing in the second and third century CE, recalls that Etruscan hunters used sweet and soft music to lure animals into their traps. A seventh-century BCE metal vessel from Chiusi has a frieze with an *aulos* player followed by a dog and a row of wild boars, seemingly portraying a similar story. The Etruscans probably did use instruments to drive game during hunts and to gather their herds. More controversial is Plutarch's suggestion in the *Moralia* that the Etruscans flogged their slaves to the accompaniment of music. Most scholars dismiss this as anti-Etruscan propaganda.[12] It's worth adding that there are references to Etruscan singing: Tages is reported

12 Niebuhr's *The History of Rome* offers this summary of Etruscan music: "The Roman music was derived from Etruria: their stage-singers too came from thence. Like the minstrels in the middle ages, the Etruscan *hister* danced and sang to instrumental music, which kept time with the verse, without any regular measure. Stringed instruments occur here and there on the monuments: but the proper native instrument was the flute" (136).

as singing "the Disciplina Etrusca to the lucumones of the twelve cities."
Emeline Richardson suggests that "in Etruria song was the preroga-
tive of the haruspex and the seer," and this may explain the lack of
lyric poetry.[13]

   Nothing in the historical record offers the audience of the *Etruscan
Concerto* a point of reference for the sound of Etruscan music. By
contrast, Camille Saint-Saëns's Concerto no. 5, op. 103, *The Egyptian*
(1896) can rely on a listener's knowledge of ancient and modern Egypt
and an awareness of the sound of ersatz Egyptian music in operas like
Aida and Hollywood movies. Hollywood has imagined Persian, Greek,
Egyptian, and Roman music for us in the scores of prolific film composers like Dimitri Tiomkin (*Land of the Pharaohs*, *The Fall of the Roman
Empire*), Alex North (*Cleopatra*, *Spartacus*), Alfred Newman (*The Egyptian*,
The Robe), and Miklós Rózsa (*Quo Vadis*, *Ben Hur*, *King of Kings*). The
Roman armies march to drums and trumpets; modern flutes and lyres
play soft arabesques in Cleopatra's chambers and provide the colour
at banquets; and dance scenes tend toward percussion and orchestra
music. If we want to hear an authentic Etruscan soundscape, or at least
a possible simulacrum, we might begin by assembling all the Etruscan
instruments listed above and have them play some Greek or Roman
music for which we have notation. Tobin points out that some scholars
have gone so far as to suggest that Etruscan music resembled Greek in
rhythms, scales, and melodic structures. Though he warns that it
"cannot be emphasized enough that this view is not built on any direct
evidence but only on the assumption that the adoption of new instruments also means the adoption of a related new repertoire of music."[14]
In other words, to play Greek music on Etruscan instruments might
bring us closer to the sounds of ancient Etruria – which was heavily
influenced by all forms of Greek culture – than any other approach.
Another alternative would be to have a composer create fanfares, songs,
marches, laments, ritual music, and perhaps a sonata or trio to be
played by the appropriate instruments, assuming that modern copies
of these can be made. This would at least bring us close to the actual
sounds of Etruscan instruments.

13 Richardson, *The Etruscans*, 227.
14 Tobin, "Music and Musical Instruments in Etruria," 843.

This is not intended as a judgment on Glanville-Hicks: like Waltari and Lawrence, she imagined the Etruscans in an original work of art based on the available materials – Etruscan antiquities, non-Western music, and *Etruscan Places*. And the *Etruscan Concerto* has lasted. I heard its most recent recorded performance on CBC Radio a few months ago, with Keith Jarrett playing the piano. It has established a place in the modern repertoire, if not for Etruscan music then for music with an affinity for the Etruscans.

PART FIVE

The Etruscans Enter Our World: The Holocaust, Modernism, the Cold War, Hollywood, Phenomenology, and Marilyn Monroe

19

Giorgio Bassani's The Garden of the Finzi-Continis *(1962):*
EtruscansJewsItalians

They resurrect the past from the distortions and injustice of oblivion.

George Steiner[1]

Every nation has one or more writers who would not have suffered as writers if they had never left the town of their birth. Almost all the novels and stories of Giorgio Bassani (1916–2000) are set in the Ferrara of his time. When he published his collected fiction in 1974, he titled the volume *Il Romanzo di Ferrara* (*The Novel of Ferrara*) as if it were one work. Despite this format there is no doubt that *The Garden of the Finzi-Continis* (1962) is Bassani's greatest book and his major claim to fame. It is a work of emotional and intellectual power and artistic distinction. Vittorio De Sica's film version, which Bassani disliked, extended his international reputation. The novel is at once a story of unrequited love, a portrait of the writer as a young man, and a novel of the Holocaust, which we never witness directly. Like Giuseppe Tomasi di Lampedusa's *The Leopard*, it engages the catastrophe of history obliquely, never confronting the reader with events we know to be as tragic as any in the century, perhaps in all of history. The ultimate cause of anti-Semitism may be in the politics of Rome or Berlin, but the novel presents it sifted into local terms as an insult at a tennis club or an absurd regulation at the university executed by an innocuous agent known to everyone. With small gestures as casual as the daily social forms of recognition and address, Bassani makes human the great questions the novel's events raise: Can one be an Italian Jew or

1   Steiner, *My Unwritten Books*, 20.

a Jewish Italian? On what basis do we determine a national identity? To what extent is any individual responsible for his society's evil deeds? Standing in the wings are the Etruscans, like distinguished but slightly shabby, not-quite-forgotten ancestors, represented by their tombs at Cerveteri, serving like a silenced chorus from an earlier, similarly distressed period of the Italian past.

From the beginning Bassani emphasizes the connection between the past and present, as well as the writer's role in the recuperation of a past that may seem remote but remains in view. This is not surprising since he studied art history at Bologna with the great Roberto Longhi and remembered his teacher's emphasis on the importance of the restoration of Renaissance paintings, one form of homage and recuperation. Bassani's dedication of *La Parole Preparate* (1966), a collection of essays, to Benedetto Croce points to another crucial influence: a philosopher for whom all history is present history. Though Bassani doesn't write what is traditionally thought of as historical fiction, *The Garden of the Finzi-Continis* breathes history on every page. The Finzi-Contini Mausoleum, in its combination of Egyptian, Minoan, late Roman, and Ostrogothic styles, is as much a metaphor for the stratigraphy of history as the Etruscan tombs at Cerveteri visited early in the novel. The two tombs triangulate the novel spatially in relation to a third burial site, the unknown Golgotha probably somewhere in southern Poland where Micòl and other members of the family of the title are buried in an unmarked mass grave. The novel's time scheme begins with the Etruscans, represented by their tombs, shifts to the history of the Italian Jews, and ends with the catastrophe of the Second World War which recapitulates the disappearance of the Etruscans with that of the Jews which took place on the same soil.

Bassani's interweaving of Italian and Jewish details, often using the most ordinary objects and mundane events, is subtle and incremental. Ferrara's many street names act as metaphors for the historical record going back to the Renaissance, while a sprinkling of references to Hitler, Stalin, Mussolini, and Mussolini's son-in-law Count Ciano ground the events in the 1930s and 1940s. The fictional characters may live in a provincial town and thus on history's periphery, but they are subtly embedded in historical time, whose full reach and ironic implications are evident on every page. The narrator Celestino shares both points of view since, as he writes in the prologue, the impulse to write about the past "came to me only a year ago on a Sunday in April 1957."[2] The prologue is an establishing glance backward by way of a contemporary excursion that takes a detour to Cerveteri to look at the Etruscan burial mounds. This sets in motion a casual discussion of Etruscan tombs, which inevitably suggest mortality and history. A young girl tells her parents, "In our history book the Etruscans are at the beginning, next to the Egyptians and the Jews. Tell me Papà: who do you think were more ancient, the Etruscans or the Jews?" (7). The conversation then sets the narrator wondering what significance there could be for the Etruscans "after the Roman conquest in the constant visiting of the cemetery at the edge of their city" (8). He imagines them moving among "the cone-shaped tombs, solid and massive as the bunkers that the German soldiers scattered over Europe in vain during the last war ... The world changed, of course, they must have said to themselves, it was no longer what it had once been, when Etruria, with its confederation of free, aristocratic city-states, had dominated almost the whole peninsula. New civilizations, more crude and popular, but also stronger and more inured, now reigned. But what did it matter?" (9). The drift into a conditional past unobtrusively becomes "a return in my memory to the years of my early youth, and to Ferrara, and to the Jewish cemetery at the end of the Via Montebello." And the turn in memory leads to the revelation in the section's final paragraph that only one of the Finzi-Contini family is buried in the ornate family mausoleum; the others, who are only names to us at this point, were "all deported to Germany in the autumn of '43. Who could say if they found any sort of burial at all?" (10). If we think we remember the scene of deportation it is only because De Sica insisted, over Bassani's objection, on filming one. Celestino will later tell us that after 1939 he never again saw Micòl, her brother Alberto, Signora Olga, Signora Regina, or Professor Ermano, the author of a work listing all the Jews buried in Venice's Lido cemetery. In the novel's long view of Italian history, the Etruscans are an Italian people, just like the Jews, who were removed from history when conquered by Rome. We know that Mussolini liked to think of his regime as ancient Rome reincarnate. The question that hangs over the Jews of Ferrara during the war is whether the Jews, whose history is at least as old as that of the Etruscans, will suffer a similar fate.

---

2 Bassani, *The Garden of the Finzi-Continis*, 5. All references will be to this edition.

Bassani subtly intimates the increasing menace by noting in passing the various restrictions – no tennis between Aryans and Jews – placed on Jews even prior to the introduction of the racial laws of 14 July 1938. Celestino emphasizes that he and his family "had always been very normal people, even banal in our normality" (140). They were assimilated Italian Jews who were being disenfranchised prior to being murdered. There were about 750 Jews in Ferrara before the war; 173 were deported in 1943 to German death camps by the puppet Republic of Salò set up by the Germans after Mussolini was deposed. The Finzi-Contini are the focus for the Jewish theme, which is already present in condensed form in the prologue. Even without the Holocaust, the Finzi-Contini family name would have died out since there were no male heirs. That they were already living in the past is suggested in the Professor's research in the Jewish cemetery and the family's pride in the grandmother's familiarity with the poets in the circle of Giosuè Carducci, who received the Nobel Prize in Literature in 1906. For Micòl, "the past counted more than the present, possession counted less than the memory of it. Compared with memory, all possessions can only seem disappointing, banal, inadequate" (186). That the narrator shares Micòl's Proustian attitude makes him the inevitable chronicler of their history. His novel will be their proper tomb and memorial. There is a subtle onomastic connection between Celestino and Micòl: his name means "belonging to heaven"; hers has roots in the Hebrew "queen" and "who is like God." If Micòl can be said to rise above Ferrara by ignoring its morality and politics, Celestino is her symbolic other, because he analyzes and judges it only after the war in his novel. His writing is an act of expiation and a plea for forgiveness for not having seen the family after he and Micòl separated. The novel that begins with an unexpected visit to Etruscan tombs ends with a farewell to the past, especially to the dead young woman who thought of the past as "the dear, sweet, *sainted* past" (246) and detested the idea of a future. She hovers over Bassani's novel like the murdered Jews who haunt Ferrara. Her translation of Emily Dickinson's "I died for Beauty" is placed like an anticipatory epitaph at the novel's midpoint.

I died for beauty, but was scarce
Adjusted in the tomb,
When one who died for truth was lain
In an adjoining room.

He questioned softly why I failed?
"For beauty," I replied.
"And I for truth, the two are one;
We brethren, are," he said.

And so, as kinsmen, met a night,
We talked between the rooms,
Until the grass had reached our lips,
And covered up our names.

Some readers will have noticed the absence of Dickinson's characteristic capitalization and dashes in the translation. It also occurs in the Italian text. The explanation must be that Micòl's text is an Italian translation published in the 1920s or 1930s, two decades before Thomas H. Johnson's publication of the "unreconstructed" edition in 1955 that restored what Dickinson had written.

The Garden of the Finzi-Continis is a novel of unique rooms – houses, tombs, ruins, churches, and schools. The poem's tomb is the final imagined resting place of Celestino and Micòl, one dying for Truth, and the other dead for Beauty. Neither with you nor without you? Except in Bassani's novel. Bassani changes one word in Dickinson's poem to make her tomb recall the grass-covered tombs at Cerveteri. The poet wrote, "Until the *Moss* had reached our lips." Micòl changes moss ("muschio") to grass ("erba"). The English translator, for some reason, ignores her choice and prints "moss." I have changed it back to "grass." After all, in Italian, her poem brings together Etruscans and Jews.

20

Pablo Picasso, Alberto Giacometti, and David Smith:
Etruscan Affinities, and a Note on Massimo Campigli

Great artists steal.

After T.S. Eliot[1]

Massimo Campigli (1895–1971) was one of those rare modern artists who didn't have to "steal" – in T.S. Eliot's sense – because he didn't seem to have suffered from anxiety of influence and he was more than happy to declare his artistic debts. The most notable was to the Etruscans: "What influenced me for the longest time was Etruscan art, which was a turning point for my painting in 1928. I loved that little, smiling humanity that makes one smile. I envied the blissful sleep of these terracotta odalisques on their sarcophagi, and their way of being dead. A pagan happiness entered in my paintings, both in the spirit of the subjects and in the spirit of the work, which became more free and lyrical."[2] The encounter immediately changed the direction of his painting. Previously influenced by Fernand Léger, Pablo Picasso, and Marino Marini – *Acrobati* (1926), *Zingari* (1928) – he moved almost immediately to painting two-dimensional female figures in asymmetrical, hieratic, roughly textured compositions with subdued "Etruscan" colours.[3] No

---

1 Eliot, *The Sacred Wood*, 125. Eliot writes, "Immature poets imitate; mature poets steal; bad poets deface what they take, and good poets make it into something better, or at least something different."
2 Campigli, "Massimo Campigli and the Etruscans," 61.
3 Giancarlo Serafini's *Omaggio a Campigli* offers a generous selection of paintings across his career with six perspectives on it by Campigli, Raffaele Carrieri, André Chastel, Raffaele de Grada, Jean Paulhan, and Franco Russoli.

one would mistake them for imitations of Etruscan originals but there is an unmistakable filiation or affinity with life-sized statues on temple roofs and figures on sarcophagi. These fresco-like paintings were featured in his exhibitions during the 1930s in Milan, Paris, and New York and made his reputation. A century later they were part of the Venice Biennale in 2021–22 in an exhibition titled *Massimo Campigli and the Etruscans: A Pagan Happiness*. The encounter with Etruscan art was Campigli's Damascus moment – his *coup de foudre* – in a very successful career. Like Saul/Paul he remained true to his revelation for the remainder of his life. In other words, it both made him as an artist and prevented him from developing, as is evident from even a casual glance at three works across the decades: *Le Grand Magasin* or *La Marché* (1929), *Six Women* (1945), and *Figura/Busto* (1961). He has something in common with Teddy Lloyd, the painter in Muriel Spark's *The Prime of Miss Jean Brodie*, the faces of whose female portraits all recall Jean's, the object of his hopeless love. On the other hand, one can't imagine Campigli waking up and wondering what he would paint that day.

Etruscan art played a much less important role in Picasso's career, but, as I will suggest, the encounter with it may have had significant unforeseen consequences for major sculptures by Giacometti and Smith. There is general agreement that all three created sculptures similar to the tall, elongated Etruscan statues of which the most famous is L'Ombra della Sera (Evening Shadow) in Volterra (see figure 20.1).

Picasso's (1881–1973) Etruscan debt is obvious and the creative provenance, so to speak, well documented. He moved into the Château de Boisgeloup, seventy-two kilometres northwest of Paris, in mid-summer 1930. Two bodies of work over the next year show an Etruscan influence. The etchings for a 1931 edition of Ovid's *Metamorphoses* show an awareness of the Etruscan mirrors with mythological scenes incised on their backs that he saw at the Louvre. He might have known that Jean-Auguste-Dominique Ingres, whose drawings he admired, had studied them a century earlier. Other sources have been suggested, but the mirrors seem the most important. We also know that among his books and magazines he had *Antiquités étrusques, grecs et romaines* (1786), engraved by François-Anne David, and the recent May 1930 issue of the magazine *Documents* with reproductions of Etruscan sculpture from the Villa Giulia. John Richardson, his biographer, suggests that Picasso was inspired by these reproductions and by his wife, Marie-Thérèse Walter, to whittle sixteen long wooden carvings of her which

20.1 L'Ombra della Sera, third century BCE.

"predict" (his verb) the later, similarly elongated figures of Alberto Giacometti (1901–1966).[4] Picasso used mostly canvas stretchers and branches found in the park. There is a close resemblance between these thin, long wooden figures and the eccentric Villa Giulia statues. The latter are not, however, as long and attenuated as those in Volterra or Perugia, copies of which are often on sale today in the piazzas of the major Italian cities. While Richardson is confident that Alberto Giacometti learned something from Picasso's tall figures, he is unwilling

4 John Richardson, *A Life of Picasso*, 3:421–2. (Sculptures of Marie-Thérèse, 1930. Carved wood, ht. 48 cm, 51 cm, and 55.7 cm. Musée Picasso, Paris.)

to claim more than that Giacometti's slim, tall figures are "closely related" to Volterra's L'Ombra della Sera. In other words, he stops short of suggesting Picasso's influence.

This seems wise since doubt continues to hang over discussions of influence in the creation of the thin walking and standing figures that first appear in Giacometti's work after his 1948 show at the Pierre Matisse Gallery in New York. It is worth recalling that L'Ombra della Sera is not a unique figure in this elongated style, though it is the tallest. Rome's Villa Giulia has a similar male figure at 40 centimetres and a female at 28 centimetres. The Louvre has another, smaller version which Giacometti might have seen during its 1955 Etruscan exhibition. Opinion remains divided over whether he did or not. And if he did, did the statues influence the crucial postwar turn in his sculpture? James Lord, his biographer, is confident that "though vaguely reminiscent of certain Etruscan figurines, [Giacometti's] are not derived from them, being far closer in spirit to Egyptian deities."[5] This isn't convincing, though I assume Lord is thinking of the thin 1932 statue *Femme qui marche*. David Sylvester, however, nods in the Etruscan direction in discussing the same sculptures, but even he doesn't see a *decisive* influence: "It is often said that these proportions were derived from Etruscan sculptures, but, while certain particular works, such as *The Chariot* of 1950, *must have been based* [my italics] on Etruscan images, their famous attenuation was probably not a stylistic influence: those sculptures were far too relaxed in form to appeal to an artist whose eye had been educated by the Egyptian, the Sumerian and the Cycladic."[6] This is a curiously self-contradicting statement: how can one work be based on another without being influenced by it?

I expected the issue to be settled by the 2011 exhibition *Giacometti and the Etruscans* at the Pinacothèque in Paris. The catalogue, however, features far too many short notes and articles written in what might be called the "one step forward, half step back" school of rhetoric. Everyone agrees that the young Giacometti must have been aware of the Etruscans, that he saw the Louvre's Etruscan exhibition in 1955 (without L'Ombra della Sera), that he must have seen L'Ombra della Sera in Volterra on a later trip, and that there must be something between affinity and

5 Lord, *Mythic Giacometti*, 85.
6 Sylvester, *Looking at Giacometti*, 149.

20.2 Alberto Giacometti, *The Chariot*, 1950.

influence at play in the relationship between his figures and the relevant Etruscan ones. Unfortunately, no one can avoid the fact that the sculptor probably saw L'Ombra della Sera and other relevant Etruscan pieces only after creating figures like *Walking Man* (1947), *Staggering Man* (1950), *The Chariot* (1950) (see figure 20.2), and *Standing Woman* (1952). Sylvester's "must have been based" suggests a doubt echoed to some degree by almost every contributor to *Giacometti and the Etruscans.*

The visual evidence looks convincing, but the individual arguments fall short and key dates don't quite match. My eye wants to believe in a direct line from the Etruscans to Giacometti's later body of work, but the confirming evidence isn't there. At least, not as decisively as between Cycladic art and *Tête qui regarde* or *Spoon Woman* (1926). Giacometti's interest in Cycladic sculpture began early and stayed with him throughout his life.

It is worth noting in passing that we still don't have a convincing explanation of L'Ombra della Sera's function or an account of its aesthetic or cultural aetiology. Jean MacIntosh Turfa makes an interesting connection to the Brontoscopic Calendar – a rare Etruscan document – which predicts for 29 December that "if it thunders, it signifies the most healthful leanness for bodies." She mentions that a few figures and models depict slimness without implying ill health and points to "fine bronze figures of gods (Diana) and priests (haruspices) [that] are thin and attenuated but with healthy faces ... and a number of terracotta statues of partial figures ... rather thin and elongated." She suggests that the exaggeration was "for artistic effect."[7] Alessandro Furesi ventures in *Giacometti et les Étrusques* that the anorexic figure is either a votary offering on behalf of a young man suffering from something like gigantism or it represents Tages, the wise young man, who came out of the earth with his revelation. Sybille Haynes suggests, however, that "the stylization of the latter's elongated flat body goes back to an older level of popular cult in Italy, documented by boardlike, wood ex-votos and thin figurines cut from sheet metal, a formal tradition untouched by Classical and Hellenistic proportions."[8] Whatever the tall bronze statue in Volterra means, it has stood erect since at least 1731. A century and a half later, Gabriele D'Annunzio named it L'Ombra della Sera.

7 Turfa, "Health and Medicine in Etruria," 864–5.
8 Haynes, *Etruscan Civilization*, 374.

Three other instances of Etruscan influence on modern sculpture should be mentioned. John Rewald sees an Etruscan presence in Giacomo Manzù's (1908–1981) early "coloured stucco relief *Annunciation,* a tinted terra-cotta *Gatekeeper,* and a *Pillar of Solomon* in marble, his first work in stone."9 Henry Moore's (1898–1986) stylized, horizontal *Three Piece Reclining Figure: Draped* of 1975 is the artist's tribute to an Etruscan predecessor, though *Three Standing Pieces* (1953) had already shown affinities. And I would add David Smith (1906–1965) because of a possible connection between his eleven stand-alone *Forgings* (see figure 20.3) and Giacometti. These are slender, vertical columns of various widths, 1.7 to 1.8 metres in height, made of flat steel bars that, Joan Pachner writes, "suggest kinship with [Barnett] Newman's signature, abstract, vertical 'zips,' and Giacometti's tall, thin figures."10 Rosalind Kraus points out that Smith's library at the time of his death had several copies of *Cahiers d'art* from 1929 with reproductions of Giacometti's early work, and she suggests a relationship between the latter's *Woman with Her Throat Cut* (1932) and Smith's *Suspended Figure* (1935). We also know that he was aware of Picasso as early as 1932 when he saw his *Construction in Metal Wire* in *Cahiers d'art* (no. 4, [1929]) and responded to it in 1936 with *Aerial Construction.*11 I mention these creative vectors simply to indicate Smith's nearly lifelong awareness of these two major predecessors. To return to the Etruscans: if – and it is a large "if" – Giacometti was at all influenced by L'Ombra della Sera or even by Picasso's Etruscan-inflected wooden Marie-Thérèse figures, then Smith's *Forgings* may have an Etrurian lineage.

There is an austere winter photograph by Dan Budnik, from 1962, of Smith sitting on a bench without a jacket, his back to the camera, looking at nineteen tall pieces of sculpture in a variety of styles standing in a snow-covered field at Bolton Landing in upper New York State.12 Looking at the picture I imagine an exhibition of sculpture in which one could walk from the elongated Etruscan figures to Picasso's carvings of Marie-Thérèse, Giacometti's walking men and women, and Smith's towering *Forgings.* The four bodies of work belong together. They speak to each other across time, whatever their degree of Etruscan filiation. Let's imagine David Smith's bench with four sculptors on it. Let's call

9 Rewald, *Giacomo Manzù,* 15.
10 Pachner, *David Smith,* 63.
11 Kraus, *Terminal Iron Work,* 36.
12 It is reproduced in Pachner, *David Smith,* 139.

20.3 David Smith, "Forging IV, Forging III, Forging I, Untitled, Forging IX, Forging XI, Construction in Rectangles, Forging II, Construction with Forged Neck," 1955.

the Etruscan Vulca, after a decorator of the Temple of Jupiter Capitolinus, and place him beside Picasso, next to Giacometti, beside Smith.[13]

---

13 Georges Braque almost found a place in this book with his 1953 ceiling for the Louvre's Etruscan gallery. Unfortunately, his motif of giant white birds had nothing to do with the Etruscan artifacts. The most obvious Etruscan note in Braque's body of work appears in the engraved plaster panels he designed for Paul Rosenberg's Paris apartment. These echoed his illustrations for an edition of Hesiod – perhaps his answer to Picasso's recent etchings for Ovid's *Metamorphoses* – and "were executed in a rhythmic, cursive hand, patterned on the ornamentation of the ancient Greek and Etruscan pieces he had studied in the Louvre thirty years earlier" (Danchev, *Braque*, 198). In the end Braque, despite his reputed Etruscan affinities, produced fewer works of Etruscan-inflected art than Picasso.

21

Zbigniew Herbert and Wisława Szymborska: Etruscans, Poles, and "Peoples Unlucky in History"

A political organism which requires the permanent, forcible subjection
of large groups of its population is likely to end by totally brutalizing
and stultifying itself. I am not saying that it will therefore destroy itself
physically, only that it may destroy itself morally and culturally,
which is not the same thing.

M.I. Finley[1]

Few twentieth-century poets were as interested in the classical world
as Zbigniew Herbert (1924–1998). References, allusions, and quotations from the ancients – various etymologies of respect and
remembrance – appear throughout his essays and poems, from *Chord
of Light* (1956), his first book, to *Epilogue to a Storm* (1998), his last.
The Etruscans appear as early as 1965 in the Polish essay "O Etruskach,"
and references to them are never merely decorative or ornamental,
either in an Orientalizing fashion or as figures intimating high culture
and moral seriousness. Herbert is a humanist for whom the answer
to the question "Why the classics?" is as self-evident as it was to
Winckelmann, to Burckhardt, and to Herbert's mentor, the philosopher Henryk Elzenberg. Herbert had no illusions about the sweetness
and light of classical Greece, but he believed that the past had posed
the right questions about human values and the meaning of history.
He was a troubled Catholic who went to school more often to
Thucydides and Marcus Aurelius than to Augustine and Aquinas. Some
of the lyrics concerned with the ancients are among his finest and best

---

1 Finley, *Aspects of Antiquity*, 145.

known, including "To Marcus Aurelius," "The Rain," "Why the Classics," "The Envoy of Mr Cogito," "Livy's Metamorphoses," and "Journey."

Because these poems about the past exist in his collections within a matrix of poems of contemporary life and history, we tend to read them as inflected by Herbert's life and Poland's historical situation in the twentieth century. The classics provide a reflective matrix of historical details, works of art, and, in the case of the Etruscans, the topos of a people who disappeared from history and historical memory for over a millennium before slowly returning. Etruscans and people like them function like a personal code for the poet, combining a historical fact and a set of images that are simultaneously cognate with events and emotions from Polish history. I sense this potent doubling even in passages from essays concerned solely with the past: "It may be that the image of the Etruscans' fate is a result of our seeing them exclusively in the light of foreign sources. It is as if they are the object of history, not a conscious subject, justifying themselves, explaining their defeats, appealing to their heirs to judge them kindly, to grant them the grace of understanding."[2] If we change "Etruscans" to "Poles" nothing else needs adjustment in this passage. Two nations that disappeared; two minor languages known only to native speakers; histories of catastrophic defeats at the hands of powerful empires; and the need to explain oneself to other more successful nations and to your own progeny. Herbert's ambivalence toward Etruscan art and his own tragic view of history inoculate him against Lawrentian assertions about Etruscan joie de vivre or a vision of a prelapsarian society without alienation or civilizational chaos. He keeps clear what we know about Etruria from what we don't. The language, for instance: "Instead of the epic poems and sacred books whose existence we have every right to assume, this rich civilization hands down to us a hopelessly dull collection of obituaries" (*CPr*, 521). He allows that the art is interesting and sui generis but not much more than an "an adventure worth recommending to the impatient as well as to lovers of classification" (523). Not quite the enthusiastic endorsement the Etruscan artists had awaited for two millennia.

---

2 Herbert, *Collected Prose*, 513. All quotations from the prose, unless otherwise indicated, will be from this edition.

Nothing holds Herbert's interest as strongly as resistance, defeat, and disappearance. This is the emotional matrix – from pain to humiliation and grief – that gathers all the other ancient orphan threads in his writing. The Etruscans are usually the hinge between past and present, ancient history and Poland. Herbert writes to his historical situation, however, without surrendering his poetry to an agenda, morality, or ideology – to "a tyranny of dichotomies chopping up complicated human reality" (*CPr*, 606). He thinks an engaged art, whether Stalinist socialist realism or Sartrean *engagement*, leads the artist "into the realm of banality" as "political kindheartedness [or denunciation] cancels out a work's artistic value" (*CPr*, 606). Herbert insists on the "paradoxical pluriformity and contradictoriness of the spirit in its relation to the problem of man" (*CPr*, 607). He also suggests that the human spirit can find itself as easily on the left as on the right; neither is intrinsically preferable, and both are responsible for totalitarianisms. As he suggests in "To Ryszard Krynicki – A Letter" (356), whether poets write against a tyrant or in praise of a tyrant, they produce bad poetry.[3]

Herbert draws the following lesson from redrawn maps: "History does not know a single example of art or an artist anywhere ever exerting a direct influence on the world's destiny – and from this sad truth follows the conclusion that we should be modest, conscious of our limited role and strength" (*CPr*, 606). He praises, for instance, Leonardo because "the peculiarity of Leonardo's disquiet is that it does not manifest itself in violent gestures. It is disquiet that respects the line, disquiet controlled and therefore doubly disquieting. How great is it and how great is he who mastered it?" (*CPr*, 587). Similarly, Horace mentions that he turned and ran at Philippi in 42 BCE, but he doesn't disturb the poem's Alcaic metre (Odes 2.7).

The poet's sphere of action, if he has a serious attitude toward his work, is not the present, by which I mean the current state of socio-political and scientific knowledge, but *reality*, man's stubborn dialogue with the concrete reality surrounding him, with this stool, with that person, with this time of day – the cultivation of the vanishing capacity for contemplation.

---

3 Herbert, *The Collected Poems*, 356. All quotations of the poetry will be from this edition.

And above all – building values, building a set of values, determining their hierarchy, which means a conscious moral choice with all the consequences in life and art that it entails – this seems to me the fundamental and most important function of culture. (*CPr*, 607)

One way of reading Herbert's poems is as a lifelong assertion of values and order in life and art during an era when "the fundamental values of European culture have been drawn into question" or openly attacked (*CPr*, 596). Whenever Herbert comments on poetry he emphasizes the need for an irony that he associates with morality, conscience, a historical consciousness, and humanist values. Before the fall of the Soviet empire, this necessitated Herbert's own version of Stephen Dedalus's "silence, exile, and cunning." Much of the Polish past had to be addressed indirectly or symbolically – a hint, an ambiguous word, or an image that winked at the Polish reader of the postwar generation.

Herbert's best-known and poetically most versatile gambit in the complex dialogue with history is the creation of his alter ego, Mr Cogito, a flexible and adaptable persona who gives his name to fifty poems, many of them among Herbert's best, over the last three decades of Herbert's life. "The Envoy of Mr Cogito," from 1974, can stand for the many poems of testimony before the imagined chair of justice and history. The Etruscans aren't mentioned here but they are a felt absent presence, so to speak, in the topos of the doomed, defeated, and forgotten (see "Those Who Lost" about the first Americans). Anyone familiar with the body of work understands the interchangeability of the names of the defeated and forgotten in the poems in which defeat is predominant: one people is a synecdoche for all. As mentioned earlier, Herbert's Polish readers had already met the Etruscans in the essay "O Etruskach" in 1965. He emphasizes that, unlike the Sumerians, Franks, and Trojans, the Etruscans left behind no heroic names to be eulogized in a poem. This is not to suggest that they are carelessly interchangeable, only that there is a historical affinity in their fates and in Herbert's references to them.

By 1965, when he wrote his essay "On the Etruscans," they were no longer "this mysterious civilization," but they remained elusive, with continuing scholarly disputes about their origin, art, language, customs, and religion. Even Stephen L. Tuck, who titled his 2016 filmed lecture series *The Mysterious Etruscans*, had enough material to fill over twenty

hours.[4] The poet who lost his natal city, Lwów, to the postwar redrawing
of boundaries has a sympathy for exile, vanished or renamed cities and
kingdoms, and, as he puts it, "little-known peoples, who have left only
their names and the memory of their defeat. We, the heirs of the crime
and the cover up, try to mete out justice to the past; *to give back a voice
to history's great mutes, the peoples who had bad luck in history*" (my italics,
CPr, 510–11).[5] It is worth noting that Adam Zagajewski's poetry of exile
also begins in postwar Lwów, which remains a motif throughout his
body of work even though he left it a year after his birth.

Part of the Etruscans' bad luck, as I wrote earlier, was the disappearance of their literature, history, and religious texts. Herbert's "The
Divine Claudius" notes that the emperor "devoted nights to study /
wrote a history of the Etruscans" (*CP*, 373). As we know, this has gone
the way of the lost Etruscan writings. Like the timeless voice that offers
a "Report from a Besieged City" beset by various conquerors across
centuries, an Etruscan ghost might lament that "if we lose our ruins
we will be left with nothing" (*CP*, 416). But the remains are like a
partial sketch or a historical wall painting much of which has faded
beyond retrieval. If Herbert can't quite write the Etruscans back into
history, he can name them occasionally in protest against those who
destroyed them, turned them into an *object* of history, and then wrote
them into another nation's record of triumph. The key Etruscan poem,
one of Herbert's finest and most ambitious, is "Livy's Metamorphoses,"
which is about many nations, at least two monolithic empires, and
several periods of history. Herbert begins by wondering "How did my
grandfather and his father understand Livy / for they surely read him
at their classical gymnasium." He notes that the classroom had a
"portrait of the emperor / for there was an emperor then / and the
empire like all empires / seemed eternal." The adverb "then" is like
a temporal agitator reminding the reader of the unspoken "now" in
which another emperor and another foreign empire look over the
shoulders of students – Stalin or a successor instead of Franz Joseph.

---

4 See Tuck, *Course Guidebook*, The Great Courses, 2016. The Florentine Leonardo
Bruni (1369–1444) anticipated Herbert in using Livy to read against Livy in his *Historia
Florentina*, which resurrects the Etruscans as Florentine ancestors.

5 Adam Zagajewski writes in "I Dreamt of My City": "I dreamt of my former city /
it spoke the language of children and the wronged, / it spoke in various voices ..."
Zagajewski, *Niewidzialna ręka*, 17.

The implied present arrives a few verses later when the speaker describes how he and his father read Livy. The father's presence is as touching as Horace's reference to his in the sixth of his *Satires*.

Not until my father and I after him did anyone
read Livy against Livy
studying closely what lies under the fresco
that's why Scaevola's theatrical gesture did not reverberate in us
nor did the centurions' cries or triumphal marches
and we tended to feel moved by the ruination
of the Samnites Gauls or Etruscans

we counted the many names of peoples the Romans trampled to dust
those buried without praise those who for Livy
were not worth even a ripple of style
those Hirpins Apuleans Lucanaians Osunanas
and residents of Tarentum Metapontis Locri

So far in the poem two empires have fallen, the Austro-Hungarian and the Roman. The transition to the present tense and the turn to a new geography in the final stanza create the expectation of others. This is, after all, a poem by a Polish poet haunted by his nation's failed resistance against empire. Herbert confirms the expectation obliquely with a new set of place names and two predictive clauses.

My father knew and I know too
that one day on the farthest outskirts
without any signs from the heavens
in Pannonia Sarajevo or Trebizond
in a city on the cold sea
or in the valley of Panshir
a local fire will break out
and the empire will fall (*CP*, 423–4)

The last line in Polish runs "I runie imperium" ("and falls the empire" or "and collapses the empire") and has a classic concision that holds off the essential word until the end. I like accidental compacted puns that occur between languages, in this instance, the concealed English "ruin" and "rune" in the Polish "runie."

Most readers will ask "Which empire?" Herbert answers "All," except for "the kingdom without bounds," the human ideal mentioned in passing in "Report from a Besieged City," by which the poet judges historical empires. Panshir (or Panjshir) directs our attention to Afghanistan, which, in the years prior to the poem's publication, had been the scene of the Soviet army's "Vietnam." In 2021 I read the poem aware of another empire that suffered defeat in the same country. History does repeat itself without meaning. Empire and *imperium* are not on Herbert's list of favoured words. He prefers to think smaller: small nations, peoples, tribes, cities, families, all of which know their existence to be communal and provisional. In a manner of speaking, an empire can fall, but it can't suffer anything other than what might be called the anguish of the powerful and affluent. Think of the United States in the years since Vietnam.

Wisława Szymborska (1923–2012), not usually discussed as a political or historical poet, captures the "tone" of imperial domination in "Voices," a poem surprising both in its form – a combination of a catalogue and a dramatic monologue – and in its political and historical edge. It provides a perfect codicil to the work of Herbert – her almost exact contemporary – with its evocation of an invading Roman army on the march. History's chosen are damned by their own words in a rolling series of brief dialogues:

Tarquinians where you'd least expect them, Etruscans on all sides.
If that weren't enough, Volsinians and Veientians.
The Aulertians, beyond all reason. And, of course,
the endlessly vexatious Sapinians, my dear Sextus Oppius.

Little nations do have little minds.
The circle of thick skulls expands around us.
Reprehensible customs. Backward laws.
Ineffectual gods, my dear Titus Vilius.

Heaps of Hernicians. Swarms of Marrucinians.
Antlike multitudes of Vestians and Samnites.
The farther you go, the more there are, dear Servius Follius.

These little nations are pitiful indeed.
Their foolish ways require supervision
with every new river we ford, dear Aulus Iunius.

Every new horizon threatens me.
That's how I'd put it, my dear Hostius Melius.

To which I, Hostius Melius, would reply, my dear
Appius Papius: March on! The world has got to end somewhere.[6]

The conquering and colonizing Romans are all named; the others remain an anonymous mass, characterized only by belittling qualities: they are "antlike," "thick as flies," and possess "little minds," "reprehensible laws," and "ineffectual gods." Many are now part of a "circle of thick skulls," an echo of *Heart of Darkness* and Golgotha. The ironic conclusion is that these people need Roman civilization to become fully human. The Romans, like Kipling's Englishmen and the Americans of Manifest Destiny, have a duty to govern the less civilized, a notion raised surprisingly even in John Stuart Mill's *On Liberty*. Kipling's poems of empire capture this sentiment as a duty to mankind and history. Joseph Conrad, a small player in the spread of the British empire, had no illusions about the march of history. Looking around him in *Heart of Darkness*, Marlow is clear-eyed about the objectives of European colonialization: "They were no colonists; their administration was merely a squeeze, and nothing more, I suspect. They were conquerors, and for that you want only brute force – nothing to boast of, when you have it, since your strength is just an accident arising from the weakness of others."[7] Appalled by what he sees, including mounds of skulls, Marlow is almost matter-of-fact in describing scenes that condemn the makers of empires: this is the way things are; these are the unspoken assumptions of the conquerors; these are their blind spots. Like Conrad and Herbert, Szymborska comes from a place that knows all one needs to

6 Szymborska, *Map*, 245. In her essay "What's Dreaming?" (*Nonrequired Reading*) Szymborska comments, "There's a scene in one of Fellini's films [*Roma*] where the workers extending a subway line come upon an Etruscan crypt covered with dazzling paintings. Unfortunately, as soon as other people rush to the scene, as soon as the photographers take out their cameras, the paintings begin to dim, fade, turn gray. Finally, after a brief moment, bare walls appear before the eyes of the mute, helpless onlookers. It's the same thing with dreams: they scatter and vanish irretrievably the moment we wake up." Unfortunately, the paintings aren't Etruscan, as Szymborska acknowledges in a later version of the essay printed in her collected prose, *Wszystkie Lektury nadobowiązkowe*, 2015.

7 Conrad, *Heart of Darkness* in *The Complete Short Fiction of Josef Conrad* 3:5.

know about history. Her country was ground zero, as one might call it, for the worst five years of the twentieth century. Her tone is measured, her stance a little to the side of events – "slant," to use Dickinson's term – as she lets the Romans damn themselves.

Herbert is equally attentive to tone, equally allergic to adjectives and nouns that may distort or exaggerate. His problem with the Etruscans is how to bring them into focus for modern readers without simplifying or idealizing. He may prefer the Etruscans to the Romans, but, as I wrote earlier, he resists Lawrence's idealized vision of a vivid, life-accepting people, who must have lived with real fullness. He insists on some inconvenient details. The fate of the slaves under the Etruscans, he reminds us, "was no better than it was in any other ancient state; the bloodily suppressed rebellions testify to that. One should not put any faith in tales of the Etruscans' gentleness told by sentimental novelists or scenes from frescoes (like films of upper-class life among the ancients), where wine tasters, flutists, and dancers bustle around a feast table" (*CPr*, 514). In other words, let's admire what is admirable and let's lament their disappearance, but let's not falsify the record by forgetting the slaves or the scenes of human sacrifice. Herbert's memory and his art are open, inclusive, and democratic: even a people that might not have been life-affirming deserve to be remembered simply because they existed. History is incomplete without them.

Herbert's farewell to Etruria in 1965 can serve as his farewell here: "A melancholy promenade: Cerveteri, Tarquinia, Volterra, Veii; hills of stone tombs completely overgrown with grass. In the kingdom of pines, crickets, and cypresses, not far under the earth, feasts, hunts, and dance are immortalized on walls. The tomb carvings engrave themselves deepest in memory. A man leaning on an elbow, head held high, draped in a garment revealing his torso, as if eternity were a long, hot summer night" (*CPr*, 524).

Rika Lesser's Etruscan Things (1983):
If Stones Could Speak or Lithic Prosopopoeia

There are some European words you can never translate properly into another language. *Felhomály*. The dusk of graves. With the connotation of intimacy there between the dead and the living.

Michael Ondaatje, *The English Patient*[1]

Within two years of each other, two books were published – a historical novel and a closely organized sequence of poems – that offer factually reliable contemporary perspectives on the Etruscans. Sybille Haynes's *The Augur's Daughter* (1981) presents the decline of the Etruscan people over roughly the same period as Mika Waltari's *The Etruscan*. The viewpoint in Haynes's novel is that of a young girl connected to the royal family who observes as Thefarie Velianas (a historical character) usurps power from the reigning family. Rika Lesser's *Etruscan Things* structures its twenty-four monologues following the map of the Etruscan sky, a drawing of which can be found in the richly detailed notes. The intention is to bring the Etruscans and their world of statues and ruins to life against the full background of a sky filled with their gods in their appropriate sections. The Rasenna speak to us between life and death, earth and cosmos, body and spirit, and humans and gods. The American poet's approach is synchronic, a cross-section of representative objects and people addressing us after a silence of two millennia. The two books are so thoroughly researched that they can be recommended as reliable introductions to the Etruscans. Having covered the historical period of Haynes's novel in my chapter on Waltari, I will focus here on Lesser's remarkable sequence, which recalls poems as diverse as lyrics from the *Greek Anthology*, Propertius's last poem (4.11), Robert Browning and

---

1 Ondaatje, *The English Patient*, 150.

Richard Howard's dramatic monologues, and modern poets as different as Thomas Hardy and Edgar Lee Masters.

Each of Lesser's poems is spoken by an object or a dead Etruscan. Among the speaking objects are canopic jars, sculptures, ruins, and sarcophagi. As mentioned, the twenty-four poems are faithfully arranged according to the Etruscan ordering of the *templum caeleste* (the vault of the heavens) following the positions of the various gods. Tinia, the Etruscan Zeus, is at the apex in the north. Each quadrant is auspicious to a different degree between fortunate and unfortunate. I suspect that much of the impressive research Lesser has done will be lost on most readers unless they are disciplined enough to read her detailed notes. The entry on lucumones is representative.

Lucumones (pl., sg. *lucumo*): The priest-kings of Etruria. Four times a year the *lucumo* of each city would show himself in public, riding forth in a chariot drawn by white horses, and then performing sacrifices. In the Fifth War between Veii and Rome, the Veientes joined the rest of the Etruscan "League," but were defeated by Tarquinius Priscus (a Roman king of Etruscan extraction) and were forced to sue for peace. In token of submission the cities of the "League" had to send him the Etruscan insignia of authority, which included the purple robe, the *corona aurea*, the scepter surmounted by an eagle, the *sella curulis* (an ivory folding seat), and the twelve *fasces* of the lictors. Following the expulsion of the Tarquins, the Roman Republican magistrates took up these symbols. (77)

Not all of this is necessary to understand "Aplu" (Apollo), the poem in question, but it contributes to what might be called the thick description of the Etruscan background in which Lesser's poems are embedded. As a group they offer a memorable speaking mosaic from the distant past. I think the poems will best reward those who read them as follows: first the poem, then its notes, then the poem again. They repay the attention. Richard Howard's introduction suggests something similar. Recognizing that some of the Etruscan details might get in the way of the poetry, he advises that "the first way of dealing with this new guide to the ruins is to read it through, notes and all … without trying to 'figure out' what the 'intellectual intentions' might be" (xi–xii). If one reads straight through, as Howard suggests, I find that there isn't enough differentiation in voice between the poems to prevent them from running one into the next. They are written under the sign of lament and elegy and are predominantly sombre, monotoned, and, even when personal, they remain curiously formal and lacking in intimacy, as if they were copied from epitaphs. This is part of their intriguing strangeness or otherness. The difference between Lesser's Etruscans and Lawrence's couldn't be greater. His are fluid, kinetic, and polychrome; hers have the stern gravitas of monuments or very old black-and-white photographs.

Sybille Haynes reminds us that, from the seventh century BCE, Etruscan writing "appears mostly on pottery vessels and occasionally on objects of precious metal. The text normally gives the name of the owner in the genitive, while *the object bearing it appears to speak* [my italics]. For example, on two oinochoai from Cerveteri, dating from about 675, we read: *mi qutun karkanas* = I (am) the jug of Karkana."[2] This is roughly like an epigram in the *Greek Anthology* from the early third century BCE, perhaps by Anyte of Tegea:

I, Hermes, have been set up
Where three roads cross, by the windy
Orchard above the grey beach.
Here tired men may rest from travel,
By my cold, clean, whispering spring.[3]

In Lesser's "Tomb of the Augurs" the speaking object – a painted figure – is combined with an ekphrasis of the painting. "Aplu" gives the dynamic, larger-than-life, polychrome Apollo of Veii (c. 515–490 BCE) (see figure 14.1) a voice. Like Keats's Hyperion he is a neglected, homeless god looking at a world that has abandoned or destroyed his temples and no longer worships him and his fellow deities. Counterpointed to his verses are those of the poet, who breathes life into him for a reader who may not know him from the statue at the Villa Giulia:

His face is frightening, the eyes
almonds bursting from their shells.
The right one bulges larger, glares
like Death. From the winged eyebrows
down his nose the lines are sharp as
a knife, cut through more than air. (30)

2 Haynes, *Etruscan Civilization*, 67.
3 Jay, *The Greek Anthology*, 78. Kenneth Rexroth is the translator.

The face has fascinated and intimidated me on every visit, and the effect is somehow connected to the god's enigmatic, impersonal, and amoral smile. It is the same smile we see on the head of Hermes, from the same period from Veii, in the same museum. They smile and live in a world of laughter without concern for mortals. For me, the least believable sections of Homer and Virgil show gods concerned about humans. Why would they bother? How could they possibly care which warrior wins a battle? And yet, with some suspension of disbelief, we believe them, for the moment. Lesser's Aplu is refreshingly disdainful of the all-too-human: his only concern is the fate of his temples. Yet, at the end, he is again merely a statue shaped by the sculptor Vulca, and it is Vulca's touch he needs: "I do not / long for the soil, but for / the touch, the call of the hand / that made me." His power now resides in the effect he has on the viewer, toward whom he seems to stride, right arm extended and right leg forward, awe-inspiring, almost threatening, certainly intimidating:

(His hands are lost, but the biceps
burn with strength. The pectorals high
and developed. On the muscular
legs the veins stand out. Supported
by the lyre, he is walking towards me.) (32)

Vulca, it is worth recalling, was a terracotta specialist from Veii who was commissioned to work in Rome's Temple of the Capitoline Jupiter, traditionally dedicated in 509 BCE. I wish Lesser had used at least one poem to bring to life a painter, sculptor, or potter in the way that Waltari does in *The Etruscan* when he shows Turms watching the painter Aruns painting on a tomb wall. Both in the novel and in this poem, the non-English name separates the artist not only from Greeks and Romans but also from ourselves. I felt a similar disorienting effect reading Etruscan rather than Latin or English words and names in the notes: "netśvis," the word for the haruspex or interpreter of the liver; "Tinia" rather than Jupiter. These are small details, but they help to restore Etruscan "otherness." Whatever we may think of their paintings, they show a people who do not resemble Greeks or Romans, and it is a category error to think so. A few more words in the language of the Rasenna would have been welcome.

Lesser echoes Giorgio Bassani's comparison of the Etruscans and the Jews in "God's Breath," but the effect, though the comparison is oblique, seems forced and anachronistic and suffers from the imbalance between the subjects compared. The poem is about the firing of bucchero, the polished black pottery that looks almost metallic and which was destroyed by Lucien Bonaparte's diggers because it might flood the market for Etruscan ware and bring the price down for the painted vases.

Children of ovens. Receptacles
on feet. Our provenance? We will
speak true. Among Etruscan ware
we are the Jews: Survivors
bound by god-given laws.
Shem's sons, misunderstood because
form free of context, bygone
ritual, is seen as evil
or made trivial. (48)

The poem seems to lose its way after "Children of ovens." The reference is clearly to the pottery but "ovens" and "feet" seem to trigger in the poet's mind a line from the so-called Lamentations of Jeremiah ("our skin was black like an oven of the terrible famine [or terrors]") that nudges her into a figurative connection between the bucchero ware and "the Jews." This then takes her farther afield to Shem's sons who, we know, are Semites, and one of whom is the father of Abraham. Furthermore, Shem's sons are then aligned with misunderstanding, bygone ritual, and evil. The pottery and the Etruscans have disappeared, and a new and very different field of intellectual and emotional force is present. It, in turn, disappears with the next line. In his novel, Bassani juxtaposes the Etruscans and the Jews in a reference to a history book. The implications of the comparison are developed by Etruscan and Jewish cemeteries and tombs and the theme of disappearance. There is an unforced credibility in the interdependence of the two peoples in that both are present in the novel's historical time and joined by their identity as "Italians." In Lesser's poem I sense something willed, and it is more than the warning sounded by the anachronism introduced by the suggestion of the Holocaust. The stanza regains its focus with "*Bucchero nero e pesante* / clay breathed black and deep" and closes with a brief catalogue of objects that shine "silver-black" and "break into song."

Lesser's sequence ends with "Degli Sposi," The Sarcophagus of the Married Couple (figure 11.1), which offers a wonderfully peaceful afterimage, but it might just as easily and perhaps more appropriately have ended with "La Banditaccia, 1979," a poem in the poet's voice about a visit to Cerveteri. This would have helped the book make a transition back to the present. On the other hand, "Degli Sposi" is a stronger poem and leaves the reader with a more evocative and memorable image – the Villa Giulia terracotta married couple smiling across the centuries in what the poem calls "conjugal bliss." But is it really conjugal bliss? Or is it possibly a reflection of conventional Northern Ionian models? Of course, it could be both: the artist relying on a traditional form and style to express the bliss and serenity he wants to suggest with the sarcophagus.

Thinking back to Lesser's book after not having read it for a few months, I realize that my mind's eye pictures it not according to the fascinating diagram on its final page (the poems arranged in a circle around the north-south axis of the heavens) but as a crowded tomb, something like the Inghirami Tomb from Volterra recreated in Florence's Archaeological Museum, or the more recently discovered Cai Cutu family tomb on display in the National Archaeological Museum of Umbria in Perugia, where the heavy-set son, with a slight resemblance to Liam Neeson, looks confidently at the entrance as if waiting for visitors offering gifts and homage. (For the image, see figure 0.1.)

23

Don Siegel's The Killers *(1964)*
and William Gibson's Idoru *(1996):*
When Is an Etruscan Not an Etruscan?

But still – there stands Etruscan, undeciphered. Who would
not be fascinated by that?

Anne Carson[1]

One of the pleasures of doing research for this book was never knowing
where and when I might stumble onto something Etruscan. A visit
two decades ago to the Cleveland Museum of Art gave me Henri Matisse's
Interior with Etruscan Vase (1940), in which the terracotta vase provides
another shape, colour, and set of patterns to an already highly figured
scene. The colour is picked up by three smaller flowerpots on the floor
and some of the peaches (?) on the table. The vase serves an aesthetic
or formal purpose as a work of art within a work of art. Nothing more
seems intended by the Etruscan motif if, indeed, it is an Etruscan vase.
A more serendipitous encounter took place on an afternoon when I
turned on a classic movie channel just as Vincent Sherman's *The Damned
Don't Cry* (1950) was beginning. It proved to be a forgettable movie
except for an exchange between Joan Crawford and a gangster played
by David Brian. He looks around her boss's apartment and comments,
"He has a nice flowerpot." Crawford's reply probably surprises everyone: "It's an Etruscan vase, not a flowerpot." So far as I know, that's
the Hollywood debut of the Etruscans.

Fourteen years later, in 1964, they make a slightly more auspicious
and longer appearance in director Don Siegel's classic *The Killers*. The
movie is a very free adaptation of Ernest Hemingway's story of the same

1 Carson, "Interview with Anne Carson," 23.

title which, incidentally, doesn't mention the Etruscans. In the film, with a screenplay by Gene L. Coon, Lee Marvin and Clu Gulager are two killers searching for money that disappeared a few years earlier, after a holdup. They trace it to Jack Browning (Ronald Reagan), the mastermind of the robbery, who is now a successful businessman. When they walk into his office, the camera is behind his desk to the left and shows, as we pan left to right, the windows, the door, and – probably to the confusion of most of the audience – a large, framed, colour reproduction (though it could pass for a painting) of the lithe young male dancer in a short blue cloak from Tarquinia's Tomb of the Triclinium (c. 470 BCE), which my readers will remember from chapter 17 and the discussion of Mika Waltari's *The Etruscan*. In the tomb, he is one of five dancing figures painted on an underground wall with images of ceremonies in honour of the deceased. Some consider it among the finest paintings of the Etruscan era. That it may be, but what is it doing in a B movie in 1964? All the other paintings in the film are undistinguished period landscapes, city scenes, and floral arrangements.

Let's assume for the moment that Coon, Siegel, or his set designer was responsible for the poster, knew it was Etruscan, and was aware that the original was on the wall of a tomb in Tarquinia. We can then assume the dancer is an intended ironic commentary on the scene taking place in Jack Browning's office. The moment the killers come through the door, the dancer changes from a figure of freedom and pleasure to an ironic Etruscan harbinger of death. If we think of him as a symbol for Browning, his significance shifts with the opening of the door. Until that moment Browning has gotten away with the money from the heist – as the song has it, "he's in the money." With the killers' arrival he becomes a man living on borrowed time. The movie's title tells us all we need to know about how the story will end. The only surprise is that the killers die as well. Hemingway's story ends with the killers still looking for their victim, who, we know, has stopped running and is waiting for them in a rooming house.

I can imagine a reader familiar with the conventions of film noir pausing here and thinking, "This is just a 1950s noir movie – it's Siegel, not Truffaut. They don't pay that sort of attention to decor. Certainly not to the paintings." With most noir movies I would agree, but I would cite *The Damned Don't Cry* and writer-director Robert Rossen's *Johnny O'Clock* (silly name and silly title) as exceptions that justify my lingering over the Etruscan in *The Killers*. Rossen made his movie in 1946. He places a copy of José Clemente Orozco's well-known painting *Zapatistas,* from 1931, on the wall over the fireplace in Johnny's apartment. When the gambler, played by Dick Powell, is asked about it by a visiting small-time actress, played by Evelyn Keyes, he turns to it and says that he saw it in Mexico, liked it, and bought it. The revolutionary painting appears in several scenes and has little to do with the movie's story or theme. But since the director is Robert Rossen, who had joined the Communist Party in 1937, it is not a stretch to suggest that it is his political nod to the those in the know that even in a B movie a Hollywood director can be sympathetic to social and political change.

A final thought about Siegel's Etruscan. The poster is too eccentric to have been placed so prominently in an important scene without Siegel understanding what it was. But even if he did, he must have known that very few, if any, in the audience would recognize the Tomb of the Triclinium, now in the National Archaeological Museum at Tarquinia. For those who didn't, it would remain a puzzle, like the black rectangle in Giotto's "Joachim's Dream" or "the man in the macintosh" in the "Hades" chapter of James Joyce's *Ulysses.* A hermeneutic black hole. Whatever the case, when a major work of Etruscan art appears prominently on an office wall in a cult American gangster movie, I take it as a clear suggestion that the Etruscans have returned and are becoming a permanent part of the furniture of mass culture. And anyone still unconvinced by my suggestion that these movies argue for the "arrival" of the Etruscans in popular culture need only look to the next two decades, when three Italian zombie movies appear – *L'etrusco uccide ancora* (1972), *Le notti del terrore* (1981), and *Neverlake* – to be followed in 2000 by an Etruscan new age novel, *Etruscans: Beloved of the Gods.* These are definitely not the Etruscans of Lawrence, Pallottino, Jacques Heurgon, Nancy Thomson de Grummond, and Stephen L. Tusk, but they are what might be classified as a branch of the family that has made it into popular culture. If I knew contemporary music as well as I know mid-century rock and jazz, I am confident I would find, in one of the varieties of contemporary music, references to the Rasenna – Fufluns or Turan? – as ostentatiously unexpected and as difficult to interpret as Don Siegel's poster.

William Gibson's Etruscan reference is as inexplicable as Don Siegel's. The DNA of Gibson's character "the Etruscan" in his novel *Idoru* would find no match in ancient Etruria. The character's genealogy looks back to Raymond Queneau's proto-Derridean *The Bark Tree* (1933) (discussed in chapter 16), which also refers to "the Etruscans," but empties the sign of everything it traditionally signified – or, to put it another way, of its inherited semantic content. In an Oxford English Dictionary edited by Gibson and Queneau, the entry would read: "ETRUSCAN: hapax legomenon (a thing said once) or *unknown*." Gibson's "the Etruscan" has no historical, semantic, or connotative relationship to the Etruscans, nor does any character in the novel seem to have heard of them. It's as if Gibson chose the name to create semantic expectations the character would not fulfill. This is also the case with the young immigrant to Sweden named "Montenegro" in Dušan Makavejev's 1981 film of the same title, who is not from that Balkan country. Gibson's character is an electronic image or hologram of an agent without any visual definition, identity, or depth. He is "a voice unlike any Chia had heard, a weird, attenuated rasp that might have been compiled from a library of faint, dry, random sounds."[2]

Introduced late in novel, "the Etruscan" is one of the saviours of the teenage girl on a quest to save a rock star in love with a "woman" who is an entirely virtual media creation. His name, like the names of almost all of Gibson's characters, doesn't resonate within an onomastic order of significations that would contribute to the novel's meaning or its style: set it beside Waverley, Uriah Heep, Raskolnikov, Isabel Archer, Razumov, Micòl, Del Jordan, or "the mechanic" (*Smilla's Sense of Snow*) and you see the difference. Gibson could have named him the Sumerian, the Hittite, or the Mayan without affecting the novel's aesthetic or thematic equilibrium. The name creates a free-floating *momentary* aura or sense of strangeness before letting it fade like a hologram. The name is a misleading sign (a false clue) whose content will be provided by the novel, not by the reader's knowledge of the Etruscans. To paraphrase a once fashionable philosopher, "In Gibson's world there is nothing outside the novel." Well, almost. The readers stand outside the novel, and they bring their knowledge about the Etruscans to bear on "the Etruscan." It's a vain effort. At novel's end they discover that their knowledge is irrelevant in this instance because he isn't an *Etruscan* Etruscan – he's an Etruscan from the Gibson branch of the family. The name is a free-floating signifier with only a serendipitous connection to the Etruscans. Blake's "Etruscan Column" at least has a source in Vitruvius and eighteenth-century books on architecture.

2 Gibson, *Idoru*, 207.

2 4

Anne Carson:
"Canicula di Anna" (1984)
and Norma Jeane Baker in Etruria

Now Paris, our black classic, breaking up / Like killer kings
on an Etruscan cup.

Robert Lowell, "Beyond the Alps"[1]

The few Etruscan instances in the work of Anne Carson (born 1950)
are as suggestive and elusive as the three in Emily Dickinson's poems
and the one quoted above, from Robert Lowell. The early poem
"Canicula di Anna" has a thin bronze boy with elongated arms, and an
old Etruscan whose speech is cut off as he falls from a parapet. The
noun "Etruria" is dropped dead centre into "Wrong Norma" (2016), a
very different poem, published thirty-two years later. And there are
Etruscans in dialogue with Marilyn Monroe in a recent poem, "Detail
from the tomb of the diver (Paestum 500–433 BCE) second detail."

I begin with "Canicula di Anna," the most substantial of the three,
an academic fable that circles around a Perugia-based phenomenological conference concerned with the nature of the self and freedom.[2]
Anna walks around old Perugia after seemingly failing to register for
the event. (If I use "seem" more than usual in this chapter, I can only

1 Lowell, "Beyond the Alps," in *Life Studies / For the Union Dead*, 4.
2 The conference was the Collegium Phaenomenologicum and took place in
July 1981 in the Casa del Sacro Cuore. See Paul Meyer, "She] {Ha?} She," 93. All my
information about Carson's research and life comes from this brilliant thesis. I can
best describe Meyer's work as an attempt to read Carson in the same thorough and
creative way as she had read Sappho and the Greek lyric poets. The Etruscans are also
mentioned in passing in "The Fall of Rome: A Traveller's Guide": "Now, / Orvieto. //
The city is of Etruscan origin." In Carson, *Glass, Irony and God*, 95.

plead that Carson, like Stéphane Mallarmé, Rainer Maria Rilke, Wallace Stevens, and John Ashbery, does that to readers.)

Within the medieval walls
are considerable remains of the lofty
terrace walls of the Etruscan period.
Some old Etruscan calling, "Ah ... " in the rain,
is it possible? Doubled
and fell off the parapet,
gone by now in the sea.[3]

Since Perugia is far inland, it is unlikely that someone might fall off the walls into the sea. But since the poem takes place in several time periods and is without a fixed narrator, it is best to keep one's mind open to art as well as geography. As Paul Meyer points out, there is a painted seaside Perugia in Benedetto Bonfigli's (1420–1496) *Miracle of the Merchant Who Found his Purse Lost during a Shipwreck in the Stomach of a Fish* on view in the National Gallery of Umbria in Perugia. Perhaps the impossible image of Perugia on the sea – a deliberate confusion of the real and the imagined – stayed with Carson. But there is more. In Carson's archive there is a postcard of another painting by Bonfigli, *Totila's Siege of Perugia and the Burial of Saint Herculanus*. The painting shows Herculanus, the bishop of Perugia, being hurled from the ramparts by Totila the Gaul in 549. That takes care of the sea and the fall, but why an "old Etruscan"? Meyer suggests that much of poet's information about Perugia comes from the eleventh edition of the *Encyclopedia Britannica* (1911), which explains some cruces: first the encyclopedia; then Carson's version.

---

3 Carson, "Canicula di Anna," in *Plainwater*, 51. All quotations will be from this edition. Thomas Mann's *The Magic Mountain* has a scene which shows how difficult it is to describe or interpret an "Ah ... " or an "Ahhh –": "The moment the priest set foot over the threshold, a hue and cry starts up inside, first a shriek like nothing you've ever heard, three or four times in a row, and then just screaming without a pause or break, like a mouth gaping wide open, I suppose, 'Ahhh –' and with such misery and terror and defiance in it that I can't describe it, and such ghastly pleading mixed in, too, and then all of a sudden it turns hollow and muffled, as if it has sunk down into the earth or is coming from a deep cellar" (52). The scream comes from a young, dying tubercular patient at the sanatorium.

PERUGIA (ancient *Perusia*) ... situated 1444 ft. above sea-level ... upon a group of hills nearly 1000 ft. above the valley of the Tiber. Its outline is very irregular ... This is the extent enclosed by the medieval walls; within them are considerable remains of the lofty terrace walls of the Etruscan period.

Perugia (ancient Perusia)
is situated 1444 feet above sea-level
on a group of hills overlooking the Tiber:
1000 feet below.
Its outline
is irregular. Within the mediaeval walls
are considerable remains of the lofty
terrace-walls of the Etruscan period. (8)

The "old Etruscan" may be a way of introducing the Rasenna past, a synecdochic way of evoking the ghostly Etruscans who were silenced in mid-sentence, so to speak, by the Romans when their world was absorbed into Rome's.

Having invented "Anna," the author whose name is Anne now plays with textual freedom, temporal freedom, and phenomenological freedom, shifting through the various time periods available in Perugia: Etruscan, Perugino's (whose paintings dominate the local gallery), her life, and the conference. The narrator exercises the freedoms available to her and in the process embodies and enacts the conference's topic. Since this is Anne Carson, the situation is not without its sly humour.

Famous phenomenologists of *tutta l'Italia*
have foregathered here.
They take things back to the sophists
then climb the stone stairs
for a heavy lunch.
Their foreheads are not so tall
as the foreheads
of the French phenomenologists
but they are much more good-natured. (53)

The humour has a light touch, closer to David Lodge's *Changing Places* than to Laurent Binet's recent philosophical novel *La septième fonction du langage.* Of course, the French phenomenologists would have the tallest foreheads, just as they have the most original, if questionable, ideas and write the longest books.

The Etruscans are good for one more turn in the poem. The National Archaeological Museum of Umbria has its own L'Ombra della Sera (Evening Shadow), one of the tall, very thin, elongated bronze figures that some suggest were resurrected by Alberto Giacometti and which I related earlier to Picasso and David Smith. Anna stops in front of it:

Her wings gleam and fold shut.
She pauses
before an Etruscan boy
of green bronze. Leaves
nod heavily on his head.
He looks down, just
discovering
that his arms, if he lets them,
extend to the
soles of his feet.
his delight is total (75–6)

Carson is fond of wings, as we see later in her career. Here I assume that they are Anna's imagined angelic wings, similar to the numerous wings in Perugino or the wings of the Etruscan female spirit Vanth – since she is interested in the Etruscan boy – or, perhaps, Geryon's red wings in *Autobiography of Red* (1998)? But the question is, to what point? *Which may be precisely the wrong question to ask a writer who avoids points altogether, preferring several simultaneous points of view or layers or themes or genres.* Her normal procedure is to retreat from a single viewpoint toward a set of possibilities. She acknowledges the boy and nothing more. With his giant hands he is almost a *lusus naturae*, a violation of realism, and a challenge to phenomenological descriptions of reality. In the conference's descriptions of the *lebenswelt* (the world we live in and try to describe) where does he fit in ("belong" is too humanizing), with his leafed head, his anorexic body and arms stretching like Plasticine to the ground? Is he like Geryon, Michel Foucault might ask, an exception to the totalizing explanatory claims of philosophy and our classifying systems? If we turn to the past: where did he fit into the more flexible, often bisexual Etruscan cosmology? The publication of Carson's *Nox* (2010) two decades later allows a sliver of possibility that the mysterious, distant, unapproachable boy is in part an Etruscan version of her troubled brother Davey, who seemed never to fit in anywhere. If only *Nox* mentioned Etruscans instead of Athenians and Spartans, there would be a more explicit link.

Names in Carson are always under pressure. Why "Canicula," why "Anna," and why the shifty Italian "di"? If in doubt, Gérard Genette suggests, squeeze the names. The Latin "canicula" is a diminutive for dog and the Dog Star, the herald of the season of oppressive heat in Italy. Packs of dogs wander the streets in the poem's Perugia, though not in the city I have visited several times to see the museum's Etruscans and to pay homage to Piero and Perugino in the National Gallery of Umbria. But "canicula" can also refer to "a violent woman," and the poet Persius extends the meaning to the "worst throw of the dice." If we keep on, we find that Anna is "grace" in Hebrew, but it is also a slippery name: Anne, Anna, Hannah, Ana, Anita. Anne isn't named in the New Testament but is described in the apocryphal Gospel of James as the mother of the Virgin Mary and therefore the grandmother of Jesus. Anna is also a prophetess (Luke 2:36). If the "I" of the narrator is hiding behind a name, she has chosen an unstable one, which would be appropriate for a conference on being and freedom whose three main texts sound like Martin Heidegger's *Poetry, Language, Thought* and Maurice Merleau-Ponty's "Eye and Mind" and "Cézanne's Doubt."[4]

Behind everything one senses the problem of presence: Greek "Parousia" is almost a homonym for Perugia/Perusia and also has the theological meaning of "the Second Coming." One asks, "Who is present?" The poem itself is as unstable and as impossible to pin down as Anna, as identities, as perceptions, as judgments, as philosophical searches after meaning, as searches for influence … and, finally, *as the Etruscans*. How can we comprehend the world view of a people who produced an elongated statue, with arms that reach to the ground, whose function we don't understand? Is the dying Etruscan's last not-quite-word – "'Ah …' in the rain" – a summons to Anna to … to do what? "Remember me"? Write about the Etruscans in a poem about death and dying? This makes sense if Paul Meyer is right that "it is a

---

4 Again, as throughout, my source is Meyer, "She] {Ha?} She."

poem, without a story, about death."[5] Perhaps Freud should have the last word, again, when he suggests that even in "the best-interpreted dreams, one often needs to leave a particular passage obscure, having become aware, during the work of interpretation, that a knot of dream-thoughts rises there that refuses to unravel."[6] Carson, like Lowell, has many such moments that remain knotted, polysemous, and ungiving while suggesting not just more but perhaps too much. So far as I know, no one has given a satisfying interpretation of Lowell's couplet at the head of this chapter. It sits like a singularity in physics, so densely compacted that its component parts are not available for inspection. Like Lowell's polysemous lines, Carson's poem seems to bring together multiple origins related only by their presence in the poet's consciousness. I'm not complaining.

Carson returns to Etruria in "Wrong Norma," a weary and intensely introspective poem about remorse, aging, and death by way of pre-dawn reflections on Billy Wilder's *Sunset Boulevard* or, more precisely, Norma Desmond / Gloria Swanson / Marilyn Monroe. Our questions begin with the title: If this is the "Wrong Norma," who is the right one? When I recently reread the poem, I imagined a triptych by Edward Hopper titled *Woman Smoking at Night Window, New York,* with each of the panels focused on one of the women and Carson reflected in all. In the work of both artists, precariousness is a felt presence. The poem's setting is a murky New York City which, at this moment and for this woman, is a trope for Hades with "the giant white smoke Miltoning / to heaven." In other words, New York is Hell, and the female speaker is at this moment a fallen angel remorseful about a "wrong" choice that landed her here rather than there.

Wrong night, wrong city, wrong movie, wrong
ambulances caterwauling past and drowning out
wrong dialogue of wrong Norma Desmond, what
could be more wrong she's the same age as me
this tilted wreck with deliquescent chin, I turn it

---

5 Ibid., 9. The death of an ancient people returns in "Cheapjack Stack" which mentions some of the accomplishments of the Phoenicians before noting that they "vanished / from / history" while the Greeks stole their alphabet "and sat down to write / the classics of Western civilization" In Carson, *Float.*

6 Freud, *Interpreting Dreams,* 540.

off, eat soup and read a novel. Thoughts trickle
in and out. No one phones. I am safe but that
won't last. I drift to the past, even 20 years ago
wasn't it possible to be pure? To just close the
door and think about one thing, the moon, curbs,
Etruria. The self wins anyway. The "s" in self
wins. I used to love making "s" in cursive style on
the blackboard in school, it's different every
time, every shell on the beach, do they even have
blackboards, teach cursive anymore, I can't wait
for morning, Sunday morning on West 3rd my
favourite time, no cars, branches stark.
Daybreak greenish and cold and on a rooftop
across from me the legendary water towers of
New York City, the giant white smoke Miltoning
to heaven.

Each time I come to the "giant white smoke" of the ending, I'm sure
that there is an earlier line setting this one up in which she holds a
cigarette and watches the smoke rise against the window like a woman
in film noir. There isn't. A nervous, sardonic agitation is the poem's
motor. Everything is in motion, even the absent cars just outside the
frame. The speed of thought is both electric and slow motion. The mind
is in a panic, scurrying to list everything that is wrong – night, city, movie,
ambulances – but if these are the *wrong* ones, which ones would satisfy?
Perhaps all those in the past, "even 20 years ago," when it might have
been "possible to be pure" and when one "was safe," when "curbs" (Thou
shalt / Though shalt not) were respected, perhaps most attentively when
violated. That period is the antithesis to this one in which there is a
vertiginous "smoke Miltoning / to heaven," though many readers will
think both Hell and Eden into the frame, and Proust's suggestion that
the only paradises are the lost ones. Even as she expresses the desire to
"think about one thing" she fails, with three, and seems to be in vertigo
toward absolute desolation. Her sleeplessness recalls Pascal's eternal
night of waking. The moon as an image of singularity is almost
commonplace, the stark, gleaming, elusive circle in the sky at once an
image of perfection, purity, and nothingness. To think about Etruria is
to reflect on something that no longer exists, like memories less vivid
with each passing moment. But if "the self wins anyway" – that is, even

if it fails to "think about one thing" – it does so because of what might be called life's existential cunning: in seeming to lose, we win. The "s" in "self" points in two directions, Janus-like, to the past and into the future. My guess is that the speaker is poised between the named "wrong" Norma of *Sunset Boulevard* (1950) and the "right" but unnamed actress (Norma) of Wilder's *Some Like It Hot* (1959): Marilyn Monroe (née Norma Jeane Mortenson), who plays Sugar "Kane" Kowalczyk.[7] Twenty years ago the speaker looked in the mirror and saw Marilyn – the *right* Norma; today the same mirror shows Gloria, the wrong Norma, unwelcome because old and washed up. Gloria Swanson was born in 1897 and was fifty-three when she starred in *Sunset Boulevard* in 1950. Anne Carson, born on 21 June 1950, would have been fifty-three in 2003. Marilyn (Norma) Monroe, born in 1926, is the absent presence in this poem, waiting to make her entry in "Detail from the tomb of the diver (Paestum 500–433 BCE) second detail," where she meets Etruscans.

Carson is a master of unobtrusive numerical forms and cadenced space. In "Wrong Norma," "Etruria" appears dead centre in the poem: eleven lines from the first line and eleven from the last. The loosely arranged content is held in place, like filings, by the antithetical magnetic pulls of Etruria (is it "pure"?) and New York. The poem begins in New York, flows toward the lost Etruria of the mind, and then back again to New York and the wisp of deferred hope in the poem's last word, "heaven." The poem moves toward "Etruria" and then away, an equal distance in each direction. Hollywood to Etruria to New York. Etruria seems called up by the echo in "to be pure," just as perhaps Milton may come to mind because of "Thick as autumnal leaves that strew the brooks / In Vallombrosa, where the Etrurian shades / High overarched imbower" (*Paradise Lost* 1.302). Etruria is the antitype of New York, historical but also sufficiently unknown to be a sort of never-never land – a haven – for anyone looking for a place of escape, a "somewhere" onto which a writer or reader can project whatever they wish. Etruria is also aurally close to Perugia/Perusia in her mind, the site of "Canicula di Anna," her first longer work, published in 1984, when the world lay all before her and *Eros the Bittersweet* would be forthcoming from Princeton University Press two years later. Like the

---

7 For another woman artist interested in the possibilities in "s / S" see Sophie Taeuber-Arp's painting *Composition à Formes de "S"* (1927).

poem, the book from Princeton would be spare and clear but also layered, learned, playful, witty, unpredictable, elusive, and a genre-bender (or "curb"-breaker). Neither gives anything away to the lazy reader. Though there is always the possibility with Carson that "Etruria" holds some random association for her in her dictionary of private meanings. That leads me to wonder whether the hinge or connection is "red." If Etruria has a colour in our imaginations, it is probably the red of terracotta and the red-coloured males of the tomb paintings, like the musician in the Tomb of the Triclinium. Red is also the colour of the several volcanoes in Carson's work – see the cover art for *Autobiography of Red* (1998). I'm surprised that "alizarin" or "madder" doesn't appear in her work – both words have rich poetic possibilities. *Eros the Bittersweet* (1986) had a red cover, as did *Grief Lessons*, terracotta again. The colour may have associations we won't understand until the biography is written. I sense a deep emotional syntax binding together what seem like scattered motifs.

The Paestum diver in the two poems titled "Detail from the tomb of the diver (Paestum 500–433 BCE) first detail" and "Detail from the tomb of the diver (Paestum 500–433 BCE) second detail" is also red and therefore probably Etruscan, though the painting itself isn't. (See figure 24.1.) It is Greek and has been dated to c. 470.[8] A similar diving figure appears in the Etruscan Tomb of Hunting and Fishing (Tarquinia c. 505–500 BCE). The Paestum diver is in a tomb made of five limestone slabs with a painting of an all-male banquet. The poem suggests that each of its two sections is related to a different detail from the painting. The first section begins with what might be a sketch of the ceiling (or, in another interpretation, the underside of the lid of a chest), which leads to Marilyn's entry into the poem, though at this point only the reader who remembers the songs she sang in Wilder's *Some Like It Hot* will realize that the star is in the room: "*Through with love* she sings Naked except for a." Two lines later the poet appears as herself – "swimming at noon always reminds me of Marilyn Monroe / Etruscan saying." I take this as both a personal detail – "I'm a Monroe fan and I too am through with love" – and as another example of Carson's humour. First, however, we need to ask, is this an Etruscan

8 The painting is from a Greek tomb discovered in 1968 at Paestum. The walls are decorated with images of a banquet; the ceiling shows the diver ("tuffatore"). For the poem, see *Believer*, no. 1 (1 March 2003).

"saying" (as in an apothegm) or is it an Etruscan (man or woman) *saying* something about swimming at noon? Or is it both? If we don't quite understand the meaning intended, Carson might shrug and remind us that the Etruscans are as "mysterious" as she is, and we have only a partial knowledge of the language. The reader also has only partial knowledge of the poet/speaker and inevitably wonders what her relationship is to Monroe beyond swimming. What aspects of the actress's life overlap with the speaker's? The remainder of the poem is a dialogue between "Etruscans" and "Marilyn," though these "Etruscans" are more closely related to Queneau's "Etruscoches" than to Etruria. The doomed movie star confesses that she likes to "go underwater" when "blue," inquires why the Etruscans bother with language when they don't write anything, and is about to dive underwater or *go under*, either literally or metaphorically, as the poem ends. The poem's colour is blue, the temperature is chilly, and the language is minimalist. Language is needed, the Etruscans tell her, because of inscriptions on tombstones (another Carson smile). I wonder whether Carson and her Etruscans know that at Monroe's death there was a copy of *Etruscan Places* in her library of approximately four hundred books.[9] Though Marilyn is "a little blue" and refers to her "pain self," she also asserts, in an echo of *Gone with the Wind*, that "Tomorrow will certainly be." That may be true, though David Hume warned us not to bet on it if we're doing logic. The diver at Paestum is just a diver, and we assume that, after entering the water, he will resurface and swim. Monroe and the "Etruscans" are ghosts communing in another dimension. *Both went under never to return.* Did Carson remember the well-known colour photographs taken in 1962 on the set of the ill-fated *Something's Got to Give* showing Marilyn swimming naked? In the most famous, she holds on to the pool's edge with one leg up against the background of the pool's water with many shades of blue. A few days later, on 8 June, the studio fired her. On 4 August she died by suicide. Blue is by far our most popular colour.[10]

---

9 Open Culture, "The 430 Books in Marilyn Monroe's Library: How Many Have You Read?," https://www.historians.org/about-aha-and-membership/aha-history-and-archives/presidential-addresses/theodore-roosevelt.

10 Several of the photographs are reproduced in Norman Mailer's *Marilyn*, 219–25. For "blue" see Pastoureau, *The Colours of our Memories*, 119. Between 40 to 50 per cent of people say blue is their favourite colour. Green trails with 15 to 20 per cent.

24.1 Tomb of the Diver (Paestum), c. 470 BCE. Of the Greek tombs dated to between 700 and 400 BCE, this is the only one with a fresco of a human figure. Discovered in 1968.

The "me" in the "Etruscan saying" suggests the elusive poet who likes to write autobiographically but without showing herself, like a fan dancer of Marilyn's era, Sally Rand or Faith Bacon or Gypsy Rose Lee. It's worth keeping in mind Carson's warning in "Essay on What I Think About Most" – "I am uneasy with any claim to know exactly / what a poem means to say."[11]

11 Carson, *Men in the Off Hours*, 34.

Afterword:
Nostos

It is not the past that determines the future. Rather, the converse is true.

Leszek Kołakowski

Il reino muerto vive todavia. (The dead kingdom is still alive.)

Pablo Neruda[1]

Kołakowski reminds us that all history is inevitably present history when we discuss it. *The Etruscans in the Modern Imgination* argues that once forgotten or ignored Etruscan matters have gradually become more present to us over the past four centuries. I have traced their gradual return or *nostos*. Rasenna civilization and culture are now displayed widely in the following forms: museums, modern works of art and intellect, travel guides, postcards, online sites, works of art, fashion, jewellery and silverware, T-shirts, company names like Etruscan Resources, academic conferences, and books. Prominent among the last two, and I name only a handful, are the declaration in Italy of 1985 as "The Year of the Etruscans," the holding of the Second International Etruscan Conference in Florence in that same year, and the publication of several blockbuster volumes like *La civiltà degli Etruschi* (Mauro Cristofani, 1985),

---

1 Kołakowski, "Esau, or the Relation of Philosophy to Trade," in *The Key to Heaven*, 24; Neruda, "The Heights of Machu Picchu," in *The Poetry of Pablo Neruda*, 155. With Neruda in mind, see also Hugo von Hofmannstahl's "Manche freilich müssen drunten sterben": "I cannot put off from my eyelids the weariness of totally / forgotten peoples, nor can I ward off from my horrified soul / the silent fall of distant stars" in Forster, *Penguin Book of German Verse*, 32.

Fortuna degli Etruschi (Franco Borsi, 1985), *The Etruscan World* (Jean MacIntosh Turfa, 2013), and *Etruscology* (Alessandro Naso, 2017). The groundwork, as I suggested at the outset, was laid by eighteenth-century scholars, antiquarians, gemologists, and collectors, with the seminal help of a "potter" of genius; it was developed in the nineteenth century by writers in various literary genres and a steady flow of both frivolous (especially on origins and language) and serious Etruscan studies; and it was brought to fruition in the past century by nearly countless scholars and creative artists who restored the Etruscans to their proper place beside the Greeks and Romans in our history and in our general culture. The appendix adds to the argument with an anthology of references to the Etruscans, from Hesiod's poems to Jhumpa Lahiri's fiction. Together with the body of the volume it contributes to what the social scientists call a "thick description" of the field.

I suggest that we now have at least five kinds of knowledge of the Etruscans. The first might be called the "Livy" version: the Etruscans as most Romans saw them. I write "most" because there is the chance that others agreed with Tacitus's suggestion that what the Romans called peace in Gaul, the Gauls saw as devastation. The second is the overall state of our knowledge of the Rasenna, which is greater than what has been known since the early years of the first millennium of our era. The third is a weaker and more casual version of this: the degree to which they are present today to an average educated individual. When we think about any of the ancient peoples other than the Egyptians, Greeks, or Romans, we rarely know more than a handful of facts picked up from documentaries, movies, serendipitous reading, and the occasional media buzz that surrounds an exhibition. Our historical knowledge is often more limited than we know; yet, taken individually, this is the present history of a particular past that each of us carries. In the fourth category is the presentness offered by each of this book's chapters where the Etruscans are present in and known through scholarship or a work of art. When an ancient people find themselves in a popular movie or a very popular television quiz show, we might suggest with some confidence that they have arrived. The presence of Lawrence's *Etruscan Places* among the books in Marilyn Monroe's small library is a telling instance. And, finally, if one of the meanings of "canonic" is timeless and therefore perennially present, I suggest that some Etruscan antiquities have become canonical over the same period as the study of the Etruscans has achieved recognition as a discipline. As expected, some works have a larger presence than others, whether among artists or the population at large, though perhaps only the Sarcophagus of the Married Couple has the standing of a work like the Apollo Belvedere or Euphronios's Sarpedon Krater – which, it is worth recalling, was found in an Etruscan tomb. Other Etruscan artifacts that have attracted attention are the following: Tarquinia's tomb paintings; the Apollo of Veii; the Chimaera of Arezzo; The Orator; the various elongated bronzes, especially L'Ombra della Sera at Volterra; vases; group tombs like those of the Inghirami and Cai Cutu; and the wonderful mirrors which, with the publication of Nancy Thomson de Grummond's *Etruscan Myth, Sacred History, and Legend* (2006), have a chance to come into their own – after all, Picasso paid them the compliment of imitation. Though there is general agreement that it is difficult to isolate specifically Etruscan elements in Etruscan art, the works above suggest that a defining criterion might lie in the extent to which they differ from Greek art.

Popular culture has found a place for many Etruscan antiquities – as stolen artifacts and forgeries – in the mystery novels of writers like Iain Pears, Michael Gilbert, Valerio Massimo Manfredi, Lyn Hamilton, and Lindsey Davis. The last deserves special mention, having written twenty novels set in Ancient Rome, most featuring an Etruscan detective named Marcus Didius Falco.[2] Other genres that feature things Etruscan are science fiction novels, travel novels set in Italy, general fiction, poetry, the plastic arts, and music. I sometimes think of the novels and poems dealing with Etruscan subjects as substitutes for the texts lost in the centuries after conquest and assimilation. While the assiduous archaeologists, historians, and linguists have given us much in the past two centuries, it is doubtful we shall ever have an Etruscan literary text, a historical narrative, a list of lucumones, a chronicle, or a biography. We can be even more certain that we shall never see again the two thousand bronzes from Volsinii (Orvieto) that the Romans looted in 264 BCE and melted down for coins, or the nearly three thousand kilograms of antique bronzes from Corneto (Tarquinia) that the papal authorities melted for the decoration of pillars of the church of Saint

---

2 See Gilbert, *The Etruscan Net* (1969); Hamilton, *The Etruscan Chimera* (2002); Manfredi, *The Ancient Curse* (2010); and Lindsey Davis's series of twenty Marcus Didius Falco detective novels (1989–2010). The Etruscan details in the last three show the authors have done their historical homework. Davis's detective discusses dentistry as well as rumours about Maecenas's sex life.

John Lateran in Rome.[3] One way of reading Anne Carson's "Some old Etruscan calling, 'Ah …' in the rain," is as a lament for the Roman triumph and the consequent disappearance of works such as these. We can also think the "Ah …" as an enigmatic gasp or interjection from "a pale messenger from the wordless world," like the Egyptian mummy Charles Wright sees in the Etruscan Museum at Cortona (not Corneto).[4] Perhaps, finally, the ejaculation might be an exclamation of anticipated pleasure at the modern return implicit in the Etruscan theory of cycles, though it is not precisely what was predicted. Whatever it is, it reminds us of both how much we still don't know about the Etruscans and how very different they were from us. Thinking about the difficulties confronting anyone attempting to understand them, I am reminded of Fustel de Coulanges's comment that "Rien dans les temps modernes ne leur [Grèce et Rome] ressemble. Rien dans l'avenir ne pourra leur ressembler" ("Nothing in our time is like them. Nothing in the future will resemble them").[5] This is even more true of the Etruscans than of their peers.

D.H. Lawrence, Mika Waltari, and Rika Lesser seem to me the writers most acutely aware of the tremor of otherness in the Etruscan world separating us from them. Each describes that world in contemporary language and imagines the often alien categories and concepts within which ancient peoples lived their lives.[6] We have a strong hint of the ontic "otherness" of their way of being not only from the importance accorded the interpretation of signs but also from their foundational myth. The chthonic appearance of Tages presents problems to modern sensibility as grave as those surrounding Romulus and Remus's wolf "mother" or Jesus's virgin birth and resurrection. But these problems didn't exist in a world where the border separating gods and humans was porous, where heroes were often of mixed divine-human parentage, and where people met various kinds of spiritual beings, from gods to dryads and satyrs. The three writers make the effort to evoke what it might have felt like to have direct, unprocessed contact with reality, closer to direct apprehension of otherness than to comprehension of it.

3 Spivey, *Etruscan Art*, 184.

4 Wright, "To the Egyptian Mummy in the Etruscan Museum at Cortona," in *Oblivion Banjo*, 338.

5 Quoted in Finley, *Aspects of Antiquity*, 13.

6 The historian Greg Anderson calls this an "ontology of their history" in *The Realness of Things Past*.

If I have turned often to Lawrence, it is both because he has been so widely influential – he's a staple of the travel books – and because he takes the Etruscans as seriously as Europeans took the Romans and Greeks in the eighteenth and nineteenth centuries. He appropriates the Etruscans with empathy and enthusiasm – in a manner of speaking, he needs them as much as they need him – as if they are a living presence across the centuries, not just a historical fact surviving in the congeries of material ruins and culture. There is a fit in *Etruscan Places* between the sensibility of an artist, the subject, and what he perceives as his own needs and those of his time. Lawrence's version of the Etruscans takes liberties with history, but it has rhetorical force and is a great gesture of an imagination possessed by life's sacredness and mystery. And he reads them as if our lives depend on it. He risks imagining what it might have been like to have a unified (pre-Socratic and pre-Cartesian) sense of identity that allowed permeability between human and non-human worlds. His use of the Etruscans is as unapologetic and unembarrassed as Rousseau's and Lévi-Strauss's of pre-modern societies. As I wrote earlier, Lawrence didn't need to be reminded that we can't go "back to the garden." His emphasis falls on what he thinks the Etruscans had that we increasingly lack: a joyous, sensitive intelligence; an animistic vision of the cosmos as one which "made men live to the depth of their being"; and an organic view of society inseparable from the sacred.[7] No alienation, deracination, and disenchantment of the world. And no priest-curated narratives. *Etruscan Places* is a plea to his contemporaries to at least imagine an alternative to post–First World War Europe – capitalist, industrialist, imperialist, Christian, and racist – in which, to quote the young Marx, "the *increasing value* of the world of things proceeds in direct proportion [to] the *devaluation* of the world of men" (Marx's italics).[8] He understood the intellectual, emotional, and epistemological distance separating our era from the Etruscans, but he was certain that much might be learned about spontaneity, tenderness, reverence, wholeness, community, the place of the spiritual in our lives, and the essential goals to be pursued. I think of his Etruscans as *exempla* to be imitated by those looking for new ways of being. They suggest a eudemonistic approach to life whose goal is human fulfillment and

7 Lawrence, *Apocalypse*, 37.
8 Marx, *The Economic and Philosophic Manuscripts of 1844*, 107.

wholeness rather than endless "progress," industrial inhumanity, and ecological devastation.

Of the writers in this book – other than Huxley and Drabble – I think Bachofen would have been most sympathetic to Lawrence's outreach to the past. Among Lawrence's contemporaries Heidegger comes to mind, with his emphasis on the need "to be open to Being" and the belief that, in George Steiner's words, "the ancient deities, or the agencies of vital order which they image, are inherent in earth and in forest, and they can be resurrected and induced into dynamic play."9 There is no evidence that Heidegger and Lawrence were aware of each other, but their mutual search for the roots of Being or presence led them by parallel paths to roughly the same period of history: from the century of the pre-Socratic thinkers to the fall of the Etruscans. In his last book, *Apocalypse,* Lawrence looks back again to a pre-Christian and pre-Greek world that is religious *without* a monotheistic god. This is his Protestantism running free: Why stop with cleansing the modern church? Why not look all the way back to the primordial time when a person could stand in an unmediated, numinous relationship with the gods? But since there is no evidence in the historical record of a society in this pure state, an Etruscan compromise or metaphor is the best he could hope for. When anyone asks me what they should read about the Etruscans I inevitably answer *Etruscan Places* and, after a pause, Pallottino's *The Etruscans* to bring us back to Leopold von Ranke's "wie es eigentlich gewesen" ("how things really were"). They are complementary and equally indispensable.

As I approach the end of the book, I think back to the gaps in the record – the lost bronzes, writings, and temples – especially the legendary gigantic mausoleum of Lars Porsena at Clusium, if it existed. There are also the lost non-Etruscan books about the Rasenna that testify to their importance: Aristotle's *Nómina Tyrrhenôn* and Theophrastus's *Perí Tyrrhenôn*; Claudius's twenty-volume *Tyrrhenika,* published in Greek in multiple copies. If this were a wish list, I would choose Claudius's book as the one to be discovered. Mediterranean archaeology throws up a surprise at least once a decade that makes some scholar's dream come true. The Punic-Etruscan gold tablets were found at Pyrgi (Santa Severa) in 1964; the non-Etruscan Riace bronzes were

9 Steiner, *Heidegger,* 142.

pulled out of the Mediterranean in 1972; the Tomb of Cai Catu was discovered in 1983 and the Tomb of the Blue Demons in 1985. The scans done by the Lerici Foundation have revealed that there are still six thousand buried tombs. The odds are very good that there will be further surprises, though, as I wrote earlier, I doubt they will involve the lost writings. These will remain as inaccessible as the lost plays of Aeschylus, Sophocles, and Euripides. But as *The Etruscans in the Modern Imagination* shows, we do have a new significant body of creative writing that includes the Etruscans, and I have no doubt that there are more examples than the ones I discuss. France, Germany, and Italy alone could probably provide enough material for another, similar volume.[10]

The Etruscan return is unique in history in so far as no classical or medieval nation has returned from the dead *in this way* and to this extent through an aesthetics of the dispossessed. What we might describe as the material and symbolic body of the Etruscans – a composite of all available traces – now survives in the following: their material remains, the classical written record, the anthropological and historical record between their disappearance and the present, and "the imagined Etruscans" of the arts of the West, from Giotto to Anne Carson. I suggested at the outset that we think of the Etruscan narrative in terms of the topos of "the return." Its conclusion is appropriately modernist: an ending that resolves many of the threads and currents in the plot without overlooking unresolved issues. If history can be defined as what we agree deserves to be remembered, then it is obvious from scholarship and the arts that the Etruscans are once again historical – alive both in universities and in our culture. They have achieved an unpredicted and unexpected afterlife in the imagination of the West.

---

10 FICTION: Honoré de Balzac, *The Wild Ass's Skin* (1831); Edward Bulwer-Lytton, *The Last Days of Pompeii* (1834); H.W. Herbert, *Roman Traitor* (1846); Ouida [Maria Louise Ramé], *In Maremma* (1882); Gabriele D'Annunzio, *Forse che si forse che no* (1910); Robert Graves, *I, Claudius* and *Claudius the God* (both 1934); Antal Szerb, *Journey by Moonlight* (1937); Ray Bradbury, *The Martian Chronicles* (1950); Barbara Pym, *Some Tame Gazelle* (1950); Ethel Wilson, *Love and Salt Water* (1956); J.I.M. Stewart, *The Use of Riches* (1983); Cynthia Ozick, "An Education" (1976); Anthony Burgess, *ABBA ABBA* (1977); Marguerite Yourcenar, *The Dark Brain of Piranesi and Other Essays* (1984); Iain Pears, *The Raphael Affair* (1990); Morgan Llywelyn and Michael Scott, *Etruscans: Beloved of the Gods* (2000); Jim Crace, *The Devil's Larder* (2001).

I leave the last word to Richard Wilbur, whose poem "To the Etruscan Poets" describes the Rasenna's disappearance and in doing so transcends it:

Dream fluently, still brothers, who when young
Took with your mothers' milk the mother tongue.

In which pure matrix, joining world and mind,
You strove to leave some line of verse behind

Like a fresh track across a field of snow,
Not reckoning that all could melt and go.

POETRY: Petrarch, *Africa* (1341); William Gibson, "On an Etruscan Tomb" (1844?); William Gilmore Sims, "The City of the Silent" (1850); Phyllis Hawtrey, "Ballad of a Mirror Found in an Etruscan Tomb" (1897); Constantine Cavafy, "The Poseidonians" (1906); Rainer Maria Rilke, *Duino Elegies* (1923); Gunnar Ekelof, "Tomba dei Tori, Tarquinia" (1951); Robert Lowell, "Falling Asleep over the Aeneid" (1951), "Beyond the Alps" (1959), "A Roman Sarcophagus" (1967); Anna Świrszczyńska, "Tears Are Falling" (1961); Antonio Porta, "Visit to the Necropolis of Norchia" (1974); Irving Layton, "Etruscan Tombs" (1987); Al Purdy, "Etruscan Tombs" (1999); Jan Haag, "Etruscan Goddess" (2000); Ezra Pound, *Posthumous Cantos* (2002); Gianna Patriarca, *My Etruscan Face* (2007); Derek Mahon, "5 Geronimo" (2008); Jack Gilbert, "The Forgotten Dialect of the Heart" (2012); Charles Simic, "Terror" (2018).

ART: Dorothy Shakespear, *Etruscan Gate: Notebook with Drawings and Watercolours* (1910–11); Carlo Carrà; Jean Cocteau; Barbara Hepworth; Sorel Etrog, Alex Colville.

PROSE: Johann Gottfried Herder, *Outlines of a Philosophy of a History of Man* (1784–91); Alexander Herzen, *My Past and Thoughts* (1855).

FILM: *The Golden Salamander* (1954); Italian zombie movies *L'Etrusco Uccide Ancora* (1972), *La Notte de Terrore* (1981), *Neverlake* (1983), *The Etruscan Smile* (2018).

Appendix:

Etruscan Sightings

c. 700 BCE Hesiod
And Circe, daughter of Helios, the son
Of Hyperion, loved Odysseus, patient-souled,
And bore great good Latinus and Agrius,
And they, in the midst of holy islands, ruled
The famous Tyrsenians, so far away.
(*Theogony*, 1005–9)

518–c. 446 BCE Pindar
Grant, I beg,
O son of Kronos, that the Phoenician
and the Tyrrhenians' war-cry
keep quiet at home: it has seen what woe to its ships
came of its pride before Kyma …
(Pythian 1.4)

c. 490–c. 425 BCE Herodotus
In the days of Atys, the son of Manes, there was a great scarcity
through the whole land of Lydia. For some time the Lydians bore
the affliction patiently, but finding that it did not pass away, they
set to work to devise remedies for the evil … The plan adopted
against the famine was to engage in games one day so entirely as not
to feel any craving for food, and the next day to eat and abstain
from games. In this way they passed eighteen years. Still the affliction
continued and became more grievous. So the king determined
to divide the nation in half, and to make the two portions draw lots,
the one to stay, the other to leave the land … the emigrants would

have his son Tyrrhenus for their leader. The lot was cast, and they who had to emigrate went down to Smyrna, and built themselves ships, in which, after they had put on board all needful stores, they sailed away in search of new homes and better sustenance. After sailing past many countries they came to Umbria, where they built cities for themselves, and fixed their residence. Their former name of Lydians they laid aside and called themselves after the name of the king's son, who led the colony, Tyrrhenians. (*The Histories of Herodotus*, 1.94)

c. 376–after 323 BCE Theopompus

[Theopompus] says … that the women of the Tyrrhenians are common property; they take great care of their bodies and exercise in the nude, often together with men … because they don't consider it shameful to show themselves in that state. At table they lie down not with their own husbands but with the first to come of the other participants and they even drink toasts to whomever they wish … To make love in public is not considered shameful by the Tyrrhenians, for that, too, is the habit of the country. (Sybille Haynes, *Etruscan Civilization*, 256–7)

98–c. 55 BCE Titus Lucretius Carus

Here then is a plain and intelligible account of the fiery thunderbolt and how it does what it does. It is a fruitless task to unroll the Tuscan scrolls, seeking some revelation of the god's hidden purpose. That is no way to study from which quarter the darting fire has come or into which other it has passed; how it has entered a closed building, and how after working its will it has slipped out again. (*De Rerum Natura* 6. 412–16)

39–65 Marcus Annaeus Lucanus

Therefore it was resolved to follow ancient custom and summon seers from Etruria. The oldest of these was Arruns who dwelt in the deserted city of Luca; the course of the thunderbolt, the marks on entrails yet warm, and the warning of each wing that strays through the sky, had no secrets for him. First, he bids the destruction of monsters, which nature, at variance with herself, had brought forth from no seed, and orders that the abominable fruit of a barren womb shall be burned with wood of evil omen. Next, at his bidding the scared citizens march right round the city; and the pontiffs, who have license to perform the ceremony, purify the walls with solemn lustration and move round the outer limit of the long sacred boundary. (*De Bello Civili / Pharsalia*, 1.584–95)

1265–1321 Dante Alighieri
Backing up to this one's chest comes Aruns,
who in the hills of Luni, worked by peasants
of Carrara dwelling in the valley's plain,

lived in white marble cut into a cave,
and from this site, where nothing blocked his view,
he could observe the sea and stars with ease.
(*The Divine Comedy*: Inferno, XX, 46–51)

1534 François Rabelais (1494?–1553?)
Here, as they were cleaning the ditches, the diggers struck with the picks against a great tomb of bronze, so immeasurably long that they never found the end of it. For it stuck out too far into the sluices of the Vienne. Opening this tomb at a certain place which was sealed on the top with the sign of a goblet, around which was inscribed in Etruscan letters, HIC BIBITUR. (*The Histories of Gargantua and Pantagruel*, 42)

1580 Michel de Montaigne (1533–1592)
That much celebrated art of divination of the Tuscans originated in this way: A laborer, piercing the ground deeply with his plough, saw Tages emerge from it, a demigod with the face of a child but the wisdom of an old man. Everyone came on the run, and his words and knowledge, containing the principles and methods of this art, were collected and preserved for many centuries … I would rather regulate my affairs by the chance of the dice than by such dreams. ("Of Prognostications," 28–9)

1699 François de Salignac de La Mothe-Fénelon (1651–1715)
"Why," said Mentor, "would you concern yourself with sacred things? Leave the decision of them to the Etrurians, who have the traditions of the most ancient oracles, and are qualified by inspiration to be the interpreters of the gods." (*Telemachus, Son of Ulysses*, 305)

1765 Louis de Jaucourt (1704–1779)
[The Etruscans] continued nevertheless to regard the image of Priapus as a powerful protector. They did not see it as more than a ridiculous object which disarmed the envious and distracted their attention, weakening their grievous stares. Gori ... assures us that the cabinets of curiosities in Tuscany are filled with these amulets which the Etruscan women carried and attached to the necks of their children ...

Etruscan divination included soothsayers and fortune tellers. The college of Auguries instituted by Romulus and confirmed by Numa was revered by the consuls who succeeded the kings; augury was thus a ruling establishment, a dignity and power, that one could not exercise without being avowed in that state ... In Rome one was trained in divination: that famous soothsayer who proved his science to Tarquin the Elder by cutting a stone with a razor, Attius Navius, was indoctrinated under an Etruscan master, the most able there was, and afterward the Senate sent pupils to Etruria as to the source, students drawn from the foremost families. ("The Religion of the Greeks and Romans," Diderot's *L'Encyclopédie* [1751–76])

1765? Denis Diderot (1713–1784)
(Epitaph for the Comte de Caylus)
Here lies an antiquarian whose temper was sour and hot;
How fittingly he's buried in this Etruscan pot!

1770 Daines Barrington (1727–1800)
(On Mozart's sight-reading abilities at age eight)
"Suppose then a capital speech in Shakespeare never seen before, and yet read by a child of eight years old, with all the pathetic energy of a Garrick. Let it be conceived likewise, that the same child is reading, with a glance of his eye, three different comments on this speech tending to its illustration; and that one comment is written in Greek, the second in Hebrew, and the third in Etruscan characters ... When all this is conceived, it will convey some idea of what this boy is capable of." ("Account of a Very Remarkable Young Musician," Maynard Solomon, *Mozart: A Life*, 3)

1773 Edward Gibbon (1737–1794)
The middle part of the peninsula that now comprises the duchy of Tuscany and the ecclesiastical state, was the ancient seat of the

Etruscans and Umbrians; to the former of whom Italy was indebted for the first rudiments of civilised life. (*The History of the Decline and Fall of the Roman Empire, Volume I: The Turn of the Tide,* 46)

1797(?) Peter Pindar (Dr John Wolcot 1738–1819)
... the world reports (I hope it is untrue),
That half Sir William's Mugs and Gods are *new,*
Himself the *baker* of the "Etrurian Ware"
That made our British Antiquarians stare:
Nay, that he means ere long to cross the main,
And at his *Naples oven* sweat again.
("Peter's Prophecy; or the President [Joseph Banks] and Poet,"
    Complete Works [1824], 235)

1818 Byron (1788–1824)
But where repose the all Etruscan three –
Dante and Petrarch, and, scarce less than they,
The Bard of Prose, creative spirit! he
Of the Hundred Tales of Love ...
(*Childe Harold's Pilgrimage,* 4.lvi)

1822 François-René de Chateaubriand (1768–1848)
The island of Graciosa, before which we were moored, displayed to us hills that were a little swollen in outline like the ellipses of an Etruscan amphora: they were draped in the green of their cornfields and gave off a pleasant smell of wheat peculiar to the harvests of the Azores. (*Memoirs from Beyond the Tomb,* 89)

1873 Anthony Trollope (1815–1882)
"Where did that Delph bowl come from?" "It is one of Mortlock's finest Etruscan vases," said Mrs Carbuncle. "Oh, – I thought that Etruscan vases came from – from somewhere in Greece or Italy," said Sir Griffin. "I declare that you are shocking," said Mrs Carbuncle, struggling to maintain her good humour. (*The Eustace Diamonds,* 504)

1881 Thomas Hardy (1840–1928)
"This lad resembled the Etruscan youth Tages ..." (*The Laodicean: A Story of Today,* 197)

1887 Rider Haggard (1856–1925)

"These vases are of a very ancient manufacture, and of all sizes. None such can have been made in the country for hundreds, or rather thousands, of years. They are found in the rock tombs, of which I shall give a description in their proper place, and my own belief is that, after the fashion of the Egyptians, with whom the former inhabitants of this country may have had some connection, they were used to receive the viscera of the dead. Leo, however, is of the opinion that, as in the case of Etruscan amphorae, they were placed there for the spiritual use of the deceased. They are mostly two-handled, and of all sizes, some being nearly three feet in height, and running from that down to as many inches. In shape they vary, but are all exceedingly beautiful and graceful, being made of a very fine black ware, not lustrous, but slightly rough. On this groundwork were inlaid figures much more graceful and lifelike than any others I have seen on antique vases. Some of these inlaid pictures represented love-scenes with a child-like simplicity and freedom of manner which would not commend itself to the taste of the present day. Others again were pictures of maidens dancing, and yet others of hunting scenes." (*She*, 97)

1891 Roger Fry (1886–1934)

I've got very keen on Etruscan things and think of going to Corneto to see the painted tombs. I think they will throw some light on Greek painting because what is so interesting is the extraordinary way in which they accepted Greek art. But there is also much that is original in their art and I think I can trace all that I formerly thought the Romans added to Greek art (namely something grotesque and picturesque) to an Etruscan origin, so much so that I think what the Italians of the Renaissance selected for their model was rather what was Etruscan in Roman art than anything else. I daresay this is rather wild or else has been said before but at present I'm rather mad on them. It is so interesting to discover a whole civilization of which one was ignorant and which has had an enormous effect on the course of modern civilization through the great plagiarists of the world, the Romans. (*Letters of Roger Fry*, I, 132)

27 December 1912 Theodore Roosevelt (1858–1919)

The least imaginative is moved by the simple inscription on the Etruscan sarcophagus, I THE GREAT LADY; a lady so haughty that no other human being was allowed to rest near her; and yet now nothing remains but this proof of the pride of the nameless one. ("History as Literature")

1912 George Bernard Shaw (1856–1950)
Stage direction: The Call Boy returns with a *man* in a *hideous Etruscan mask, carrying* a *whip* ... Two slaves in Etruscan masks, with ropes and drag hooks, hurry in. (*Androcles and the Lion*, Act 2, 464)

1923 Rainer Maria Rilke (1875–1926)
Look at the half-assurance of the bird ...
like one of those Etruscan souls, escaped
from a dead man enclosed within a space,
on which his resting figure forms a lid.
(*Duino Elegies*, 8.56–60)

1936 T.S. Eliot (1888–1965)
[I]t is only upon readers who wish to see a Christian civilization survive and develop ... that I am urging the importance of the study of Latin and Greek. If Christianity is not to survive, I shall not mind if the texts of the Latin and Greek languages become more obscure and forgotten than those of the language of the Etruscans. (*Essays Ancient and Modern*, 184)

1944 George Seferis (1900–1971)
In this Etruscan village, behind the sea of Salerno
behind the harbours of our return ...
We come from Arabia, Egypt, Palestine, Syria;
the little state of
Kommagene, which flickered out like a small lamp,
comes to mind,
and great cities that lived for thousands of years
and then became pastures for cattle,
Fields for sugar-cane and corn.
("Last Stop")

1947 Herbert Read (1893–1968)
D.H. Lawrence called Etruscan art the supreme art of all times and all nations. The statement is no doubt considered as a wilful exaggeration

by all those scholars and critics who value a reputation for objectivity, but I think it needs very little amendment to be acceptable. Etruscan art undoubtedly belongs to the most supreme art of all times and nations. Like Oriental art and Gothic art, it is what is perhaps best described as a transcendental art. (*A Coat of Many Colours: Occasional Essays*, 237)

1953 Saul Bellow (1915–2005)
His old sire, gruff and mocking, deeply tickled, lay like the Buffalo Bill of the Etruscans in the beach chair and bath towel drawn up burnoose-wise to keep the dazzle from his eyes – additionally shaded by his soft, flesh-heavy arm – his bushy mouth open with laughter. (*The Adventures of Augie March*, 63)

1956 Bernard Berenson (1865–1959)
The Etruscan problem remains as enigmatic as ever. The theory now gaining credence is that the Etruscans were autochthons, relatively little affected by Aryans, but having affinity linguistically with Basque and Georgian. Now I do not know any Georgian, but Basques have nothing somatically in common with the present Tuscans. So I remain on the fence with regard to the origin of Etruscan speech and of the race. Perhaps all these speculations are mere pass-time, idle curiosity, getting us nowhere. (*Sunset and Twilight*, 202)

1956 Ethel Wilson (1888–1980)
"I know you pay altogether too much attention to people," said Nora, stretching her arms lazily and smiling her sideways Etruscan smile. (*Love and Salt Water*, 108)

1959 Pamela Hansford Johnson (1912–1981)
The church bells began to ring in their sweet mournfulness, each note rounded as an O. They were playing *Dixie*, an air so foreign to the tongue of the carillon that it took on all the gnomic charm of a language still undeciphered, like Etruscan or Minoan. (*The Unspeakable Skipton*, 173)

1965 Jean Renoir (1894–1979)
I wonder whether in primitive times, all objects, not just art, were beautiful. It's a disturbing question. When we look at ancient Etruscan

pottery, it's all beautiful. And don't tell me that every Etruscan potter was a genius. (Interview with Jacques Rivette, included in DVD edition of the film *French Cancan*)

1965 Muriel Spark (1918–2006)
[Ricky] said, "My aunts never told me my mother was a Catholic. Anyway, they were not really my aunts. Perhaps my father was a Catholic, too. An Irish couple, I expect, whoever they were. I know more about the Etruscans than I do about my own parents, and in fact I've got no curiosity about them at all, whereas the Etruscans –" (*The Mandelbaum Gate*, 265)

1973 Anthony Powell (1905–2000)
"On the contrary," said Dr Brightman. "The Greeks did not know what being rich meant until they came in contact with the Lydians, now thought to be ancestors of the Etruscans." (*Temporary Kings*, 9)

1976 Eugenio Montale (1896–1981)
I came back
with the group after visiting the tombs
of Lucumos, dens of aristocrats
disguised as thieves, the prison-like street
à la Piranesi in old Leghorn.
("After a Flight")

1990 Milan Kundera (b. 1929)
Even though he spent so much of his time in galleries, it took Kennedy's photographs to make Rubens realize this simple fact: the great painters and sculptors from classic days to Raphael and perhaps even to Ingres avoided portraying laughter, even smiles. Of course, the figures of Etruscan sculpture all have smiles, but this smile isn't a response to some particular, momentary situation but a permanent state of the face, expressing eternal bliss. For classical sculptors as well as for painters of later periods a beautiful face was imaginable only in its immobility. (*Immortality*, 322)

1991 Colin Dexter (1930–2017)
After gaining his pre-ordained First in both parts of the Classical Tripos, Jimmy had been awarded a Junior Research Fellowship at

Oxford to study early Etruscan epigraphy; and then, three years later, he had died of Hodgkin's disease. (*The Jewel That Was Ours*, 12)

1995 Alice Munro (b. 1931)
The regular customers who had changed into something like friends were: a middle-aged woman who was a chartered accountant but preferred such reading as *Six Existentialist Thinkers*, and *The Meaning of Meaning*; a provincial civil servant who ordered splendid, expensive works of pornography such as I had not known existed (their elaborate Oriental, Etruscan connections seemed to me grotesque and uninteresting, compared to the simple, effective, longed-for rituals of myself and Nelson). ("The Albanian Virgin," *Selected Stories*, 488)

1997 Barry Unsworth (1930–2012)
Silence settled around them and Cecilia thought how strange it was that she and Harold should be standing here, so glum and divided, among these ancient hills where the pleasure-loving Etruscans had grown their grapes and pressed their wine. "These were the heartlands of the Etruscans," she said. "They made their wine and danced and had their games and celebrations all around here. You can see it in their paintings on the walls of their tombs. They were a very hedonistic –" (*After Hannibal*, 176)

2008 Jhumpa Lahiri (b. 1967)
The Etruscans were her focus now. A few months ago she had attended a lecture in Boston about Etruscan references in Virgil, and this had ushered her headlong into that mysterious civilization prior to Rome, people who had possibly wandered from Asia minor to central Italy and flourished for four centuries, who had ruled Rome for one hundred years before turning obsolete. Their literature was nonexistent, their language obscure. Their primary legacy was tombs and the things that were put in them: jewels, pottery, weapons to accompany the dead. She was learning about the *haruspices*, augurs who interpreted the will of the gods through the entrails of animals, lightning bolts, dreams of pregnant women, flights of birds. She wanted to put a seminar together when she returned to Wellesley, about Etruscan influence in Roman antiquity, and possibly, based on her research a proposal for a second book. She had gone to the Vatican to see the Etruscan collection at the Gregorian Museum, and

also to the Villa Giulia. She was combing through Cicero and Seneca, Livy and Pliny, reading fragments of the occultist senator Nigidius Figulus, typing notes into her laptop, marking up the many books she read. ("Going Ashore," *Unaccustomed Earth*, 299–300)

2009 John Updike (1932–2009)
Fiesole – its little Roman stadium, its charming Etruscan museum built in the form of a first-century Ionic temple – ("My Father's Tears," *My Father's Tears and Other Stories*, 209)

Bibliography

Adams, J.N. *Bilingualism and the Latin Language*. Cambridge: Cambridge
University Press, 2003.

Alter, Robert. *A Lion for Love: A Critical Biography of Stendhal*. New York: Basic
Books, 1979.

Anderson, Greg. *The Realness of Things Past: Ancient Greece and Ontological History*.
Oxford: Oxford University Press, 2018.

Applebaum, Anne. *Gulag: A History*. New York: Doubleday, 2003.

Aristotle, *The Politics*. Translated by T.A. Sinclair. Harmondsworth: Penguin
Books, 1975.

Artaud, Antonin. *Œuvres complètes*. Paris: Gallimard, 1956–94.

Bachofen, J.J. *Myth, Religion, and Mother Right: Selected Writings of J.J. Bachofen*.
Translated by Ralph Mannheim. With a preface by George Boas and an
introduction by Joseph Campbell. Princeton: Princeton University Press, 1967.

Baker, Paul R. *The Fortunate Pilgrims: Americans in Italy 1800–1860*. Cambridge:
Harvard University Press, 1964.

Balzac, Honoré de. *The Wild Ass's Skin*. Translated by Helen Constantine.
London: Oxford University Press, 2012.

Barańczak, Stanisław. *A Fugitive from Utopia*. Cambridge, MA: Harvard University
Press, 1987.

Barker, Andrew D. "Music in Greek and Roman Life." In *The Oxford Companion
to Classical Civilization*, edited by Simon Hornblower and Antony Spawforth,
477–9. Oxford: Oxford University Press, 1998.

Barnes, Jonathan. "The Same Again: The Stoics and Eternal Recurrence."
In *Method and Metaphysics: Essays in Ancient Philosophy I*, 412–78. Oxford:
Clarendon Press, 2011.

Barnes, Julian. "Robespierre's Chamber Pot." *London Review of Books* 42, no. 7
(2 April 2020): 3–6.

Baron, Hans. *From Petrarch to Leonardo Bruni: Studies in Humanistic and Political Literature.* Chicago: University of Chicago Press, 1968.

Bassani, Giorgio. *Dentro le mura.* Milan: A. Mondadori, 1973.

– *The Garden of the Finzi-Continis.* Translated by William Weaver. New York: Everyman's Library, 2005.

– *Il Giardino dei Finzi-Contini.* Torino: Einaudi, 1962.

Beckett, Wendy. *Peggy Glanville-Hicks.* Pymble, Australia: Angus & Robertson, 1992.

Bedford, Sybille. *Aldous Huxley: A Biography.* 2 vols. London: Chatto & Windus, 1973–4.

– *Aldous Huxley: A Biography.* London: Papermac, 1993.

Bellow, Saul. *The Adventures of Augie March.* New York: Penguin Books, 1984.

Benelli, Enrico. "Alphabets and Language." In *Etruscology,* edited by Alessandro Naso, 246–70. London: Routledge, 2017.

Benjamin, Walter. *The Correspondence of Walter Benjamin, 1910–1940.* Edited and annotated by Gershom Scholem and Theodor W. Adorno. Translated by Manfred R. Jacobsen and Evelyn M. Jacobsen. Chicago: University of Chicago Press, 1994.

– "Johann Jakob Bachofen." In *Walter Benjamin: Selected Writings, Volume 3, 1935–1938,* edited by Howard Eiland and Michael W. Jennings, 11–24. Translated by Edmund Jephcott, Howard Eiland, and others. Cambridge, MA: Belknap Press of Harvard University Press, 2002.

– "Paralipomena to 'On the Concept of History: The Now of Recognizability.'" In *Walter Benjamin: Selected Writings, Volume 4, 1938–1940,* edited by Howard Eiland and Michael W. Jennings, 389–400. Translated by Edmund Jephcott and others. Cambridge, MA: Belknap Press of Harvard University Press, 2002.

– *Walter Benjamin's Archive: Images, Texts, Signs.* Translated by Esther Leslie. Edited by Ursula Marx, Gudrun Schwarz, Michael Schwarz, Erdmut Wizisla. London: Verso, 2007.

Bentley, G.E., Jr. *The Stranger from Paradise: A Biography of William Blake.* New Haven: Published for the Paul Mellon Centre for Studies in British Art by Yale University Press, 2001.

Berenson, Bernard. *Sunset and Twilight: From the Diaries of 1947-1948.* New York: Harcourt, Brace & World. 1963.

Berger, John. *Selected Essays.* Edited by Geoff Dyer. New York: Pantheon Books, 2001.

Binet, Laurent. *The Seventh Function of Language.* Translated by Sam Taylor. New York: Farrar, Straus and Giroux, 2017.

Blake, William. *Complete Writings.* Edited by Geoffrey Keynes. London: Oxford University Press, 1972.

Blessington, Marguerite, Countess of. *The Idler in Italy: Journal of a Tour.* 2 vols. Philadelphia: Carey and Hart, 1839.

Boardman, John. *Greek Art.* London: Thames and Hudson, 1996.

Bonaparte, Lucien. *Catalogue d'antiquités choisies trouvées au cours des fouilles faites par le prince Canino.* Rome: 1822.

– *Muséum étrusque de Lucien Bonaparte: fouilles de 1828 à 1829.* Viterbe: 1829.

Bonfante, Larissa. *Etruscan.* London: University of California Press / British Museum, 1990.

– ed. *Etruscan Life and Afterlife.* Detroit: Wayne State University Press, 1986.

– "The Women of Etruria." *Arethusa* 6 (1973): 91–101.

Bonnefoy, Yves. *The Arrière-pays.* Translated and introduced by Stephen Romer. New York: Seagull Books, 2012.

Brennan, Joseph. *Thomas Mann's World.* New York: Russell & Russell, 1962.

Brown, Frederick. *Flaubert: A Biography.* New York: Little, Brown and Co., 2006.

Browne, Thomas. *Religio Medici, Hydriotaphia, and The Garden of Cyrus.* Edited by Robin Robbins. Oxford: Clarendon Press, 1972.

Bruni, Leonardo. *History of the Florentine People.* Edited and translated by James Hankins. Cambridge, MA: The I Tatti Renaissance Library / Harvard University Press, 2001.

Bulwer-Lytton, Edward. *The Last Days of Pompeii,* London: Collins Clear-Type Press, 1902.

Burke, Janine. *The Sphinx on the Table: Sigmund Freud's Art Collection and the Development of Psychoanalysis.* New York: Walker & Co., 2006.

Burke, Kenneth. *The Philosophy of Literary Form: Studies in Symbolic Action.* Baton Rouge: Louisiana State University Press, 1967.

Byres, James. *Hypogaei, Or Sepulchral Caverns on Tarquinia.* Edited by Frank Howard. London: Frank Howard, 1842.

Cairns, Francis. *Sextus Propertius: The Augustan Elegist.* Cambridge: Cambridge University Press, 2006.

Cameron, Alan. *The Last Pagans of Rome.* New York: Oxford University Press, 2011.

Campbell, Joseph. *Goddesses: Mysteries of the Feminine Divine.* Edited by Safron Rossi. Novato, CA: New World Library, 2013.

Campigli, Massimo. "Massimo Campigli and the Etruscans." *Minerva* (September/October 2021): 61.

Camus, Albert. *Lyrical and Critical Essays.* Edited by Philip Thody. Translated by Ellen Conroy Kennedy. New York: Vintage Books, 1970.

Canetti, Elias. *The Secret Heart of the Clock: Notes, Aphorisms, Fragments 1983–1985.* New York: Farrar Straus Giroux, 1989.

Čapek, Karel. *Italské Listy: Fejetony.* Praha: Československý Spisovatel, 1970.

Carey, John. *The Unexpected Professor: An Oxford Life in Books*. London: Faber & Faber, 2014.

Carne-Ross, D.S. *Pindar*. New Haven: Yale University Press, 1985.

Carson, Anne, "Detail from the tomb of the diver (Paestum 500–433 BCE) first detail" and "Detail from the tomb of the diver (Paestum 500–433 BCE) second detail." *Believer*, no. 1 (1 March 2003), n.p.

– *Eros the Bittersweet: An Essay*. Princeton: Princeton University Press, 1986.

– *Float*. Toronto: McClelland & Stewart, 2016.

– *Glass, Irony and God*. With an introduction by Guy Davenport. New York: A New Directions Book, 1995.

– "Interview with Anne Carson." *The White Review*, no. 20 (June 2017).

– *Men in the Off Hours*. New York: Alfred A. Knopf, 2000.

– *Norma Jeane Baker of Troy*. New York: New Directions, 2019.

– *NOX*. New York: A New Directions Book, 2010.

– *Plainwater: Essays and Poetry*. New York: Alfred A. Knopf, 1995.

– "Wrong Norma." *London Review of Books* 38, no. 17 (8 September 2016).

Chadwick, John. *The Decipherment of Linear B*. Harmondsworth: Penguin Books, 1961.

Chateaubriand, François René. *Memoirs from Beyond the Tomb*. Translated by Robert Baldick. Harmondsworth: Penguin Books, 1961.

Cicero. *De Senectute, De Amicitia, De Divinatione*. Translated by W.A. Falconer. Cambridge, MA: Harvard University Press, 1964.

Clark, Kenneth. *The Nude: A Study in Ideal Form*. Princeton: Princeton University Press; Bollingen Series 35:2. 1990.

Conrad, Joseph. *The Complete Short Fiction of Joseph Conrad*. Vol. 3, *The Tales*, edited by Samuel Hynes. Hopewell, NJ: Ecco Press, 1992.

Conway, R.S. "Etruria," in the *Encyclopedia Britannica*, 1911 edition. https://en.wikisource.org/wiki/1911_Encyclopedia_Britannica.

Cornell, Tim. *The Beginnings of Rome: Italy and Rome from the Bronze Age to the Punic Wars (c. 1000–264 BCE)*. London: Routledge, 1995.

Craft, Robert. *Present Perspectives: Critical Writings*. New York: Alfred A. Knopf, 1984.

Danchev, Alex. *Braque: A Life*. London: Hamish Hamilton, 2005.

Dante. *Inferno*. Translated by Allen Mandelbaum. Berkeley: University of California Press, 1980.

Darwin, Erasmus. *The Botanic Garden: A Poem in Two Parts*. London: Jones & Company, 1824.

Davenport, Guy. *7 Greeks*. Translated by Guy Davenport. New York: New Directions Books, 1995.

Davies, Norman. *Vanished Kingdoms: The Rise and Fall of States and Nations.* New York: Viking, 2012.

Davis, Lindsey. *Ode to a Banker.* London: Arrow, 2001.

– *Poseidon's Gold.* New York: Berkeley Prime Crime, 2011.

de Angelis, Francesco. "The Reception of Etruscan Culture: Dempster and Buonarroti." In *The Etruscan World*, edited by Jean MacIntosh Turfa, 130–5. London: Routledge, 2013.

Debussy, Claude. *Debussy Letters.* Selected and edited by François Lesure and Roger Nichols. Translated by Roger Nichols. London: Faber and Faber, 1987.

de Grummond, Nancy Thomson, ed. *An Encyclopedia of the History of Classical Archaeology.* New York: Routledge, 1996.

– *Etruscan Myth, Sacred History, and Legend.* Philadelphia: University of Pennsylvania Museum of Archaeology and Anthropology, 2006.

– "Etruscan Tombs." In *An Encyclopedia of the History of Classical Archaeology*, edited by Nancy Thomson de Grummond, 409–10. New York: Routledge, 1996.

– "Haruscipy and Augury: Sources and Procedures." In *The Etruscan World*, edited by Jean MacIntosh Turfa, 539–44. London: Routledge, 2013.

– "Rediscovery." In *Etruscan Life and Afterlife*, edited by Larissa Bonfante, 18–46. Detroit: Wayne State University Press, 1986.

Delacroix, Eugène. *The Journal of Eugène Delacroix.* Translated by Walter Pach. New York: Hacker Art Books, 1980.

Della Fina, Giuseppe M. "History of Etruscology." In *Etruscology*, edited by Alessandro Naso, 53–68. London: Routledge, 2017.

Dennis, George. *The Cities and Cemeteries of Etruria.* 2 vols. London: John Murray, 1883.

– *Westminster Review* 41, (March–June 1844): 145–77.

Derrida, Jacques. *Points … : Interviews.* Edited by Elisabeth Weber. Translated by Peggy Kamuf and others. Stanford: Stanford University Press, 1995.

Dexter, Colin. *The Jewel That Was Ours.* London: Pan Books, 1991.

Dickinson, Emily. *The Complete Poems of Emily Dickinson.* Edited by Thomas H. Johnson. Boston: Little Brown and Company, 1960.

– *Selected Letters.* Edited by Thomas H. Johnson. Cambridge, MA: Harvard University Press, 1986.

Diderot, Denis. *Encyclopédie ou dictionnaire raisonné des sciences, des arts et des métiers.* Paris: Briasson, 1765.

Dolan, Brian. *Wedgwood: The First Tycoon.* New York: Viking, 2004.

Donne, John. *The Complete Poetry and Selected Prose.* Edited by Charles M. Coffin. New York: Modern Library, 1952.

Doolittle, Hilda [H.D.]. *Tribute to Freud.* New York: New Directions, 2012.

Drabble, Margaret. *The Dark Flood Rises.* London: Canongate, 2017.

− *The Radiant Way.* Toronto: McClelland & Stewart, 1987.

Dumas, Alexandre. *The Black Tulip.* [No translator.] London: Everyman's Library, 1971.

Dumas, Ann, Colta Ives, Susan Alyson Stein, and Gary Tinterow. *The Private Collection of Edgar Degas.* New York: Metropolitan Museum of Art, 1997.

Dunlop, Ian. *Degas.* New York: Harper & Row, 1979.

"Early Roman History: Barthold Niebuhr, *The History of Rome,* Thomas Arnold, *History of Rome.*" *Western Review* 1 (April 1846): 211–72.

Eckermann, Johann Peter. *Conversations with Goethe.* Translated by John Oxenford. Edited by J.K. Moorhead. London: Dent, 1971.

Edwards, Owen Dudley. *Macaulay.* London: Weidenfield and Nicolson, 1988.

Eliot, George. *Daniel Deronda.* London: Oxford World Classics, 1988.

Eliot, T.S. *Essays Ancient and Modern.* New York: Harcourt, Brace and Co., 1936.

− *The Sacred Wood.* London: Methuen & Co., 1967.

− *Selected Essays.* London: Faber and Faber, 1932.

Emerson, Ralph Waldo. *Emerson in His Journals.* Selected and edited by Joel Porte. Cambridge, MA: Harvard University Press, 1982.

− *Essays and Lectures.* Selected by Joel Porte. New York: Library of America, 1983.

− *The Journals and Miscellaneous Notebooks of Ralph Waldo Emerson.* Vol. 7, *1838–1842.* Edited by A.W. Plumstead and Harrison Hayford. Cambridge, MA: Harvard University Press, 1969.

− *The Journals of Ralph Waldo Emerson.* Edited by Robert N. Linscott. New York: Modern Library, 1960.

− *The Journals of Ralph Waldo Emerson.* Vol. 14, *1854–1861.* Edited by Ronald A. Bosco and Glen M. Johnson. Cambridge, MA: Harvard University Press, 1860.

− *The Journals of Ralph Waldo Emerson.* Vol. 16, *1866–1882.* Edited by Ronald A. Bosco and Glen M. Johnson. Cambridge, MA: Harvard University Press, 1982.

− *Selected Journals 1820–1842.* Edited by Lawrence Rosenwald. New York: Library of America, 2010.

− *The Topical Notebooks of Ralph Waldo Emerson.* Vol. 3. Edited by Glen M. Johnson. Columbia: University of Missouri Press, 1994.

England, Martha W. "Apprenticeship at the Haymarket?" In *Blake's Visionary Forms Dramatic,* edited by David V. Erdman and John E. Grant, 3–29. Princeton: Princeton University Press, 1970.

Erdman, David. *Blake: Prophet Against Empire.* New York: Anchor Books, 1969.

Fagan, Brian M. *Returning to Babylon: Travelers, Archeologists and Monuments in Mesopotamia.* Boston: Little, Brown and Co., 1979.

Fairbank, Ronald. *3 More Novels: Vainglory, Inclinations, Caprice.* New York: New Directions, 1986.

Fénelon, François de. *Telemachus, Son of Ulysses.* Edited and translated by Patrick Riley. Cambridge: Cambridge University Press, 1994.

Finley, M.I. "The Etruscans and Early Rome" and "Etruscheria." In *Aspects of Antiquity: Discoveries and Controversies.* London: Chatto & Windus, 1968.

– *The Use and Abuse of History.* London: Hogarth Press, 1986.

Flaubert, Gustave. *Bouvard and Pécuchet / The Dictionary of Received Ideas.* Translated by A.J. Krailsheimer. Harmondsworth: Penguin Books, 1976.

– *Flaubert in Egypt.* Translated and edited by Francis Steegmuller. Chicago: Academy Chicago, 1979.

– "Flaubert to Louise Colet, 1851–4." Translated by Francis Steegmuller. *Grand Street* 2, no. 2 (Winter 1983): 136–49.

– *Salammbô.* Translated by A.J. Krailsheimer. Harmondsworth: Penguin Books, 1977.

– *The Sentimental Education.* Translated by Patricia Burlingame. New York: New American Library, 1972.

Forster, Leonard W., ed. *Penguin Book of German Verse.* Harmondsworth: Penguin Books, 1990.

Fothergill, Brian. *Sir William Hamilton: Envoy Extraordinary.* New York: Harcourt, Brace & World, 1969.

Fowles, John. *Daniel Martin.* Toronto: Collins, 1977.

France, Anatole. *The Gods Will Have Blood.* Translated by Frederick Davies. Harmondsworth: Penguin Books, 1983.

– *Oeuvres.* 4 vols. Edition established, presented, and annotated by Marie-Claire Bancquart. Paris: Gallimard, 1984–91.

– *Prétextes: Suivi de Nouveaux Prétextes.* Paris: Mercure de France, 1963.

– *The Red Lily.* [No translator.] New York: Boni and Liveright. n.d.

Freud, Sigmund. *The Complete Letters of Sigmund Freud to Wilhelm Fliess, 1887–1904.* Edited by Jeffrey Moussaieff Masson. Cambridge, MA: Harvard University Press, 1985.

– *The Interpretation of Dreams.* Translated by James Strachey. New York: Discus Books, 1970.

– *Interpreting Dreams.* Translated by J.A. Underwood. London: Penguin Books, 2006.

Fromm, Erich. *The Forgotten Language.* New York: Grove Press, 1957.

Fry, Roger. *Last Lectures.* Edited with an Introduction by Kenneth Clark. New York: Macmillan, 1939.

- *Letters of Roger Fry.* 2 vols. Edited by Denys Sutton. London: Chatto
  & Windus, 1972.
- *Transformations.* London: Chatto & Windus, 1926.

Gamwell, Lynn, and Richard Wells, eds. *Sigmund Freud and Art: His Personal
  Collection of Antiquities.* London: State University of New York in association
  with Freud Museum, London, 1989.

Gautier, Théophile. *My Fantoms.* Selected, translated, and introduced
  by Richard Holmes. New York: New York Review of Books, 2008.

Gay, Peter. *Freud: A Life for Our Time.* London: J.M. Dent and Sons, 1988.

Gibbon, Edward. *The History of the Decline and Fall of the Roman Empire.* Vol. 1,
  The Turn of the Tide. Edited by Betty Radice. London: Folio Society, 1983.
- *The History of the Decline and Fall of the Roman Empire.* Vol. 3, *The Revival and
  Collapse of Paganism.* Edited by Betty Radice. London: Folio Society, 1983.

Gibson, William. *Idoru.* New York: G.P. Putnam's Sons, 1996.

Gide, André. "Journal sans dates." In *Prétextes: Suivi de Nouveaux Prétextes.* Paris:
  Mercure de France, 1963.
- *Self-Portraits: The Gide-Valéry Letters 1890–1942.* Edited by Robert Mallet.
  Abridged and translated by June Guicharnaud. Chicago: University of Chicago
  Press, 1966.

Gilbert, Michael. *The Etruscan Net.* London: Companion Book Club, n.d.

Glanville-Hicks, Peggy. *Etruscan Concerto.* Musical Heritage Society 2005 [1992].
  Keith Jarrett, piano, Brooklyn Philharmonic Orchestra, Dennis Russell Davies,
  conductor, 13' 55".
- "Musical Explorers: Six Americans Who Are Changing the Musical
  Vocabulary." *Vogue* 116 (15 November 1950).

Gooch, G.P. *History and Historians in the Nineteenth Century.* London: Longman's,
  1952.

Grafton, Anthony. "A Passion for the Past." *New York Review of Books*
  (8 March 2001): 50–1.

Graves, Robert. *I, Claudius.* London: Arthur Baker, 1934.

Gray, Mrs. Hamilton. *Tour to the Sepulchres of Etruria, in 1839.* London: J. Hatchard
  and Son, 1841.

Haggard, H. Rider. *She.* London: Oxford University Press, 1991.

Hajkalovà, Markéta. *Mika Waltari: The Finn.* Translated by Gerald Turner.
  Helsinki: Werner Söderström Osakeyhtio, 2008.

Hall, Claire. "The Day a God Rode In." *London Review of Books*
  (20 February 2020): 11–12.

Hall, John T., ed. *Etruscan Italy: Etruscan Influences on the Civilizations of Italy from
  Antiquity to the Modern Era.* Provo, Utah: Brigham Young University, 1996.

Hamilton, Lyn. *The Etruscan Chimera.* New York: Berkley Prime Crime, 2002.

Harari, Maurizio. "Etruscan Art or Art of the Etruscans?" In *Etruscology,* edited by Alessandro Naso, 70–7. London: Routledge, 2017.

Harloe, Katherine. *Winckelmann and the Invention of Antiquity: History and Aesthetics in the Age of Altertumswissenschaft.* Oxford: Oxford University Press, 2013.

Harper, Kyle. *The Fate of Rome: Climate, Disease, and the End of an Empire.* Princeton University Press, 2017.

Harrison, Robert Pogue. "A New Kind of Woman." *The New York Review of Books* (25 April 2013): 36–8.

Haven, Cynthia L., ed. *The Invisible Rope: Portraits of Czesław Miłosz.* Athens, Ohio: Ohio University Press, 2011.

Hawthorne, Nathaniel. *The Marble Faun.* New York: Signet, 1961.

– *The Marble Faun: or, The Romance of Monte Beni.* Edited with an introduction by Richard H. Broadhead. New York: Penguin Books, 1990.

– *The Scarlet Letter: A Romance.* New York: Penguin Books, 1973.

Hawthorne, Sophia Peabody. *Notes in England and Italy.* Boston: G.P. Putnam & Son, 1869.

Haynes, Sybille. *The Augur's Daughter: A Story of Etruscan Life.* London: Rubicon Press, 1987.

– *Etruscan Civilization: A Cultural History.* London: British Museum Press, 2000.

Heaney, Seamus. "In Gratitude for All the Gifts." In *The Invisible Rope: Portraits of Czesław Miłosz,* edited by Cynthia L. Haven, 206–11. Athens, Ohio: Ohio University Press, 2011.

Hegel, G.W.F. *Aesthetics: Lectures on Fine Art.* 2 vols. Translated by R.M. Knox. Oxford: Clarendon Press, 1975.

– *Aesthetik.* Edited by H.G. Hotho. Berlin, 1842.

– *The Philosophy of History.* Translated by J. Sibree. New York: Dover, 1956.

Hemingway, Ernest. *The Sun Also Rises.* New York: Scribner's, 1970.

Herbert, Zbigniew. *The Collected Poems 1956–1998.* Translated and edited by Alissa Valles. New York: Ecco Press, 2007.

– *The Collected Prose 1948–1998.* Translated and edited by Alissa Valles. New York: Ecco Press, 2010.

– *Labirynt nad morzem.* Warszawa: Zeszyty Literackie, 2000.

– *Węzeł Gordyjski: oraz inne pisma rosproszone 1948–1998.* Edited by Paweł Kądziela. Warszawa: Biblioteka Więzi, 2001.

Herder, Johann. *Selected Early Works 1764–67.* Edited by Ernest A. Menze and Karl Menges. Translated by Ernest A. Menze with Michael Palma. University Park: Pennsylvania State University Press, 1992.

Herodotus. *The Histories of Herodotus*. Translated by George Rawlinson. Edited by E.H. Blakeney. New York: Dutton (Everyman's Library), 1954.

Hesiod. *Hesiod and Theognis*. Translated by Dorothea Wender. Harmondsworth: Penguin Books, 1973.

Heurgon, Jacques. *Daily Life of the Etruscans*. Translated by James Kirkup. London: Phoenix Press, 2002.

– "The Date of Vegoia's Prophecy," *The Journal of Roman Studies* 49 (1959): 41–5. https://www.jstor.org/stable/297621.

Hillard, George Stillman. *Six Months in Italy*. Boston: Ticknor and Fields, 1865.

Hobsbawm, Eric. *On History*. London: The New Press, 1997.

Hobson, J. Allan. *Dreaming: An Introduction to the Science of Sleep*. New York: Oxford University Press, 2002.

Hofmann, Michael. "Heine's Heartmobile." *The New York Review of Books* (22 July 2021): 42.

Hollier, Denis, ed. *A New History of French Literature*. Cambridge, MA: Harvard University Press, 1989

– "Plenty of Nothing." In *A New History of French Literature*, edited by Denis Hollier, 894–900. Cambridge, MA: Harvard University Press, 1989.

Holub, Robert C. "Constance School of Reception Aesthetics [Reception Theory]." In *Encyclopedia of Contemporary Literary Theory: Approaches, Scholars, Terms*, edited by Irene R. Makaryk, 14–18. Toronto: University of Toronto Press, 1993.

Horace. *Odes and Epodes*. Translated by C.E. Bennett. Cambridge, MA: Harvard University Press, 1968.

– *Satires, Epistles, and Ars Poetica*. Translated by H.R. Fairclough. Cambridge, MA: Harvard University Press, 1978.

Hornblower, Simon, and Antony Spawforth, eds. *The Oxford Companion to Classical Civilization*. London: Oxford, 1998.

Howatson, M.C., ed. *The Oxford Companion to Classical Literature*. London: Oxford, 1990.

Humbert, Jean-Marcel, Michael Pantazzi, Christiane Ziegler. *Egyptomania: Egypt in Western Art*. Ottawa: National Gallery of Canada, 1994.

Huxley, Aldous. "Aldous Huxley, Interview." In *Writers at Work: The Paris Review Interviews, Second Series*. Introduction by Van Wyck Brooks, 193–214. New York: The Viking Press, 1963.

– *Antic Hay*. Harmondsworth: Penguin Books, 1975.

– *Brave New World*. New York: Bantam Books, 1962.

– *Brief Candles*. Harmondsworth: Penguin Books, 1973.

– *Complete Essays.* Vol. 3, *1930–1935.* Edited with commentary by Robert S. Baker and James Sexton. Chicago: Ivan R. Dee, 2001.

– *Eyeless in Gaza.* Harmondsworth: Penguin Books, 1974.

– *Point Counter Point.* Harmondsworth: Penguin Books, 1967.

– *Selected Letters of Aldous Huxley.* Edited with an introduction by James Sexton. Chicago: Ivan R. Dee, 2007.

– *Those Barren Leaves.* London: Chatto & Windus, 1950.

Hyde Minor, Heather. "G.B. Piranesi's *Diverse manière* and the Natural History of Ancient Art." In *Memoirs of the American Academy in Rome.* Vols 56–7 (2011/2012), 323–51.

Ives, Colta. "Degas, Japanese Prints, and Japonisme." In *The Private Collection of Edgar Degas,* edited by Ann Dumas, Colta Ives, Susan Alyson Stein, and Gary Tinterow, 247–62. New York: Metropolitan Museum of Art, 1997.

James, Henry. *Italian Hours.* New York: Ecco Press, 1987.

– *Literary Criticism: Essays on Literature, American Writers, English Writers.* Edited by Leon Edel. New York: Library of America, 1984.

– *Literary Criticism: French Writers, Other European Writers, the Prefaces to the New York Edition.* Edited by Leon Edel. New York: Library of America, 1984.

– *Selected Letters.* Edited by Leon Edel. Cambridge, MA: Harvard University Press, 1987.

– *Traveling in Italy with Henry James: Essays.* Edited by Fred Kaplan. New York: William Morrow, 1994.

James, William. *Writings 1902–1910.* New York: Library of America, 1987.

Janson, H.W., and Anthony F. Janson. *History of Art.* New York: Harry N. Abrams, 1997.

Jarry, Alfred. *Tout Ubu.* Paris: Le Livre de Poche, 1962.

Jaucourt, Louis de. "The Religion of the Greeks and Romans." Translated by Susan Emanuel. Ann Arbor: Michigan Publishing, University of Michigan Library, 2005. http://hdl.handle.net/2007/2017/spo.did2222.0000.431.

Jay, Peter, ed. *The Greek Anthology: And Other Ancient Greek Epigrams.* Harmondsworth: Penguin Books, 1981.

Jefferson, Thomas. Letter to John Adams, 5 May 1817. https://founders. archives.gov/documents/Jefferson/03-11-02-0271.

Jenkins, Ian, and Kim Sloan. *Vases & Volcanoes: Sir William Hamilton and His Collection.* London: British Museum Press, 1996.

Jenkyns, Richard. *The Victorians and Ancient Greece.* Oxford: Basil Blackwell, 1980.

Jerome. *Chronicon.* https://www.tertullian.org/fathers/jerome_preface_ chronicles.htm.

Johnson, Pamela Hansford. *The Unspeakable Skipton.* London: Hodder and Stoughton, 2018.

Jones, Brian W. *The Emperor Domitian.* London: Routledge, 1992.

Joyce, James. *Ulysses.* New York: Modern Library, 1961.

Kähler, Heinz. *The Art of Rome and Her Empire.* New York: Greystone Press, 1965.

Kennedy, William Sloane. *Reminiscences of Walt Whitman, and Extracts from Letters and Remarks on His Writings.* New York: Haskell House Publishers, 1973.

– *Reminiscences of Walt Whitman, and Extracts from Letters and Remarks on His Writings.* Walt Whitman Archive: Whitman Archive ID: med. 00567.

Kinkead-Weekes, Mark. *D.H. Lawrence: Triumph to Exile 1912–1922.* Cambridge: Cambridge University Press, 1996.

Kirk, G.S., and J.E. Raven. *The Presocratic Philosophers.* Cambridge: Cambridge University Press, 1970.

Kołakowski, Leszek. *The Key to Heaven ... and Conversations with the Devil.* New York: Grove Press, 1972.

Korenjak, Martin. "The Etruscans in Ancient Literature." In *Etruscology,* edited by Alexander Naso, 35–52. London: Routledge, 2017.

Kraus, Rosalind. *Terminal Iron Works: The Sculpture of David Smith.* Cambridge, MA MIT Press, 1973.

Kulikowski, Michael. "A Very Bad Man." *London Review of Books* (18 June 2020): 15–16.

Kundera, Milan. *The Curtain: An Essay in Seven Parts.* Translated by Linda Asher. New York: HarperCollins, 2005.

– *Encounter.* Translated by Linda Asher. New York: HarperCollins, 2017.

– *Immortality.* Translated by Peter Kussi. New York: Grove Weidenfeld, 1990.

Lahiri, Jhumpa. *Unaccustomed Earth.* New York: Alfred A. Knopf, 2008.

Lancel, Serge. *Carthage: A History.* Translated by Antonia Nevill. Oxford: Blackwell, 1995.

Lanchester, John. *The Debt to Pleasure.* Toronto: McClelland & Stewart, 1996.

Latifau, Joseph François. *Mœurs des sauvages Amériquains comparés aux mœurs des premiers temps.* Paris, 1724.

Lawrence, D.H. *Apocalypse.* Edited by Mara Kalnins. New York: Viking Press, 1982.

– *The Collected Letters of D.H. Lawrence.* Edited with an introduction by Harry T. Moore. 2 vols. London: Heinemann, 1970.

– *Etruscan Places.* Foreword by Massimo Pallottino. London: Olive Press, 1994.

– *Lady Chatterley's Lover.* London: William Heinemann, 1961.

– *The Letters of D.H. Lawrence.* Vol. 2, *1913–16.* Edited by George J. Zytaruk and James T. Boulton. Cambridge: Cambridge University Press, 1981.

– *The Letters of D.H. Lawrence.* Vol. 6, *1928–1930.* Edited by Keith Sagar
     and James T. Boulton. Cambridge: Cambridge University Press, 1993.
– *Sketches of Etruscan Places and Other Italian essays.* Edited by Simonetta de
     Filippis. Cambridge: Cambridge University Press, 1992.
– *St Mawr* and *The Virgin and the Gipsy.* Harmondsworth: Penguin Books, 1950.
– *Studies in Classic American Literature.* Harmondsworth: Penguin Books, 1971.
– *Women in Love.* Edited by David Farmer, Lindeth Vasey, and John Worthen.
     Cambridge: Cambridge University Press, 1987.
Leavis, F.R. *The Critic as Anti-Philosopher.* Athens, Georgia: University of Georgia
     Press, 1983.
Leppmann, Walter. *Winckelmann.* New York: Alfred A. Knopf, 1970.
Lesser, Rika. *Etruscan Things.* New York: George Braziller, 1983.
Lévi-Strauss, Claude. *Tristes Tropiques.* Translated by John Weightman and Doreen
     Weightman. Introduction and notes by Patrick Wilcken. London: Penguin
     Books, 2012.
Li Castro, Emiliano. "Musical Instruments." In *Etruscology,* edited by Alessandro
     Naso, 505–21. London: Routledge, 2017.
Lilla, Mark. "The Writer Apart." *The New York Review of Books* (13 May 2021):
     18–21.
Lives of the Later Caesars. Translated by David Magie. Introduction by A.R. Birley.
     London: Folio Society, 2005.
Livy. *The Early History of Rome.* Translated by Aubrey de Sélincourt. Introduction
     by R.M. Ogilvie. London: Penguin Books, 2002.
Llywelyn, Morgan, and Michael Scott. *Etruscans.* New York: TOR, 2000.
Lord, James. *Mythic Giacometti.* New York: Farrar, Straus and Giroux, 2004.
Lowell, Robert. *Collected Poems.* Edited by Frank Bidart and David Gewanter.
     New York: Farrar, Straus and Giroux, 2003.
– *Life Studies / For the Union Dead.* New York: Farrar, Straus and Giroux. 1964.
Lucan. *Pharsalia.* Translated by J.D. Duff. Cambridge, MA: Harvard University
     Press, 1969.
Lucretius. *On the Nature of the Universe.* Translated by Ronald Latham.
     Harmondsworth: Penguin Books, 1981.
Macaulay, Thomas Babington. *Lays of Ancient Rome.* London: Longmans, Green,
     and Co., 1881.
Macfarlane, Roger T. "'*Tyrrhena Regum Progenies*': Etruscan Literary Figures from
     Horace to Ovid." In *Etruscan Italy: Etruscan Influences on the Civilizations of Italy
     from Antiquity to the Modern Era,* edited by John F. Hall, 241–65. Provo, Utah:
     Brigham Young University, 1996.

Mailer, Norman. *Marilyn: A Biography.* New York: Grosset & Dunlap, 1973.

Manfredi, Valerio Massimo. *The Ancient Curse.* Translated by Christine Feddersen-Manfredi. London: Macmillan, 2010.

Maras, Daniele F. "Religion." In *Etruscology,* edited by Alessandro Naso, 277–316. London: Routledge, 2017.

Marchand, Suzanne L. *Down from Olympus: Archaeology and Philhellenism in Germany, 1750– 1970.* Princeton: Princeton University Press, 1996.

Marx, Karl. *The Economic and Philosophic Manuscripts of 1844.* Translated by Martin Milligan. Edited with an introduction by Dirk J. Struik. New York: International Publishers, 1973.

Matthiessen, F.O. *American Renaissance: Art and Expression in the Age of Emerson and Whitman.* London: Oxford University Press, 1968.

McMullen, Roy. *Degas: His Life, Times, and Work.* London: Secker & Warburg, 1985.

Mencken, H.L. *Prejudices: Third Series.* New York: A.A. Knopf, 1924.

Mérimée, Prosper. *Carmen and Other Stories.* Translated with an introduction and notes by Nicholas Jotcham. Oxford: Oxford University Press, 1989.

Meyer, Paul. "She] {Ha?} She." PhD Thesis, University of Toronto, 2016.

Miłosz, Czesław. *Unattainable Earth.* Translated by the author and Robert Hass. New York: Ecco Press, 1986.

Momigliano, Arnaldo. *Alien Wisdom: The Limits of Civilization.* Cambridge: University of Cambridge Press, 1975.

– *The Classical Foundations of Modern Historiography.* Berkeley: University of California Press, 1990.

Montaigne, Michel de. *The Complete Works of Montaigne.* Translated by Donald M. Frame. Stanford: Stanford University Press, 1965.

Montale, Eugenio. *Collected Poems: 1920–1954.* Translated and annotated by Jonathan Galassi. New York: Farrar, Straus and Giroux, 2000.

– *New Poems.* Translated by G. Singh with an introduction by F.R. Leavis. London: Chatto & Windus, 1976.

Montserrat, Dominic. *Akhenaten: History, Fantasy and Ancient Egypt.* London: Routledge, 2000.

Munro, Alice. *Selected Stories.* Toronto: McClelland & Stewart, 1996.

Murdoch, Iris. *The Flight from the Enchanter.* London: Chatto & Windus, 1956.

Naso, Alessandro, ed. *Etruscology.* London: Routledge, 2017.

Neruda, Pablo. *The Poetry of Pablo Neruda.* Edited with an introduction by Ilan Stavans. New York: Farrar, Straus and Giroux, 2003.

Niebuhr, B.G. *The History of Rome.* Translated by Julius Charles Hare and Connor Thirlwall. London: Taylor and Walton, 1837.

Nietzsche, Friedrich. *Twilight of the Idols / The Anti-Christ.* Translated by R.J. Hollingdale. Harmondsworth: Penguin Books, 1969.

Nin, Anaïs. *The Diary of Anaïs Nin: 1947–1955.* New York: Harcourt Brace Jovanovich, 1974.

Nussbaum, Martha. *The Cosmopolitan Tradition: A Noble But Flawed Idea.* Cambridge, MA: Belknap Press of Harvard University Press, 2019.

O'Brien, Geoffrey. "Magic Sayings by the Thousands," *New York Review of Books* (4 November 2021): 34–6.

Ogilvie, R.M. *A Commentary on Livy, Books 1–5.* Oxford: Clarendon Press, 1965.

– *Early Rome and the Etruscans.* Hassocks, Sussex: Harvester Press, 1976.

– "Introduction to Livy." In *The Early History of Rome.* London: Penguin Books, 2002.

– *The Romans and Their Gods: In the Age of Augustus.* London: Chatto & Windus, 1969.

Ondaatje, Michael. *The English Patient.* Toronto: McClelland & Stewart, 1992.

Orwell, George. *Animal Farm.* New York: Harcourt, Brace and Co., 1946.

– *The Collected Essays, Journalism and Letters of George Orwell.* 4 vols. Edited by Sonia Orwell and Ian Angus. Harmondsworth: Penguin Books, 1970.

Ovid. *Metamorphoses,* 2 vols. Translated by Frank Justus Miller. Cambridge, MA: Harvard University Press, 1971.

Pachner, Joan. *David Smith.* London: Phaidon-Focus, 2013.

Pallottino, Massimo. *The Etruscans.* Edited by David Ridgway. Translated by J. Cremona. Bloomington: Indiana University Press, 1975.

– "In Search of Etruria: Science and Imagination." In D.H. Lawrence, *Etruscan Places,* 9–28. London: Olive Press, 1994.

Parsons, Peter. *City of the Sharp-Nosed Fish: Greek Lives in Roman Egypt.* London: Weidenfield and Nicolson, 2007.

Pastoureau, Michel. *The Colours of our Memories.* London: Polity, 2012.

Perkins, Philip. "DNA and Etruscan Identity." In *Etruscology,* edited by Alessandro Naso, 109–20. London: Routledge, 2017.

Petrarch. *Selections from the Canzoniere and Other Works.* Translated with an introduction and notes by Mark Musa. Oxford: Oxford University Press, 1985.

Pietromarchi, Antonello. *Lucien Bonaparte: Prince Romain.* French translation by Reine Carducci Artensio. Paris: Librairie Académique Perrin, 1985.

Piggott, Stuart. *Ancient Europe.* Edinburgh: Edinburgh University Press, 1965.

Pindar. *The Odes of Pindar.* Translated by C.M. Bowra. Harmondsworth: Penguin Books, 1969.

Pindar, Peter [Dr John Woolcott]. *Poems: Selected from the Poems of Peter Pindar, Esquire.* Philadelphia: M. Jones, 1807.

Pinkard, Terry. *Hegel: A Biography*. Cambridge: Cambridge University Press, 2000.

Plato. *The Republic of Plato*. Translated with notes and an interpretive essay by Allan Bloom. New York: Basic Books, 1968.

Pliny the Elder. *Natural History: A Selection*. Translated with an introduction and notes by John F. Healy. London: Penguin Books, 1991.

Poe, Edgar Allan. *Complete Stories and Poems of Edgar Allan Poe*. New York: Doubleday & Co., 1964.

– "Review of *Reminiscences of an Intercourse with Mr. Niebuhr, the Historian, during a Residence with him in Rome.*" *The Southern Literary Messenger* 2, no. 2 (January 1836, 2): 126–7.

Pollock, Griselda. *Mary Cassatt: Painter of Modern Women*. London: Thames & Hudson, 1998.

Polybius. *The Histories*. Translated by Robin Waterfield. Introduction and notes by Brian McGing. London: Oxford University Press, 2010.

Potts, Alex. "Introduction" to Johann Joachim Winckelmann, *History of the Art of Antiquity*. Translated by Harry Francis Mallgrave. Los Angeles: Getty Publications, 2006.

Powell, Anthony. *Temporary Kings*. London: Heinemann, 1973.

Propertius. *Elegies*. Translated by G.P. Gould. Cambridge, MA: Harvard University Press, 1990.

Proust, Marcel. *À la recherche du temps perdu*. Edited and presented by Pierre Clarac and André Ferré. Paris: Bibliothèque de la Pléiade, 1954.

– *Cities of the Plain*. Translated by C.K. Scott Moncrieff. London: Chatto & Windus, 1973.

– *Finding Time Lost*. Translated by Ian Patterson. London: Penguin Books, 2002.

– *The Guermantes Way*. Part 2. Translated by C.K. Moncrieff and Terence Kilmartin. New York: Random House, 1981.

– *Jean Santeuil*. Translated by Gerard Hopkins. London: Penguin Books, 1955.

– *Selected Letters: 1880–1903*. Translated by Ralph Mannheim. New York: Doubleday & Co., 1983.

– *Time Regained*. Translated by Andreas Mayor. London: Chatto & Windus, 1972.

– *Within a Budding Grove*, Part 2. Translated by C.K. Scott Moncrieff. London: Chatto & Windus, 1972.

Purdy, Al. "Purdy among the Etruscans." *Canadian Forum* (June 1998): 18–19.

– *Rooms for Rent in the Outer Planets 1962–1996*. Edited and selected by Al Purdy and Sam Solecki. Madeira Park, BC: Harbour Publishing, 1996.

Queneau, Raymond. *The Bark Tree*. Translated by Barbara Wright. New York: New Directions, 1968.

– *Le Chiendent*. Paris: Gallimard, 1933.

Quinn, Josephine. "Caesar Bloody Caesar." *New York Review of Books*
(22 March 2018): 25–6.
– *In Search of the Phoenicians*. Princeton: Princeton University Press, 2018.
Rabelais, François. *The Histories of Gargantua and Pantagruel.* Translated by J.M.
Cohen. London: Penguin Books, 1967.
Raitt, A.W. *Prosper Mérimée.* London: Eyre & Spottiswoode, 1970.
Raphael, Frederic. *Antiquity Matters.* New Haven: Yale University Press, 2017.
Rasmussen, Tom B. "The Imagery of Tomb Objects (Local and Imported) and Its
Funerary Importance." In *The Etruscan World,* edited by Jean MacIntosh Turfa,
674–5. London: Routledge, 2013.
Read, Herbert. *A Coat of Many Colours: Occasional Essays.* London: Routledge, 1947.
Reilly, Robin. *Wedgwood: The New Illustrated Dictionary.* Woodbridge, Suffolk:
Antique Collectors' Club, 1995.
Renoir, Jean. Interview with Jacques Rivette. Included in DVD edition of the film
French Cancan (1954), produced by The Criterion Collection (released 2004).
Reveley, Edith. *The Etruscan Couple and Other Stories.* London: Victor
Gollancz, 1976.
Rewald, John. *Giacomo Manzù.* London: Thames and Hudson, 1967.
Richardson, Emeline. *The Etruscans: Their Art and Civilization.* Chicago:
University of Chicago Press, 1964.
Richardson, John. *A Life of Picasso: The Triumphant Years.* Vol. 3, *1917–1932.*
New York: Alfred A. Knopf, 2007.
Ridgway, David. "James Byres and the Definition of the Etruscans." In *Etruscan
by Definition: Papers in Honour of Sybille Haynes, MBE,* edited by Judith Swaddling
and Philip Perkins, 2–8. London: The British Museum, 2009.
Rilke, Rainer Maria. *Ahead of All Parting: The Selected Poetry and Prose of Rainer
Maria Rilke.* Translated by Stephen Mitchell. New York: Random House, 1995.
– *Duino Elegies.* Translated by J.B. Leishman and Stephen Spender. New York:
W.W. Norton, 1963.
Roazen, Paul. *Freud and His Followers.* New York: Meridian, 1974.
Rogers, Victoria. *The Music of Peggy Glanville-Hicks.* Farnham, England:
Ashgate, 2009.
Roosevelt, Theodore. "History as Literature." *American Historical Review* 18, no. 3.
Or https://www.historians.org/about-aha-and-membership/aha-history-and-
archives/presidential-addresses/theodore-roosevelt.
Rosenblum, Robert. *Transformations in Late Eighteenth Century Art.* Princeton:
Princeton University Press, 1969.
Rowland, Ingrid D. *The Scarith of Scornello.* Chicago: University of Chicago
Press, 2004.

Ruether, Rosemary. *Goddesses and the Divine Feminine: A Western Religious History*. Berkeley: University of California Press, 2005.

Ruskin, John. *Modern Painters*. Edited and abridged by David Barrie. London: Andre Deutsch, 1987 .

Safranski, Rüdiger. *Goethe: Life as a Work of Art*. New York: Liveright-Norton, 2017.

Sartre, Jean-Paul. *Life/Situations: Essays Written and Spoken*. Translated by Paul Auster and Lydia Davis. New York: Pantheon Books, 1977.

Scholz-Strasser, Inge. *Sigmund Freud: Vienna IX, Bergstrasse 19*. Vienna: Universe Publishing, 1998.

Schoolfield, George C. *A History of Finland's Literature*. Lincoln, Nebraska: University of Nebraska Press, 1998.

Seferis, George. *Collected Poems*. Translated by Edmund Keeley and Philip Sherard. Princeton: Princeton University Press, 1995.

Seneca. *Naturales Quaestiones*. 10 vols. Translated by Thomas H. Corcoran. Cambridge, MA: Harvard University Press, 1971–72.

Serafini, Giancarlo, ed. *Omaggio a Campigli*. Rome: Carlo Bestetti Edizioni d'Arte – Galleria "Il Collezionista d'Arte Contemporanea," 1972.

Shaw, George Bernard. *Complete Plays with Prefaces*. New York: Dodd, Mead & Co., 1963.

Shipley, Lucy. *The Etruscans: Lost Civilizations*. London: Reaktion Books, 2017.

Shrimpton, Gordon S. *Theopompus the Historian*. Montreal: McGill-Queen's University Press, 1991.

Simmons, Laurence. *Freud's Italian Journey*. Amsterdam: Rodopi, 2006.

Simonnet, Claude. *Queneau déchiffré*. Paris: Julliard, 1962.

Smollett, Tobias. *Travels through France and Italy*. London: Tauris Parke, 2010.

Solomon, Maynard. *Mozart: A Life*. New York: HarperCollins, 1995.

Spark, Muriel. *The Mandelbaum Gate*. London: Macmillan, 1965.

Spengler, Oswald. *The Decline of the West: Perspectives on World History*. Translated by Charles Francis Atkinson. London: George Allen & Unwin Ltd, 1928.

Spivey, Nigel. *Etruscan Art*. London: Thames and Hudson, 1997.

Spivey, Nigel, and Simon Stoddart. *Etruscan Italy*. London: B.T. Batsford, 1960.

Sprenger, Maria, and Gilda Bartoloni. *The Etruscans: Their History, Art, and Architecture*. Translated from the German and Italian by Robert Erich Wolf. New York: Harry N. Abrams, 1983.

Steiner, George. *Heidegger*. London: Fontana/Collins, 1978.

– *My Unwritten Books*. New York: New Directions, 2008.

Steingräber, Stephan, ed. *Etruscan Painting: Catalogue Raisonné of Etruscan Wall Paintings*. Translated by David Ridgway and Francesca Ridgway. New York: Harcourt Brace Jovanovich, 1986.

– "Etruscan Rock-cut Tombs: Origins, Characteristics, Local and Foreign Elements." In *Etruscan by Definition: Papers in Honour of Sybille Haynes*, MBE, edited by Judith Swaddling and Philip Perkins, 64–8. London: The British Museum, 2009.

Stendhal. *Correspondance*, Vols 1–3. Preface by V. del Litto. Edited and annotated by Henri Martineau and V. del Litto. Paris: Gallimard, 1968.

– *Italian Chronicles*. Translated by Raymond N. MacKenzie. Minneapolis: University of Minnesota Press, 2017.

– *Lucien Leuwen*. Translated by H.L.R. Edwards. Woodbridge, Suffolk: Boydell Press, 1984.

– *Napoléon: Vie de Napoléon; Mémoires sur Napoléon*. Edited and presented by Catherine Mariette. Paris: Stock, 1998.

– *Oeuvres intimes*, Vol. 1. Edited by V. Del Litto. Paris: Gallimard, 1981.

– *The Private Diaries of Stendhal*. Edited and translated by Robert Sage. New York: W.W. Norton & Co., 1962.

– *Rome, Naples and Florence*. Translated by Richard Coe. New York: George Braziller, 1960.

– *Voyages en Italie*. Edited, presented, and annotated by V. Del Litto. Paris: Gallimard, 1973.

Stevens, Wallace. *Opus Posthumous*. Edited by Milton J. Bates. New York: Alfred A. Knopf, 1989.

Stewart, Susan. *The Ruins Lesson: Meaning and Material in Western Culture*. Chicago: University of Chicago Press, 2020.

Stoddart, Simon K.F., ed. *Historical Dictionary of the Etruscans*. Lanham, MD: Scarecrow Press, 2009.

Stump, Jordan. *Naming & Unnaming: On Raymond Queneau*. Lincoln: University of Nebraska Press, 1998.

Suetonius. Translated by J.C. Rolfe. Cambridge, MA: Harvard University Press, 1959.

Swaddling, Judith, and Philip Perkins, eds. *Etruscan by Definition: Papers in Honour of Sybille Haynes*, MBE. London: The British Museum, 2009.

Sylvester, David. *Looking at Giacometti*. London: Chatto & Windus, 1994.

Syme, Ronald. *Sallust*. Berkeley: University of California Press, 1964.

– *Tacitus*. Oxford: Clarendon Press, 1958.

Szymborska, Wisława. *Map: Collected and Last Poems*. Translated by Claire Cavanaugh and Stanisław Barańczak. Boston: Houghton Mifflin Harcourt, 2015.

– *Wszystkie Lektury nadobowiązkowe*. Kraków: Wydawnictwo Znak, 2015.

Tacitus. *The Complete Works of Tacitus*. Translated by Alfred John Church and William Jackson Brodribb. Edited by Moses Hadas. New York: Modern Library, 1942.

Tadié, Jean-Yves. *Proust: A Life*. New York: Penguin Books, 2000.

Tayler, Christopher. "For Want of a Dinner Jacket." *London Review of Books* (6 May 2021): 35–8.

Thiher, Allen. *Raymond Queneau*. Boston: Twayne Publishers, 1985.

Thomas, Keith. "Success on a Plate." *Times Literary Supplement* (10 September 2021): 8–9.

Thucydides. *The Landmark Thucydides*. Translated by Richard Crawley. Edited by Robert B. Strassler. New York: Simon & Schuster, 1996.

Thuillier, Jean-Paul, and Claudia Zevi, eds. *Giacometti et les Étrusques*. Florence: Giunti, 2011; Paris: Pinacothèque de Paris, 2011.

Tobin, Fredrik. "Music and Musical Instruments in Etruria." In *The Etruscan World*, edited by Jean MacIntosh Turfa, 841–54. London: Routledge, 2013.

Toloudis, Constantin. *Queneau and the Agony of Presence*. New York: Peter Lang, 1995.

Trilling, Lionel. *Beyond Culture*. New York: Harcourt Brace Jovanovich, 1979.

– *The Liberal Imagination*. New York: Anchor Books, 1953.

Trollope, Anthony. *The Eustace Diamonds*. London: Oxford University Press, 2011.

Tuck, Stephen. *Course Guidebook*. The Great Courses [DVD series], 2016. https://www.thegreatcourses.com/.

Turfa, Jean MacIntosh, ed. *The Etruscan World*. London: Routledge, 2013.

– "Health and Medicine in Etruria." In *The Etruscan World*, edited by Jean MacIntosh Turfa, 855–84. London: Routledge, 2013.

Ulf, Christoph. "An Ancient Question: The Origin of the Etruscans." In *Etruscology*, edited by Alessandro Naso, 11–34. London: Routledge, 2017.

Unsworth, Barry. *After Hannibal*. New York: Doubleday, 1997.

Updike, John. *My Father's Tears & Other Stories*. London: Penguin Books, 2009.

Valerius Maximus. *Memorable Doings and Sayings*. Edited and translated by D.R. Shackleton Bailey. Cambridge, MA: Harvard University Press, 2000.

Virgil. 2 vols. Translated by H. Rushton Fairclough. Cambridge: Harvard University Press, 1965.

– *The Aeneid*. Translated by Robert Fitzgerald. New York: Random House, 1983.

Volpe, Sandro. "Sur des Thèmes de Henry James: François Truffaut, Jean Gruault et *La Chambre verte*." In *Narrare / Rappresentare*, edited by Francesca Torchi, 101–14. Bologna: CLUEB, 2003.

von Vacano, Otto Wilhelm. *The Etruscans in the Ancient World*. Bloomington: Indiana University Press, 1965.

Vout, Caroline. *Classical Art: A Life History from Antiquity to the Present.* Princeton: Princeton University Press, 2018.

Waltari, Mika. *The Egyptian.* Translated by Naomi Walford. New York: Buccaneer Books, 1976.

– *The Etruscan.* Translated by Lily Leino. New York: G.P. Putnam's Sons, 1956.

– *The Roman.* Translated by Naomi Walford. New York: G.P. Putnam's Sons, 1966.

Walton, Loring Baker. *Anatole France and the Greek World.* Durham: Duke University Press, 1950.

Weber, Max. *From Max Weber: Essays in Sociology.* Translated and edited by H.H. Gerth and C. Wright Mills. New York: Oxford University Press, 1978.

– *The Protestant Ethic and the "Spirit" of Capitalism and Other Writings.* Edited and translated by Peter Baehr and Gordon C. Wells. New York: Penguin Books, 2002.

Wellard, James. *The Search for the Etruscans.* London: Thomas Nelson & Sons, 1973.

Wells, H.G. *The Outline of History: Being a Plain History of Life and Mankind.* Toronto: Doubleday, Doran & Gundy, 1929.

Whitney, W.D. *The Life and Growth of Language.* New York: Appleton, 1888.

Wilbur, Richard. *New and Collected Poems.* San Diego, CA: Harcourt Brace Jovanovich, 2017.

Williams, Dyfri. "The Hamilton Gray Vase." In *Etruscan by Definition: Papers in Honour of Sybille Haynes, MBE,* edited by Judith Swaddling and Philip Perkins, 10–20. London: British Museum, 2009.

Wilson, Ethel. *Love and Salt Water.* Toronto: McClelland & Stewart, 1990.

Winckelmann, Johann Joachim. *History of the Art of Antiquity.* Translated by Harry Francis Mallgrave. Introduction by Alex Potts. Los Angeles: Getty Publications, 2006.

Wiseman, T.P. *The Myths of Rome.* Exeter: University of Exeter Press, 2004.

Wright, Charles. *Oblivion Banjo: The Poetry of Charles Wright.* New York: Farrar, Straus and Giroux, 2019.

Yourcenar, Margaret. *The Dark Brain of Piranesi and Other Essays.* Translated by Richard Howard. New York: Farrar, Straus and Giroux, 1984.

Zagajewski, Adam. *Another Beauty.* Translated by Clare Cavanagh. Athens, GA: University of Georgia Press, 2002.

– *Niewidzialna Ręka.* Kraków: Znak, 2009.

– *Slight Exaggeration: An Essay.* Translated by Clare Cavanagh. New York: Farrar, Straus and Giroux, 2017.

– *Solidarity, Solitude.* New York: Ecco Press, 1990.

Zevi, Claudia. "Giacometti, the Last of the Etruscans." *The Independent* (17 September 2011).

Index